HARDEN'S

Top UK Restaurants

2000

Where to buy Harden's guides

Harden's guides are on sale in most major bookshops
in the UK, and many major bookshops in the US.
In case of difficulty, call Harden's Guides on
(020) 7839 4763.

**Customised editions –
the ideal corporate gift**

Harden's Top UK Restaurants and *Harden's London
Restaurants* are available in specially customised
corporate gift formats. For information, please call
(020) 7839 4763.

To register for the Update and the Survey
- **return the reply-paid card or**
- **send an e-mail to mail@hardens.com**
  (Don't forget to include your postal address.)
- **visit our new website www.hardens.com**

Text and London maps © Harden's Guides, 1999
UK maps © Maps in Minutes, 1998

ISBN 1-873721-29-3 (paperback)
ISBN 1-873721-33-1 (bonded leather)

British Library Cataloguing-in-Publication data:
a catalogue record for this book is available from
the British Library.

Printed and bound in Finland by
Werner Söderström Corporation

Research and editorial assistant: Antonia Russell

Harden's Guides
14 Buckingham Street
London WC2N 6DF

Distributed in the United States of America by
Seven Hills Book Distributors,
1531 Tremont Street, Cincinnati, OH 45214

CONTENTS

RATINGS & PRICES

We see little point in traditional rating systems, which generally tell you nothing more than that expensive restaurants are 'better' than cheap ones because they use costlier ingredients and attempt more ambitious dishes. You probably knew that already – our system assumes that, as prices rise, so do diners' expectations.

Prices and ratings are shown as follows:

£ Price
The cost of a three-course *dinner* for one person. We include half a bottle of house wine, coffee and service (or a 10% tip if there is no service charge).

Food
The following symbols indicate that, ***in comparison with other restaurants in the same price-bracket***, the cooking at the establishment is:

★★   **Exceptional**
★   **Very good**

Ambience
Restaurants which provide a setting which is very charming, stylish or 'buzzy' are indicated as follows:

𝔸   **Particularly atmospheric**

Small print

Telephone number – *all UK numbers are shown in the new (post-Easter 2000) style. Until then, the numbers for London (and some other cities) will work only if dialled in their entirety. Irish numbers are shown for dialling within Eire (the international code for which is + 353).*

Sample dishes – *these dishes exemplify the style of cooking at a particular establishment. They are merely samples – it is unlikely that these specific dishes will be available at the time of your visit.*

Value tip – *if we know of a particularly good-value set menu or some similar handy tip, we note this. Details change, so always check ahead.*

Details – *the following information is given where relevant.*

Directions – *to help you find the establishment.*

Last orders time – *at dinner (Sunday may be up to 90 minutes earlier).*

Opening hours – *unless otherwise stated, restaurants are open for lunch and dinner seven days a week.*

Credit and debit cards – *unless otherwise stated, Mastercard, Visa, Amex and Switch are accepted.*

Dress – *where appropriate, the management's preferences concerning patrons' dress are given.*

Smoking – *cigarette smoking restrictions are noted. Pipe or cigar smokers should always check ahead.*

Children – *if we know of a specified minimum age for children, we note this.*

Accommodation – *if an establishment has rooms, we list how many and the minimum price for a double.*

HOW THIS BOOK IS ORGANISED

As response to the format of our London guide has generally been very favourable, we have tried, to the extent possible, to observe the same principles here.

London is covered first, and, in recognition of the scale and diversity of its restaurant scene, has an extensive introduction and indexes, as well as its own maps. After the London section, the guide is organised strictly by place name – we could see no logic in separating England from Scotland, Wales, Northern Ireland or the Republic of Ireland, so Chester, Clachan and Cork alike appear under 'C'.

For *cities and larger towns*, you can therefore turn straight to the relevant section. In the major restaurant centres you will find an introduction summarising key attractions.

In *less densely populated areas*, you will generally find it easiest to start with the map of the relevant area at the back of the book, which will guide you to the appropriate place names.

HOW THIS BOOK IS RESEARCHED

This book is the result of a research effort involving some 7,000 people – our 'reporters'. This year, over 4,000 contributed to our ninth annual survey of London restaurant-goers. Our second survey of restaurant-goers outside the capital attracted 3,500 participants (with some 500 people participating in both surveys).

The density of the feedback on London (where many of the top places attract several hundred reviews each) is such that the ratings for the metropolitan restaurants included in this edition are almost exclusively statistical in derivation. We have, as it happens, visited all the restaurants in the London section, anonymously, and at our own expense, but we use our personal experiences only to inform the standpoint from which to interpret the consensus opinion.

In the case of the more commented-upon provincial restaurants, we have adopted an approach very similar to London. In the case of less visited provincial establishments, however, the interpretation of survey results owes as much to art as it does to science. In our experience, smaller establishments are – for better or worse – generally quite consistent, and we have therefore felt able to place a relatively high level of confidence in a lower level of commentary. Conservatism on our part, however, will undoubtedly have led to some smaller places being under-rated compared to their more visited peers.

FROM THE EDITORS

Although we have been in the business of publishing restaurant guides (to London) for the past nine years, this is only the second edition of our guide to the whole of the UK (and, now, Eire).

Just as the restaurants in the capital have undergone a transformation during the period over which we have been publishing guides about them, it is quite possible that we are seeing the stirring of a similar revolution across the British Isles as a whole. It is exciting to play a part in recording what on any analysis is an important period of evolution and improvement of the British and Irish restaurant scenes.

It would be a very arrogant publisher who claimed any guide book as perfect, and we certainly make no such claim for this one. However, this second edition of the guide is bigger and, we believe, better than the first, and we hope that readers will think so too.

In this edition, we have considerably expanded the number of entries (all of the increase coming from outside London) and, as noted above, have begun to include places in the Republic of Ireland. Initially at least, our coverage in this new territory is not as comprehensive as we would like, and doubtless there is still room to expand the number of UK entries. If there are names which you think have been unfairly passed over, please remember that the solution lies partially in your own hands.

Assembling a large number of people interested to contribute their views on restaurants is no easy task, and we are once again most grateful to readers of the *Observer* and the *Guardian* who completed survey forms distributed with those newspapers. We are no less grateful, of course, to the growing band of our "own" reporters who also took part.

All restaurant guides are the subject of continual revision. This is especially true when the restaurant scene is undergoing a period of rapid change, as at present. **Please help us to make the next edition even more comprehensive and accurate.** If you register for your free update (by returning the reply-paid card at the back of the book, by e-mail, or on the web at our new site www.hardens.com) you will be invited, in the spring of 2000, to participate in our next survey. **If you take part you will, on publication, receive a complimentary copy of *Harden's Top UK Restaurants 2001*.**

Richard Harden   **Peter Harden**

LONDON INTRODUCTION

LONDON INTRODUCTION

There is no doubt that the 1990s have seen a great
revolution in dining out in the capital. Some effects of
the revolution have been extremely benign: there is now
a range of places to eat – especially in the inner suburbs
– which would have been unthinkable a decade ago.
However not all recent developments can be classed
as progress. The number of places, especially in the
West End, where you can be parted from large sums
of money and receive remarkably little in return is
now larger than ever.

To help to guide you through the minefield, see the
results from our London survey. Results start on page
16. Do note that we publish the Most Mentioned list
because it seems to us that it is genuinely of interest
to know which are the restaurants which are attracting
popular attention. It means just what it says though:
inclusion on the list is not necessarily any kind of guide
to a restaurant's quality, just an indication of its profile.

Owing to the sheer breadth of the London scene, this
initial review is very selective. The 'Area overviews'
(starting on page 58) will help you identify many
excellent places not mentioned below.

Fine dining

There are few truly world-class restaurants in London.
Arguably, there are only two – *Gordon Ramsay* (the new
'enfant terrible' on the block) and *Le Gavroche* (the
oldest, and perhaps most traditional 'grand restaurant').
There are pretenders of course, most obviously
Chez Nico at Ninety and the *Oak Room Marco Pierre White*,
but some may find them rather joyless affairs. Knocking
on the door of greatness is the *Square* – an emerging
success of the last decade.

Grandeur and tradition

Though perhaps not generally in quite the same league
for cooking as the Fine Dining restaurants, some of the
top hotel dining rooms are worth seeking out for their
stylish and comfortable settings and very good service.
The *Connaught* is often held up as the capital's benchmark
of culinary consistency. Its less culinarily ambitious
Mayfair competitor, the *Dorchester Grill*, is now also back
on top form. At a more modest price-point, London's
oldest restaurant, *Rules,* still has a lot to recommend it,
and, if money is no particular object, *Wilton's* typifies
a certain traditional style.

'In' places

The most perennially 'in' restaurants in London are the (very difficult to book) duo, *The Ivy* and *Le Caprice*. A year old (in its new guise), the *Mirabelle* looks set similarly to become a modern classic. The media and fashion world currently has a quandary – should it stick with the undoubted virtues of *Nobu* or prefer this season's look, *Asia de Cuba*? For the international set, Knightsbridge's upmarket Italian restaurants remain the destinations of choice.

Mega-brasseries

Almost entirely a creation of the 1990s, these very large establishments endeavour to deliver modern British cooking in a stylish setting of such size that dining becomes a spectacle in itself. The Conran group, usually identified as the originator of the concept, runs three such establishments – *Bluebird, Mezzo* and *Quaglino's* – which are all very expensive indeed for what they offer. If you want to eat in a large modern brasserie, but are still seeking good value, only the relatively unpretentious *Palais du Jardin* can honestly be recommended.

Key cuisines

Here are some foreign cuisines in which London excels.

Modern Italian
London's Italian cooking has in recent years emerged with a vengeance from the Anglicised torpor which has dominated since the '50s. Modern Italian establishments now offer the most exciting continental cuisine available in London. Notable followers of the new school include *Assaggi, Cibo, Tentazioni* and *Zafferano.*

Indian
London has the finest selection of Indian restaurants in the world, with outstanding places at all price-levels. At the grander end of the market, the best names include the new *Zaika* and the emerging *Vama,* as well as the more established *Salloos, Star of India* and *Tamarind.* Some of the best subcontinental food in London is incredibly cheap – see the list on page 19 for the best inexpensive places.

Thai
London's most consistently successful grand ethnic restaurant is the *Blue Elephant*, which offers a lot of theatre, as well as some very good, if not inexpensive, cooking. There are concentrations of good, less expensive Thai restaurants in Soho, south west London and west London. A London speciality is the adoption of Thai cooking by pubs or places which, by day, are 'greasy spoons' – Kensington's *Churchill* is an excellent example.

East-meets-West

'Fusion'-cooking is an idea to which many places pay lip service, but which few imbue with any great meaning. Three fashionable US-originated restaurants, however – *Nobu* (Japanese/South American), *Vong* (French/Thai) and *Asia de Cuba* (self-explanatory) – have opened in the last few years. The first two mentioned, at least, have made a considerable success of offering cooking combining the culinary traditions of different continents. The same can be said of the excellent and home-grown *Sugar Club,* now located in Soho, and also the *Birdcage,* which has developed a great following, despite an unlikely and out-on-a-limb location.

Gastropubs

Gastropubs are an area of undoubted improvement over the past few years. The original 'super-pub', *The Eagle,* in ever-trendier Clerkenwell, is still one of the best, but there is now a host of worthy imitators. *The Havelock Tavern* and the *Angelsea Arms* (both Hammersmith or Shepherd's Bush way) and Battersea's *Mason's Arms* are further top examples.

Budget ethnics

Ethnic restaurants are almost invariably the top choice for budget dining. The best of them tend to cluster in particular parts of town. Chinatown is in the heart of the West End. There are several concentrations of Indian restaurants, of which the most accessible are in the Little India by Euston Station and the East End's Brick Lane – the southern Indians of Tooting are a little further away. There are many good, inexpensive Thai restaurants around Hammersmith and Chiswick.

Vegetarians

Most London restaurants (some of the classic French establishments aside) provide some form of vegetarian option, perhaps explaining the existence of relatively few specialist vegetarian restaurants of any note – *Blah!Blah!Blah!* and *The Gate* are among notable exceptions. Some of the best vegetarian food is ethnic. Southern Indian restaurants offer some delicious and extremely inexpensive cooking. Fine examples of the type include *Kastoori* and *Rasa*. Veggies should also be very happy with the meze dishes available at Middle Eastern restaurants – the *Maroush* group being notable in this respect.

LONDON SURVEY RESULTS

LONDON – MOST MENTIONED

These are the restaurants which were most frequently mentioned by reporters. (Last year's position is given in brackets. An asterisk* indicates a first appearance in the list of a recently opened or re-launched restaurant.)

1	The Ivy (2)
2	Oxo Tower (1)
3	Mirabelle*
4	Bank (4)
5	Le Caprice (12)
6=	Livebait (14)
6=	Bluebird (3)
8	Quaglino's (6)
9	Le Pont de la Tour (5)
10	The Square (18)

11	Blue Elephant (11)
12	The River Café (13)
13	Nobu (23)
14	Belgo (17)
15	Bibendum (15)
16	Vong (20)
17	The Criterion (9)
18	Zafferano (26)
19	Mezzo (8)
20	Le Palais du Jardin (10)

21=	Gordon Ramsay*
21=	The Sugar Club (38)
23	Coq d'Argent*
24	Chez Bruce (-)
25	Le Gavroche (25)
26	City Rhodes (19)
27=	Chutney Mary (35)
27=	Axis*
29	La Poule au Pot (-)
30	La Tante Claire (22)

31=	Andrew Edmunds (32)
31=	Titanic*
33	The Avenue (36)
34	Café Spice Namaste (27)
35	Rules (-)
36	L'Oranger (16)
37	Savoy Grill (-)
38	fish!*
39	1 Lombard Street*
40	Kensington Place (28)

LONDON – NOMINATIONS

Ranked by the number of reporters' votes for:

Top gastronomic experience
1 Gordon Ramsay*
2 The Ivy (2)
3 Mirabelle*
4 The Square (4)
5 Le Gavroche (6)
6 Chez Bruce (-)
7 Nobu (-)
8 The River Café (8)
9 Zafferano (-)
10 Club Gascon*

Favourite
1 The Ivy (1)
2 Le Caprice (2)
3 Chez Bruce (8)
4 The River Café (7)
5 Nobu (-)
6 Mirabelle (-)
7 Zafferano (6)
8 Le Palais du Jardin (4)
9 The Square (-)
10 Clarkes (-)

Best for business
1 City Rhodes (1)
2 Bank (4)
3 Savoy Grill (5)
4 Oxo Tower (3)
5 1 Lombard Street*
6 Le Pont de la Tour (2)
7 The Ivy (7)
8 Square (6)
9 Coq d'Argent*
10 Axis*

Best for romance
1 La Poule au Pot (1)
2 Andrew Edmunds (2)
3 The Ivy (6)
4 Julie's (7)
5 Oxo Tower (3)
6 Launceston Place (5)
7 The Blue Elephant (4)
8 Odette's (-)
9 Le Caprice (10)
10 The Criterion (8)

LONDON – HIGHEST RATINGS

These are the restaurants which received the best average food ratings.

We have divided the most represented restaurant cuisines (opposite) into two price-brackets – under and over £35.

Where the less represented cuisines (below) are concerned just the best three performers in the survey are shown.

British, Traditional
1 Connaught
2 Dorchester Grill
3 Wiltons

Vegetarian
1 The Gate
2 Blah! Blah! Blah!
3 Food for Thought

Burgers, etc
1 Ed's Easy Diner
2 Wolfe's
3 Hard Rock Café

Pizza
1 Pizza Metro
2 Pizzeria Castello
3 Eco

East/West
1 Nobu
2 The Birdcage
3 Vong

Thai
1 Chiang Mai
2 Latymers
3 Esarn Kheaw

Fish & Chips
1 Faulkner's
2 Toff's
3 Brady's

Fish & Seafood
1 Chez Liline
2 Lobster Pot
3 Back to Basics

Greek
1 Vrisaki
2 Halepi
3 Lemonia

Spanish
1 Cambio de Tercio
2 Gaudi
3 Lomo

Turkish
1 Gallipoli
2 Iznik
3 Sarcan

Lebanese
1 Ranoush
2 Maroush
3 Al Hamra

Modern British

£35 and over
1 Chez Bruce
2 Clarke's
3 City Rhodes
4 The Glasshouse
5 755

Under £35
1 Mesclun
2 The Havelock Tavern
3 The Anglesea Arms
4 The Mason's Arms
5 The Apprentice

French

£35 and over
1 Gordon Ramsay
2 Pied à Terre
3 Aubergine
4 Chezmax
5 The Square

Under £35
1 Monsieur Max
2 Club Gascon
3 The White Onion
4 Les Associés
5 Bleeding Heart

Italian/Mediterranean

£35 and over
1 Assaggi
2 Zafferano
3 Tentazioni
4 Grissini
5 Cibo

Under £35
1 Del Buongustaio
2 The Green Olive
3 Luigi's Delicatessen
4 Aglio e Olio
5 Made in Italy

Indian

£35 and over
1 Zaika
2 Vama
3 Tamarind
4 Salloos
5 Star of India

Under £35
1 Lahore Kebab House
2 Shree Krishna
3 Kastoori
4 Battersea Rickshaw
5 Rasa

Chinese

£35 and over
1 Ken Lo's Memories
2 Mao Tai
3 Dorchester, Oriental
4 Zen
5 Mr Wing

Under £35
1 Fung Shing
2 Royal China
3 Mandarin Kitchen
4 Mr Kong
5 Hunan

Japanese

£35 and over
1 Shogun
2 Tatsuso
3 Matsuri
4 Miyama
5 Suntory

Under £35
1 Inaho
2 Café Japan
3 Kulu Kulu
4 Ikkyu
5 Itsu

LONDON DIRECTORY

Aglio e Olio SW10   **£ 24**   ★

194 Fulham Rd   (020) 7351 0070   4–3B
"Delicious, basic Italian food" that's *"good-value"* (by the
standards of Chelsea's 'Beach') has already made this *"noisy"*
newcomer a popular stand-by. / **Sample dishes:** *antipasti; spaghetti
with clams; panna cotta with fresh berries.* **Details:** *11.30 pm.*

Al Hamra W1   **£ 39**   ★

31-33 Shepherd Mkt   (020) 7493 1954   2–4B
"Top-notch", if pricey, cooking is the highlight at this long-
established Lebanese, characterfully located in Shepherd Market
(with great outside tables in summer); *"unless you speak Arabic,
you may be treated like a tourist".* / **Sample dishes:** *tabbouleh;
Lebanese mixed grill; honey & cream cheese halva.* **Details:** *11.30 pm;
no Switch.*

Alounak   **£ 20**   ★★

10 Russell Gdns, W14   (020) 7603 1130
44 Westbourne Grove, W2   (020) 7229 0416
"Great kebabs and BYO economy" provide *"excellent value for
money"* at this *"authentic"* Persian duo, near Olympia and in
Bayswater. / **Sample dishes:** *yoghurt & cucumber dip; lamb & tomato
skewers; Persian sweets.* **Details:** *Midnight; no Amex.*

Andrew Edmunds W1   **£ 30**   𝔸

46 Lexington St   (020) 7437 5708   2–2D
"Once introduced, you return many times as an old friend" to this
"fun", *"squashed"*, *"no-fuss"* *"charmer"*, in a candlelit Soho
townhouse; the modern British cooking is *"usually good value"*,
and the amazing wine list a *"great draw".* / **Sample
dishes:** *houmous with asparagus & artichokes; sea bass with banana leaf &
Thai rice; citrus tart.* **Details:** *10.45 pm.*

The Anglesea Arms W6   **£ 26**   ★★

35 Wingate Rd   (020) 8749 1291
"Great ingredients, imaginatively prepared" guarantee that *"seats
are in short supply"* at this *"buzzy"*, Brackenbury Village
gastropub; it's *"smoky"*, though, and service is *"still so slow"* –
"you'll be drunk before you get your dinner". / **Sample dishes:** *deep-
fried courgette flowers with goat's cheese; char-grilled lamb, green salad &
chips; lemon & ricotta tart with raspberries.* **Details:** *10.45 pm; no Amex;
no booking.*

Anglo Asian Tandoori N16   **£ 19**   𝔸★

60-62 Stoke Newington Ch St   (020) 7254 9298
Low-lit Stoke Newington Indian whose *"courteous"* service, *"well
prepared"* traditional cooking and *"reasonable"* prices make it a
top local choice. / **Sample dishes:** *samosas; chicken tikka masala; Indian
ice cream.* **Details:** *11.45 pm, Fri & Sat 12.30 am; no Switch.*

The Apprentice SE1   **£ 27**   ★

31 Shad Thames   (020) 7234 0254
"Well-presented food" at *"great-value"* prices attracts many
willing 'guinea pigs' to the dining room of this South Bank
catering school; that *"service varies widely"* is all part of the fun,
but you must *"bring your own atmosphere".* / **Sample dishes:** *seared
scallops in tomato & parsley purée; pork with lemon grass boulangère; banana
ravioli with apricot sauce.* **Details:** *8.30 pm; closed Sat & Sun;
no smoking area.*

Asia de Cuba WC2   £ 55   A

45 St Martin's Ln   (020) 7300 5500   3–4C

*The off-the-wall décor of Ian Schrager's (he of NY's Studio 54, Royalton, etc) Manhattanite new Covent Garden hotel is certainly impressive (as is the number of style police in attendance); on a day two visit, the pricey fusion fare in the restaurant did little to distract from the scene, and the beautiful people were already out in force. / **Sample dishes:** Thai beef salad; pan-roasted spiced duck; chocolate pecan tart. **Details:** Midnight, 1am Sat; closed Sat L.*

Assaggi W2   £ 40   A★★

39 Chepstow Pl   (020) 7792 5501

*A cult following ensures "you can never get a table" at this "terrific" dining room above a Bayswater pub, where "original and different" regional cooking and "very friendly" service make this now the highest-rated Italian in town. / **Sample dishes:** pecorino with carpegna & rocket; fillet of beef with spinach; panna cotta. **Details:** 11.30 pm; closed Sun.*

Les Associés N8   £ 32

172 Park Rd   (020) 8348 8944

*"Lovely, little local", beloved of Crouch Enders, thanks to charming service and the "great value for money" of its "classic French" menu. / **Sample dishes:** pheasant terrine; beef in red wine sauce; chocolate mousse. **Value tip:** set Sun L £22(FP). **Details:** 10 pm; closed Mon & Sat L; no Amex.*

The Atlas SW6   £ 23   A★

16 Seagrave Rd   (020) 7385 9129   4–3A

*"A new start-up worthy of support" – this "Eagle-spawned foodie pub", near Earl's Court 2, offers "generously portioned" Mediterranean grub in a "convivial" setting; "great garden", too. / **Sample dishes:** spinach soup; pork chops with confit garlic; chocolate mousse cake. **Details:** 10.30 pm; no Amex; no booking.*

Aubergine SW10   £ 59   A★★

11 Park Wk   (020) 7352 3449   4–3B

*Gordon Ramsay's move may have robbed this Chelsea address of its headlines, but William Drabble's "tantalising" cooking still makes a visit here a "special treat" – the "unobtrusive" service and "relaxed" setting both outrank the old master's new place. / **Sample dishes:** scallops wrapped in dried bacon; duck with creamed confit cabbage; roast figs in honey & lime sauce. **Value tip:** set weekday L £34(FP). **Details:** 10.30 pm; closed Sat L & Sun.*

L'Aventure NW8   £ 38   A★★

3 Blenheim Ter   (020) 7624 6232

*"What a lovely restaurant", typifies reactions to this "evergreen" St John's Wood "romantic" favourite, where the Gallic fare is "beautifully presented, and as tasty as it looks". / **Sample dishes:** scallops in basil oil; leg of rabbit stuffed with sesame sauce; gratin of pear with sabayon. **Details:** 11 pm; closed Sat L (and Sun in winter); no Switch.*

The Avenue SW1   **£ 44**

7-9 St James's St   (020) 7321 2111   2–4D

"Airy", "bright" and "buzzy" St James's establishment, whose
performance is quite good, judged by the standards of West End
mega-brasseries – that is to say that it's a touch "overpriced" and
service is "erratic". / **Sample dishes:** Mozzarella, Parma ham & salami
bruschetta; seared salmon with aubergine gratin & marinated squid; blackberry
& apple pie. **Value tip:** pre-th. £30(FP). **Details:** Midnight, Fri & Sat
12.30 am, Sun 10 pm.

Axis WC2   **£ 47**

1 Aldwych   (020) 7300 0300   1–2D

"Smart and sleek" West End basement ("bunker"?) yearling,
whose modern British cooking is often hailed as "mouthwatering"
and "beautifully presented" (though it can sometimes "fail to
ignite"); the slightly "clinical" ambience especially suits business.
/ **Sample dishes:** potato terrine with truffles; seared tuna in Indian spices;
summer berries with peach sorbet. **Details:** 11.15 pm; closed Sat L & Sun.

Babur Brasserie SE23   **£ 26**   ★★

119 Brockley Rise, Forest Hl   (020) 8291 2400

"Lovely and delicate" Indian cooking – with excellent regional
specialities – justifies the trip to this Forest Hill subcontinental.
/ **Sample dishes:** lamb with fennel, ginger & saffron; tuna with red chilli &
palm vinegar; banana, apricot & roast almond pie. **Value tip:** set Sun L
£14(FP). **Details:** 11.15 pm; closed Fri L; no smoking area.

Back to Basics W1   **£ 35**   ★★

21a Foley St   (020) 7436 2181   1–1B

"Great fresh fish" wins universal praise for this "cramped and
basic" Fitzrovian, even though sometimes "sniffy" service
contributes to an atmosphere many find "grim". / **Sample
dishes:** mushroom stuffed with crab, spinach & Parmesan; baby monkfish with
crayfish salsa; bread & butter pudding with whisky. **Details:** 10 pm; closed Sat
& Sun.

Bah Humbug SW2   **£ 27**   Ⓐ

St Matthew's Church   (020) 7738 3184

"Atmospheric, cool and trendy" Brixton veggie, where the "very
good" ambience – if you like Gothic church crypts – is a greater
strength than the "too wholesome to be tasty" cooking. / **Sample
dishes:** avocado mousseline; Cantonese mock duck; strawberry crepes with
chocolate fondue. **Details:** 11.30 pm; D only, Sat & Sun open L & D;
no Amex.

Bank WC2   **£ 47**

1 Kingsway   (020) 7379 9797   1–2D

The "best of the mega-brasseries" is "great for a quick business
dinner" (and also popular for breakfast); many now think it
"oversized and overpriced", though (and "don't forget your
earplugs"). / **Sample dishes:** chicken with mango & coriander; seared
mullet with sesame dressing; sticky toffee pudding with honey ice cream. **Value
tip:** pre-th. £29(FP). **Details:** 11 pm; no Switch.

Bar Italia W1   **£ 6**   Ⓐ

22 Frith St   (020) 7437 4520   3–2A

"Where else is there at 3 am?" – this "irresistible" 24-hour Soho
"classic", famous for the "best coffee anywhere" is a "great place
to people-watch" and soak up the "after-movies or after-
clubbing" atmosphere. / **Sample dishes:** salami sandwich; spaghetti
carbonara; tiramisu. **Details:** 4 am, Fri & Sat 24 hours; no credit cards;
no booking.

Battersea Rickshaw SW11   £ 22
15-16 Battersea Sq   (020) 7924 2450   4–4C
"All the ambience of a three-star hotel in Slough" does little to dent locals enthusiasm for this Battersea stalwart, with its "very good and consistent" curries and "smiley" service. / **Sample dishes:** quail in ginger & tomato sauce; sour lime chicken; Indian ice cream. **Details:** 11.30 pm; D only.

Belgo   £ 30
50 Earlham St, WC2   (020) 7813 2233
124 Ladbroke Grove, W10   (020) 8982 8400
72 Chalk Farm Rd, NW1   (020) 7267 0718
Though some still "like the concept" of this Belgian moules/frites (and beer) chain, for many the "gimmick" is now just "old hat"; for 'formula-food' it is amazingly "expensive", especially given the "squashed" conditions and utterly "indifferent" service, charged for at a shocking 15%. / **Sample dishes:** bacon & egg warm salad; mussels in wine & garlic sauce; vanilla ice cream with ginger biscuits. **Details:** 11.30 pm.

Bibendum SW3   £ 59   🅐
81 Fulham Rd   (020) 7581 5817   4–2C
Hold the front page – Brompton Cross Landmark Stages Comeback!; it's rather exciting to see this once great modern French restaurant beginning to regain its old form; it's still "overpriced" and a bit "snotty", but then it always has been. / **Sample dishes:** sautéed foie gras with redcurrant sauce; chicken in tarragon sauce; chocolate Pithiviers. **Details:** 10.30 pm.

Bibendum Oyster Bar SW3   £ 34   🅐★
81 Fulham Rd   (020) 7589 1480   4–2C
"Great shellfish, prawns and other tasty cold fruits de mer" win high praise at this "elegant" bar in the foyer of the Conran Shop. / **Sample dishes:** oysters; avocado & brown shrimp salad; crème brûlée. **Details:** 10 pm; no booking.

The Birdcage W1   £ 56   🅐★
110 Whitfield St   (020) 7323 9655   1–1B
It's "weird and wonderful" to find this "exotic" and "intimate" yearling in such an "awful" location (near Warren Street tube); the "innovative" and "spicy" fusion menu is exciting too, but soaring prices mean some now find it just "too expensive". / **Sample dishes:** Thai soup with couscous spring rolls; skate wing with penne & ginger sauce; kumquats with honey & orange juice. **Details:** 11.15 pm; closed Sat L & Sun; no smoking area.

Blah! Blah! Blah! W12   £ 23   🅐★
78 Goldhawk Rd   (020) 8746 1337
"Incredibly flavoursome" veggie food, "that never fails to impress carnivores", wins high praise for this "dark" and "friendly" Shepherd's Bush fixture; BYO. / **Sample dishes:** tarte Tatin; potato & tomato rosti; passion fruit tart. **Details:** 11 pm; closed Sun; no credit cards.

Blakes Hotel SW7   £ 88   🅐
33 Roland Gdns   (020) 7370 6701   4–2B
"She (or he) had better be worth it", if you're contemplating a visit to this opulent, "dark" and rather "naughty" South Kensington townhouse hotel basement, famed for its aphrodisiac qualities; the cooking may be "wonderfully creative" but it's also "far too expensive". / **Sample dishes:** wild mushroom risotto; crispy chicken & ginger sauce; millefeuille with praline sauce. **Details:** 11.30 pm.

Bleeding Heart EC1   **£ 33**   A★

Bleeding Heart Yd, Greville St   (020) 7242 8238
*"It's a delight to introduce new diners" to this "difficult-to-find",
"cramped" and "cosy" Holborn cellar, which is as popular for
business lunches as for "romantic" evenings; "solid" French fare
and an "excellent wine list" complete the package. / Sample
dishes: smoked salmon with sweet mustard sauce; venison with fresh figs
& Merlot sauce; coconut mousse with roast banana compote.
Details: 10.30 pm; closed Sat & Sun.*

Blue Elephant SW6   **£ 44**   A★

4-6 Fulham Broadway   (020) 7385 6595   4–4A
*It's not only the "unique" and spacious setting – "a bit like
Fantasy Island" – that makes this "great fun" and "romantic"
Fulham Thai once again London's most talked-about ethnic; the
food is "consistently good" (if "expensive"), and service "friendly"
and "attentive". / Sample dishes: prawns & chicken in rice paper with
plum sauce; stir-fried pork with mushrooms & baby corn; fresh fruits with
raspberry sauce. Details: Midnight, Sun 10.30 pm; closed Sat L; smart casual.*

Bluebird SW3   **£ 45**

350 Kings Rd   (020) 7559 1000   4–3C
*"Conran Restaurants should be ashamed" of this "very
overpriced" and "increasingly disappointing" Chelsea hangar –
"for such a lovely-looking restaurant, it's so incredibly average".
/ Sample dishes: tomato tart; smoked rabbit with mushrooms; chocolate
mousse. Value tip: pre-th. £27(FP). Details: 11 pm.*

Bombay Palace W2   **£ 32**   A★

50 Connaught St   (020) 7723 8855
*"Consistently good", if "somewhat impersonal", Indian, just north
of Hyde Park, whose "fresh and tasty" cooking merits greater
recognition than it achieves. / Sample dishes: lamb & lentil kebabs;
chicken in yoghurt & black peppercorns; carrot halva. Details: 11.30 pm;
no smoking area.*

Brady's SW18   **£ 20**   ★

513 Old York Rd   (020) 8877 9599
*"Plump, moist fish and big fat chips" attract "weekend queues"
at this "unpretentious" Wandsworth bistro. / Sample dishes: smoked
salmon; cod & chips; treacle tart. Details: 10.30 pm; closed Sun;
no credit cards; no booking.*

La Brasserie SW3   **£ 34**   A

272 Brompton Rd   (020) 7584 1668   4–2C
*"Improved after the revamp" – admittedly from a low base – this
atmospheric South Kensington institution still specialises in
"standard", Gallic fare, served rather "lazily"; "great" weekend
breakfasts are a highlight. / Sample dishes: stuffed provençale
mushrooms; pan-fried monkfish in white wine; crème brûlée.
Details: 11.30 pm; no booking Sat L or Sun L.*

Brasserie 24 EC2   **£ 39**   A

International Financial Centre   (020) 7877 7703
*"Sensational views" – which can now also be enjoyed at night –
ensure the 24th-floor dining room at the building formerly known
as the NatWest Tower is "consistently full"; the food is "not
exciting, but well cooked". / Details: 9 pm; closed Sat & Sun.*

Café 209 SW6   **£ 17**
209 Munster Rd   (020) 7385 3625
*"Relaxed, no-fuss, BYO" Thai, which younger Fulhamites
pronounce "always a hoot" – indeed, all the hooting makes it
"noisy"; the "bantering" owner is Joy – "by name and nature".
/ **Sample dishes**: tom yum soup; Thai green curry; banana fritter ice cream.
Details: 10.45 pm; D only; closed Sun; no credit cards.*

Café du Marché EC1   **£ 36**   Ⓐ★
22 Charterhouse Sq   (020) 7608 1609
*"Relax – forget the City for a couple of hours", at this "very
attractive", "rustic" favourite on the fringe of Smithfield, which
offers "reliable" French cooking and "friendly" service; it's "very
different in the evenings", when romantics replace suits, and
there's jazz. / **Sample dishes**: tomato, anchovies & tuna salad; roast
partridge in red wine sauce; prune and armagnac pudding. **Details:** 10 pm;
closed Sat L & Sun; no Amex.*

Café Japan NW11   **£ 24**   ★
626 Finchley Rd   (020) 8455 6854
*You're "enthusiastically greeted" at this Golders Green oriental,
which is "always busy", thanks to a "wide range of dishes at
reasonable prices", not least "top-quality sushi". / **Sample
dishes**: seafood tempura; Japanese crispy duck; green tea ice cream.
Details: 10.30 pm; closed Mon L & Tue L; no Amex; no smoking area.*

Café Spice Namaste   **£ 31**   ★
247 Lavender Hl, SW11   (020) 7738 1717
16 Prescot St, E1   (020) 7488 9242
*Cyrus Todiwala's "very interesting" (and often "exceptional")
Indian cooking justifies the trip to the large, "bright" and
"modern" original, near Tower Bridge; the inferior Battersea
offshoot is a bit of a red herring. / **Sample dishes**: pan-fried chicken
with chutney; tiger prawns, crab & squid curry; coconut & pineapple ice cream.
Details: 10.30 pm, Sat 10 pm; E1 closed Sat L & Sun - SW11 D only
except Sun when L & D.*

Cambio de Tercio SW5   **£ 33**   Ⓐ
163 Old Brompton Rd   (020) 7244 8970   4–2B
*"Really good fun" – this stylish South Kensington spot serves
some "good Spanish food", and has a "friendly" attitude.
/ **Sample dishes**: sweetcorn & prawn ravioli; grilled tuna with caramelised
vinegar; citrus sorbets. **Details:** 11 pm.*

The Canteen SW10   **£ 39**   Ⓐ★
Chelsea Harbour   (020) 7351 7330   4–4B
*"Only the location in dismal Chelsea Harbour is a let-down", at
this "brilliant", if nowadays slightly unsung, modern British "all-
rounder"; it reliably delivers "top food and top service" in a
"unique" setting. / **Sample dishes**: quail, pancetta & brioche salad; lobster
tempura, Asian greens & Chinese noodles; crème brûlée. **Details:** 11 pm, Fri
& Sat midnight; closed Sat L & Sun.*

Capital Hotel SW3   **£ 75**
22-24 Basil St   (020) 7589 5171   4–1D
*"Formal" and pricey Knightsbridge hotel dining room, whose quiet
competence has long offered a "consistent" culinary benchmark;
initial reports give cause to question whether new chef Eric
Chavot is keeping up standards. / **Sample dishes**: onion velouté with
chorizo tortellini; lamb & tomato risotto; iced tea parfait. **Value tip:** set
weekday L £36(FP). **Details:** 11 pm; dinner, jacket & tie.*

Le Caprice SW1   £ 47   Ⓐ★

Arlington Hs, Arlington St   (020) 7629 2239   2–4C

*The engine purrs so smoothly at this ultra-"chic" modern British "perennial" near the Ritz that there are always doubters who "can't understand the fuss"; to its legions of devotees, though, it's just "overall wonderful" – "surviving its new ownership with flying colours" – and "always booked". / **Sample dishes:** crispy duck & watercress salad; rabbit with rosemary & pumpkin polenta; bread pudding with cinnamon ice cream. **Details:** Midnight.*

Caraffini SW1   £ 34   Ⓐ★

61-63 Lower Sloane St   (020) 7259 0235   4–2D

*"Good value for money" and "fun waiters who are professionals" make this "bustling" and "friendly" Italian near Sloane Square a great local favourite – "in spite of the noise". / **Sample dishes:** Parma ham & melon; veal in lemon sauce; tiramisu. **Details:** 11.30 pm; closed Sun.*

Chelsea Bun Diner SW10   £ 18

9a Lamont Rd   (020) 7352 3635   4–3B

*"Titanic fry-ups" at "good-value" prices make this "fun and lively" diner Chelsea's number one "hangover breakfast" point – at other times, the BYO policy is the principal attraction; they "need a no-smoking area". / **Sample dishes:** stuffed potato skins; cheeseburger & chips; banana split. **Details:** 11 pm; no Amex.*

The Chelsea Ram SW10   £ 26   Ⓐ★

32 Burnaby St   (020) 7351 4008   4–4B

*"Delicious pub grub at reasonable prices" and an "attractive interior" guarantee that this obscurely located Chelsea "hang-out" is often "too busy"; the food has "slipped" slightly, though. / **Sample dishes:** ham hock salad with lentils; herb-crusted lamb & macaroon ragoût; bread & butter pudding. **Details:** 10 pm; no Amex; no booking.*

Chez Bruce SW17   £ 38   Ⓐ★★

2 Bellevue Rd   (020) 8672 0114

*This "great neighbourhood restaurant" overlooking Wandsworth Common elicits a hymn of praise – from reporters right across London – for its "top quality", "inventive" and "good value" modern British cooking and its "lovely, friendly" service. / **Sample dishes:** smoked haddock mousse with pickled cucumber; stuffed leg of rabbit with tomato, ceps & noodles; poached figs with almond cake. **Details:** 10.30 pm; closed Sun D; booking: max 6.*

Chez Liline N4   £ 30   ★★

101 Stroud Green Rd   (020) 7263 6550

*Arguably "the best exotic fish restaurant in town" may have a "lousy" Finsbury Park location, "uninspiring" décor and sometimes "slow" service, but it offers "excellent value" and is "worth a detour". / **Sample dishes:** tiger prawns with ginger & spring onions; plateau of shellfish & crustacea; fresh tropical fruits. **Details:** 10.30 pm; closed Sun.*

Chez Nico at Ninety
Grosvenor House Hotel W1   £ 89   ★
90 Park Ln   (020) 7409 1290   2–3A
Even those lauding "exceptional" food at Nico Ladenis's Mayfair
temple of gastronomy admit that it's a "very dull" place, and
increasingly the view is that the whole performance is "very
ordinary, for the price". / **Sample dishes:** *griddled foie gras; veal cutlets*
with roast garlic; lemon tart. **Details:** *11 pm; closed Sat L & Sun; no Switch;*
jacket & tie.

Chezmax SW10   £ 41   𝔸★★
168 Ifield Rd   (020) 7835 0874   4–3A
"Superb" and "inspired" Gallic cooking and "amazing" service –
the maître d' is "awesome" – are carving out a notable
reputation for this obscurely sited Chelsea-fringe basement; "it's
equally good for romance or a good night out". / **Sample**
dishes: *goat's cheese tart; lobster with caramelised root vegetables; fresh figs in*
amaretto. **Details:** *11 pm; closed Mon & Sun.*

Chiang Mai W1   £ 32   ★★
48 Frith St   (020) 7437 7444   3–2A
This Soho stalwart's "authentic", "imaginative" and "subtle" Thai
cuisine is the best of its type in the West End; the catch? – the
atmosphere can be "deathly". / **Sample dishes:** *Thai fishcakes; chicken*
with lemon grass curry; sorbets. **Details:** *11 pm; closed Sun L; no Amex.*

Churchill Arms W8   £ 15   ★
119 Kensington Ch St   (020) 7792 1246
"The best Thai food ever, and as cheap as anything" ensures it's
"impossible to get a table" at this very well known Kensington
pub-annexe; beware – "if you haven't booked, the waitresses can
be scary". / **Sample dishes:** *won tons; prawns with stir-fried noodles; apple*
pie. **Details:** *9.30 pm; closed Sun D; no Amex; no lunch bookings.*

Chutney Mary SW10   £ 42   ★
535 King's Rd   (020) 7351 3113   4–4B
"Consistently good" cooking, which "may not all be authentic, but
is exciting and delicious", has made this "spacious and airy"
Indian "with a twist" the best known subcontinental in town, in
spite of its distant-Chelsea location. / **Sample dishes:** *chilli calamari;*
lamb chops with apricot; bitter chocolate kulfi. **Value tip:** *set weekday L*
£27(FP). **Details:** *11.30 pm; no smoking area.*

Cibo W14   £ 40   ★
3 Russell Gdns   (020) 7371 6271
"Intimate" (if vaguely "weird") Olympia Italian whose "delicious"
(if pricey) cooking and "unusual" wines make it quite a
"favourite"; "make sure you get a good table – some are
cramped". / **Sample dishes:** *deep-fried courgette flowers; lobster spaghetti;*
amaretto semifreddo. **Details:** *11 pm; closed Sat L & Sun D; smart casual.*

City Miyama EC4   £ 51   ★
17 Godliman St   (020) 7489 1937
This "stark" City Japanese is "expensive but worth it"; the
teppan-yaki and sushi bars find most favour – "the restaurant
itself is fine, but atmosphere-free". / **Sample dishes:** *chicken yakitori*
skewers; salmon teriyaki; green tea ice cream. **Details:** *9.30 pm; closed Sat D*
& Sun.

City Rhodes EC4   £ 55   ★
New Street Sq   (020) 7583 1313
"Exquisite" modern British cooking and "extremely helpful" and "efficient" staff create "a very good atmosphere for business" at Gary R's dining room, just off Fleet Street – reporters' top choice for an "expensive" City lunch. / Sample dishes: tomato terrine with peppered goat's cheese; rabbit with parsley & garlic tart; baked custard with nutmeg ice cream. Details: 9 pm; closed Sat & Sun.

Claridges Restaurant W1   £ 70   🄰
Brook St   (020) 7629 8860   2–2B
"Impressive and elegant" it may be, but the charming Art Deco dining room of Society's favourite hotel only really sets pulses racing at breakfast, which is "exceptional in every way". / Sample dishes: oak-smoked Scottish salmon; roast rack of lamb; apple sorbet. Details: 10.45 pm; jacket & tie.

Clarke's W8   £ 46   🄰★★
124 Kensington Ch St   (020) 7221 9225
Sally Clarke's "always spot-on" cooking offers "simplicity at its best" from "focussed" modern British menus (which, at dinner, offer no choice); many find her "very pleasant" restaurant, near Notting Hill Gate, "romantic" – especially upstairs. / Sample dishes: Mozzarella with spiced aubergines; chicken with polenta & wilted spinach; bitter chocolate & prune soufflé. Details: 10 pm; closed Sun; no smoking area.

Club Gascon EC1   £ 33   🄰★★
57 West Smithfield   (020) 7796 0600
"Foie gras in every conceivable permutation" is part of the "exceptional and different" repertoire which has made this unusual newcomer – specialising in Gascony's "gutsy" cuisine – the foodie hit of the year; an "excellent and unusual wine list" is a bonus. / Sample dishes: char-grilled foie gras & sweet onion marmalade; cassoulet of veal sweetbreads; crème Catalan. Details: 11 pm; closed Sat L & Sun; no Amex.

Connaught W1   £ 70   🄰
Carlos Pl   (020) 7499 7070   2–3B
"Splendid", panelled Mayfair dining room whose dependable Anglo-French cooking remains resolutely "unfashionable and calorific"; service is legendarily "perfect". / Sample dishes: smoked fish pâté; fillet steak with green peppercorn sauce; burnt Cambridge cream. Details: 10.45 pm; Grill closed Sat L; jacket & tie for dinner; jacket for lunch.

Coq d'Argent EC3   £ 49
1 Poultry   (020) 7395 5000
"Typically Conran" City yearling – albeit one with a "fantastic" 6th-floor location – offering cooking which is "nothing special" at "bank robbery" prices; "crazy" table-turning demands are a recurrent complaint. / Sample dishes: artichoke & walnut salad; steak with bordelaise sauce; passion fruit cheesecake. Value tip: set Sun L £32(FP). Details: 10 pm; closed Sat L & Sun D.

The Criterion W1   £ 43   🄰
Piccadilly Circus   (020) 7930 0488   2–3D
It's a pity that "disobliging" and "elusive" service mars so many visits to this "exquisite" neo-Byzantine chamber – its school-of-MPW cooking may not be remarkable, but it is competent by the standards of the larger West End places. / Sample dishes: smoked salmon with sauce vierge; roast pork with sage mash; crème brûlée. Details: Midnight, Sun 10.30 pm.

Cross Keys SW3   £ 33   𝔸

1 Lawrence St   (020) 7349 9111   4–3C
*"Not very pub-like", former Chelsea boozer, whose rear
conservatory houses "such a lovely restaurant", serving fairly good
modern British fare in a "fun" and "buzzy" atmosphere. / Sample
dishes: duck liver terrine; salmon & couscous salad; roast nectarines with
ginger crunch. Value tip: set weekday L £20(FP). Details: 11 pm.*

Del Buongustaio SW15   £ 33   𝔸★★

283 Putney Br Rd   (020) 8780 9361
*"Original" and "consistently excellent" cooking (and "exciting
wines", too) makes this externally unpromising but "intimate"
Putney Italian a very popular southwest London destination.
/ Sample dishes: wild mushrooms sautéed with pears; roast tuna with peanut
& herb crust; coffee tart with chocolate ice cream. Value tip: set weekday L
£22(FP). Details: 10.30 pm; closed Sat L.*

Dorchester Grill
Dorchester Hotel W1   £ 59   𝔸★

53 Park Ln   (020) 7629 8888   2–3A
*With its "sumptuous, old-fashioned" Spanish Baronial décor,
"impressive" (but "not condescending") service and "dependable"
cooking, this "grand" Mayfair grill is a worthy representative of
"English tradition at its best". / Sample dishes: dressed Cornish crab;
steak & kidney pie; bread & butter pudding. Value tip: pre-th. £40(FP).
Details: 11 pm; smart casual.*

Dorchester, Oriental
Dorchester Hotel W1   £ 70

53 Park Ln   (020) 7629 8888   2–3A
*The cooking – "on a par with Hong Kong" – is "almost worth the
prices" at this swanky Mayfair Chinese; some think the décor
"chic" – we're with those who find it "silkily off-putting". / Sample
dishes: prawn & chicken dumplings with ginger; stir-fried prawns with spinach
& chilli; chilled mango pudding. Value tip: set weekday L £25(FP).
Details: 11 pm; closed Sat L & Sun; smart casual.*

The Eagle EC1   £ 22   𝔸★

159 Farringdon Rd   (020) 7837 1353
*"Fight to get a table" if you want to enjoy the "gutsy"
Mediterranean cooking which has won fame for this "cramped
and smoky" gastropub (it was London's first), on the fringe of
Smithfield. / Sample dishes: pumpkin, chilli & Parmesan risotto; scallops on
bruschetta with rocket & peppers; Portuguese custard tart. Details: 10.30 pm;
closed Sun D; no credit cards; no booking.*

Eco   £ 25   ★

162 Clapham High St, SW4   (020) 7978 1108
4 Market Row, Brixton Market, SW9   (020) 7738 3021
*"Electric atmosphere and top pizzas" have made the oddly
decorated, 'original' Clapham branch a "very trendy" (if "noisy",
"smoky" and "uncomfortable") south London phenomenon; the
Brixton Market branch – where you can BYO – actually came
first (as Pizzeria Franco), and was re-badged this year. / Sample
dishes: marinated aubergines with anchovies; pizza Florentina; tiramisu.
Details: SW4 11 pm, Sat 11.30 pm - SW9 L only; SW9 closed Wed & Sun;
SW4 Mon-Fri no smoking area; SW9 no booking.*

Ed's Easy Diner ✳   £ 21   𝔸

12 Moor St, W1   (020) 7439 1955
Trocadero, W1   (020) 7287 1951
362 King's Rd, SW3   (020) 7352 1956
O2 Centre, 255 Finchley Rd, NW3   (020) 7431 1958
*"You can't go far wrong" perching on a stool at these "retro"
American diners – they offer "perfect burgers" and "milkshakes
to die for".* / **Sample dishes:** crispy onion rings; bacon & cheeseburger with
chips; Oreo sundae. **Details:** Midnight - SW3 & NW3 11 pm - all branches
1 am, Fri & Sat; no booking.

Elistano SW3   £ 26   𝔸★

25-27 Elystan St   (020) 7584 5248   4–2C
*It's the "perfect local Italian", say devotees of this "crowded",
"noisy" and "fun" Chelsea backstreet trattoria.* / **Sample
dishes:** baked aubergine with Parmesan; veal with artichokes & mushrooms;
tiramisu. **Details:** 11 pm; closed Sun.

The Engineer NW1   £ 35   𝔸

65 Gloucester Ave   (020) 7722 0950
*"Overcrowded", Primrose Hill gastropub hailed for its "great,
relaxed atmosphere", "beautiful garden" and "beautiful punters";
"everything is fresh, and portions are generous", with the "great
Sunday brunch" perhaps the leading attraction.* / **Sample
dishes:** parsnip soup; roasted sea bass; pomegranate parfait.
Details: 10.30 pm; no Amex.

The Enterprise SW3   £ 32   𝔸

35 Walton St   (020) 7584 3148   4–2C
*"Always lively, always fun" – this "easy-going" converted pub is
usually "packed to the gills" with quite a "wacky" crowd (well, by
Knightsbridge standards); the food is not really the point.* / **Sample
dishes:** spinach gnocchi; peppered lamb fillet; sticky toffee pudding.
Details: 11 pm; smart casual; booking: Mon-Fri L only.

Esarn Kheaw W12   £ 23   ★

314 Uxbridge Rd   (020) 8743 8930
*Shepherd's Bush "gem", offering "great, spicy and authentic"
north Thai cooking "at a bargain price"; as a place, it's "not fun",
though, and service is very "indifferent".* / **Sample dishes:** northern
Thai sausages; pan-fried pomfret with noodles; ice cream. **Details:** 11 pm;
closed Sat L & Sun L.

L'Escargot W1   £ 40   𝔸★

48 Greek St   (020) 7437 2679   3–2A
*"Excellent cooking", "friendly and attentive" service and a
"charming" atmosphere have finally come together again at this
reviving Gallic classic in the heart of Soho – now a top all-round
West End choice; upstairs, the suitably adorned Picasso Room
offers pricier fine dining.* / **Sample dishes:** Scottish langoustines with
caviar; lamb chump with butter beans; champagne fruit jelly.
Details: 11.30 pm; closed Sat L & Sun.

Faulkner's E8   £ 19   ★★

424-426 Kingsland Rd   (020) 7254 6152
*"Except for the impossible location", this eminent East Ender
wins consistent acclaim thanks to "the best fish and chips
around"; BYO.* / **Sample dishes:** prawn cocktail; cod with chips & peas;
rhubarb crumble. **Details:** 10 pm; no Amex; no smoking area.

fish! SE1   £ 30   ★
Cathedral St   (020) 7836 3236
*The "greenhouse-like" Borough Market prototype of this
ambitious new chain, has made a good start with its "fresh and
simple" fish and "efficient" service; coming soon – openings in
Battersea, Canary Wharf, Marylebone and Smithfield. / Sample
dishes: prawn cocktail; grilled halibut with butter sauce; treacle tart.
Details: 11 pm; closed Sun; no smoking area.*

Floriana SW3   £ 53   ★
15 Beauchamp Pl   (020) 7838 1500   4–1C
*It's a shame that the "divine" Italian cooking at this
"sophisticated" Knightsbridge newcomer is "aimed at the cost-
insensitive" and comes in such "small portions"; "the chief
obstacle to enjoyment", however, is the "exceptionally slooooow
service". / Sample dishes: Scottish lobster salad; grilled salmon with
hollandaise; lavender sorbet. Value tip: set weekday L £35(FP).
Details: 11 pm; closed Sun.*

Food for Thought WC2   £ 16   ★
31 Neal St   (020) 7836 0239   3–2C
*"Some of the best, wholesome veggie food in London" maintain
the continuing crush at this "tiny" Covent Garden basement café;
"scrummy puddings somehow undo all the good work of the
other dishes". / Sample dishes: green salad with croutons; Indonesian
casserole; apple & plum crumble. Details: 8.15 pm; closed Sun D;
no credit cards; no smoking; no booking.*

Fox & Anchor EC1   £ 22   𝔸★
115 Charterhouse St   (020) 7253 4838
*"Guinness and a full English breakfast, perfect", say fans of the
"astounding" fry-ups – "you can feel your arteries clogging up" –
at this Smithfield institution. / Sample dishes: prawn cocktail; fillet steak
with mushrooms; apple pie. Details: 10 pm, weekends 10.30 pm; closed Sun.*

Frederick's N1   £ 38   𝔸★
106 Camden Pas   (020) 7359 2888
*"A sense of occasion" attaches to this old Islington warhorse, with
its lofty conservatory; the "good-value" modern British cooking
has improved of late, and "slick" service contributes to a
"smooth" overall experience. / Sample dishes: lobster with pak choy;
roast lamb with mustard crust; milk chocolate mousse. Value tip: set Sat
Lunch £24(FP). Details: 11.30 pm; closed Sun; smart casual;
no smoking area.*

French House W1   £ 32   𝔸★
49 Dean St   (020) 7437 2477   3–3A
*The "food is back on form" – with a vengeance – at this "cosy",
"intriguing" and "romantic" dining room, above the famous Soho
pub; as at its sibling, St John, the modern British menu is
"uncompromising". / Sample dishes: ox tongue with sauce vierge; rabbit
& chicory in mustard sauce; burnt Cambridge cream. Details: 11.15 pm;
closed Sun.*

Fung Shing WC2   £ 32   ★★
15 Lisle St   (020) 7437 1539   3–3A
*"The best Chinese food in Chinatown" ("excellent seafood", in
particular) is consistently found at this "exceptional oriental";
there's "no real atmosphere", though. / Sample dishes: steamed
scallops with ginger; stir-fried ostrich with spring onions; mango pudding.
Details: 11.30 pm.*

Gallipoli   £ 22   Ａ★

102 Upper St, N1   (020) 7359 0630
120 Upper St, N1   (020) 7226 8099

*An "amazing-value" combination of "fresh" Turkish food (served
in "huge portions"), supremely "friendly" staff and a "lively"
atmosphere makes these "wonderfully cheap and cheerful"
Islington cafés "deservedly popular" – "it's best to book".*
/ **Sample dishes:** mussels in beer batter; fish & seafood brochettes; baklava.
Details: 11 pm; Fri & Sat 11.30 pm; no Amex.

The Gate W6   £ 27   Ａ★★

51 Queen Caroline St   (020) 8748 6932

*"Revolutionary" cooking makes this "hard-to-find" Hammersmith
spot – with its "great staff" and "laid back" atmosphere – "the
best veggie in London".* / **Sample dishes:** red pepper & sun dried tomato
roulade; teriyaki aubergine with pan-fried noodles; blueberry & lemon tart.
Details: 10.45 pm; closed Sat L & Sun.

Gaudi EC1   £ 42

63 Clerkenwell Rd   (020) 7608 3220

*Is the Spanish cooking at this Clerkenwell two-year-old "sublime",
or is it "difficult to find such bad food nowadays"?; is the
ambience "wonderful" or "terrible"?; does "everything work" or is
the service "dodgy"? – rarely does a place inspire such a
cornucopia of contradictory comments.* / **Sample dishes:** gazpacho
with creamed lobster; grilled swordfish with coriander; summer fruit tartlet.
Value tip: set weekday L £26(FP). **Details:** 10.30 pm; closed Sat L & Sun.

Le Gavroche W1   £ 97   ★

43 Upper Brook St   (020) 7408 0881   2–2A

*For traditionalists, "the best French food in town" (not to mention
"the best wine list") makes this "slightly stuffy" Mayfair stalwart
"a true corner of paradise"; "outrageous" prices irritate some,
making "the best quality set lunch in London" all the more
attractive.* / **Sample dishes:** lobster & champagne mousse; medallions of
veal; white chocolate parfait. **Details:** 11 pm; closed Sat & Sun; jacket & tie.

Giraffe   £ 22   Ａ★

6-8 Blandford St, W1   (020) 7935 2333
46 Rosslyn Hl, NW3   (020) 7435 0343

*Can these "cool", "sparkily decorated", "'70s ambience"
newcomers revolutionise our perception of chain restaurants?;
with their "enthusiastic young staff" and "enormous portions" of
"surprisingly good" food, they could… if they can keep it up.*
/ **Sample dishes:** minted couscous with roast vegetables; spicy Moroccan lamb
with red lentils; apple & pecan crumble. **Details:** NW3 11.30 pm - W1
11.15 pm; no smoking; no booking.

The Glasshouse TW1   £ 37   ★★

14 Station Parade, Kew   (020) 8940 6777

*"Following in the footsteps of Chez Bruce" (same owner), this
"superb" newcomer is already "well worth the drive to Kew" on
account of its "brilliant" menu of "imaginative" modern British
cooking; "service doesn't match up", though.* / **Sample dishes:** pear,
endive & Roquefort in pastry; confit duck breast with red cabbage; orange
parfait with bitter chocolate sorbet. **Details:** 10.30 pm; closed Sun D.

Gordon Ramsay SW3   £ 68   ★★
68-69 Royal Hospital Rd   (020) 7352 4441   4–3D
The TV "hysterics" may be difficult to stomach, but not so Ramsay's "perfect and masterful" cooking which has clearly established his Chelsea yearling as the capital's culinary number one; service is so good it's "nearly intrusive", though, and the special charm of the 'old' Aubergine has not been transplanted to here. / **Sample dishes:** roast scallops with cauliflower purée; pigeon stuffed with ceps; hot chocolate fondant with caramel ice cream. **Value tip:** set weekday L £43(FP). **Details:** 11 pm; closed Sat & Sun.

Gordon's Wine Bar WC2   £ 19   𝔸
47 Villiers St   (020) 7930 1408   3–4D
"Great as ever", London's oldest wine bar offers a good, inexpensive wine selection to accompany its "super cheeses" and "reasonable" and "freshly cooked" plats du jour; its dark corners are ideal "for illicit encounters", and there's a wonderful terrace. / **Sample dishes:** smoked salmon mousse; fish lasagne & salad; treacle tart. **Details:** 9 pm; closed Sun; no Amex; no booking.

Grano W4   £ 42   ★
162 Thames Rd   (020) 8995 0120
The team from Tentazioni have hit the ground running at this "excellent" newcomer, near Kew Bridge, delivering some "imaginative" (and "deceptively filling") modern Italian cooking; it's "expensive for the location", though, and some complain of a "lack of atmosphere". / **Sample dishes:** asparagus ravioli; roast beef with wild mushrooms & radicchio; zabaglione. **Details:** 10.30 pm; closed Mon L, Sat L & Sun D.

Great Eastern Dining Room EC2   £ 30   𝔸★
54 Great Eastern St   (020) 7613 4545
"Cool" new Italian bar/restaurant which is already "too popular" with Shoreditch hipsters; the surprise is that the "simple" cooking is "well prepared", and that service is "friendly". / **Sample dishes:** field mushroom risotto; sea bream with lemon parsley sauce; plums with amaretto Mascarpone. **Details:** 10.30 pm; closed Sat L & Sun.

The Green Olive W9   £ 34   𝔸★
5 Warwick Pl   (020) 7289 2469
"A real surprise in Maida Vale", this "terrific neighbourhood Italian", by Clifton Nurseries, impresses with its "good food", "nice wines", "caring service" and "value for money"; it can be "romantic" too, but "you must sit upstairs". / **Sample dishes:** Mozzarella, aubergine & tomato salad; braised pork belly with mustard mash; chocolate mousse. **Details:** 10.45 pm; D only Mon-Fri; Sat & Sun open L & D.

Grissini SW1   £ 42   ★
Hyatt Carlton Tower, 2 Cadogan Pl   (020) 7858 7171   1–4A
"Stylish" Belgravia hotel restaurant whose "fantastic" Italian cooking and "obliging" service don't get the following which fans think it merits; the culprits seem to be the expense and, to some, "a lack of ambience". / **Sample dishes:** tuna carpaccio; scorpion fish with chick peas; pear & plum crumble. **Details:** 10.45 pm; no smoking area.

Halcyon Hotel W11 £ 61 ★
129 Holland Pk Ave (020) 7221 5411
There's no 'right answer' about the dining room of this discreet Holland Park villa hotel, beloved of celebs; for fans, it's a "romantic" place ("especially al fresco"), with "terrific" modern British food and "charming" service – for detractors, it's "expensive", "hotely" and "dull". / Sample dishes: warm artichoke & chicken liver salad; sea bass with oyster fritters; chocolate tart with orange ice cream. Value tip: set weekday L £39(FP). Details: 10.30 pm, Fri & Sat 11 pm; closed Sat L; smart casual.

Halepi £ 30 𝔸
18 Leinster Ter, W2 (020) 7262 1070
48-50 Belsize Ln, NW3 (020) 7431 5855
An odd duo comprising a "dark and intimate" Bayswater Greek taverna and its new, shinier Hampstead offshoot; fans applaud the "lively" spirit at both sites – sceptics just can't see it. / Sample dishes: chicken & lemon broth; lamb souvlaki; baklava. Details: W2 12.30 am - NW3 10 am.

Hard Rock Café W1 £ 27 𝔸
150 Old Park Ln (020) 7629 0382 2–4B
"The queue says it all", proclaim fans of this Mayfair "legend" – the original of the worldwide chain – which is "still rocking" ("too loud"); standards, though, are being "diluted". / Sample dishes: nachos with salsa & cheese; hamburger & chips; Heath Bar sundae. Details: 12.30 am, Fri & Sat 1 am; no Switch; no smoking area; no booking.

The Havelock Tavern W14 £ 27 𝔸★★
57 Masbro Rd (020) 7603 5374
"Arrive early to nab your table" to enjoy the "imaginative" and "consistent" cooking at this "relaxed" and "buzzy" Olympia gastropub – it can be "impossibly crowded and smoky" and service is "shambolic". / Sample dishes: smoked herring salad with mustard dressing; rump steak with horseradish & caper butter; treacle pudding with ginger ice cream. Details: 10 pm; no credit cards; no booking.

Hilaire SW7 £ 51 𝔸★
68 Old Brompton Rd (020) 7584 8993 4–2B
"Friendly" and "reliable" bourgeois South Kensington spot, where a loyal fan club hails "consistently excellent" French cooking; it's "comfortable" but "a little cramped", which some find "romantic". / Sample dishes: grilled scallops with relish; wild salmon with pea mash; chocolate marquise. Details: 11 pm; closed Sat L & Sun.

Hunan SW1 £ 29 ★★
51 Pimlico Rd (020) 7730 5712 4–2D
"There is much happy slurping" at this idiosyncratic and intimate Chinese near Pimlico Green – the cooking is "excellent", especially if you "leave the choice to them"; "slapdash" service is not unknown. / Sample dishes: pan-fried octopus with pak choy; pork with fried rice; pancakes. Details: 11.15 pm; closed Sun.

Ikeda W1 £ 53 ★
30 Brook St (020) 7629 2730 2–2B
"Superb sushi" is the mainstay of Mr Ikeda's long-established Mayfair Japanese. / Sample dishes: deep-fried bean curd with spinach; salmon sashimi; green tea ice cream. Value tip: set weekday L £34(FP). Details: 10.30 pm, Sat 10 pm; closed Sat L & Sun; no Switch; smart casual.

Ikkyu £ 24 ★

67 Tottenham Ct Rd, W1 (020) 7636 9280
7 Newport Pl, WC2 (020) 7439 3554
"Authentic Japanese neighbourhood restaurants", well known, in particular, for their "good and cheap sushi"; the original (W1) branch is "much the better of the two". / **Sample dishes:** miso soup; Pacific pike with pak choy; fresh fruit. **Details:** 10.30 pm - WC2 Fri & Sat 11.30 pm; W1, closed Sat & Sun L; W1 no Switch; WC2 no smoking area.

Inaho W2 £ 29 ★★

4 Hereford Rd (020) 7221 8495
"The long waits are for a good reason" at this "tiny" and "cramped" Japanese café in Bayswater – the chef is preparing "impeccable", very "affordable" sushi and other "exceptional" dishes; "you get warm service... when it finally comes". / **Sample dishes:** chicken yakitori; assorted sushi; green tea ice cream. **Value tip:** set weekday L £15(FP). **Details:** 11 pm; closed Sat L & Sun; no Amex & no Switch.

Isola SW1 £ 60

145 Knightsbridge (020) 7838 1044 4–1D
First announced over a year ago, Oliver Peyton's Knightsbridge newcomer has been a long time in coming, so lets hope this large Italian (overseen by Frenchman Bruno Loubet) is worth the wait; the basement is to house the slightly less ambitious Osteria d'Isola (£45). /

Itsu SW3 £ 25

118 Draycott Ave (020) 7584 5522 4–2C
Glossily gimmicky, conveyor-belt bar/restaurant, near Brompton Cross (formerly called t'su); its "interesting sushi" concept is "quite expensive", but the "new menu is a great improvement". / **Sample dishes:** prawn sushi with Asian pesto; grilled chicken with green soba noodles; coffee. **Details:** 11 pm; smoking only in bar; no booking.

The Ivy WC2 £ 47 A★

1 West St (020) 7836 4751 3–3B
"Without peer"; this "consistently satisfying" Theatrelander is still (new owners notwithstanding) reporters' No 1 Favourite, thanks to its "simple" and "reliable" modern British cooking and "superb" service (and "you can watch the stars", too); "it would be even better if you could get in". / **Sample dishes:** caramelised onion tart; chicken stuffed with foie gras in truffle sauce; Scandinavian iced berries. **Value tip:** set Saturday lunch £28(FP). **Details:** Midnight.

Iznik N5 £ 21 A★

19 Highbury Pk (020) 7354 5697
"Much loved" Islington Turk; it has "good-value" cooking and "welcoming" service, but it's the "superb", "romantic" atmosphere which earns its cult following. / **Sample dishes:** courgettes & feta with mint; chicken in cream & mustard; rice pudding. **Details:** 11 pm; no Amex.

Jason's W9 £ 38 A★

Opposite 60 Blomfield Rd (020) 7286 6752
"Sitting with a view of the canal" (near Little Venice) is the best place to enjoy "fabulous fish" (with "imaginative" Mauritian twists), according to the many devotees of this "small" and "friendly" fixture. / **Sample dishes:** crab salad with avocado & mango; seafood à la crème; chocolate mousse. **Details:** 10.30 pm; closed Sun D.

Julie's W11   £ 44   𝔸

135 Portland Rd   (020) 7229 8331

*"Sexy, crazy, great" – the "lovely nooks and corners" of this
"intimate", Gothic/Baroque Holland Park labyrinth make "a
wonderful place to hide away with your loved one"; even the
starry-eyed, though, can see the cooking's "past it". / Sample
dishes: lobster risotto with Parmesan; sea bass with spiced lime pickle &
Japanese ginger; crème brûlée. Details: 11.15 pm; closed Sat L.*

Kastoori SW17   £ 19   ★★

188 Upper Tooting Rd   (020) 8767 7027

*"An absolute delight – who needs meat?"; the "refreshingly
different" vegetarian fare at this "well-run" Tooting South
Indian/East African is as "fabulous" as the atmosphere is "dull".
/ Sample dishes: chick pea samosas; chilli banana curry; rice pudding.
Details: 10.30 pm; closed Mon L & Tue L; no Amex & no Switch.*

Ken Lo's Memories SW1   £ 40   ★

67-69 Ebury St   (020) 7730 7734   1–4B

*Fans forgive the "decidedly dated décor" of this eminent and
long-established Belgravian, thanks to the notably "high standard"
of its Chinese cuisine. / Sample dishes: braised aubergine; bang bang
chicken; yellow bean cake with lychees. Details: 10.45 pm; closed Sun L;
smart casual.*

Kensington Place W8   £ 39   𝔸

201-205 Kensington Ch St   (020) 7727 3184

*Loyal fans say we're "harsh" about this seminal, if
"uncomfortable" and "noisy", modern British 'goldfish bowl', just
off Notting Hill, but the fact is that its ratings have been
inexorably heading south; can recent purchasers the
Avenue/Circus group turn it round? – time will tell. / Sample
dishes: scallops with pear purée & mint viniagrette; roast partridge with onion
squash & thyme; baked tamarillos with vanilla ice cream. Value tip: set
weekday L £22(FP). Details: 11.45 pm, Sun 10.15 pm.*

Kulu Kulu W1   £ 18   ★

76 Brewer St   (020) 7734 7316   2–2D

*"Top quality" conveyor-belt sushi "at good prices" make this tiny
Soho café a great place to "eat and run". / Sample dishes: nigiri
sushi; tempura with udon noodes; green tea. Details: 10 pm; closed Sun;
no Amex; no smoking; no booking.*

The Ladbroke Arms W11   £ 24   𝔸

54 Ladbroke Rd   (020) 7727 6648

*"A real pub, with good food and beer, and without pretensions" –
which is all the more remarkable, as it's on the fringe of Notting
Hill; when it's sunny, arrive early to "grab a table" outside.
/ Sample dishes: Greek dips; sautéed lambs liver with mash; hot chocolate
fondant. Details: 9.45 pm; no Amex.*

Lahore Kebab House E1   £ 18   ★★

2 Umberston St   (020) 7488 2551

*"If you can ignore the squalor", it's "seriously worth journeying
across town" for the "incredible food at rock bottom prices" –
"the best kebabs in the world!" – at this infamous East Ender;
BYO. / Sample dishes: lamb tikka; Karahi lamb; rice pudding.
Details: 11.45 pm; no credit cards.*

The Lanesborough W1   £ 52   𝔸

Hyde Pk Corner   (020) 7259 5599   1–3A

*"They don't seem to pull it off, foodwise", but the large
conservatory-restaurant of this mega-swanky hotel, with "enough
plants to rival Kew", offers consolation in the form of "good-value
set menus", "terrific English breakfasts" and "very good
afternoon teas". /* **Sample dishes:** *crab spring rolls; spiced barbecue
salmon with coconut rice; chocolate & coconut millefeuille.* **Details:** *Midnight.*

Langan's Bistro W1   £ 30

26 Devonshire St   (020) 7935 4531   1–1A

*"Inconsistent" Marylebone bistro, whose intimate scale and
tranquillity present a stark contrast with its Mayfair stable-mate.
/* **Sample dishes:** *rocket salad with smoked bacon & mushrooms; grilled
lemon sole with citrus butter; orange compote with lavender sorbet.*
Details: *11 pm; closed Sat L & Sun.*

Latymers W6   £ 20   ★

157 Hammersmith Rd   (020) 8741 2507

*"Great Thai food for a fiver" and "very good" service make it
worth braving the "smoky" back room of this "grim-looking"
Hammersmith gin palace. /* **Sample dishes:** *mint chicken & prawn
toast; pork stir-fry with noodles; Thai pancake.* **Details:** *10 pm; closed Sun;
no booking at lunch.*

Launceston Place W8   £ 41   𝔸★

1a Launceston Pl   (020) 7937 6912   4–1B

*This "delightful" gem – "tucked away" in a Kensington townhouse
– was bought by the Avenue/Circus group in mid '99; with its
"grown-up", "drawing room" ambience, it's long been one of the
capital's most enjoyable modern British restaurants – let's hope
they don't wreck it! /* **Sample dishes:** *goat's cheese soufflé with poached
pears; lamb chump with pumpkin ravioli; orange sponge pudding.* **Value
tip:** *pre-th. £27(FP).* **Details:** *11.30 pm; closed Sat L & Sun D.*

Leith's W11   £ 48   𝔸★

92 Kensington Pk Rd   (020) 7229 4481

*Notting Hill gastronomic stalwart, which won much more support
this year for its "excellent" modern British cooking, "superb" wine
list, "solid" service and "romantic" setting; for a vocal minority,
though, the whole approach remains "a bit '80s". /* **Sample
dishes:** *crab & shiitake mushroom couscous; Morteaux sausage ravioli with
oyster mushrooms; raspberry & pistachio soufflé.* **Details:** *11.30 pm;
closed Mon L, Sat L & Sun.*

Lemonia NW1   £ 25   𝔸

89 Regent's Pk Rd   (020) 7586 7454

*"As welcoming as ever" – the long-serving and "very friendly"
staff are what really make this "popular" and "noisy" Primrose
Hill fixture; the Greek fare is "reasonable", if not up to its past
best. /* **Sample dishes:** *Greek cheese & spinach pie; calamari with sweet
chilli sauce; baklava.* **Value tip:** *set weekday L £15(FP).* **Details:** *11.30 pm;
closed Sat L & Sun D; no Amex.*

Lindsay House W1   £ 48   𝔸★★

21 Romilly St   (020) 7439 0450   3–3A

*Richard Corrigan has really hit his stride at this "beautiful" Soho
townhouse, whose "unusual" (ring-to-enter) set-up is part of its
"intimate" and "discreet" appeal; on a good day, his "gorgeous,
superbly executed" modern British grub is among the best in
town. /* **Sample dishes:** *sweetbreads with pistachios; pork with apricots &
cabbage; chocolate cake with port sauce.* **Details:** *11 pm; closed Sat L & Sun.*

Lisboa Patisserie W10   £ 6   ★★
57 Golborne Rd   (020) 8968 5242
"Custard tarts to die for" have brought fame to this *"grotty"* but
trendy Portuguese pâtisserie in North Kensington. / *Sample*
dishes: cheese croissant; tuna salad; custard tart. **Details:** *8 pm;
no credit cards; no booking.*

Livebait   £ 42
21 Wellington St, WC2   (020) 7836 7161
43 The Cut, SE1   (020) 7928 7211
"This fish has gone off"; Groupe Chez Gérard continues its
"disastrous" devaluation of this once *"fresh and lively"* concept,
which is now really *"beginning to feel like a chain"* – *"expensive"*,
"noisy", *"too casual"* and with *"indifferent"* cooking; Waterloo is
still much better than Covent Garden. / *Sample dishes: honey-roast
octopus with razor clams & olives; char-grilled sea bass with plum tomato
compôte; Victoria plums with cherry sabayon.* **Value tip:** *set weekday L
£28(FP).* **Details:** *11.30 pm; closed Sun; no smoking areas.*

Lobster Pot SE11   £ 41   ★★
3 Kennington Ln   (020) 7582 5556
We think the *"very surreal"* discovery of a *"wonderfully kitsch"*,
"authentically French" fish restaurant hard by the Elephant &
Castle leads reporters to over-egg their appreciation of its
cooking; we're with the minority who find it *"rather expensive"* for
what it is, if of a *"high standard"*. / *Sample dishes: seafood platter;
fish stew; pink grapefruit sorbet.* **Details:** *11 pm; closed Mon & Sun;
smart casual.*

Lomo SW10   £ 21   𝔸
222-224 Fulham Rd   (020) 7349 8848   4–3B
"Chic" but *"laid-back"*, this *"excellent modern tapas café"* –
newly washed up on the Chelsea 'Beach' – is *"really friendly"* and
"trying hard". / *Sample dishes: prawns in garlic; sweet peppers stuffed
with chorizo; pannetone bread pudding.* **Details:** *11.30 pm; no booking.*

Luc's Brasserie EC3   £ 34   𝔸★
17-22 Leadenhall Mkt   (020) 7621 0666
"Full of life" and with *"City food about as good as it gets"*, this
"excellent", *"unpretentious"* Gallic bistro makes a top choice
around Lloyds; it's *"not the place for a serious business lunch"*.
/ *Sample dishes: mushroom fricassée; scallops wrapped in bacon; apple tart
with crème anglaise.* **Details:** *L only; closed Sat & Sun; no Switch.*

Luigi's Delicatessen SW10   £ 26   ★
359 Fulham Rd   (020) 7351 7825   4–3B
"Fantastic pizzas" (and other good, simple dishes) *"in chaotic
Italian style"* make this *"cramped"* Chelsea 'Beach' deli/diner a
huge hit with *"a Eurotrash crowd that's happy to rough it"*.
/ *Sample dishes: baked aubergine; Parma ham & Mozzarella pizza;
panna cotta.* **Details:** *10.30 pm; closed Sun; no Amex; no booking.*

Made in Italy SW3   £ 26   ★
249 King's Rd   (020) 7352 1880   4–3C
"Very fresh pastas and pizza" win strong praise for this *"basic"*,
"fun" and *"friendly"* Chelsea spot, though service can be
"moody". / *Sample dishes: garlic bread; pizza Napolitana; zabaglione.*
Details: *11.30 pm; D only; no Amex; booking: parties only.*

Maggie Jones's W8   £ 33   🄰

6 Old Court Pl   (020) 7937 6462   4–1A

"For those winter days", the "dark", "cosy" and "rustic" charm of this "eccentric" Kensington fixture is just the job; it comes in "generous" portions, but the dated Anglo/French cooking is a "bit overpriced" and "complacent". / Sample dishes: avocado stuffed with prawns; roast saddle of lamb; treacle tart. Details: 11 pm.

Malabar W8   £ 24   🄰★

27 Uxbridge St   (020) 7727 8800

The feel is "upmarket", but prices offer "good value" at this wonderfully "consistent" and justifiably well-known Indian, just off Notting Hill Gate. / Sample dishes: devilled chicken livers; chicken tikka masala; mango fool. Value tip: set Sun L £13(FP). Details: 11.15 pm; no Amex.

Mandarin Kitchen W2   £ 27   ★★

14-16 Queensway   (020) 7727 9012

"Heavenly" seafood (including "the best lobster in London") makes it worth braving the "bizarre" '70s décor of this eminent Bayswater Chinese; service is "friendly", too, "considering the turnover". / Sample dishes: seafood soup; sea bass with ginger & spring onions; pancakes. Details: 11.30 pm.

Mao Tai SW6   £ 36   🄰★

58 New King's Rd   (020) 7731 2520

It may be "less personal since it doubled in size", but "you can't really fault" this long-running Parson's Green success story; it's "always full", thanks to its "delicious" Chinese cooking, "immaculate" service and "fun" atmosphere. / Sample dishes: chicken dumplings; noodles with beans & chilli; blackcurrant sorbet. Details: 11.30 pm; no smoking area.

Maroush   £ 35   ★

I) 21 Edgware Rd, W2   (020) 7723 0773
II) 38 Beauchamp Pl, SW3   (020) 7581 5434
III) 62 Seymour St, W1   (020) 7724 5024

Swanky Lebanese outfits where "everything is incredibly fresh"; the snack bars (at nos I and II) are "classic" late-night destinations, while the restaurants at all three are "expensive but good overall"; no I is "good for a party night out" (after 10.30pm music and dancing – minimum charge £48). / Sample dishes: houmous salad; garlic chicken; baklava. Details: W1 1 am - W2 1.30 am - SW3 5 am.

The Mason's Arms SW8   £ 25   🄰★

169 Battersea Park Rd   (020) 7622 2007

"Great pub food" – from a "superb" and "frequently changing" menu – makes it "worth the wait for a table" at this "trendy" Battersea boozer. / Sample dishes: Parma ham & Parmesan with baby spinach; pan-fried cajun chicken; bread & butter pudding. Details: 10.20 pm.

Matsuri SW1   £ 48   ★★

15 Bury St   (020) 7839 1101   2–3D

The "best all-round Japanese in the West End"; despite an ambience some find a mite elusive, this smart St James's teppan-yaki and sushi restaurant provides an "excellent experience", with "wonderful" food and "attentive" service. / Sample dishes: fresh salmon with wasabi sauce; duck teppan-yaki with orange sauce; fireball ice cream. Details: 10.30 pm; closed Sun; no Switch.

Mediterraneo WII   **£ 31**   A★

37 Kensington Park Rd   (020) 7792 3131

"A top package" of *"affordable"* and *"well prepared"* Italian
cooking, *"great"* service and a *"top people-watching
environment"* (*"was it the setting for 'Notting Hill'?"*) are making
Osteria Basilico's upstart offspring even more popular than its
parent. / **Sample dishes:** char-grilled smoked Mozzarella with rocket; grilled
salmon with roasted tomatoes; tiramisu. **Details:** 11.30 pm.

Mesclun N16   **£ 25**   ★★

24 Stoke Newington Ch St   (020) 7249 5029

It's *"a real surprise"* to discover this Stoke Newington venture –
it's *"so welcoming"*, and its modern British menu is *"beautifully
prepared"* and *"excellent value"*; *"the atmosphere's much better
since redecoration"*. / **Sample dishes:** grilled sardines with provençale
sauce; roast lamb chump with sweet red peppers; chocolate tart.
Details: 11 pm; D only; no Amex.

Mezzo W1   **£ 42**

100 Wardour St   (020) 7314 4000   2–2D

"Too big, too loud, too full of itself"; Conran's Soho behemoth
offers a lethal cocktail of *"limp"* and *"overpriced"* modern British
cooking and *"really shoddy"* and *"inefficient"* service. / **Sample
dishes:** pesto ravioli; baked halibut, fennel & clam broth; gingerbread pudding.
Value tip: pre-th. £27(FP). **Details:** Mon-Wed midnight, Thu-Sat 1 am
(crustacea till 3 am); closed Sat L.

Mirabelle W1   **£ 48**   A★

56 Curzon St   (020) 7499 4636   2–4B

A *"fantastic all-rounder"*; with its *"excellent"* modern French
cooking, *"James Bond"* setting and *"choreographed"* service – not
to mention a *"vast"* wine list, with interest *"at all prices"* –
MPW's Mayfair *"classic"* has quickly become a top choice for
practically any occasion. / **Sample dishes:** smoked salmon roulade; veal
escalope; bitter chocolate sorbet. **Value tip:** set Sun L £31(FP).
Details: Midnight; no smoking area.

Mitsukoshi SW1   **£ 60**   ★★

14-16 Regent St   (020) 7930 0317   2–3D

This *"very Japanese"* establishment in the basement of the
eponymous department store is, for some, *"the best in town"*; it's
rather a dry experience, though. / **Sample dishes:** assorted sushi; beef
teriyaki; green tea ice cream. **Details:** 9.30 pm; closed Sun.

Miyama W1   **£ 53**   ★

38 Clarges St   (020) 7499 2443   2–4B

"Top sushi" helps distinguish this Mayfair oriental, but the
atmosphere is very *"Japanese businessy"*. / **Sample dishes:** miso
soup; seafood teppan-yaki; red bean ice cream. **Details:** 10.30 pm;
closed Sat L & Sun L; smart casual.

Momo W1   **£ 38**   A

25 Heddon St   (020) 7434 4040   2–2C

"High on fashion and style, not content", this *"cool"* Moroccan,
just off Regent Street, has a *"delicious setting"* and *"great
atmosphere"* – shame about the *"indifferent"* food and
"arrogant" service. / **Sample dishes:** seafood tempura with citrus dressing;
tuna with yellow beans & noodles; red bean pudding. **Details:** 10.30 pm.

Mon Plaisir WC2　　　　　　　　**£ 34**　　　A★

21 Monmouth St　(020) 7836 7243　3–2B

*"Thank heavens it's open again"; this "delightful", old bistro –
"an oasis of resolute Frenchmen", in the heart of Theatreland –
"still has the same high standards after the fire", not least of
"honest-to-goodness" cooking; there is a particularly "good pre-
theatre dinner" (and bargain set lunch). / **Sample dishes:** snails with
garlic sauce; confit of duck; chocolate biscuit cake. **Value tip:** pre-th. £15(FP).
Details: 11.15 pm; closed Sat L & Sun.*

Monkeys SW3　　　　　　　　**£ 47**　　　A★★

1 Cale St　(020) 7352 4711　4–2C

*"Outstanding" old-school establishment, on Chelsea Green, whose
"friendly" staff help create a "very agreeable" atmosphere;
"delicious game, in season" is the highlight, complemented by a
"spectacular" wine list. / **Sample dishes:** foie gras salad; mallard with
game chips; pancakes with Cointreau. **Details:** 10.30 pm; closed Sat & Sun;
no Amex.*

Monsieur Max TW12　　　　　　**£ 34**　　　★★

133 High St, Hampton Hl　(020) 8979 5546

*"Correct cuisine du terroir", "scandalously cheap", ensures a
diverse fan club for this "superb local restaurant" in Hampton
Hill (nearest BR, Fulwell); "Max is a great character". / **Sample
dishes:** snails in white wine & black truffle sauce; pigeon with mushrooms;
chocolate millefeuille & armagnac ice cream. **Details:** 9.30 pm; closed Sat L.*

Montana SW6　　　　　　　　**£ 36**　　　A

125-129 Dawes Rd　(020) 7385 9500

*"Always a fabulous, relaxing meal", say the many fans of this
deepest-Fulham jazz bar/restaurant, cradle of the eponymous
group; it's still the best of the bunch (especially for a "great
brunch"), but – as at its siblings – the southwest USA fare is
increasingly "hit-and-miss". / **Sample dishes:** smoked catfish & cod
cakes; rib-eye steak with molasses-baked peas; fried banana tacos. **Value
tip:** set weekday L £22(FP). **Details:** 11 pm, Fri & Sat 11.30 pm; closed Mon-
Thu L.*

Moro EC1　　　　　　　　　**£ 32**　　　A★★

34-36 Exmouth Mkt　(020) 7833 8336

*"Innovative Moorish cooking" – "a treat to find something so
different" – of "consistently high quality" has put this "laid-back
and cool" Clerkenwell two-year old firmly on the map; service is
"professional and unobtrusive". / **Sample dishes:** hot yoghurt soup with
walnuts & coriander; rabbit braised in garlic & white wine; chocolate & apricot
tart. **Details:** 10.30 pm; closed Sat & Sun.*

Morton's W1　　　　　　　　**£ 48**　　　A★

28 Berkeley Sq　(020) 7493 7171　2–3B

*"Stylish", dining room on the first floor of a fashionable Mayfair
club, whose recent opening to the public has been well received;
chef Gary Holihead left in mid-1999, and it's too early to say
whether the new régime is keeping up his standards. / **Sample
dishes:** beef carpaccio with truffles & Parmesan; sea bass with bouillabaise
sauce; blueberries in Madeira sauce. **Details:** 11.30 pm; closed Sat L & Sun.*

Mr Kong WC2   £ 21   ★
21 Lisle St   (020) 7437 7341   3–3A
"Excellent Chinatown eatery" whose *"generous"* portions of *"inexpensive"* but *"high quality"* Cantonese fare – *"be brave, go for the specials!"* – are *"consistently excellent"*; *"downstairs is not nice"*. / **Sample dishes:** sesame prawn satay; salted scallops & king prawns; mint tea. **Details:** 2.45 am.

Mr Wing SW5   £ 41   𝔸★
242-244 Old Brompton Rd   (020) 7370 4450   4–2A
"Great for a rumble in the jungle!" – but it's not just the *"fun"* setting (complete with foliage and fish tanks) which makes this *"romantic"* and *"upmarket"* Earl's Court Chinese *"simply the best"*; *"the food's pretty good, too"*. / **Sample dishes:** prawns in garlic; deep-fried chilli beef; toffee apple. **Details:** Midnight.

Nautilus NW6   £ 21   ★★
27–29 Fortune Gn Rd   (020) 7435 2532
"The best fish and chips" (fried in matzo-meal) in *"good portions"* make this West Hampstead fixture one of London's best chippies; *"take away"* is safest, though – some think the interior's *"horrible"*. / **Sample dishes:** minestrone soup; stuffed lemon sole; orange sorbet. **Details:** 10 pm; closed Sun; no credit cards; no booking.

Nobu W1   £ 53   𝔸★★
Metropolitan Hotel, Old Park Ln   (020) 7447 4747   2–4A
"Sensational and original" cooking and *"amazing people-watching"* make this *"wickedly expensive but wickedly good"* Japanese/South American, NYC-to-Mayfair import *"far and away the best"* of London's trendiest dining rooms. / **Sample dishes:** yellowtail fish with jalepenos; black cod with miso; chocolate fondant bento box. **Value tip:** set weekday L £34(FP). **Details:** 10.15 pm, Sat 11.15 pm; closed Sat L & Sun; no smoking area.

Oak Room Marco Pierre White
Hotel Meridien W1   £105   ★
21 Piccadilly   (020) 7437 0202   2–3D
"Silly" prices (half the reporters who mention this place do so as their *'most overpriced'* nomination) sour appreciation of the often *"superb"* cooking at MPW's grand chandeliered chamber; the *"arrogant"* service and the *"stiff"* atmosphere also do it few favours. / **Sample dishes:** foie gras terrine; roast lamb with herb crust; blackberry soufflé. **Value tip:** set weekday L £58(FP). **Details:** 11.15 pm; closed Sat L & Sun.

Odette's NW1   £ 38   𝔸★
130 Regent's Pk Rd   (020) 7586 5486
A *"marvellous"*, *"so romantic"* dining room (mirrors everywhere) combines with *"lovely"* modern British cooking and *"courteous"* service to maintain this Primrose Hill veteran's standing as north London's top all-rounder. / **Sample dishes:** warm rabbit salad with pancetta & kidneys; cod & tiger prawns with Indian spices; prunes in saffron custard. **Value tip:** set weekday L £20(FP). **Details:** 11 pm; closed Sat L & Sun.

1 Lombard Street EC3   £ 46   𝔸
1 Lombard St   (020) 7929 6611

"This is what the City needed", say supporters of Herbert Berger's "professional" modern British yearling, near the Bank of England; "get a table upstairs" (rather than in the cheaper brasserie in the converted banking hall downstairs) to avoid the noise of the "wide-boy" bar. / **Sample dishes:** artichoke, mushroom & pumpkin seed salad; lobster, langoustine & scallops in oriental broth; chocolate, whisky & coffee praline. **Details:** 10 pm; closed Sat & Sun; bookings: max 6 (7 in restaurant).

L'Oranger SW1   £ 49
5 St James's St   (020) 7839 3774   2–4D

It's "not quite the same, since last year's debacle" (involving the acrimonious departure of many of the staff), but after some rocky months there is a feeling that this agreeable modern French dining room in St James's "has started to climb back" towards its previous heights. / **Sample dishes:** potato salad with poached egg & caviar; John Dory with crushed potatoes; Caribbean chocolate fondant. **Details:** 11.15 pm; closed Sat L & Sun.

Oslo Court NW8   £ 39   ★★
Prince Albert Rd   (020) 7722 8795

"Faultless — so long as you don't mind eating with your grandparents' generation", this "cosseting" Regent's Park institution (at the foot of an apartment block) offers "delicious", unreformed International cooking and "incredibly attentive but not suffocating" service. / **Sample dishes:** scallops wrapped in bacon; duck with three sauces; apple crêpe tart. **Details:** 11 pm; closed Sun; smart casual.

Oxo Tower SE1   £ 43   𝔸
Barge House St   (020) 7803 3888

"With views like this, the food's a bit irrelevant" at the survey's most-mentioned place — "just as well" as the "expensive" modern British grub at the brasserie of this eighth-floor South Bank landmark (again reporters' most talked about place) is "rather disappointing", and service decidedly "second rate"; the adjoining restaurant is even pricier. / **Sample dishes:** duck confit with curried lentils; roast poussin in sesame marinade; pecan pie with caramel sauce. **Value tip:** set weekday L £23(FP). **Details:** 11.15 pm.

Le Palais du Jardin WC2   £ 35   𝔸
136 Long Acre   (020) 7379 5353   3–3C

This "bright and buzzy" Covent Garden mega-brasserie is something of a surprise — "given its scale, it still manages to deliver"; that said, today's performance pales in comparison to a few years ago. / **Sample dishes:** crab cakes with sweetcorn relish; lobster & scallops with herb tagliatelle; banana tarte Tatin with caramel. **Details:** Midnight.

The Park NW6   £ 27   𝔸
105 Salusbury Rd   (020) 7372 8882

"In an area that needed a decent eatery", this large, "trendy" Queen's Park bar/restaurant is deservedly making a big splash; it's a pity that mean portions and off-hand service take the edge off the experience. / **Sample dishes:** rocket & Parmesan salad; pizza with artichokes & smoked sausage; panna cotta with blueberries. **Details:** 11 pm; no smoking area.

Pâtisserie Valerie   £ 20   A★

105 Marylebone High St, W1   (020) 7935 6240
44 Old Compton St, W1   (020) 7437 3466
RIBA Centre, 66 Portland Pl, W1   (020) 7631 0467
8 Russell St, WC2   (020) 7240 0064
215 Brompton Rd, SW3   (020) 7823 9971

*"Comforting" Gallic cafés, universally popular for their "delicious breakfasts" and "some of the best pastries and croissants in town"; the large Brompton Road branch has a broader-than-average menu, and is a hugely popular rendezvous. / **Sample dishes:** Caesar salad; club ciabatta sandwich; summer fruit tart.* **Details:** *6 pm-8 pm, Sun earlier; Portland Pl, closed Sun; no smoking area; no booking.*

Pétrus SW1   £ 43   ★★

33 St James's St   (020) 7930 4272   2–4C
*Marcus Wareing's "excellent" (and "good-value") modern French cuisine makes this St James's newcomer "a serious place for serious eating"; some find the service a little "overbearing", but most seem to like it that way, the somewhat "stilted" décor is the chief drawback. / **Sample dishes:** cauliflower soup with girolles; pan-fried brill; dark chocolate mousse.* **Details:** *10.45 pm; closed Sat L & Sun; booking, max 6.*

Pharmacy W11 ✳   £ 42

150 Notting Hl Gt   (020) 7221 2442
*"Very hit-or-miss food", poor service and general "absence of substance" win few friends for this "pretentious" Notting Hill yearling – "they should give you anti-depressants with the bill". / **Sample dishes:** salt cod with poached eggs & bacon; lamb shank with celery & spinach; blueberry tart.* **Details:** *10.45 pm.*

Pied à Terre W1   £ 55   ★★

34 Charlotte St   (020) 7636 1178   1–1C
*"Brilliant", "cutting-edge" modern French cuisine makes this "serious" (but "not too formal") Fitzrovian one of London's shrinking field of places with real, first-rank culinary ambitions; some think it feels a mite "dead". / **Sample dishes:** artichoke & foie gras terrine with truffles; roast sea bass with oyster & caviar sauce; caramelised apple filo parcel.* **Details:** *10.45 pm; closed Sat L & Sun; smart casual.*

Pizza Metro SW11   £ 25   ★★

64 Battersea Rise   (020) 7228 3812
*"Outstanding pizza" (sold by the metre) means this "cramped" and "fun" Battersea spot – beloved of Italian expats – is usually "frantic". / **Sample dishes:** baked aubergine; linguine with crayfish; Neopolitan cake.* **Details:** *11 pm; closed Mon & Tue-Fri L.*

Pizzeria Castello SE1   £ 19   ★

20 Walworth Rd   (020) 7703 2556
*"Amazing value, well worth going to the Elephant & Castle for" ensures there's often a queue for this "always buzzing" pizzeria; "park in a well-lit area". / **Sample dishes:** deep-fried Brie with blackcurrants; pizza with smoked ham & pineapple; chocolate fudge cake.* **Details:** *11 pm, Fri & Sat 11.30 pm; closed Sat L & Sun; smart casual.*

Le Pont de la Tour SE1   **£ 60**   𝔸
36d Shad Thames   (020) 7403 8403
*Fans still applaud the Tower Bridge-side 'flagship' of the Conran
empire for its "impressive setting" ("especially if you get an
outside table") and "fine cuisine"; food that is merely "OK",
though, and "slow" service are leading more and more people to
conclude that it "no longer justifies its prices". / **Sample
dishes:** roast stuffed squid with sauce vierge; lamb with black olive & herb
crust; roast peach brioche & mint ice cream. **Details:** 11.30 pm; closed Sat L.*

La Poule au Pot SW1   **£ 39**   𝔸
231 Ebury St   (020) 7730 7763   4–2D
*With its "many nooks and crannies" and the "Gallic attitude" of
the waiters – their "rudeness actually adds to the ambience" –
this Pimlico stalwart has always "dripped with romance"; its
sometimes "delicious", rustic French cuisine is currently finding
renewed favour. / **Sample dishes:** cheese quiche; rabbit with mustard
crust; crème brûlée. **Value tip:** set weekday L £25(FP). **Details:** 11.15 pm.*

Prism EC3   **£ 42**   ★
147 Leadenhall St   (020) 7256 3888
*Harvey Nics's "great new power-dining venue" has made a real
splash in the City, thanks to its "stylish", "well spaced" setting, its
"attentive" service and – most surprising of all – its "interesting"
modern British menu. / **Sample dishes:** Whitby cod tempura with pea
purée; seared scallops with Chinese duck ravioli; lemon tart with passion fruit
sorbet. **Details:** 10 pm; closed Sat & Sun.*

Quaglino's SW1   **£ 39**
16 Bury St   (020) 7930 6767   2–3D
*"How the mighty have fallen"; the St James's mega-brasserie
which even Conran-phobes used to like is now "so amateur" in all
respects – an "overpriced" and "noisy", "conveyor-belt",
delivering cooking "with no soul". / **Sample dishes:** potato & celery
soup; steak & chips; chocolate bombe. **Value tip:** set always available £26(FP).
Details: Midnight, Fri & Sat 1 am, Sun 11 pm.*

Ranoush W2   **£ 17**   ★★
43 Edgware Rd   (020) 7723 5929
*"Kebabs which just don't get any better" and "exotic fruit juices"
are among the culinary attractions of this "bustling" and "fun"
late-night Bayswater Lebanese take-away; stop at a hole-in-the-
wall first, it's 'cash only'. / **Sample dishes:** tabbouleh; lamb with salad &
pitta bread; pistachio pudding. **Details:** 3 am; no credit cards.*

Ransome's Dock SW11   **£ 39**   𝔸★
35 Parkgate Rd   (020) 7223 1611   4–4C
*This "thoughtful", "top class local", by the river in Battersea,
provides "lovely" modern British cooking, "friendly" service, a
"relaxed" setting and – last but not least – "a wide range of
interesting and reasonably priced wines". / **Sample dishes:** seared
scallops with roast beetroot; duck breast with caramelised pears; hot prune &
armagnac soufflé. **Details:** 11 pm; closed Sun D; smart casual.*

Rasa £ 28 ★★
6 Dering St, W1 (020) 7629 1346
55 Stoke Newington Ch St, N16 (020) 7249 0344
"Awesome food" from a *"genuinely different"* vegetarian Indian
menu and *"charming"* service make this dynamic Keralan duo a
force to be reckoned with; the year-old Mayfair branch (*"now in
its stride"*) is much larger than the Stoke Newington original.
/ **Sample dishes:** deep-fried spicy potato pâté; sweet mango & banana curry;
banana pancake with coconut ice cream. **Details:** 11 pm; N16 closed Mon L-
Thu L - both branches closed Sun L; no smoking.

The Real Greek N1 £ 33 ★★
15 Hoxton Market (020) 7739 8212
'True' Greek cuisine is apparently the inspiration, but 'modern
British with a Greek twist' would perhaps more aptly describe
Theodore Kyriakou's modishly sparse new venture in über-trendy
Hoxton; a very early visit found intriguing cooking as you would
hope from the man who originated the Livebait concept. / **Sample
dishes:** cured tuna with Eastern spices; Ismir style meat dumplings; rose petal
meringue with blackberries. **Details:** 10.30 pm.

Restaurant One-O-One SW1 £ 56 ★
William St, 101 Knightsbridge (020) 7290 7101 1–3A
"This man can cook!" – rare for an hotel – so it's worth braving
"strangely dressed waiters" and *"panoramic views of passing 137
buses"* for the Gallic fish and seafood served at this Knightsbridge
"goldfish bowl"; *"not everything succeeds"*, but the *"set menu is
very good value"*. / **Sample dishes:** roast scallops with pan-fried foie gras;
chicken Kiev; chocolate tart with orange custard. **Details:** 10.30 pm.

Rhodes in the Square SW1 £ 47 Ⓐ★
Dolphin Sq, Chichester St (020) 7798 6767 1–4C
Gary Rhodes's *"awesome"* modern British cooking mostly wins
rave reviews for this *"relaxed but businesslike"* yearling – a
midnight blue *"cruise ship"* dining room, lost in the bowels of a
Pimlico apartment block; for a vociferous minority, though, it's
"overhyped and overpriced". / **Sample dishes:** lobster omelette
thermidor; roast rabbit stuffed with bacon; Jaffa Cake pudding.
Details: 10 pm; closed Sat L & Sun D.

Rib Room & Oyster Bar
Hyatt Carlton Tower Hotel SW1 £ 53
2 Cadogan Pl (020) 7858 7053 1–4A
This Belgravia grill room – long a popular business lunching venue
– was relaunched in September 1999 in a more 'with it' format,
and with oysters co-starring with the beef for which the place has
long been known. / **Sample dishes:** fresh oysters; rib of Aberdeen Angus;
crème brûlée. **Details:** 11.15 pm; no Switch; smart casual.

The Ritz W1 £ 75 Ⓐ
150 Piccadilly (020) 7493 8181 2–4C
What is *"surely the most beautiful and romantic dining room in
London"* rarely stirs itself to produce cooking that's any more than
"average" (or worse – *"they can't even roast beef without
destroying it!)"*. / **Sample dishes:** goose foie gras with artichokes; beef
Wellington; tarte Tatin. **Value tip:** set Sun L £48(FP). **Details:** 11 pm;
jacket & tie.

The River Café W6 £ 52 ★

Thames Whf, Rainville Rd (020) 7381 8824

*"Great", "simple" cooking using "fantastic ingredients" still makes this "difficult-to-find" Hammersmith luminary some folk's "best Italian"; however, "astronomical" prices (and, on occasion, "charmless" service) mean there are more people than ever who'd "prefer to stay at home with the cookbook". / **Sample dishes:** spaghetti vongole with clams & chilli; char-grilled lamb with roast fennel; chocolate Nemesis. **Details:** 9.30 pm; closed Sun D.*

Royal China SW15 £ 29 ★

3 Chelverton Rd (020) 8788 0907

*Putney oriental, whose formula is similar to its illustrious central namesakes; it's under different management, and a touch more "changeable". / **Sample dishes:** sesame prawn toast; pork stir-fry; lychee ice cream. **Details:** 10.45 pm; no Visa, Mastercard or Switch; no booking for Sun L.*

Royal China £ 29 ★★

40 Baker St, W1 (020) 7487 4688
13 Queensway, W2 (020) 7221 2535
68 Queen's Grove, NW8 (020) 7586 4280

*"'Kick ass' dim sum" – "as good as Hong Kong" – help make this tacky trio (decked out like '70s discos) London's Chinese benchmark; branches are usually "crowded, noisy and chaotic". / **Sample dishes:** seaweed with pimentos; chicken in black bean sauce; toffee apple & banana. **Details:** 11 pm, Fri & Sat 11.30 pm.*

Rules WC2 £ 43 Ⓐ

35 Maiden Ln (020) 7836 5314 3–3D

*"Despite being a tourist magnet", London's oldest restaurant (1798) is "good at what it does", with highlights including "top game" and "the best Stilton in town"; the place remains generally "safe", but satisfaction slipped somewhat this year. / **Sample dishes:** smoked salmon, trout & haddock parfait; steak, kidney & oysters with suet pudding; crème caramel & armagnac prunes. **Details:** 11.30 pm.*

Salloos SW1 £ 45 ★

62-64 Kinnerton St (020) 7235 4444 1–3A

*The food's "worth the price" – no mean feat – at this discreet, "slightly odd" Pakistani "haven", long tucked away in a quiet Belgravia mews; you may wish to avail yourself of the "helpful menu guidance". / **Sample dishes:** lamb chop; Karahi chicken; kulfi. **Value tip:** set weekday L £27(FP). **Details:** 11.15 pm; closed Sun; smart casual.*

Sarastro WC2 £ 29 Ⓐ

126 Drury Ln (020) 7836 0101 1–2D

*"Incredible… the first time"; the "unique", "OTT", "junk-Baroque" setting of this Covent Garden phenomenon certainly makes for an "entertaining" experience; the "run-of-the-mill tourist food" has only a walk-on rôle. / **Sample dishes:** cheese-filled pastries; breaded chicken with asparagus; honey pudding. **Details:** 11.30 pm.*

Sarcan N1 £ 17 Ⓐ

4 Theberton St (020) 7226 5489

*"Bustling but courteous" Turkish delight, just off Islington's Upper Street, offering "wonderful grills" and "excellent-value mezze". / **Sample dishes:** falafel with tahini; shish kebab with rice; honey & nut pudding. **Value tip:** set weekday L £8(FP). **Details:** Midnight.*

Sarkhel's SW18 £ 25 ★★

199 Replingham Rd   (020) 8870 1483

"Enjoy it now, before people work out how to get there" – ex-Bombay Brasserie chef Udit Sarkhel's Southfields subcontinental may look undistinguished, but it *"rightly gets rave reviews"* for its *"fantastic cooking"* and charming service. / **Sample dishes:** prawn kebabs; braised lamb shank; kulfi. **Details:** 10.30 pm; closed Mon, Tue & Sat L; no Amex.

Savoy Grill WC2 £ 66 🄰

Strand   (020) 7836 4343   3–3D

With its elegant, *"boardroom"* ambience, and *"effortlessly smooth"* service, this famous room remains a top *"power lunch"* venue – it's *"not so good in the evenings"*; the cooking is *"always reliable, but unadventurous"* and *"not, at the price, exceptional"*. / **Sample dishes:** dressed crab; salmon with savoy cabbage; chocolate bread & butter pudding. **Value tip:** set post theatre £32(FP). **Details:** 11.15 pm; closed Sat L & Sun; jacket & tie.

Savoy River Restaurant WC2 £ 66 🄰

Strand   (020) 7420 2699   3–3D

"Insipid" and *"old-fashioned"* cooking mars this classic Thames-side dining room; it remains a *"treat"* for romance, and *"for a full English breakfast"* it's sans pareil. / **Sample dishes:** smoked salmon; grilled calves liver with bacon; caramelised pineapple. **Value tip:** set Brunch £42(FP). **Details:** 11.30 pm; jacket & tie.

755 SW6 £ 39 ★★

755 Fulham Rd   (020) 7371 0755

"A very pleasant surprise"; *"varied and very good-quality"* modern British cooking wins high praise for this unremarkable-looking Fulham spot; *"if only it were more lively!"* / **Sample dishes:** crab & smoked haddock cannelloni; roast venison fillets; hot chocolate soufflé. **Details:** 11 pm; closed Sun D & Mon.

Shogun W1 £ 50 ★★

Adam's Rw   (020) 7493 1255   2–3A

"Tokyo in W1" – *"great teriyaki"* and *"very good sushi"* win a devoted following for this Mayfair stalwart, which, by Japanese restaurant standards, has a *"lovely ambience"*. / **Sample dishes:** chicken yakitori; prawn & vegetable tempura; fresh fruit. **Details:** 11 pm; D only; closed Mon; no Switch.

Shree Krishna SW17 £ 18 ★★

192-194 Tooting High St   (020) 8672 4250

"No change", in Tooting, at what many vote *"the best curry house in south London"* (which is especially *"good for vegetarians"*); *"how do they make it so cheap?"* / **Sample dishes:** potato pancake; chicken & coriander curry; mango kulfi. **Details:** 10.45 pm; no Switch.

Simpsons-in-the-Strand WC2 £ 46 🄰

100 Strand   (020) 7836 9112   3–3D

"It's always popular with visitors, as it has a traditional feel", but this venerable institution's English cooking is *"a flop"* (except at breakfast); the recent refurb may buck things up, but our foray into the new, 'lighter' upstairs restaurant, 'Chequers', was hardly exciting. / **Sample dishes:** asparagus in chervil butter; fillet steak with herb-crusted mushrooms; bread & butter pudding. **Value tip:** pre-th. £31(FP). **Details:** 11 pm, Sun 9 pm; closed Sat L; jacket.

Sonny's SW13　　　　　　　**£ 37**　　　𝔸★
94 Church Rd　(020) 8748 0393
*This "newly revamped" Barnes star – long in the vanguard of the
"new breed of local modern British restaurant" – is a "superb all
rounder"; "definitely worth a trip, even if Hammersmith Bridge is
shut". / Sample dishes: pan-fried foie gras & mango; roast lamb & spiced
sausages with pumpkin purée; apple tarte Tatin & rosemary ice cream. Value
tip: set Sun L £25(FP). Details: 11 pm; closed Sun D.*

Sotheby's Café W1　　　　　**£ 32**　　　𝔸★
34 New Bond St　(020) 7293 5077　2–2C
*"A perfect setting in the heart of the auction house, for lunch and
a gossip" and "you overhear the most interesting conversations";
the cooking is "simple, good, and light", the wine list
"impeccable" and service "exceptional". / Sample dishes: potted
partridge with chanterelles; lobster club sandwich; marbled fudge brownie.
Details: L only; closed weekends, except May-Jul and Sep-Dec; no smoking.*

Souk WC2　　　　　　　　　**£ 23**　　　𝔸
27 Litchfield St　(020) 7240 1796　3–3B
*"It feels like you're in the casbah", at this "fun" North African
basement, near Cambridge Circus; its "lively" but cosy setting is
as "suitable for large groups" as it is for a "romantic twosome",
but this is "not a gastronomic experience". / Sample dishes: mixed
meze; chicken, olive & preserved lemon tagine; baklava. Details: 11.30 pm;
no Amex.*

Soulard N1　　　　　　　　**£ 26**　　　𝔸★
113 Mortimer Rd　(020) 7254 1314
*"Cramped but welcoming" Islington-fringe bistro, which is "always
a delight", thanks to its "authentic" cooking and the "wonderful"
attentions of mein host, Philippe. / Sample dishes: smoked haddock
terrine with watercress sauce; lamb & smoked bacon brochettes; chocolate
mousse with mint sauce. Details: 10.30 pm; D only; closed Sun & Mon;
no Amex & no Switch.*

The Square W1　　　　　　　**£ 60**　　　★★
6-10 Bruton St　(020) 7495 7100　2–2C
*Phillip Howard's "excellent" modern French cooking continues to
establish this grand and "professional" Mayfair venture in
London's gastronomic vanguard; it gets flak for being
"overpriced", however, and its style is perhaps a touch more
"formal" than is necessary. / Sample dishes: roast foie gras with
caramelised endive; lamb with garlic & rosemary confit; lemon & lime soufflé.
Details: 10.45 pm; closed Sat L & Sun L; smart casual.*

Star of India SW5　　　　　**£ 36**　　　★
154 Old Brompton Rd　(020) 7373 2901　4–2B
*Famously "not your typical curry house", this "fun", long-
established South Kensington subcontinental rejoices in striking
and "amusing" (read 'camp') décor and an "eccentric" owner;
the highlight, however, is the "interesting" menu realised to
"above average" standards. / Sample dishes: prawns in spiced batter;
quail stuffed with chicken & dried fruit; saffron & fennel infused pineapple.
Details: 11.45 pm.*

The Sugar Club W1   £ 43   ★

21 Warwick St   (020) 7437 7776   2–2D

*It's a "real treat" – and a rare one – to find cooking as "innovative" and "delicious" as Peter Gordon's fusion fare in the heart of the West End; many applaud the "buzzy" premises as "much improved on the Notting Hill original", though they are a touch "echoey". / **Sample dishes:** yellowtail with black bean & ginger salsa; roast duck with green beans; chocolate brownie terrine. **Details:** 11 pm; no smoking area.*

Suntory SW1   £ 72

72 St James's St   (020) 7409 0201   2–4D

*"Mega-pricey", "all-suits" St James's veteran, which plutocratic reporters say is still "the best" for "high-quality Japanese food"; it is a "dry and dull" experience, though. / **Sample dishes:** prawn tempura; beef & beancurd sukiyaki; green tea ice cream. **Value tip:** set weekday L £38(FP). **Details:** 10 pm; closed Sun L; smart casual.*

Sweetings EC4   £ 33   𝔸★

39 Queen Victoria St   (020) 7248 3062

*"Time-warp bliss" – it may be a Victorian "dinosaur", but this "splendid" City seafood parlour "keeps up traditions", with "the freshest, simplest fish" served in a "basic" but "unique" and "timeless" setting. / **Sample dishes:** dressed crab; salmon fishcakes & chips; jam roly-poly. **Details:** L only; closed Sat & Sun; no credit cards; no booking.*

Tamarind W1   £ 41   𝔸★★

20 Queen St   (020) 7629 3561   2–3B

*"Lovely, fresh and original flavours" are winning a growing reputation for this "unusual" and "excellent all round" Mayfair "nouvelle-Indian"; it's now London's leading subcontinental (with a Big Apple offshoot 'slated' for the 'fall'). / **Sample dishes:** chick pea, lentil, spinach & potato cake; prawns with pickle spices; carrot fudge with almonds & cashew nuts. **Details:** 11.30 pm; closed Sat L.*

La Tante Claire
Berkeley Hotel SW1   £ 81   ★

Wilton Pl   (020) 7823 2003   1–3A

*"Oh dear", Pierre Koffmann's move to Belgravia has, at a stroke, reduced his restaurant – once London's greatest – to also-ran status; there are still "fantastic" results, but for too many they're just "mediocre", and the atmosphere seems "wrong, cold and expensive". / **Sample dishes:** char-grilled foie gras; stuffed pig's trotter; millefeuille of red & blackcurrants. **Value tip:** set weekday L £42(FP). **Details:** 11 pm; closed Sat L & Sun; dinner, jacket.*

Tatsuso EC2   £ 65   ★★

32 Broadgate Circle   (020) 7638 5863

*"Make sure someone else is paying" if you visit what many hail as the "greatest Japanese in town"; it offers "perfect food at unbelievably high prices", but the ambience – in both the upstairs teppan-yaki and the basement restaurant – is "dull". / **Sample dishes:** prawn tempura; sushi & sashimi selection; green tea ice cream. **Details:** 9.45 pm; closed Sat & Sun; smart casual.*

Tentazioni SE1   **£ 40**   ★

2 Mill St   (020) 7237 1100

*"Excellent" and "very imaginative" Italian cooking is "let down by
a grim setting" at this "out of the way" bar/restaurant, near
Tower Bridge, despite the efforts of the "charming" staff. / **Sample
dishes:** pheasant tortellini with truffle oil; monkfish with celery & olives;
pancakes with amaretto-soaked candied fruits. **Details:** 11 pm; closed Sat L
& Sun.*

The Terrace W8   **£ 40**   𝔸★

33c Holland St   (020) 7937 3224   4–1A

*"Small but perfectly formed" yearling in a Kensington
"backwater", with "delicious" modern British cooking, "personal
and attentive" service and "romantic" atmosphere; its "lovely
terrace" is the icing on the cake. / **Sample dishes:** game terrine with
Cumberland sauce; partridge with cabbage, bacon & celeriac gratin; blackberry
crème brûlée. **Details:** 10.30 pm; closed Sun D.*

Titanic W1   **£ 38**

Regent Palace Hotel   (020) 7437 1912   2–3D

*"It's great for a drink and people-watching", otherwise "words
cannot describe" this vast and "electric" 'teen-scene', off Piccadilly
Circus; some reporters did try – "awful", "disaster", "dreadful",
"horrible", "no imagination", "overpriced", "ugh!" / **Sample
dishes:** potato blinis with smoked salmon; tuna with Mediterranean herbs;
chocolate Swiss roll with raspberries. **Details:** 11.30 pm.*

Toff's N10   **£ 26**   ★★

38 Muswell HI Broadway   (020) 8883 8656

*"Unsurpassed, south of Watford", this celebrated Muswell Hill
chippy offers "great fish and chips in massive portions". / **Sample
dishes:** fish soup; cod & chips; bread & butter pudding. **Value tip:** set
weekday L £15(FP). **Details:** 10 pm; closed Mon & Sun; no booking on Sat.*

Toto's SW1   **£ 40**   𝔸★

Lennox Gardens Mews   (020) 7589 0075   4–2D

*"Wonderful, traditional Italian" behind Harrods – "a great all-
rounder" with a "comfortable" and "romantic" setting, "lovely"
service and "reliable" cooking. / **Sample dishes:** squid ink spaghetti
with clams; herb-crusted lamb with confit shallots; lemon parfait with
mandarins. **Details:** 11.30 pm; smart casual.*

Tui SW7   **£ 29**   ★★

19 Exhibition Rd   (020) 7584 8359   4–2C

*"Exceptional", fiery cooking has regained its former reliability at
this "authentic" South Kensington Thai; post-refurbishment, the
setting is still "cramped" and "cold". / **Sample dishes:** chicken wings;
basil chicken curry; coconut custard. **Details:** 10.45 pm; smart casual.*

Vama SW10   **£ 36**   ★★

438 King's Rd   (020) 7351 4118   4–3B

*"Wonderful, imaginative" cooking, delivered by "polite and
timely" staff is winning ever-greater recognition for this "lovely", if
cramped, World's End Indian. / **Sample dishes:** mushroom tikka;
chicken stuffed with cashews and paneer; pancakes with fudge sauce.
Details: 11.30 pm; Sun 10 pm.*

Vong SW1   £ 42   ★
Wilton Pl   (020) 7235 1010   1–3A
*Fans rave over "brilliant" and "original" Thai/French cooking at
the Belgravia outpost of top NYC chef Jean-Georges Vongerichten;
the dining room is "smart", but a tad neutral, and some find the
whole experience "pretentious". / Sample dishes: tuna steamed in rice
paper; aromatic lamb with sautéed pak choy; chocolate cake with lemon grass
ice cream. Details: 11.30 pm; no smoking area.*

Vrisaki N22   £ 24   ★
73 Myddleton Rd   (020) 8889 8760
*"Tons of food" – "the best value meze in London" – make it
"worth the trip" to "huge buzzing Greek restaurant, hidden
behind a Bounds Green kebab shop". / Sample dishes: mixed meze;
salmon with couscous; ice cream. Details: Midnight; closed Sun; no Amex.*

The Waldorf Meridien WC2   £ 57   𝔸
Aldwych   (020) 7836 2400   1–2D
*"The space and the atmosphere are the treat" in the Palm Court
of this grand Covent Garden-fringe hotel; breakfast is "great", but
the food "then goes downhill for the rest of the day" (though tea
is a "lovely experience"). / Sample dishes: smoked salmon with vodka
crème fraîche; roast lamb with black olive mash; fruit scones with cream. Value
tip: pre-th. £34(FP). Details: 11.15 pm; closed Sat L; jacket & tie req'd for
tea dances; no smoking area.*

The Westbourne W2   £ 24   𝔸
101 Westbourne Park Villas   (020) 7221 1332
*"Get there early" – especially on a sunny day – before the food
runs out at this "fun" but shambolic Bayswater boozer; it's always
"overcrowded" with trustafarian Hillbillies. / Sample dishes: leek &
potato soup; roasted pork & tomatoes with butter beans; praline ice cream with
peaches. Details: 10 pm; closed Mon L; no Amex.*

The White Onion N1   £ 34   𝔸★★
297 Upper St   (020) 7359 3533
*"The star of Islington", on account of its "amazing" and
"interesting" modern British cooking and "attentive" service;
some find the understated setting "gloomy" – it's "nicer upstairs".
/ Sample dishes: pan fried foie gras & Mozzarella salad; duck with puy lentils
& caramelised onions; dark chocolate soufflé. Details: 11 pm; closed L, Mon-
Fri.*

William IV NW10   £ 26   𝔸★
786 Harrow Rd   (020) 8969 5944
*A "great Sunday pub lunch venue", this "out-of-the-way" Kensal
Green gastropub offers satisfying and "reasonably priced" fare,
and has an attractive courtyard garden. / Sample dishes: fresh
oysters with spicy salsa; char-grilled chicken with red lentils; banoffi pie.
Details: 10.30 pm, Fri & Sat 11 pm.*

Wiltons SW1   £ 52   𝔸★
55 Jermyn St   (020) 7629 9955   2–3C
*Notoriously "pricey" St James's stalwart, famed for its oysters and
praised for its "always reliable" seafood, meat and game; it's "too
much like a gentlemen's club", for some tastes, but it "can't be
outdone for power lunches". / Sample dishes: oyster soup; halibut with
spring greens; crème brûlée. Value tip: set Sun L £36(FP).
Details: 10.30 pm; closed Sat; jacket & tie.*

Windows on the World
Park Lane Hilton Hotel W1   £ 70   𝔸
22 Park Ln   (020) 7208 4021   2–4A
"Stunning view, but ouch!" – the cooking is *"poor and very expensive"* on the 28th floor of this Mayfair hotel; as an all-round experience, however, weekend brunches *"take a lot of beating"*, and in the evening it's *"romantic"*. / **Sample dishes:** duck liver pâté; fillet of sea bass; fruit cream with strawberry jus. **Value tip:** set Brunch £48(FP). **Details:** Mon-Thu 10.30 pm, Fri & Sat 11.30 pm; closed Sat L & Sun D; dinner, jacket & tie.

Windsor Castle W8   £ 26   𝔸
114 Campden Hl Rd   (020) 7243 9551
"A wonderful pub, inside and out"; thanks to its *"good pub food"* and *"lovely garden"*, this old Kensington inn is often *"overcrowded"* – no excuse for sometimes *"surly"* service. / **Sample dishes:** oysters; roast lamb; rhubarb crumble. **Details:** 10.30 pm; no smoking area (L only); no booking.

Wolfe's WC2   £ 26
30 Gt Queen St   (020) 7831 4442   3–1D
Homesick Yanks seek out this large, *"very American"* family restaurant in Covent Garden, known for its *"great burgers"*; the one behind Harrods has been knocked down. / **Sample dishes:** avocado & Mozzarella salad; butterfly chicken with peppercorn sauce; Wolfe's waffles. **Details:** 11.30 pm; closed Sun.

Yum Yum N16   £ 24   𝔸★
30 Stoke Newington Ch St   (020) 7254 6751
"Always-good food and welcoming service" has long proved a winning formula for this *"crowded"* Stoke Newington Thai. / **Sample dishes:** chicken & coconut soup; chicken & papaya with sticky rice; pancakes with coconut & ice cream. **Details:** 10.45 pm, Fri & Sat 11.15 pm.

Zafferano SW1   £ 44   𝔸★★
16 Lowndes St   (020) 7235 5800   1–4A
"Fight to get in", if you want to enjoy the *"awesome"* cooking at what is for many reporters *"the best Italian in town"*; only the low-key décor of its Belgravia premises inspires anything short of total adulation. / **Sample dishes:** crayfish risotto; rabbit with polenta & Parma ham; lemon tart with Mascarpone. **Details:** 11 pm; closed Sun.

Zaika SW3   £ 35   ★★
257-259 Fulham Rd   (020) 7351 7823   4–2C
"The Indian Chelsea didn't know it needed"; Vineet Bhatia's *"exciting and different"* cuisine, not to mention the supremely well-oiled service and comfortably distinctive décor, have made this newcomer (on the site of Chavot, RIP) an instant hit. / **Sample dishes:** stir-fried south Indian vegetables; crab masala; chocolate samosas. **Details:** 10.45 pm; closed Sat L & Sun.

Zen SW3   £ 44   ★
Chelsea Cloisters, Sloane Ave   (020) 7589 1781   4–2C
"Delicious food and courteous service, but a dingy room" is the current state of the *"comfortable"* Chelsea cradle of this Chinese dynasty. / **Sample dishes:** sesame prawn toast; lobster with ginger & spring onions; toffee apple & banana. **Value tip:** set weekday L £23(FP). **Details:** 11.15 pm; no Amex; smart casual.

LONDON AREA OVERVIEWS & INDEXES

CENTRAL

Soho, Covent Garden & Bloomsbury
(Parts of W1, all WC2 and WC1)

£60+	Savoy Grill	*British, Traditional*	𝔸
	Savoy River Restaurant	*French*	𝔸
£50+	Asia de Cuba	*East/West*	𝔸
	The Waldorf Meridien	*Afternoon tea*	𝔸
£40+	Lindsay House	*British, Modern*	𝔸★★
	The Ivy	*"*	𝔸★
	The Sugar Club	*"*	★
	Axis	*"*	-
	Bank	*"*	-
	Mezzo	*"*	-
	Rules	*British, Traditional*	𝔸
	Simpsons-in-the-Strand	*"*	𝔸
	Livebait	*Fish & seafood*	
	L'Escargot	*French*	𝔸★
	The Criterion	*"*	𝔸
£35+	Titanic	*British, Modern*	-
	Le Palais du Jardin	*French*	𝔸
£30+	Belgo Centraal	*Belgian*	-
	French House	*British, Modern*	𝔸★
	Andrew Edmunds	*"*	𝔸
	Mon Plaisir	*French*	𝔸★
	Fung Shing	*Chinese*	★★
	Chiang Mai	*Thai*	★★
£25+	Sarastro	*International*	𝔸
	Wolfe's	*Burgers, etc*	-
£20+	Ed's Easy Diner	*Burgers, etc*	𝔸
	Pâtisserie Valerie	*Sandwiches, cakes, etc*	𝔸★
	Souk	*North African*	𝔸
	Mr Kong	*Chinese*	★
	Ikkyu	*Japanese*	★
£15+	Gordon's Wine Bar	*International*	𝔸
	Food for Thought	*Vegetarian*	★
	Kulu Kulu	*Japanese*	★
£5+	Bar Italia	*Sandwiches, cakes, etc*	𝔸

Mayfair & St James's
(Parts of W1 and SW1)

£100+	Oak Room MPW	*French*	★
£90+	Le Gavroche	*French*	★

£80+	Chez Nico	*French*	★
£70+	Connaught	*British, Traditional*	𝔸
	Claridges Restaurant	*French*	𝔸
	The Ritz	*"*	𝔸
	Windows on the World	*"*	𝔸
	Dorchester, Oriental	*Chinese*	-
	Suntory	*Japanese*	-
£60+	The Square	*French*	★★
	Mitsukoshi	*Japanese*	★★
£50+	The Lanesborough	*British, Modern*	𝔸
	Dorchester Grill	*British, Traditional*	𝔸★
	Wiltons	*"*	𝔸★
	Nobu	*East/West*	𝔸★★
	Shogun	*Japanese*	★★
	Ikeda	*"*	★
	Miyama	*"*	★
£40+	Le Caprice	*British, Modern*	𝔸★
	Rhodes in the Sq	*"*	𝔸★
	The Avenue	*"*	-
	Pétrus	*French*	★★
	Mirabelle	*"*	𝔸★
	Morton's	*"*	𝔸★
	L'Oranger	*"*	-
	Tamarind	*Indian*	𝔸★★
	Matsuri	*Japanese*	★★
£35+	Quaglino's	*British, Modern*	-
	Momo	*North African*	𝔸
	Al Hamra	*Lebanese*	★
£30+	Sotheby's Café	*British, Modern*	𝔸★
£25+	Hard Rock Café	*Burgers, etc*	𝔸
	Rasa	*Indian*	★★

Fitzrovia & Marylebone
(Part of W1)

£50+	The Birdcage	*East/West*	𝔸★
	Pied à Terre	*French*	★★
£35+	Back to Basics	*Fish & seafood*	★★
	Maroush	*Lebanese*	★
£30+	Langan's Bistro	*French*	-
£25+	Royal China	*Chinese*	★★

LONDON AREA OVERVIEWS

£20+	Giraffe	British, Modern	A★
	Pâtisserie Valerie	Sandwiches, cakes, etc	A★
	Ikkyu	Japanese	★

Belgravia, Victoria & Pimlico
(SW1, except St James's)

£80+	La Tante Claire Berkeley Hotel	French	★
£60+	Isola	Italian	-
£50+	Restaurant One-O-One	French	★
	Rib Room	Steaks & grills	-
£40+	Vong	East/West	★
	Zafferano	Italian	A★★
	Toto's	"	A★
	Grissini	"	★
	Ken Lo's Memories	Chinese	★
	Salloos	Indian	★
£35+	La Poule au Pot	French	A
£30+	Caraffini	Italian	A★
£25+	Hunan	Chinese	★★

WEST

Chelsea, South Kensington,
Kensington, Earl's Court & Fulham
(SW3, SW5, SW6, SW7, SW10 & W8)

£80+	Blakes Hotel	International	A
£70+	Capital Hotel	French	-
£60+	Gordon Ramsay	French	★★
£50+	Hilaire	British, Modern	A★
	Aubergine	French	A★★
	Bibendum	"	A
	Floriana	Italian	★
£40+	Clarke's	British, Modern	A★★
	Launceston Place	"	A★
	The Terrace	"	A★
	Bluebird	"	-
	Chezmax	French	A★★

	Monkeys	*French*	A★★
	Mr Wing	*Chinese*	A★
	Zen	*"*	★
	Chutney Mary	*Indian*	★
	Blue Elephant	*Thai*	A★
£35+	755	*British, Modern*	★★
	The Canteen	*"*	A★
	Kensington Place	*"*	A
	Montana	*American*	A
	Maroush	*Lebanese*	★
	Mao Tai	*Chinese*	A★
	Vama	*Indian*	★★
	Zaika	*"*	★★
	Star of India	*"*	★
£30+	Maggie Jones's	*British, Traditional*	A
	Bibendum Oyster Bar	*Fish & seafood*	A★
	La Brasserie	*French*	A
	Cross Keys	*Mediterranean*	A
	Cambio de Tercio	*Spanish*	A
	The Enterprise	*International*	A
£25+	The Chelsea Ram	*British, Modern*	A★
	Elistano	*Italian*	A★
	Luigi's Delicatessen	*"*	★
	Made in Italy	*"*	★
	Windsor Castle	*International*	A
	Itsu	*Japanese*	-
	Tui	*Thai*	★★
£20+	Aglio e Olio	*Italian*	★
	The Atlas	*Mediterranean*	A★
	Lomo	*Spanish*	A
	Ed's Easy Diner	*Burgers, etc*	A
	Pâtisserie Valerie	*Sandwiches, cakes, etc*	A★
	Malabar	*Indian*	A★
£15+	Chelsea Bun Diner	*International*	-
	Churchill Arms	*Thai*	★
	Café 209	*"*	-

Notting Hill, Holland Park, Bayswater, North Kensington & Maida Vale (W2, W9, W10, W11)

£60+	Halcyon Hotel	*British, Modern*	★
£40+	Leith's	*British, Modern*	A★
	Julie's	*"*	A
	Pharmacy	*"*	-
	Assaggi	*Italian*	A★★

£35+	Jason's	Fish & seafood	A★
	Maroush	Lebanese	★
£30+	Belgo Zuid	Belgian	-
	Halepi	Greek	A
	The Green Olive	Italian	A★
	Mediterraneo	Mediterranean	A★
	Bombay Palace	Indian	A★
£25+	Mandarin Kitchen	Chinese	★★
	Royal China	"	★★
	Inaho	Japanese	★★
£20+	The Ladbroke Arms	British, Modern	A
	The Westbourne	"	A
	Alounak	Persian	★★
£15+	Ranoush	Lebanese	★★
£5+	Lisboa Patisserie	Sandwiches, cakes, etc	★★

Hammersmith, Shepherd's Bush Chiswick & Olympia (W4, W5, W6, W12, W14)

£50+	The River Café	Italian	★
£40+	Cibo	Italian	★
	Grano	"	★
£25+	The Havelock Tavern	British, Modern	A★★
	The Anglesea Arms	"	★★
	The Gate	Vegetarian	A★★
£20+	Blah! Blah! Blah!	"	A★
	Alounak	Persian	★★
	Esarn Kheaw	Thai	★
	Latymers	"	★

NORTH

Hampstead, West Hampstead, St John's Wood, Regent's Park, Kilburn & Camden Town (NW postcodes)

£35+	Odette's	British, Modern	A★
	The Engineer	"	A
	L'Aventure	French	A★★
	Oslo Court	"	★★

£30+	Belgo Noord	*Belgian*	-
	Halepi	*Greek*	𝔸
£25+	William IV	*British, Modern*	𝔸★
	Lemonia	*Greek*	𝔸
	The Park	*Italian*	𝔸
	Royal China	*Chinese*	★★
£20+	Giraffe	*British, Modern*	𝔸★
	Ed's Easy Diner	*Burgers, etc*	𝔸
	Nautilus	*Fish & chips*	★★
	Café Japan	*Japanese*	★

Islington, Highgate, Crouch End, Stoke Newington, Finsbury Park, Muswell Hill & Finchley (N postcodes)

£35+	Frederick's	*British, Modern*	𝔸★
£30+	Chez Liline	*Fish & seafood*	★★
	The White Onion	*French*	𝔸★★
	Les Associés	*"*	-
	The Real Greek	*Greek*	★★
£25+	Mesclun	*British, Modern*	★★
	Soulard	*French*	𝔸★
	Toff's	*Fish & chips*	★★
	Rasa	*Indian*	★★
£20+	Vrisaki	*Greek*	★
	Gallipoli	*Turkish*	𝔸★
	Iznik	*"*	𝔸★
	Yum Yum	*Thai*	𝔸★
£15+	Sarcan	*Turkish*	𝔸
	Anglo Asian Tandoori	*Indian*	𝔸★

SOUTH

South Bank (SE1)

£60+	Le Pont de la Tour	*British, Modern*	𝔸
£40+	Oxo Tower	*British, Modern*	𝔸
	Livebait	*Fish & seafood*	-
	Tentazioni	*Italian*	★
£30+	fish!	*Fish & seafood*	★

LONDON AREA OVERVIEWS

| £25+ | The Apprentice | British, Modern | ★ |
| £15+ | Pizzeria Castello | Pizza | ★ |

Battersea, Clapham, Wandsworth, Barnes, Putney, Brixton & Lewisham
(All postcodes south of the river except SE1)

£40+	Lobster Pot	Fish & seafood	★★
£35+	Chez Bruce	British, Modern	𝔸★★
	The Glasshouse	"	★★
	Ransome's Dock	"	𝔸★
	Sonny's	"	𝔸★
£30+	Monsieur Max	French	★★
	Del Buongustaio	Italian	𝔸★★
	Café Spice Namaste	Indian	★
£25+	The Mason's Arms	British, Modern	𝔸★
	Bah Humbug	"	𝔸
	Pizza Metro	Pizza	★★
	Eco	"	★
	Eco Brixton	"	★
	Royal China	Chinese	★
	Babur Brasserie	Indian	★★
	Sarkhel's	"	★★
£20+	Brady's	Fish & chips	★
	Battersea Rickshaw	Indian	-
£15+	Kastoori	Indian	★★
	Shree Krishna	"	★★

EAST

Smithfield & Farringdon
(EC1)

£40+	Gaudi	Spanish	-
£35+	Café du Marché	French	𝔸★
£30+	Club Gascon	French	𝔸★★
	Bleeding Heart	"	𝔸★
	Moro	North African	𝔸★★
£20+	Fox & Anchor	British, Traditional	𝔸★
	The Eagle	Mediterranean	𝔸★

**The City & East End
(All E and EC postcodes, except EC1)**

£60+	Tatsuso	*Japanese*	★★
£50+	City Rhodes	*British, Modern*	★
	City Miyama	*Japanese*	★
£40+	Prism	*British, Modern*	★
	1 Lombard Street	*"*	𝔸
	Coq d'Argent	*French*	-
£35+	Brasserie 24	*International*	𝔸
£30+	Sweetings	*Fish & seafood*	𝔸★
	Luc's Brasserie	*French*	𝔸★
	Gt Eastern Dining Room	*Italian*	𝔸★
	Café Spice Namaste	*Indian*	★
£15+	Faulkner's	*Fish & chips*	★★
	Lahore Kebab House	*Indian*	★★

INDEXES

BREAKFAST
(with opening times)

Central
Bank *(7.30)*
Bar Italia *(7)*
Claridges Restaurant *(7)*
Connaught *(7.30)*
Dorchester Grill *(7, Sun 7.30)*
Food for Thought *(9.30)*
Giraffe *(8, Sat & Sun 9)*
Grissini *(7, Sun 8)*
The Lanesborough *(7)*
Pâtisserie Valerie: *Old Compton St W1 (7.30, Sun 9); RIBA Centre, 66 Portland Pl W1 (8); Marylebone High St W1 (8, Sun 9); WC2 (9.30, Sun 9)*
Restaurant One-O-One *(7)*
The Ritz *(7)*
Savoy River Restaurant *(7)*
Simpsons-in-the-Strand *(Mon-Fri 7.30)*
Sotheby's Café *(9)*
The Waldorf Meridien *(7, Sat & Sun 7.30)*
Windows on the World *(7)*

West
Blakes Hotel *(7.30)*
La Brasserie *(8, Sun 9)*
Capital Hotel *(7, Sun 7.30)*
Chelsea Bun Diner *(7)*
Ed's Easy Diner: *SW3 (Sat & Sun only, 9)*
Halcyon Hotel *(7, Sun 7.30)*
Jason's *(9.30)*
Lisboa Patisserie *(8)*
Pâtisserie Valerie: *SW3 (7.30, Sun 9)*
Ranoush *(9)*

North
Ed's Easy Diner: *NW3 (Sat & Sun only, 9)*
Giraffe: *all branches (8, Sat & Sun 9)*
Iznik *(Sat & Sun 9)*

South
Bah Humbug *(Sat & Sun 10.30)*
Eco Brixton: *SW9 (9)*

East
Brasserie 24 *(7.30)*
Coq d'Argent *(Mon-Fri only, 7.30)*
Fox & Anchor *(7)*

BRUNCH MENUS

Central
Bank
Le Caprice
Giraffe
Grissini

The Ivy
The Lanesborough
Mirabelle
Momo
Restaurant One-O-One
The Sugar Club
Vong
The Waldorf Meridien
Windows on the World

West
Bluebird
La Brasserie
Chelsea Bun Diner
Cross Keys
Halcyon Hotel
Montana

North
The Engineer
Giraffe
The Park
The White Onion

South
Bah Humbug
Le Pont de la Tour
Ransome's Dock

BUSINESS

Central
The Avenue
Axis
Bank
Le Caprice
Chez Nico
Claridges Restaurant
Connaught
The Criterion
Dorchester Grill
Dorchester, Oriental
L'Escargot
Le Gavroche
Grissini
The Ivy
Ken Lo's Memories
The Lanesborough
Lindsay House
Mirabelle
Mitsukoshi
Miyama
Mon Plaisir
Morton's
Oak Room MPW
L'Oranger
Pétrus
Pied à Terre
Quaglino's
Restaurant One-O-One

Rhodes in the Sq
Rib Room
The Ritz
Rules
Savoy Grill
Savoy River Restaurant
Simpsons-in-the-Strand
The Square
The Sugar Club
Suntory
La Tante Claire
  Berkeley Hotel
Vong
Wiltons
Windows on the World
Zafferano

West
Aubergine
Bibendum
Bluebird
The Canteen
Capital Hotel
Clarke's
Gordon Ramsay
Launceston Place
Leith's

North
Frederick's
Odette's

South
Oxo Tower
Le Pont de la Tour

East
Bleeding Heart
Brasserie 24
Café du Marché
City Miyama
City Rhodes
Coq d'Argent
Luc's Brasserie
Moro
1 Lombard Street
Prism
Sweetings
Tatsuso

BYO
(Bring your own wine)

Central
Food for Thought

West
Alounak: *W14*
Blah! Blah! Blah!
Café 209
Chelsea Bun Diner

South
Eco Brixton: *SW9*
Monsieur Max

East
Faulkner's
Lahore Kebab House

CHILDREN
**(h – high or special chairs
m – children's menu
p – children's portions
e – weekend entertainments
o – other facilities)**

Central
Al Hamra *(p)*
Axis *(m)*
Back to Basics *(p)*
Bank *(hp)*
Belgo Centraal: *WC2 (hp)*
The Birdcage *(p)*
Claridges Restaurant *(h)*
The Criterion *(h)*
Dorchester Grill *(hm)*
Dorchester, Oriental *(h)*
Ed's Easy Diner: *Trocadero W1 (hm); Moor St W1 (m)*
L'Escargot *(h)*
Fung Shing *(h)*
Giraffe *(h)*
Hard Rock Café *(hmpo)*
The Ivy *(hp)*
The Lanesborough *(hm)*
Langan's Bistro *(p)*
Maroush: *all branches (p)*
Matsuri *(m)*
Mezzo *(h)*
Nobu *(h)*
Oak Room MPW *(h)*
Quaglino's *(h)*
Restaurant One-O-One *(h)*
Rib Room *(h)*
The Ritz *(h)*
Royal China: *all branches (hm)*
Rules *(h)*
Savoy Grill *(h)*
Savoy River Restaurant *(h)*
The Waldorf Meridien *(h)*
Windows on the World *(h)*
Wolfe's *(hm)*
Zafferano *(h)*

West
Alounak: *W14 (h)*
Assaggi *(p)*
Blah! Blah! Blah! *(p)*
Blakes Hotel *(h)*
Blue Elephant *(he)*
Bluebird *(hm)*
Bombay Palace *(hp)*

INDEXES

ENTERTAINMENT
(Check times before you go)

Central
The Avenue
(jazz, Sun L; pianist, Wed eves)
Claridges Restaurant
(dinner dance, Fri & Sat)
Grissini
(music, nightly)
The Lanesborough
(supper dances, Fri & Sat; jazz Sun brunch)
Mezzo
(music, all week)
Quaglino's
(jazz, nightly in bar)
Rib Room
(pianist Mon-Sat eves)
The Ritz
(band, Fri & Sat)
Sarastro
(opera, Mon; Turkish music, Sun)
Savoy River Restaurant
(dinner dance, nightly ex Sun)
The Waldorf Meridien
(jazz, Sun brunch)
Windows on the World
(dinner dance, Fri & Sat; jazz Sun brunch)

West
Cambio de Tercio
(guitarist, Wed)
Chutney Mary
(jazz, Sun L)
Floriana
(pianist nightly)
Maroush: *W2*
(music & dancing, nightly)
Montana
(jazz, Wed-Sun)
Mr Wing
(jazz Thu-Sat)
Star of India
(music, Thu & Fri (winter only))
William IV
(DJ, Fri & Sat)

North
Les Associés
(accordion 1st Fri of month)

South
Bah Humbug
(nightly, in adjacent Bug Bar)

East
Café du Marché
(music, nightly)

LATE
(open till midnight or later as shown; may be earlier Sunday)

Central
Asia de Cuba *(Midnight, Sat 1 am)*
The Avenue *(Midnight, Fri & Sat 12.30am, Sun 10pm)*

Bar Italia *(4 am, Fri & Sat 24 hours)*
Le Caprice
The Criterion *(not Sun)*
Ed's Easy Diner: *all central branches (midnight, Fri & Sat 1 am)*
Hard Rock Café *(12.30 am, Fri & Sat 1 am)*
The Ivy
The Lanesborough
Maroush: *W1 (1 am)*
Mezzo *(Mon-Wed midnight, Thu-Sat 1 am (crustacea till 3 am))*
Mirabelle
Mr Kong *(2.45 am)*
Le Palais du Jardin
Quaglino's *(midnight, Fri & Sat 1 am, not Sun)*

West
Alounak: *all branches*
Blue Elephant *(midnight, Sun 10.30 pm)*
The Canteen *(Fri & Sat only)*
Ed's Easy Diner: *SW3*
Halepi: *W2 (12.30 am)*
Maroush: *W2 (1.30 am); SW3 (5 am)*
Mr Wing
Ranoush *(3 am)*

North
Anglo Asian Tandoori *(Fri & Sat 12.15 am)*
Ed's Easy Diner: *NW3 (midnight, Fri & Sat 1 am)*
Rasa: *N16 (Fri & Sat only)*
Sarcan
Vrisaki

NO-SMOKING AREAS
(* completely no smoking)

Central
The Birdcage
Connaught*
Food for Thought*
Grissini
Hard Rock Café
Ikkyu: *WC2*
Kulu Kulu*
Livebait: *WC2*
Nobu
Rasa: *all branches**
Sotheby's Café*
The Sugar Club
Vong
The Waldorf Meridien

West
Bombay Palace
Chutney Mary
Clarke's
Itsu*

Mao Tai
Windsor Castle

North
Café Japan
Frederick's
Giraffe: *NW3**
The Park
Rasa: *all branches**

South
The Apprentice
Babur Brasserie
Eco: *SW4*
fish!

East
Faulkner's

OUTSIDE TABLES
(* particularly recommended)

Central
Al Hamra*
Back to Basics
Bar Italia
Caraffini
Ed's Easy Diner: *Moor St W1*
Giraffe: *W1*
Gordon's Wine Bar*
Hard Rock Café
Mirabelle*
Momo
Morton's*
Le Palais du Jardin
Pâtisserie Valerie: *RIBA Centre, 66 Portland Pl W1*; WC2*
La Poule au Pot
The Ritz*
Toto's*
Wolfe's

West
The Anglesea Arms
The Atlas*
Blakes Hotel*
Bombay Palace
La Brasserie
The Chelsea Ram
Elistano
The Enterprise
The Gate*
Halcyon Hotel*
The Havelock Tavern
Jason's*
The Ladbroke Arms*
Lisboa Patisserie
Luigi's Delicatessen
Made in Italy
Mediterraneo
The River Café*

INDEXES

The Terrace
Vama
The Westbourne*
William IV*
Windsor Castle*

North
Les Associés
L'Aventure*
The Engineer*
Frederick's*
Gallipoli: *all branches*
Lemonia
Odette's
Sarcan
Soulard

South
Babur Brasserie
Bah Humbug
Battersea Rickshaw
Café Spice Namaste: *SW11*
fish!*
Livebait: *SE1*
The Mason's Arms
Oxo Tower*
Pizza Metro
Le Pont de la Tour*
Ransome's Dock*

East
Bleeding Heart*
Coq d'Argent*
The Eagle
Moro

ROMANTIC

Central
Andrew Edmunds
The Birdcage
Le Caprice
Claridges Restaurant
Connaught
The Criterion
French House
Le Gavroche
The Ivy
Lindsay House
Mirabelle
Momo
Mon Plaisir
L'Oranger
La Poule au Pot
The Ritz
Salloos
Sarastro
Savoy Grill
Savoy River Restaurant
Shogun

Toto's
Windows on the World

West
Aubergine
Bibendum
Blakes Hotel
Blue Elephant
The Canteen
Chezmax
Clarke's
Grano
The Green Olive
Halcyon Hotel
Jason's
Julie's
Launceston Place
Maggie Jones's
Mediterraneo
Monkeys
Mr Wing
The Terrace
Zaika

North
L'Aventure
The Engineer
Frederick's
Odette's
Oslo Court

South
Bah Humbug
Chez Bruce
The Glasshouse
Oxo Tower

East
Bleeding Heart
Café du Marché

ROOMS WITH A VIEW

Central
Grissini
The Ritz
Savoy River Restaurant
Windows on the World

South
Oxo Tower
Le Pont de la Tour

East
Brasserie 24
Coq d'Argent

LONDON MAPS

MAP I – WEST END OVERVIEW

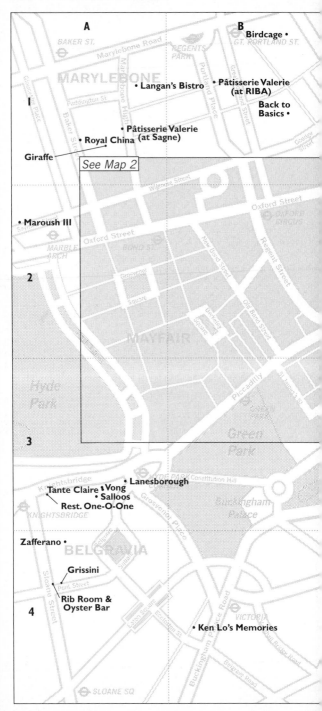

A

B

BAKER ST.

Marylebone Road

REGENTS PARK

GT. PORTLAND ST.

Birdcage •

MARYLEBONE

• Langan's Bistro

• Pâtisserie Valerie (at RIBA)

I

Paddington St

Portland Place

Back to Basics •

• Pâtisserie Valerie (at Sagne)

• Royal China

Giraffe

See Map 2

Wigmore Street

Oxford Street

OXFORD CIRCUS

• Maroush III

MARBLE ARCH

Oxford Street

BOND ST.

New Bond Street

Regent Street

Old Bond Street

2

Grosvenor Square

Berkeley Square

MAYFAIR

Piccadilly

Hyde Park

St James's St.

GREEN PARK

Green Park

3

Knightsbridge

HYDE PARK Constitution Hill

• Lanesborough

Tante Claire ₃ Vong

• Salloos

Rest. One-O-One

Grosvenor Place

Buckingham Palace

KNIGHTSBRIDGE

Zafferano •

BELGRAVIA

Grissini

Pont Street

Rib Room & Oyster Bar

Sloane Street

Eaton Square

VICTORIA

Buckingham Palace Road

Belgrave Road

• Ken Lo's Memories

4

SLOANE SQ

MAP 1 – WEST END OVERVIEW

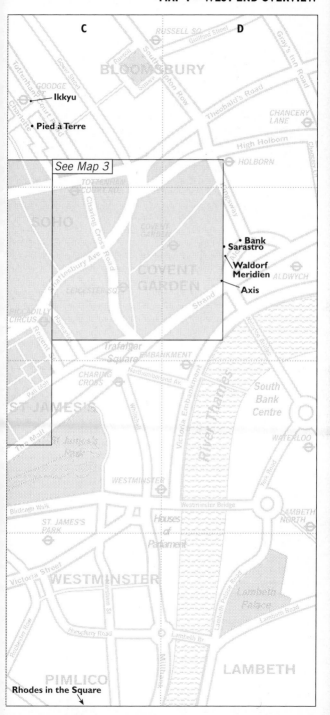

MAP 2 – MAYFAIR, ST JAMES'S & WEST SOHO

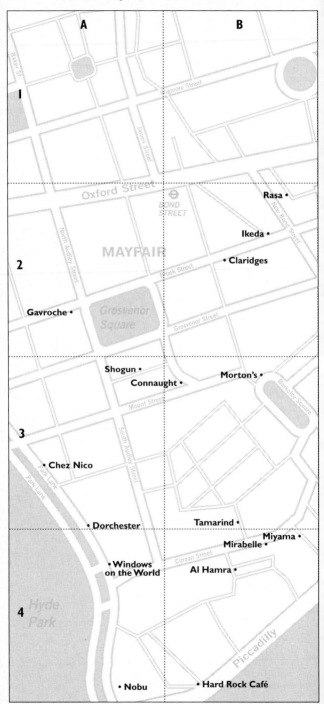

MAP 2 – MAYFAIR, ST JAMES'S & WEST SOHO

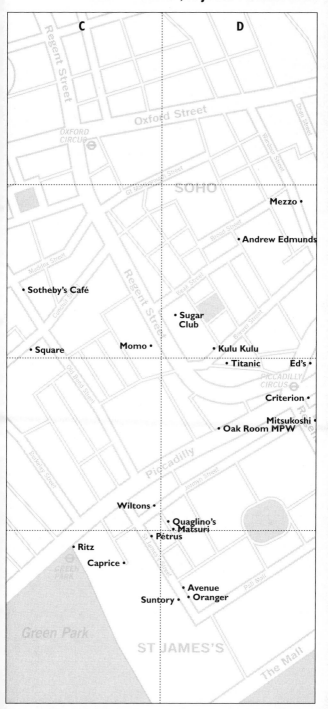

MAP 3 – EAST SOHO, CHINATOWN & COVENT GARDEN

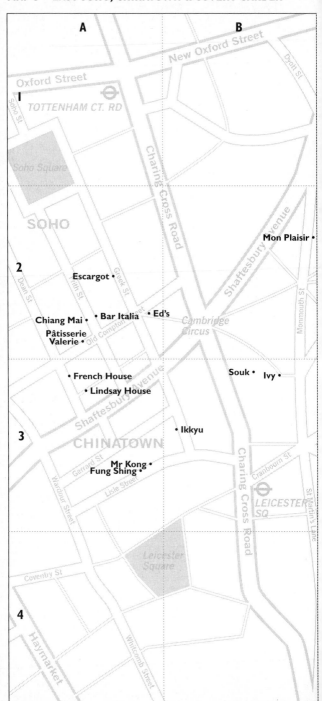

MAP 3 – EAST SOHO, CHINATOWN & COVENT GARDEN

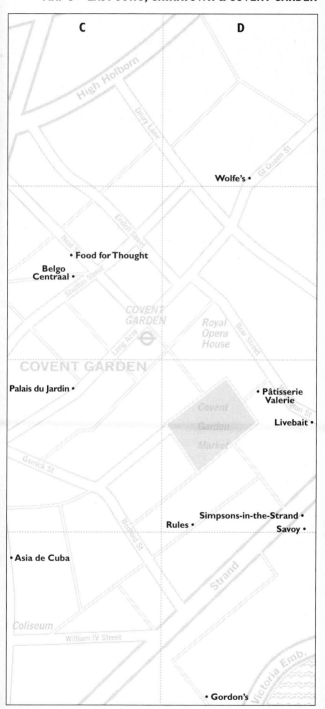

C

D

High Holborn

Drury Lane

Gt Queen St

Wolfe's •

Endell Street

Neal

• Food for Thought

Belgo
Centraal •

Shelton Street

COVENT
GARDEN

Royal
Opera
House

Bow Street

Long Acre

COVENT GARDEN

Palais du Jardin •

• Pâtisserie
Valerie

ston St

Livebait •

Covent
Garden
Market

Garrick St

Simpsons-in-the-Strand •

Rules •

Savoy •

Bedford St

• Asia de Cuba

Strand

Coliseum

William IV Street

Victoria Emb.

• Gordon's

MAP 4 – KNIGHTSBRIDGE, CHELSEA & SOUTH KENSINGTON

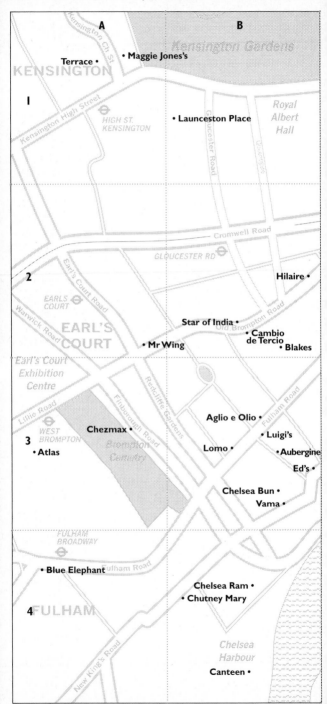

MAP 4 – KNIGHTSBRIDGE, CHELSEA & SOUTH KENSINGTON

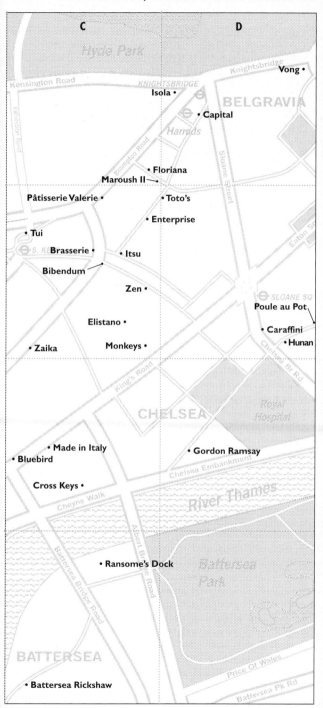

UK & EIRE
SURVEY RESULTS
& TOP SCORERS

PLACES PEOPLE TALK ABOUT

Restaurants outside London mentioned most frequently in the survey (last year's position shown in brackets):

1	Manoir aux Quat' Saisons *(1)*	*Great Milton, Oxon*
2	Seafood Restaurant *(2)*	*Padstow, Cornwall*
3	Le Petit Blanc *(3)*	*Oxford*
4	Waterside Inn *(4)*	*Bray, Berks*
5	Walnut Tree *(5)*	*Llandewi Skirrid, Mon'shire*
6	Yang Sing *(8)*	*Manchester*
7	The Angel *(7)*	*Hetton, N Yorks*
8	Whit' Oyster Fishery Co. *(12)*	*Whitstable, Kent*
9	Browns *(13=)*	*Oxford*
10	21 Queen Street *(-)*	*Newcastle upon Tyne*
11=	Heathcotes *(10=)*	*Longridge, Lancs*
11=	Hotel du Vin et Bistro *(17=)*	*Winchester, Hants*
13	Shimla Pinks *(-)*	*Birmingham*
14=	Simply Heathcotes *(10=)*	*Manchester*
14=	Sharrow Bay *(6)*	*Ullswater, Cumbria*
16=	Carved Angel *(20=)*	*Dartmouth, Devon*
16=	Chaing Mai *(-)*	*Oxford*
16=	The Crown *(17=)*	*Southwold, Suffolk*
16=	Hart's *(-)*	*Nottingham*
16=	Terre à Terre *(-)*	*Brighton*
16=	Ubiquitous Chip *(16)*	*Glasgow*

TOP SCORERS

All restaurants whose food rating is ★★; plus restaurants whose price is £50+ with a food rating of ★:

£90+ Manoir aux Quat' Saisons *(Great Milton)* ★𝔸
      Waterside Inn *(Bray)* ★

£80+ Altnaharrie Inn *(Ullapool)* ★★𝔸

£70+ Gidleigh Park *(Chagford)* ★★
      Lower Slaughter Manor *(Lower Slaughter)* ★𝔸
      Patrick Guilbaud *(Dublin)* ★

£60+ Hambleton Hall *(Hambleton)* ★★𝔸
      Lettonie *(Bath)* ★★𝔸
      Peacock Alley *(Dublin)* ★★
      Buckland Manor *(Buckland)* ★𝔸
      Gravetye Manor *(East Grinstead)* ★𝔸
      Lords of the Manor *(Upper Slaughter)* ★𝔸
      The French Horn *(Sonning)* ★𝔸
      Homewood Park *(Hinton Charterhouse)* ★
      Chester Grosvenor Hotel, Arkle *(Chester)* ★
      The Fat Duck *(Bray)* ★
      Harry's Place *(Great Gonerby)* ★

£50+ Fischers at Baslow Hall *(Baslow)* ★★𝔸
      Sharrow Bay *(Ullswater)* ★★𝔸
      Winteringham Fields *(Winteringham)* ★★𝔸
      Croque en Bouche *(Malvern Wells)* ★★
      Kinnaird House *(Dunkeld)* ★𝔸
      Llangoed Hall *(Llyswen)* ★𝔸
      Michael's Nook *(Grasmere)* ★𝔸
      Old Beams *(Waterhouses)* ★𝔸
      One Devonshire Gardens *(Glasgow)* ★𝔸
      Pink Geranium *(Melbourn)* ★𝔸
      Walletts Court *(St Margarets at Cliffe)* ★𝔸
      Carved Angel *(Dartmouth)* ★
      Number One *(Edinburgh)* ★
      Old Vicarage *(Ridgeway)* ★
      Thorntons *(Dublin)* ★
      Vineyard at Stockcross *(Stockcross)* ★

£40+ Ballymaloe Hotel *(Shanagarry)* ★★𝔸
      Clarence Hotel, Tea Rooms *(Dublin)* ★★𝔸
      Fairyhill *(Reynoldston)* ★★𝔸
      Horn of Plenty *(Gulworthy)* ★★𝔸
      The Market *(Manchester)* ★★𝔸
      The Peat Inn *(Cupar)* ★★𝔸
      Chavignol *(Chipping Norton)* ★★
      One Paston Place *(Brighton)* ★★
      Pennypots *(Falmouth)* ★★

TOP SCORERS

Walnut Tree *(Llandewi Skirrid)* ★★
The Box Tree *(Ilkley)* ★★
21 Queen Street *(Newcastle upon Tyne)* ★★
La Potinière *(Gullane)* ★★
La Terrasse *(Sandgate)* ★★

£30+ Blue Bicycle *(York)* ★★Ⓐ
Blue Lion *(East Witton)* ★★Ⓐ
Bodidris Hall Hotel *(Llandegla)* ★★Ⓐ
Inn at Whitewell *(Clitheroe)* ★★Ⓐ
Merchant House *(Ludlow)* ★★Ⓐ
Nantyffin Cider Mill *(Crickhowell)* ★★Ⓐ
Roly's Bistro *(Dublin)* ★★Ⓐ
Three Chimneys *(Dunvegan)* ★★Ⓐ
The Angel *(Hetton)* ★★Ⓐ
blue bar café *(Edinburgh)* ★★
Doyle's Seafood Bar *(Dingle)* ★★
Markwick's *(Bristol)* ★★
Mermaid Café *(Dublin)* ★★
Monsieur Max *(Hampton Hill)* ★★
Oaks Restaurant *(Ludlow)* ★★
Ramore Wine Bar *(Portrush)* ★★
Riverside *(Bridport)* ★★
Yang Sing *(Manchester)* ★★
Ivory Tower *(Cork)* ★★
Three Lions *(Stuckton)* ★★

£25+ Bell's Diner *(Bristol)* ★★Ⓐ
Blagraves House *(Barnard Castle)* ★★Ⓐ
Drum & Monkey *(Harrogate)* ★★Ⓐ
Loch Fyne Oyster Bar *(Clachan)* ★★Ⓐ
Masons Arms *(Cartmel Fell)* ★★Ⓐ
Mother India *(Glasgow)* ★★Ⓐ
Spread Eagle *(Sawley)* ★★Ⓐ
The Lime Tree *(Manchester)* ★★Ⓐ
Aziz *(Oxford)* ★★
Chaing Mai *(Oxford)* ★★
Little Yang Sing *(Manchester)* ★★
Terre à Terre *(Brighton)* ★★

£20+ Green's *(Manchester)* ★★Ⓐ
Nobody Inn *(Doddiscombsleigh)* ★★Ⓐ
Kalpna *(Edinburgh)* ★★
Salvo's *(Leeds)* ★★
The Three Crowns *(Brinkworth)* ★★
Al Shami *(Oxford)* ★★
Nirmals *(Sheffield)* ★★

£15+ Hansa *(Leeds)* ★★
Mumtaz Paan House *(Bradford)* ★★
The Mermaid Café *(Hastings)* ★★

UK & EIRE
DIRECTORY

Sawadee   **£ 27**
16-17 Bon Accord Crescent AB11 6AB   (01224) 582828
"Good Thai 'home' cooking" and *"courteous"* service makes this
superior city-centre oriental *"an oasis in an area devoid of culinary
high-spots"*. / **Sample dishes:** *Thai salad; crispy duck pancakes; ice cream.*
Details: *11 pm; no smoking area.*

Silver Darling   **£ 40**
Pocra Quay, North Pier AB11 5DQ   (01224) 576229
Even some of those who think this converted customs-house offers
"excellent" fresh fish admit this place is *"slightly pricey"* for what it is.
/ **Sample dishes:** *mussel & langoustine soup; roast monkfish with Parma ham;
apple tart with green apple sorbet.* **Value tip:** *set 3-crs L £18.50.*
Details: *9.30 pm; closed Sat L & Sun.*

Penhelig Arms   **£ 26**
LL35 0LT   (01654) 767215
"Good food and a friendly atmosphere" make this lively pub, with its
harbour view, a very useful stand-by. / **Sample dishes:** *baked stuffed
aubergines & peppers; monkfish in ginger & lime sauce; bread & butter
pudding.* **Value tip:** *set 3-crs Sun L £12.95.* **Details:** *9 pm; no Amex;
no smoking in dining room.* **Accommodation:** *10 rooms, from £68.*

Porth Tocyn Hotel   **£ 37**   A★
LL53 7BU   (01758) 713303
"Standards have been kept up over 30 years" is a typical report on
this genteel seaside hotel (nicely removed from the hubbub of the
town itself, and with lovely views); it provides *"cooking with plenty of
variety and interest"* and *"good wines"*, from a *"genial host"*.
/ **Sample dishes:** *Stilton & bacon rarebit; roast guinea fowl with tarragon
truffle sauce; Jamaican rum pie.* **Value tip:** *set 3-crs L £17.50.*
Details: *2m S of Abersoch - follow blue road signs with bed symbol; 9.30 pm;
closed mid Nov to Easter; no Amex; no smoking; children: 7+ at D.*
Accommodation: *17 rooms, from £62.*

Summer Isles   **£ 43**   A★
IV26 2YG   (01854) 622282
Stunning views (towards the islands for which it is named) and
good and imaginative cooking make a visit to this long-established
family-owned hotel, in a remote corner of the Highlands,
"truly memorable". / **Sample dishes:** *mushroom risotto; scallops
with leeks in vermouth; chocolate fudge cake.* **Details:** *25m N from
Ullapool on A835; 8 pm; no Amex; no smoking in dining room;
children: 6+.* **Accommodation:** *13 rooms, from £74.*

Café 152   **£ 25**   ★
152 High St IP15 5AX   (01728) 454152
"Wonderful fish enhanced by cleanly flavoured sauces" is one of
the strengths of the *"unusual"* menu at this unpretentious and
"good-value" bistro. / **Sample dishes:** *squid ink risotto; lamb with roast
vegetables & olives; iced nougat parfait.* **Details:** *6m from A12 on A1094
signposted Aldeburgh; 10 pm Summer, 9 pm Winter; 10pm in summer, 9pm in
winter, closed Tue (& Mon in winter); no Amex; children: restricted after 8 pm.*

Lighthouse £ 24 A★
77 High St IP15 5AU (01728) 453377
*"Consistently good food at a great price" and a "lovely", "rustic" atmosphere ensure that Peter and Sarah Hill's "very friendly" venture "rarely disappoints", and it is – by a long chalk – the most commented-upon place in town; "excellent fresh fish" is the highlight. / **Sample dishes:** parsnip & lentil soup; grilled skate wing with red pepper salsa; fresh orange sorbet. **Details:** 10 pm; closed for 2 weeks end Jan & 1 week in Oct; no Amex or Diners; children: parental control essential.*

Regatta £ 25 A
171 High St IP15 5AN (01728) 452011
*Some tip the "fresh cod and chips", in preference to other "too eclectic" choices, at this lively restaurant. / **Sample dishes:** smoked salmon; lobster thermidor; crème brûlée. **Details:** 10 pm; closed Wed, Nov-Mar; no smoking area.*

ALDFORD, CHESHIRE 5–3A
The Grosvenor Arms £ 27 A
Chester Rd CH3 6HJ (01244) 620228
*"The Duke of Westminster's local" (near gates to his estate) has suitably superior standards, and offers good portions of English cooking in a relaxed setting. / **Sample dishes:** cherry tomato, olive & feta tart; roast lamb with apricot & pepper sauce; bread pudding with apricot sauce. **Details:** 6m S of Chester on B5130; 10 pm; children: 14+ after 6 pm.*

ALLOWAY BY AYR, AYRSHIRE 9–4B
Brig O' Doon House Hotel £ 27 A★
KA7 4PQ (01292) 442466
*This "wonderful, hidden-away restaurant in Burns's birthplace" makes "innovative" use of "Scottish produce cooked to perfection". / **Sample dishes:** seared salmon; lemon & tarragon chicken; apple & sultana crumble. **Details:** 9 pm; no smoking in dining room. **Accommodation:** 5 rooms, from £85.*

ALNWICK, NORTHUMBERLAND 8–1B
The Gate £ 22 ★
Bondgate Within NE66 1TD (01665) 602607
*"Lots of garlicky, olive oily vegetables, superb fish, imaginative cheese, a good wine list and a friendly chef" combine to make this "friendly and informal but polished", "modern Mediterranean" place "an oasis in a culinary desert"; it's also tipped for its suitability for veggies. / **Sample dishes:** avocado & salmon with lime dressing; chicken & seafood in garlic butter; raspberry roulade & mango coulis. **Details:** 9.30 pm, Sat & Sun 10 pm; closed Mon (& Sun in winter); no credit cards; smoking discouraged.*

ALTRINCHAM, GREATER MANCHESTER 5–2B
French Restaurant £ 27 A
25 The Downs WA14 2QD (0161) 941 3355
*"Happy", and "lively" suburban restaurant; its style may be a bit old-fashioned, but it's a "pleasant place to eat" in an area without a huge number of good, mid-range alternatives. / **Sample dishes:** salade de foie de volaille; roast leg of lamb; apricot bavarois. **Value tip:** set 3-crs L £8.95. **Details:** 10.30 pm; closed Sat L.*

Juniper £ 47 ★
21 The Downs WA14 2QD (0161) 929 4008
*Slightly more mixed reports this year on this "unpretentious" Manchester-fringe foodie mecca; the majority still found the Gallic cooking "elegant and sophisticated", but for some it's "too clever" and "doesn't live up to the hype". / **Sample dishes:** lobster bisque; duck with juniper & spring greens; rice pudding soufflé. **Details:** 10 pm; closed Mon L, Sat L & Sun.*

Amberley Castle   £ 46   Ⓐ
BN18 9ND   (01798) 831992
*The cuisine doesn't live up to the "excellent" setting – complete with
drawbridge, portcullis, etc – of this fairy-tale castle; some find that
service which is "too flunky-like" contributes to a "false" ambience.
/ Sample dishes: quail with red cabbage; herb-crusted salmon with spinach
& capers; dark chocolate tart. Value tip: set 2-crs L £12.50. Details: N of
Arundel, on B2139; 9.30 pm; jacket & tie; no smoking; booking: max 6;
children: 12+. Accommodation: 15 rooms, from £145.*

Drunken Duck   £ 28   Ⓐ
Barngates LA22 0NG   (01539) 436347
*The "beautiful, high-ceilinged dining room" of this pub is
"always busy", thanks to the "excellent reputation" its "interesting"
cooking enjoys, and its "superb" service. / Sample dishes: chicken in
ginger & garlic; coriander crusted salmon; chocolate marquise. Details: 3m
from Ambleside, towards Hawkshead; 9 pm; no smoking.
Accommodation: 11 rooms, from £90.*

The Glass House   £ 29   Ⓐ ★
Rydal Rd LA22 9AN   (01539) 432137
*This "delightful" and "spacious" modern building, "with lots of glass
and a working water-wheel", is widely acclaimed for its "excellent"
atmosphere; the "precise", "fresh" and "interesting" cooking is almost
as great an attraction. / Sample dishes: char-grilled asparagus with
Parmesan; red mullet with deep-fried celeriac; rice pudding & glazed bananas.
Details: behind Little Bridge House; 10 pm; no Amex; no smoking.*

Zeffirelli's   £ 19
Compston Rd LA22 9DN   (01539) 433845
*"Even the keenest carnivore is satisfied" at this "informal Italian-style,
veggie pizza-and-pasta café/restaurant"; it's an "inexpensive" place,
and "you can combine a trip with a visit to the adjoining cinema".
/ Sample dishes: polenta with olive chilli; pasta with pesto & roast tomatoes;
summer pudding. Details: 9.45 pm; in winter, closed Mon & Tue; no Amex;
no smoking.*

Gilbeys   £ 28
1 Market Sq HP7 0DF   (01494) 727242
*The "straightforward" modern British cooking at this "cramped" and
"friendly" bistro is "expensive for what it is", but the "very reasonably
priced wines" (from the shop next door, with no mark-up) ensure
"immense popularity". / Sample dishes: rabbit & green peppercorn
terrine; grilled cod fillet with bubble & squeak; peanut butter parfait.
Details: in Old Amersham, 5m N of M40 J2, 1m from Amersham; 9.45 pm.*

Santhi   £ 22   Ⓐ
16 Hill Ave HP6 5BW   (01494) 432621
*Just a few yards from the Metropolitan line station, this grand Indian
boasts a "forest" and a "fountain" to add interest to its "tropical"
setting; it's praised for its "traditional but freshly cooked" fare.
/ Sample dishes: chicken chat; chicken jahllosa; mango delight.
Details: 10.45 pm; no smoking area.*

ANSTRUTHER, FIFE
Cellar £ 39 9–4D A★

24 East Green KY10 3AA (01333) 310378

In the cellar of a stone-built, 17th-century house behind the Scottish Fisheries museum, this long-established fixture produces some "beautiful" cooking using "superb" ingredients (primarily piscatorial), and has "great atmosphere" to boot. / **Sample dishes:** haddock omelette; crayfish & mussel bisque; hazelnut praline parfait. **Details:** 9.30 pm; closed Mon & Tue L (& Sun in winter); no smoking; children: 8+.

APPLECROSS, HIGHLAND
Applecross Inn £ 23 9–2B ★

Shore St IV54 8LR (01520) 744262

"However stormy the weather is outside, it's cosy within", at this "severely inaccessible" inn (at the end of one of the most picturesque drives in Scotland); "good game" and the "freshest imaginable seafood", "nice and plainly cooked", comes at "ridiculously cheap prices". / **Sample dishes:** seafood platter; scallops with crispy bacon & rice; raspberry cranachan. **Details:** off A896, S of Shieldaig; 9 pm; no Amex & no Switch; no smoking. **Accommodation:** 5 rooms, from £45.

ARNCLIFFE, N YORKS
Amerdale House Hotel £ 38 8–4B ★

BD23 5QE (01756) 770250

This "brilliant hotel", in an "idyllic", if "isolated", Dales setting wins a chorus of approval for its "four-course menus of fresh local produce"; it's "a wonderful place to stay as well as eat". / **Sample dishes:** tomato & basil tart; pan-roast sea bass; vanilla mousse. **Details:** 8.30 pm; D only, closed mid Nov to mid Mar; no Amex; no smoking; max booking 6. **Accommodation:** 11 rooms, from £66.50, incl D.

ASCOT, BERKS
The Thatched Tavern £ 34 3–3A

Cheapside Rd SL5 7QG (01344) 620874

"Fairly priced", traditional British cooking from an "upscale" menu wins consistent support for this "comfortable" and "relaxed" pub/restaurant, off the high street; some praise the staff's "personal touch" – others feel they are a little "snooty". / **Sample dishes:** goat's cheese & rocket salad; slow-roast lamb with rosemary & garlic; chocolate swirl cheesecake. **Value tip:** set 3-crs Sun L £17.95. **Details:** 10 pm.

ASENBY, N YORKS
The Crab & Lobster £ 36 8–4C A★

Dishforth Rd YO7 3QL (01845) 577286

Highly popular, "pretty, thatched pub", whose "extraordinary" interior is a "unique environment where every surface and hanging space is packed" with miscellaneous "nick nacks"; the "imaginative" cooking (available in bar and restaurant) is notable too, with "terrific fresh fish" the highlight (and good provision for veggies). / **Sample dishes:** scallops in garlic butter; fish platter with lobster beurre blanc; sticky toffee pudding. **Value tip:** set 2/3-crs L £11.50/£14.50 (Sun £16.95). **Details:** junction of Asenby Rd & Topcliffe Rd; 9 pm; no smoking in dining room; no booking in the bar. **Accommodation:** 10 rooms, from £80.

ASKRIGG, N YORKS
The King's Arms £ 39 8–4B A

Market Pl DL8 3HQ (01969) 650258

This "fine country pub" ('The Drovers' in 'All Creatures Great & Small') is a "very friendly and welcoming" spot, with "imaginative" food and "good beer". / **Sample dishes:** fricassée of wild mushrooms; roast quails; hot chocolate soufflé. **Details:** 9 pm; no smoking; children: 12+. **Accommodation:** 11 rooms, from £79.

ASTON CANTLOW, WARKS   2–1C
King's Head   £ 38

Bearley Rd B95 6HY   (01789) 488242

"A bright and cheerful evening out" is to be had at this *"brightly
decorated"*, *"converted pub"*, at the centre of the village; it's praised
for its well-prepared Mediterranean-influenced grub and *"friendly
staff"*. / **Sample dishes:** pan-fried squid with radicchio; duck with spring
onion & mango noodles; raspberry & cassis crème brûlée. **Details:** 9.45 pm.

ASTON CLINTON, BUCKS   3–2A
The Bell Inn   £ 39

London Rd HP22 5HP   (01296) 630252

"Considering its reputation", this *"solid"* old-timer (half a
century under the same ownership) can seem *"tired and dated"* –
"self-conscious" and *"poor value for money"*; *"it fluctuates between
'nice' and 'dreadful', depending on the day"*. / **Sample dishes:** rabbit
boudin with stewed tomatoes; monkfish with mussel & chilli fritters; apple
& prune tarte Tatin. **Value tip:** set 2/3-crs L £12/£14.50. **Details:** on A41
between Tring & Aylesbury; 9.45 pm; no smoking in dining room; children: 10+
on Sat eve. **Accommodation:** 20 rooms, from £65.

AYLESBURY, BUCKS   3–2A
Hartwell House   £ 51

Oxford Rd HP17 8NL   (01296) 747444

"Very grand", part-Jacobean country house hotel, which is praised by
its supporters for its *"excellence in all respects"*; a vocal minority,
though, decries *"unforgivable"* standards; *"the Emperor of Japan
stayed recently – he must have left much poorer, and hungry!"*
/ **Sample dishes:** wood pigeon, venison & quail; roast duck with wild
mushrooms & salsify; pear & pecan tart. **Value tip:** set 2/3-crs L £22/£29.
Details: 2m W of Aylesbury on A418; 9.45 pm; no Amex; jacket & tie;
no smoking in dining room; children: 8+. **Accommodation:** 46 rooms,
from £205.

AYSGARTH, N YORKS   8–4B
George & Dragon   £ 24

DL8 3LZ   (01969) 663358

"A good-value-for-money pub restaurant" offering pub-grub-and-more
food, *"and plenty of it"*. / **Sample dishes:** chicken & duck liver pâté;
chicken stuffed with prawns; marinated pear sundae. **Details:** 9 pm;
no Amex; no smoking area. **Accommodation:** 7 rooms, from £28.

BAKEWELL, DERBYS   5–2C
Renaissance   £ 30   ★

Bath St DE45 1BX   (01629) 812687

"Superbly run by a Frenchman and his English wife", this
"converted barn" provides a *"friendly"* setting in which to enjoy
some *"flavoursome"* cooking – *"Norman cuisine in the hands of a
high quality Norman chef"*. / **Sample dishes:** lobster & chicken sausage;
pan-fried noisettes of lamb; saffron meringue & lime syllabub.
Details: 9.30 pm; closed Mon & Sun D; no Amex; no smoking.

BALLATER, ABERDEEN   5–2C
Green Inn   £ 40   ★

9 Victoria Rd AB35 5QQ   (013397) 55701

*"Marvellous fresh local ingredients in imaginative and substantial
dishes"* is a modern Scottish recipe which makes many return
"year after year" to this *"excellent"*, *"husband-and-wife set-up"*.
/ **Sample dishes:** tomato & basil soup with langoustines; loin of venison; pear
& frangipane tart. **Details:** in centre of village, on the green; 9.30 pm; D only,
closed Sun & Mon Oct-Mar, closed 2 weeks Oct; no smoking during dinner.
Accommodation: 3 rooms, from £64.

BALTIMORE, CO CORK, *EIRE* 10–4A
The Customs House IR £ 27 ★
(028) 20200
"Fresh fish, caught by the locals and cooked simply with real intelligence and creativity" makes a visit here an *"uplifting"* experience; the husband-and-wife team that runs this place *"takes great pride in the quality of the cooking".* / **Sample dishes:** crab claws with lemon mayonnaise; roast duck in red wine sauce; crème brûlée. **Details:** 10 pm; D only, Wed-Sun; closed Nov-Easter; no credit cards; no smoking; max booking 6.

BAMFORD, LANCS 5–2B
Egerton Arms £ 24
Ashworth Rd OL11 5UP (01706) 646183
"Lovely views" and *"large portions"* of *"good modern British cooking"* win praise for this pub restaurant on the moors. / **Sample dishes:** moules marinière; Normandy pork leg; amaretto peach tiramisu. **Value tip:** set 2-crs L £6.95. **Details:** on top of hill, off Bury-Rochdale old road; 10 pm; no Amex; no smoking area.

BANBURY, OXON 2–1D
Thai Orchid £ 24
56 Northbar St OX16 OTL (01295) 270833
Fans say it's worth persevering to find this slightly "off-the-beaten-track" Banbury Thai, and particularly commend the "wonderful mixed starters" and the "veggie banquet". / **Sample dishes:** barbecue spare ribs; stir-fried vegetables; sherry trifle. **Details:** next to St Marys church; 10.30 pm; closed Sat L & Sun; no smoking area.

BANGOR, CO DOWN 10–1D
Shanks £ 43 ★
150 Crawfordsburn Rd BT19 1GB (01247) 853313
It's odd to find a "sophisticated" menu at a golf course club-house, however smartly designed (à la Conran) it may be; few, however, doubt the quality of the "good-value, imaginative and well-prepared" modern British cooking. / **Sample dishes:** foie gras with grilled figs; turbot with morels & chive velouté; warm coconut tart. **Value tip:** set 2-crs L £13.95. **Details:** A2 to Bangor, follow signs for The Blackwood; 10 pm; closed Mon, Sat L & Sun.

BARNARD CASTLE, CO DURHAM 8–3B
Blagraves House £ 26 Ⓐ★★
30 The Bank DL12 8PN (01833) 637668
This beautifully located 17th-century residence offers "an historic setting" ("Cromwell stayed here"), and its "delicious", "creative" and "reasonably priced" cooking makes for "a truly excellent night out". / **Sample dishes:** crab tart with calvados; pan-fried venison with sloe jelly; chocolate torte & coffee bean sauce. **Details:** 9.30 pm; D only, closed Mon & Sun; no Amex; no smoking in dining room; children: 8+.

BASLOW, DERBYS 5–2C
Fischers at Baslow Hall £ 50 Ⓐ★★
Calver Rd DE45 1RR (01246) 583259
"Wonderful", "sublime", "exquisite" – the plaudits for the *"inventive"* Gallic cooking at Max and Susan Fischer's *"beautifully refurbished"* Edwardian Gothic pile keep on coming; the atmosphere is perhaps a touch *"quiet and restrained"*, but that's just how the punters seem to like it, and service is *"incredibly kind and caring".* / **Sample dishes:** scallops with Jerusalem artichoke purée; roast Derbyshire lamb in thyme jus; dark & white chocolate mousse. **Details:** on A623 Stockport Rd, 0.5m past village church; 9.30 pm; closed Sun D; jacket in dining room; no smoking; children: 12+ after 7 pm. **Accommodation:** 6 rooms, from £100.

Clos du Roy   £ 32
1 Seven Dials, Saw Close BA1 1EN   (01225) 444450
*"Stylish" (going on tacky) "musical instrument décor" distinguishes this long-established venue (complete with a pianist to get you in the mood) — a local favourite, especially "for a pre-theatre dinner"; the place is known for its "good, truly French food", but some have found standards "not up to expectations" on recent visits. / **Sample dishes:** scallops & bacon in Pernod sauce; roast duck with morello cherry sauce; coconut & mango crème brûlée. **Value tip:** set 2/3-crs L & pre-th £9.95/£13.95. **Details:** 10.30 pm; no Switch.*

Demuths   £ 25   ★
2 North Parade Passage BA1 1NX   (01225) 446059
*"Friendly", "colourful" and "laid-back" central venture whose "interesting" cooking is "so good you wouldn't know it was veggie". / **Sample dishes:** green vegetable marinade; almond & asparagus strudel; black rice pudding & coconut cream. **Details:** off Abbey Green; 10 pm; no Amex; no smoking; Fri & Sat max booking 4.*

Firehouse Rotisserie   £ 28   ★
2 John St BA1 2JL   (01225) 482070
*"Great wood oven-cooked pizzas" are just part of the "unusual selection" of dishes at this already "very popular" and "lively" new Cal/Ital bistro, which has a "pleasant, rustic interior". / **Sample dishes:** Chinese chicken salad; char-grilled salmon with olive mash; caramelised lemon tart. **Details:** 10.30 pm; closed Sun.*

Lettonie   £ 62   A★★
35 Kelston Rd BA1 3QH   (01225) 446676
*"Consistently awesome" — the "spectacular originality" of Martin Blunos's cooking makes this a "world-class" restaurant, and it's a "relaxed", "down-to-earth" place, too, despite being housed in a "beautiful" mansion on the fringe of the city; "I was told it was good", fumes one reporter, "but that was a major understatement". / **Sample dishes:** scrambled duck egg with Sevruga caviar; John Dory with salsify & potato gâteau; strawberry & vanilla parfait ice. **Value tip:** set 2-crs L £15. **Details:** 2m W of Bath on A431; 9 pm; closed Mon & Sun; no smoking. **Accommodation:** 4 rooms, from £95.*

Moody Goose   £ 38   ★
74 Kingsmead Sq BA1 2AB   (01225) 466688
*The atmosphere can indeed seem "a touch moody", but "it improves on acquaintance" of this earnest two-year old, city-centre basement venture; chef-patron Stephen Shore's "pleasing" modern British cooking, makes good use of "seasonal ingredients" and is earning the place quite a reputation. / **Sample dishes:** pan-fried scallops with spinach noodles; duck cassoulet with haricot beans; iced nougat parfait with figs. **Value tip:** set 2/3-crs L & early eve £10/£14. **Details:** down hill from Theatre Royal, bear right into Kingsmead Square; 9.30 pm; closed Sun; no smoking in dining room.*

Moon & Sixpence   £ 32
6a Broad St BA1 5LJ   (01225) 460962
*Thanks to its "consistently good French-influenced" food and "very pleasant surroundings" (in an interesting modern re-development), it's "essential to book" for dinner at this "lively" central restaurant-cum-wine bar. / **Sample dishes:** rillettes of smoked fish; confit of duck with mixed bean & tomato salsa; torte of chocolate mousse. **Details:** nr Podium shopping centre; 10.30 pm; no smoking area.*

Olive Tree, Queensberry Hotel   £ 36   ★
Russel St BA1 2QF   (01225) 447928
"Very popular" Mediterranean restaurant, in a modishly decorated
basement, with quite a reputation for *"first class cuisine"*; most
applaud the *"superbly executed"* fare, but some say the place is
"over-praised", and many feel the *"cool"* setting *"lacks atmosphere"*.
/ **Sample dishes:** seared scallops with lemon risotto; braised pork belly with
smoked bacon; soft meringue with muscat poached fruit. **Value tip:** set 2/3-crs
L £12.50/£14.50. **Details:** nr Assembly Rooms; 10 pm; closed Sun L;
no Amex; no smoking. **Accommodation:** 29 rooms, from £135.

Pump Rooms   £ 28   🅰
Abbey Church Yard BA1 1LZ   (01225) 444477
The *"standard of food is not up to the beauty of the building"* but
it's *"nevertheless a good experience"* to visit these *"very lovely and
relaxing"* Georgian rooms in the heart of the town – *"one of the
most enjoyable places in the country for afternoon tea"*.
/ **Sample dishes:** spinach & Roquefort soufflé; cod & fennel in l
emon parsley sauce; dark chocolate & orange torte. **Details:** by Abbey;
L only, open until 10pm in Aug; no smoking area.

Rajpoot   £ 27   🅰
Argyle St BA2 4BA   (01225) 466833
Atmospheric premises – a lavishly decorated basement, near the
Pulteney Bridge – and *"attentive"* service help make this *"the best
local Indian"* for many reporters. / **Sample dishes:** chicken chat; chicken
mughlai; sorbet. **Value tip:** set 2-crs L £6.95. **Details:** 11 pm, Fri & Sat
11.30 pm.

Woods   £ 33
9-13 Alfred St BA1 2QX   (01225) 314812
"A long wait for mediocre food" or *"not bad but high-priced and
uninteresting"* – such is the tone of far too much of this year's
commentary on this popular, long-established fixture. / **Sample
dishes:** smoked chicken with garlic croutons; roast herb-crusted monkfish with
shallots; steamed lemon & ginger sponge. **Value tip:** set 2-crs L £7, set 2-crs
early eve £8. **Details:** 11 pm; closed Sun D; no Switch.

BEAUMARIS, ANGLESEY   4–1C
Ye Olde Bull's Head   £ 38   ★
Castle St LL58 8AP   (01248) 810329
"Good food, a wide choice and an historic atmosphere" make this
splendid old coaching inn an ever-useful stopping-off point for today's
traveller; Sunday lunch is a particular recommendation. / **Sample
dishes:** scallops with warm tomato vinaigrette; sea bass with basil & orange
butter sauce; rhubarb & stem ginger tiramisu. **Details:** 9.30 pm; closed Sun;
no smoking; children: 7+. **Accommodation:** 15 rooms, from £81.

BECKENHAM, KENT   3–3B
Chateau D'If   £ 34
61 High St BR3 1AW   (020) 8650 2291
"Welcoming" genuine Gallic bistro, *"worth a visit"* for its *"very good"*
cooking and no-nonsense style. / **Sample dishes:** Mediterranean fish
soup; roast lamb with sweet peppers; warm chocolate savarin. **Value tip:** set
2-crs L £12.50. **Details:** 10.30 pm; closed Sat L & Sun.

BEDFORD, BEDS   3–1A
The Swan Hotel   £ 25
The Embankment MK40 1RW   (01234) 346565
Town-centre riverside hotel, whose *"good-value"* modern British
cooking (from a *"limited menu"*) makes it a more exciting culinary
destination than you might expect. / **Sample dishes:** hot tiger prawns;
rack of lamb; meringue. **Details:** 9 pm. **Accommodation:** 110 rooms,
from £59.50.

Deane's   £ 30   A★
34-40 Howard St BT1 6PD   (01232) 331134
*For an "exciting" metropolitan-style ambience, Ulster has nowhere to
beat this large, rather OTT city-centre brasserie; the cooking is
"superb", too — both downstairs and in the more hushed 'fine dining'
restaurant (£45) above — and service throughout is "friendly and
knowledgeable".* / **Sample dishes:** *goat's cheese tart; roast duck with bok
choi & noodle cakes; chocolate fondant tart.* **Details:** *nr Grand Opera House;
9.30 pm; closed Sun; no smoking area.*

Nick's Warehouse   £ 30   A★
35 Hill St BT1 2LB   (01232) 439690
*With its "humming" atmosphere, "happy, interested staff" and —
not least — "good and fresh" modern British cooking, Belfast's original
modern eatery continues to deliver all-round satisfaction; "lunchtime
fish dishes" (in the "more grown up" 'business' restaurant, upstairs)
are especially approved.* / **Sample dishes:** *smoked bacon risotto
with Parmesan; salmon with parsley pesto; baked banana cheesecake.*
Details: *behind St Anne's Cathedral, nr Waring St; 9.30 pm; closed Mon D,
Sat L & Sun; children: not after 9 pm.*

The Other Place   £ 23
179 Botanic Ave BT17 1JG   (01232) 207200
*"Lively and entertaining", open-all-day lynchpins of the three major
restaurant concentrations of South Belfast — there are other branches
at 537 Lisburn Road and 135 Stranmill Road — serving solid fare at
"reasonable prices".* / **Sample dishes:** *steamed chilli mussels; Indonesian
chicken & bell pepper stir-fry; Bailey's cheesecake.* **Details:** *nr Botanic Railway
Station; 11 pm; no Amex.*

Roscoff   £ 40
7 Lesley House, Shaftesbury Sq BT27 7DB   (01232) 331532
*The many fans of TV celeb' Paul Rankin's "bright" city-centre
venture continue to praise modern British cooking that "matches his
reputation"; there's quite a minority which finds "a tendency to rest
on past laurels", though, and some find the place "wildly overpriced".*
/ **Sample dishes:** *spicy mussel soup with coconut milk; crispy duck confit with
lentils; banana & chocolate bread pudding.* **Value tip:** *set 2/3-crs set
L £14.95/£17.50.* **Details:** *nr Botanic Railway Station; 10.30 pm; closed Sat
L & Sun; no smoking area.*

The Laughing Buddha   £ 24
198-200 Broadway DA6 7BD   (020) 8303 6290
*"Consistently good food and service" make this "pleasant" and
"enjoyable" Chinese restaurant, in the centre of town, a reliable
choice.* / **Sample dishes:** *mussels with black bean sauce; deep-fried chilli
beef with carrots; toffee apple.* **Details:** *off A2; 11 pm, Fri & Sat midnight.*

Druid Inn   £ 24
Main St DE4 2BL   (01629) 650302
*There's "always something interesting" on the "huge blackboard
menus" at this "always very busy" pub, which offers "a very warm
atmosphere at the end of a walk".* / **Sample dishes:** *deep-fried prawns
with soy dip; honey-roast saddle of lamb; summer pudding.* **Details:** *NE of
Ashbourne, off B5056; 9 pm; no smoking area; children: 10+.*

Kingshead House £ 39 ★
GL4 8JH (01452) 862299
"Well established" restaurant, whose attractions include *"up-to-date cooking, drawn from 'old' recipes"*, a *"very knowledgeable proprietor"* and a *"great wine list"*. / **Sample dishes:** *salmon mousse; fillet steak with red wine sauce; roast peach melba.* **Details:** *off A417; 9.45 pm; closed Mon, Sat L & Sun; no Switch; no smoking during D; children: 9+.*
Accommodation: *1 room, at about £70.*

BIRMINGHAM, W MIDLANDS 5–4C

There are some signs of life (most notably the recent opening of the city's first major brasserie, *Le Petit Blanc*), but what remains striking about the restaurant scene of "England's second city" is how little of it there actually is.

The most celebrated restaurant near the centre of the city is a modern Indian (*Shimla Pinks*, now a national chain), and Brum's greatest culinary claim to fame is its balti houses, which cluster in the inner suburbs of Moseley and Sparkbrook. For the visitor, they offer an interesting experience which is at least cheap (especially as you take your own booze). We've chosen five of the best examples. There is also a Chinatown, but only the *Chung Ying* duo really stand out.

Those looking for a dinner with a touch of grandeur might like to consider a trip to Sutton Coldfield, where the oldest moated manor-house in England, *New Hall*, offers a venue of some charm. Closer to the centre, *Jonathan's* offers Victorian comfort.

Adils £ 12 ★
148-150 Stoney Ln B12 8AJ (0121) 449 0335
"Great balti dishes in an authentic environment", with *"lots of flavour, not just heat"*; *"unbelievable value"* – BYO. / **Sample dishes:** *shish kebab; tropical tandoori fish selection; kulfi.* **Details:** *3m from city centre on A41; 12.30 am.*

Beau Thai £ 26 ★
761 Olde Lode Ln B92 8JE (0121) 743 5355
"Lots of choice" from a *"well balanced"* and *"imaginative"* Thai menu wins unanimous support for this small Solihull spot, run by an English husband and Thai wife team. / **Sample dishes:** *prawns in filo pastry; chicken with chilli & basil; fresh fruit salad.* **Details:** *10 pm; closed Mon L, Sat L & Sun; no smoking area.*

Chez Jules £ 19 ★
5a Ethel St, Off New St B2 4BG (0121) 633 4664
With its *"lively, young ambience"* and *"groovy staff"*, this *"vibrant"* and *"enthusiastic"* central canteen in a *"Spartan, hall-like"* setting may have a few rough edges, but is widely praised for its *"simple French food"* at *"good-value"* prices. / **Sample dishes:** *steamed mussels with shallots; steak with oyster mushrooms; tarte Tatin.* **Value tip:** *set 2/3-crs L £4.90/£5.90.* **Details:** *off New Street; 11 pm; closed Sun; no smoking area.*

Chez Julien
£ 28

1036-1044 Stratford Rd B90 4EE   (0121) 744 7232

*We note this bourgeois Gallic spot for its usefulness – it's eight minutes' drive from the NEC; the limited and negative commentary it received this year would not otherwise justify its inclusion. / **Sample dishes:** Lyon sausage in brioche dough; braised partridge with savoy cabbage; cheese of the day. **Value tip:** set 3-crs L £10, set 3-crs £ £13.50. **Details:** nr M42, J4; 10.30 pm; closed Sat L & Sun L.*

Chung Ying Garden
£ 29   ★

17 Thorp St B5 4AT   (0121) 666 6622

*"The best Chinese restaurant in Birmingham's Chinatown"; together with its nearby sister the Chung Ying (16-18 Wrottesley St, tel 622 5669), these "huge" and "frantic" emporia are highly popular destinations, on account of their "consistently good" and "generous" cooking. / **Sample dishes:** aromatic duck with pancakes; steamed halibut in black bean sauce; ice cream. **Details:** next to Hippodrome Theatre; 11.30 pm; no smoking.*

Giovannis
£ 28

27 Poplar Rd B14 7AA   (0121) 443 2391

*Quality Italian fish dishes are the keystone of this successful "small local" – a "reliable" and "busy", if rather "suburban", spot. / **Sample dishes:** aubergine with Parmesan; fish with tomato & fennel; tiramisu. **Value tip:** set 3-crs L £11.80. **Details:** from city centre take A435, opp Cross Guns pub; 10.30 pm; closed Mon & Sun.*

Imrans
£ 13   ★

264-266 Ladypool Rd B12 8JU   (0121) 449 6440

*"First-class budget food" and "an atmosphere all of its own" make this Sparkbrook balti-house our top recommendation for first-timers – it's smarter than average, and offers a wide range of sweetmeats. / **Sample dishes:** chicken pakora; balti chicken tikka masala; mango kulfi. **Details:** opp Training & Development Centre; midnight; no smoking area.*

Jonathans
£ 33   Ⓐ

16-24 Wolverhampton Rd B68 0LH   (0121) 429 3757

*"Traditional British food with an upmarket twist" is on offer at this "famous" Brummie spot; it's the "exceptional" atmosphere created by the "beautiful Victorian setting" which makes it special, though – the "food is good, but definitely overpriced". / **Sample dishes:** baked Welsh goat's cheese parcels; beef marinated in Glenmorangie; bread & butter pudding. **Value tip:** set 2/3-crs set D £13.90/£15.90. **Details:** on junction with Hagley Road; 10 pm; closed Sun D; no jeans; no smoking area. **Accommodation:** 48 rooms, from £88.*

Jyoti
£ 14   ★

569-571 Stratford Rd B11 4LS   (0121) 766 7199

*"Unusual and brilliant food" – and "extremely cheap", too – makes the "superb" vegetarian cooking at this Sparkhill BYO Gujerati well worth seeking out. / **Sample dishes:** vegetable samosas; potato & aubergine curry; kulfi. **Details:** 9.15 pm; closed Mon; no Amex; no smoking.*

Kabibish
£ 21

29 Woodbridge Rd B13 8EH   (0121) 449 5556

*Popular Moseley Kashmiri, touted by some as the best balti stop in town. / **Sample dishes:** stuffed mushrooms; chicken paneer masala; mango delight. **Details:** A435, nr go-karting club; 11.15 pm; closed Sun D.*

Maharaja
£ 22   ★

23 Hurst St B5 4SA   (0121) 622 2641

*"Always reliable and fresh food, beautifully spiced" has made this "welcoming" city-centre Indian a local favourite for over a quarter of a century. / **Sample dishes:** tandoori chicken; spiced lamb with spinach; lychees. **Details:** 11 pm; closed Sun.*

Le Petit Blanc £ 29 new

9 Brindleyplace B1 2HS (0121) 633-7333

The third branch of Monsieur Blanc's (and Mr Branson's) expanding metropolitan-style Gallic brasserie chain opened in August 1999 (too late for reporters to rate); even if the form suggests it will be fairly unremarkable, the sheer fact of its existence – in Brum – must portend something. / **Sample dishes:** *herb pancakes with mushrooms; cod with lemon & caper butter; chocolate fondant.* **Details:** *facing Icon Gallery; 11.30 pm; no smoking area.*

Pranees Thai £ 21

816 Bristol Rd B29 6NA (0121) 744 1111

A meal at this Selly Oak Thai feels "like eating in someone's front room"; service is "warm" and "friendly", and the "interesting" dishes are "delicately" flavoured. / **Sample dishes:** *spicy Thai fishcakes; stir-fried chilli & garlic chicken; steamed Thai custard.* **Details:** *opp Bristol St Motors; 10.30 pm; D only; no Amex; no smoking area.*

Restaurant Gilmore £ 30

27 Warstone Ln B18 6JQ (0121) 233 3655

"Real food, beautifully presented, and served by friendly and relaxed staff" makes Mr Gilmore's modern British restaurant in Hockley's "jewellery quarter" pretty popular, though some people find prices a touch "steep". / **Sample dishes:** *grilled sausage of salmon & crayfish; Welsh lamb with minted pea risotto; vanilla seed & Mascarpone torte.* **Value tip:** *set 2/3-crs L £12.50/£15.50.* **Details:** *9.30 pm; closed Mon, Sat L & Sun; no smoking area.*

Royal Naim £ 16 ★

417-419 Stratford Rd B11 4JZ (0121) 766 7849

These large, "plain" and "friendly" Sparkhill premises are some reporters' "balti favourite in the heart of balti land". / **Sample dishes:** *chicken tikka; mushroom balti with garlic naan; pistachio kulfi.* **Details:** *2 mins from city centre on A34; 1 am; need large group to book.*

San Carlo £ 38

4 Temple St B2 5BN (0121) 633 0251

The food is "brilliant" ("especially fish"), say fans of this glitzy city-centre trattoria; some find service can be "arrogant" and "slow" (especially "when there are 'star' guests about"), but others say it's "comforting". / **Sample dishes:** *lobster tails; grilled swordfish with salsa verde; tartufo flambée.* **Details:** *behind cathedral; 10.45 pm; children: 5+.*

Shimla Pinks £ 31

214 Broad St B15 1AY (0121) 633 0366

"The most stylish restaurant in town" (not a demanding standard) – this forebear of a national chain is a "light and bright curry house de luxe"; with its "central location", it remains "very popular", but only some say the cooking is "a treat" – for others, it's just "ordinary food at twice the price of a balti house". / **Sample dishes:** *tandoori king prawns; chicken korma; mango curd.* **Details:** *nr Symphony Hall; 11 pm; closed Sat L & Sun L.*

St Pauls £ 25 A★

50-54 St Paul's Square B3 1QL (0121) 605 1001

This "original" Hockley spot – "a super showcase for local artists" as well as a restaurant – makes "a refreshing addition to Brum's restaurant scene"; its thoughtful modern British cooking offers "great value for money". / **Sample dishes:** *Thai beef salad with cashew nuts; rack of lamb with redcurrant; chocolate bread & butter pudding.* **Details:** *10 pm, Sat 11 pm; closed Sat L & Sun.*

Normandie £ 28 ★

Elbut Ln, Birtle BL9 6UT   (0161) 764 3869

*"Excellent" modern British cooking (with Gallic overtones) makes
this long-established hotel and restaurant "well worth its reputation";
its premises on the moors do not please everyone – "if only the place
had a bit of atmosphere, this would be a first-class night out".
/ **Sample dishes:** trio of goat's cheeses; brill with king prawn ravioli; banana
crème brûlée. **Value tip:** set 3-crs L £12.50. **Details:** off B6222, 3m NE of
Bury; 9.30 pm; closed Sat L & Sun. **Accommodation:** 23 rooms, from £69.*

Mallory Court £ 60

Harbury Ln CV33 9QB   (01926) 330214

*The "lovely location" and the "formal but pleasant" service are
both mentioned in the (limited number of) reports on this luxurious
country house hotel; there is some praise for the "well balanced"
cooking too, but it comes at a hefty price. / **Sample dishes:** grilled
asparagus with Parmesan; rabbit stuffed with langoustines; Grand Marnier
soufflé. **Value tip:** set 2/3-crs L £21/£28. **Details:** 2m S of Leamington Spa,
off B4087; 10 pm, Sat 10.30 pm; no smoking in dining room; children: 9+.
Accommodation: 18 rooms, from £185.*

September Brasserie £ 30 ★

15-17 Queen St FY1 1PU   (01253) 623282

*"A first-class establishment in a gastronomic desert", this small,
first-floor restaurant offers "never-changing standards" of
modern British cooking, often using organic ingredients. / **Sample
dishes:** seafood gratin; organic salmon with spinach; white chocolate terrine.
Value tip: set 2-crs L £5. **Details:** just past North Pier, opp Senate House;
10 pm; closed Mon & Sun.*

Crown Inn £ 32

High St GL56 9EX   (01386) 700245

*"The best pub Sunday lunch" is the sort of meal which is the forte of
this "15th-century coaching inn, converted to a great little hotel and
pub". / **Sample dishes:** skate wing & rocket salad; poached halibut
& scallops with artichoke; Baked Alaska. **Details:** off A44 between Moreton-in-
Marsh and Broadway; 10 pm; no Switch; no smoking. **Accommodation:** 21
rooms, from £99.*

Devonshire Arms £ 48 Ⓐ

Grassington Rd BD23 6AJ   (01756) 710441

*This "modern eaterie" in a "very imposing" coaching inn offers a
"Mediterranean feel in a rural setting"; many find it "excellent in
every way", but the complaints of those who find the cooking
"really disappointing and very expensive" are just too voluble to
ignore. / **Sample dishes:** salmon terrine with grapefruit syrup; Périgord duck;
pineapple upside-down cake. **Details:** on A59, 5m NE of Skipton; 10 pm;
D only, ex Sun open L & D; jacket & tie; no smoking. **Accommodation:** 41
rooms, from £155.*

BOTTISHAM, CAMBS

Stocks £ 34

76-78 High St CB5 9BA (01223) 811202
*Useful spot, with a "good location, opposite the church" of a Fenland
borders village; the modern British cooking from a husband-and-wife
team "continues to please", and service is "helpful". / **Sample
dishes:** tiger prawns in garlic butter; loin of venison; chocolate mocha tart.
Details: between Newmarket & Cambridge; 9.30 pm; D only, closed Mon
& Sun; no Amex.*

BOUGHTON LEES, KENT

Eastwell Manor £ 50 𝔸

Eastwell Pk TN25 4HR (01233) 213000
*The "beautiful setting" of this manor house hotel restaurant (with its
"delightful gardens") has been wasted of late – "such an impressive
hotel needs better cooking" being a too-common view about the
"pricey" cuisine; perhaps the forthcoming addition of a brasserie
heralds a shake up. / **Sample dishes:** lobster linguini with spinach purée;
pork cutlet on Swiss chard & marjoram jus; trio of poached pears. **Value
tip:** set 2-crs L £10. **Details:** 3m N of Ashford on A251; 9.30 pm; no jeans;
no smoking in dining room. **Accommodation:** 23 rooms, from £180.*

BOWNESS, CUMBRIA

Miller Howe £ 48 𝔸★

Rayrigg Rd LA23 1EY (01539) 442536
*A new owner (installed in 1998) has pepped up the coooking at the
dining room of this well-known hotel, with its "fantastic location"
overlooking the lake; there is the odd gripe of "dated" décor and
"over-fussy" cooking, but most reporters pronounce the overall
experience "simply wonderful". / **Sample dishes:** smoked haddock with
pink ginger; duck with cinnamon sauce; chocolate soufflé. **Value tip:** set 3-crs
L £15 (Sun £18.50). **Details:** on A592 between Windermere & Bowness;
8 pm; no smoking; children: 8+. **Accommodation:** 12 rooms, from £150,
incl D.*

Porthole £ 35 𝔸★

3 Ash St LA23 3EB (01539) 442793
*"Fabulous, family-run" Lakeland rarity, offering "carefully prepared",
mainly Italian dishes in a "cosy" and "very relaxing" ambience;
"amicable" service, a "fabulous wine selection" and "great puddings"
complete the winning package. / **Sample dishes:** antipasti; veal with
mushrooms; vanilla crème brûlée. **Details:** 10.30 pm; closed Tue & Sat L.*

BRADFORD, W YORKS

Kashmir £ 14 ★

27 Morley St BD7 1AG (01274) 726513
*It's not only that this is "the cheapest curry house in town",
this "Bangladeshi café" offers "good choice and fast service"; it's
"for trenchermen", though, "not gourmets". / **Sample dishes:** mixed
kebab; vegetable masala; coconut ice cream. **Details:** nr Alhambra Theatre;
3 am; no credit cards; no smoking area.*

Mumtaz Paan House ✳ £ 18 ★★

Great Harton Rd BD7 3HS (01274) 571861
*That it's perceived as "the curry restaurant most likely to be
frequented by Asian people in Bradford" must be "a good sign",
and the "simple choice of dishes excellently cooked and with well-
judged spicing" elicits a hymn of praise; we're talking "authentic"
here – "no alcohol". / **Sample dishes:** chicken samosas; Karahi fish with
pomegranates; mango lassi. **Details:** nr Alhambra Theatre and Photographic
Museum; 1 am; no smoking area.*

Nawaab £ 21 A★

32 Manor Rw BD1 4QE (01274) 720371

*"For a 'posh' curry experience" ("count the mobile phones"), fans praise this "handsomely housed" establishment, with its "considerate" service and "top dishes". / **Sample dishes:** onion bhaji; chicken masala; kulfi. **Value tip:** set 3-crs L £7.99. **Details:** nr station; 11 pm; no smoking area.*

BRADFORD ON AVON, WILTS 2–2B

Thai Barn £ 25 A

24 Bridge St BA15 1BY (01225) 866443

*"All the usual favourites, and some original tastes as well", are served at this "new but very good Thai" in the centre of this Cotswolds town. / **Sample dishes:** spicy fishcakes; green chicken curry; baked custard. **Value tip:** set 2/3-crs L £6.95/£7.95. **Details:** opp Bridge St car park; 10.30 pm; no Amex; no smoking area.*

BRAUNSTON, RUTLAND 5–4D

Blue Ball Inn £ 22

6 Cedar St LE15 8QS (01572) 722135

*A village pub/restaurant which is "always a reliable choice", thanks to its consistent French cooking and "pleasant" service – "the wait is worth it!" / **Sample dishes:** goat's cheese & tomato salad; lamb with rosemary sauce; nougatine parfait. **Details:** next to church; 9.30 pm; closed Sun D; no smoking.*

BRAY, WINDSOR 3–3A

The Fat Duck £ 66 ★

1 High St SL6 2AQ (01628) 580333

*Heston Blumenthal is something of a "culinary alchemist", and the "inspired combinations" on offer at his "reworked old pub" can offer "rare and memorable taste experiences"; his concoctions may also be "so bizarre as to be off-putting", though, and sometimes "pretentious" service contributes to some reports expressing "total disappointment". / **Sample dishes:** crab feuilleté with foie gras; veal sweetbreads with cockles & truffle cream; chocolate & thyme sorbet. **Value tip:** set 3-crs L £23.50. **Details:** 9.30 pm, Sat 10 pm; closed Mon & Sun D; closed 2 weeks at New Year; no smoking area.*

Fish £ 30 A★

Old Mill Ln SL6 2BG (01628) 781111

*This "excellent fish restaurant" may "officially be a pub", but it's as the former that it's making waves, not just for its "outstanding" cooking and reasonable prices, but also for its "good, friendly service". / **Sample dishes:** smoked haddock & spinach fishcake; squid & king scallops on black spaghetti; caramelised sharp lemon tart. **Details:** 9.15 pm; closed Mon & Sun D; no smoking area; children: 12+ at D.*

Waterside Inn £ 95 ★

Ferry Rd SL6 2AT (01628) 620691

*"Good weather and a table facing the river" are the best circumstances in which to enjoy "gastronomic delights of the first order" at Michel Roux's "very French" and "effortlessly luxurious" Thames-side fixture; there's no discounting the minority, though, which finds the atmosphere needlessly "snobbish" and "stuffy". / **Sample dishes:** seared scallops & apples; duck with lemon & thyme jus; peach soufflé. **Details:** 10 pm; closed Mon & Tue L (& Sun D, Oct-Apr); children: 12+. **Accommodation:** 9 rooms, from £135.*

BREARTON, N YORKS   8–4B
The Malt Shovel   £ 19   𝔸★

HG3 3BX   (01423) 862929

*"A very characterful pub, justly famed for the quality of its meals",
whose setting is a "wonderfully converted barn"; it offers "excellent
food", "well presented" from an "eclectic" menu; "fine beer" too.
/ Sample dishes: seafood platter; liver, bacon & black pudding with mash;
lemon tart. Details: off A61, N of Harrogate; 9 pm; closed Mon;
no credit cards; need 8+ to book.*

BRIDPORT, DORSET   2–4B
Riverside   £ 33   ★★

West Bay   DT6 4EZ   (01308) 422011

*An "excellent-quality fish restaurant", whose standards are
"unexpected", given its "seaside café"-style premises; "exceptional",
"simply cooked" dishes are universally praised, and they are
"not expensive, either". / Sample dishes: hot shellfish in chilli & tomato
jus; brill with crispy spinach; gooseberry & elderflower fool. Details: in centre
of West Bay; 9 pm; closed Mon & Sun D; no Amex; smoking discouraged.*

BRIGHTON, E SUSSEX   3–4B

Particularly in the diversity of its culinary scene, "London by
the Sea" in some ways mimics that of the capital, even if
most establishments are comparatively modest in scale.
The selection below includes good but quite inexpensive
Italian, Lebanese, Chinese, Thai and Indian options.

The city's culinary claim to fame is as veggie heaven.
Terre à Terre – probably the best vegetarian restaurant in the
UK – heads a fair list of notable, no-meat dining places.

The top of the market is thinly served, with *One Paston Place*
the only 'player'. The cooking of one of its former chefs can
now be enjoyed, in more modest surroundings, at the less
pricey *Gingerman*.

Al Duomo   £ 17

7 Pavilion Bldg BN1 1EE (01273) 326741

*"Dustbin-lid-size pizzas" and "the best veggie cannelloni ever" are
among the dishes which commend this buzzing Italian, near the
Royal Pavilion. / Sample dishes: calamari; pizza primavera; crème caramel.
Details: 11.30 pm.*

Black Chapati   £ 29

12 Circus Pde, New England Rd BN1 4GW (01273) 699011

*An "eclectic mix" of dishes – Indian, Arabic and British – has
long made this "dreadfully located" ("take a map"), "sparse"
and "uncomfortable" dining room something of a foodie
destination; recent reports, though, range from "fabulous" to
"mega-disappointing", and "abrupt" service is a recurrent problem.
/ Sample dishes: pan-fried Cornish scallops; roast duck with spring onion
mash; cardamon crème brûlée. Details: 10 pm; D only, closed Mon & Sun.*

Bombay Aloo   £ 13   ★

39 Ship St BN1 1AB (01273) 771089

*"No wonder there's often a queue" – this is one of Brighton's best
veggies – a "novel" subcontinental in "bizarre, Mediterranean style";
"adequate Indian nosh" just "doesn't come any cheaper".
/ Sample dishes: mixed starters; spinach & potato curry; ice cream.
Details: opp main post office; 11 pm; no Amex; no smoking area;
need 6+ to book; children: under-8s eat free.*

Chilka House £ 18 ★

69 St James St BN2 1PJ (01273) 677085
"Good Indian staples, with excellent Goanese specialities" make this
a local curry house of more-than-local note. / **Sample dishes:** samosas;
lamb kofte; mango kulfi. **Details:** towards Marina, before hospital; 10 pm;
D only; no Switch.

China Garden £ 20 ★

88-90 Preston St BN1 2HG (01273) 325124
"Superb dim sum" helps distinguish this *"very good"* Chinese;
its fairly formal setting makes it *"useful for special occasions"*.
/ **Sample dishes:** hot hors d'oeuvres; lobster with sweet & sour sauce;
ice cream. **Details:** 11 pm; closed Sun.

Cripes! £ 20 𝔸

7 Victoria Rd BN1 3FS (01273) 327878
Crêpes (geddit?) are the staple at this *"cheap and cheerful"* Breton
establishment, near the Dials – it's *"light and airy at lunch, intimate
and fun in the evening"*. / **Sample dishes:** no starters; Camembert, ham
& mushroom gallette; crêpes with white chocolate sauce. **Details:** 11.30 pm;
closed Mon; no smoking area.

Donatello £ 19

1-3 Brighton Pl BN1 1HJ (01273) 775477
"Huge", *"good-value"* trattoria in the centre of the town, which offers
"enormous portions" and a *"great, busy atmosphere"*; not a great
culinary experience, but a *"cheap"* one. / **Sample dishes:** moules
marinière; veal escalopes cooked with Parma ham; Italian apple tart.
Details: 11.30 pm; no smoking area.

English's £ 28 𝔸

29-31 East St BN1 1HL (01273) 327980
Some traditionalists love the *"wonderful range of seafood"* (washed
down by *"Guinness in a chilled pewter mug"*), the *"great building"*
and the *"wonderful"* location (with good outside tables) of this Lanes
institution; there's a feeling that it lives on its reputation, though, and
some people find it a *"total let-down"*. / **Sample dishes:** clam chowder;
grilled Dover sole; chocolate timbale. **Value tip:** set 2-crs L £6.95.
Details: 10 pm.

Gars £ 25

19 Prince Albert St BN1 1HF (01273) 321321
"Consistently high standards" make this *"excellent"* Peking/Szechuan
establishment, with its *"welcoming"* service, reporters' most popular
Chinese in town. / **Sample dishes:** sesame prawns; chicken with garlic
& wine; toffee banana. **Value tip:** set 2-crs L & Sun L £5.95, set 3-crs early
eve £10.95. **Details:** 11 pm; children: 7+ after 7 pm.

Gingerman £ 30 ★

21a Norfolk Square BN1 2PD (01273) 326688
The *"imaginative"* new chef at this Lanes restaurant trained at
One Paston Place, and it shows – thanks to the *"interesting and
very well presented menu"*, the place is *"already full"*. / **Sample
dishes:** summer truffle risotto with broad beans; pan-fried veal with cider;
chocolate soufflé with Bailey's ice cream. **Value tip:** set 2/3-crs weekday
L £12.95/£14.95. **Details:** off Norfolk Square towards seafront; 10 pm; closed
Mon, Tue L & Sun D.

Havana £ 35

33 Duke St BN1 1AG (01273) 773388
This *"airy"*, *"nicely decorated"* and *"child-friendly"* bar/restaurant
makes a pleasant place to hang out around the Lanes (*"for breakfast,
lunch or dinner"*); the food (more British than Cuban) can be *"very
good"* too, but consistency is a problem. / **Sample dishes:** chilled crab
cannelloni; roast pork fillet; double caramelised apple bavarois.
Details: 11 pm; children: 6+ after 6pm.

Kambi £ 20 ★

107 Western Rd BN1 2AA (01273) 327934

An "exciting range" of "excellent" Lebanese dishes (not least "the best kebabs in the South East") make this busy local, near Hove seafront, worthy of mention; the BYO policy contributes to "great value". / **Sample dishes:** houmous & aubergine; mixed grill with rice; baklava. **Details:** 11.30 pm.

One Paston Place £ 46 ★★

I Paston Pl BN2 1HA (01273) 606933

"The best South Coast restaurant" offers "seriously good" modern French cooking, "eclectically inspired, but never discordant"; for a vociferous few, the "brightly lit" Kempstown townhouse setting makes a visit a "joyless" experience, notwithstanding the "friendly" service. / **Sample dishes:** roast asparagus with pancetta; halibut with salsify & brown shrimps; milk chocolate crème brûlée. **Value tip:** set 2/3-crs L £14.50/£16.50. **Details:** halfway between pier and marina; 10 pm; closed Mon & Sun; children: 2+.

Pinocchio £ 20 A★

22 New Rd BN1 1HJ (01273) 677676

"Pizza like Naples" (and "exceptional-value set meals") ensure that this "friendly" trattoria is always "bustling and noisy". / **Sample dishes:** melon & Parmesan; lasagne; torta al tartufo. **Details:** nr Theatre Royal; 11.30 pm; closed Mon.

Quentin's £ 30 ★

42 Western Rd BN3 1JD (01273) 822734

"A totally reliable local restaurant" in Hove, offering a "stylish", "well-presented" modern British menu in a cosy "scrubbed pine" setting. / **Sample dishes:** paella fishcakes with tomato sauce; beef with horseradish mash & port sauce; chocolate crème brûlée. **Value tip:** set 2-crs L £9.95. **Details:** 10 pm; closed Mon & Sun.

Regency £ 17 ★

131 Kings Rd BN1 2HH (01273) 325014

It may be a "'70s time-warp", but this "fabulous fish restaurant on the seafront" has many fans for its "very extensive" menu of dishes – from "brilliant" fish and chips to "very fresh" seafood – all served in "ample portions". / **Sample dishes:** prawn cocktail; whole grilled plaice; coffee & petit fours. **Details:** opp West Pier; 11 pm; no smoking area. **Accommodation:** 25 rooms, from £40.

Terre à Terre £ 28 ★★

71 East St BN1 1NQ (01273) 729051

"Total gastronomic fulfilment, with a perfect balance of tastes in every dish" is rare enough – in a veggie restaurant, it's extraordinary; admittedly, service at this "chic" Lanes spot can be "slow", but "the wait is worth it" for the "labour-intensive" cooking. / **Sample dishes:** foccacia bread; Camembert soufflé; rhubarb & raspberry sabayon trifle. **Details:** 10.30 pm; closed Mon L; no smoking area.

Trogs £ 28 ★

124 Kings Rd BN1 2FA (01273) 204655

"Worth going to Brighton for, even if you eat meat", this basement restaurant ("thankfully unconnected with the hotel above") offers "imaginative" and "superbly presented" veggie fare, and exceptional service. / **Sample dishes:** roasted marinated courgettes; marinated seared tofu with plum sauce; banana & butterscotch bundles. **Details:** opp West Pier, by Metropole Hotel; 9.30 pm; no smoking.

Wai Kika Moo Kau £ 16 ★

11a Kensington Gdns BN1 4AL (01273) 671117

"Cheap and very cheerful" Lanes veggie, praised especially for its breakfasts. / **Sample dishes:** garlic mushrooms; Stilton bake; ice cream & sorbets. **Details:** 5 pm, Sat 6 pm; L only; no credit cards.

The Three Crowns   £ 24   ★★
The Street SN15 5AF (01666) 510366
"Fabulous food every time", from an *"extensive"* menu, makes this
friendly hostelry, not far from the M4, *"a step up from even the
better end of usual pub restaurants"*; unsurprisingly, it's *"very busy"*,
and service can be *"variable"*. / **Sample dishes:** no starters; rack of lamb
with garlic breadcrumbs; Scotch mist. **Details:** 9.30 pm; no smoking area;
no booking.

BRISTOL, CITY OF BRISTOL   2–2B

Prosperous Bristol is relatively well served for good-quality
restaurants with a decent selection of establishments at
most levels.

At the top end of the market, *Harveys* is arguably the name
best known to visitors, though the cognoscenti head for the
(less expensive) *Markwicks*.

At the mid-price level, *Bell's Diner* is a very well-liked,
long-established all-rounder, while the year-old, strikingly
designed *River Station* (whose owners previously ran Bell's)
is on the road to becoming one of the city's landmarks.

The majority of restaurants are located in and around the
centre of the town. Genteel Clifton is well served for quality
'every-day' places (of which *Rocinantes, and Red Snapper* are
the best-known foodie destinations).

Bell's Diner   £ 29   𝔸★★
1 York Rd BS6 5QB (0117) 924 0357
"A unique little spot that does what it does very well" – this
long-established, highly *"popular"*, and *"very cosy and intimate"*
institution employs *"great"* staff who deliver both *"quality"* staples
(such as *"great burgers"*) and *"thoughtful"*, more ambitious dishes,
all at *"reasonable prices"*. / **Sample dishes:** scallops with pea & mint
risotto; roast Trelough duck; cherry & almond tart. **Details:** 10.30 pm; closed
Mon L, Sat L & Sun D; no smoking.

Bouboulina   £ 27   ★
9 Portland St BS8 4JA (0117) 973 1192
The *"meze is a real celebration"* at this *"lovely"*, *"spacious"* spot,
near the suspension bridge; it wins consistent praise for its *"fresh"*
Greek cooking. / **Sample dishes:** stuffed vine leaves; kleftiko; orange
baklava. **Value tip:** meze 12.95 for 15 dishes. **Details:** 11.30 pm;
no smoking area.

Browns   £ 30   𝔸
38 Queens Rd BS8 1RE (0117) 930 4777
In spite of its *"terrible"*, *"formulaic"* food, this huge outpost of Bass's
English brasserie chain retains a depressingly broad following on
account of its *"good interior (lots of panelling and palms)"* and
"lively" atmosphere. / **Sample dishes:** gravadlax; steak, mushroom
& Guinness pie; lemon tart. **Value tip:** set 2-crs early eve £5. **Details:**
next to Bristol Museum; 11.30 pm; no smoking area.

Byzantium £ 36 Ⓐ

2 Port Wall Ln BS1 6NB (0117) 922 1883

This "fantastically opulent" and trendy yearling, in a fringe-location near Redcliffe Bridge, certainly offers a "visual extravaganza"; the "concept is intriguing", but sadly "they can't quite pull it off", and the "quite expensive" cooking can be "very mediocre". / **Sample dishes:** Middle Eastern meze; chicken & guinea fowl fricasée; trio of chocolate desserts. **Details:** 11.30 pm; closed Sun L; no smoking area.

A Cozinha £ 31 ★

33 St Stephens St BS1 1JX (0117) 922 5505

"Fantastic Portuguese food" is ecstatically praised at this "intimate" spot, which serves "traditional" dishes (prepared with "great attention to detail") and "excellent" Hispanic wines. / **Sample dishes:** goat's cheese & olive roulade; fish, pork & seafood casserole; almond tart. **Value tip:** set 2-crs L £8.50. **Details:** 9.30 pm; no Amex.

Glasnost £ 24 ★

1 William St, Totterdown BS3 4TU (0117) 972 0938

"Varied and interesting" venture, whose eclectic menu (including "rarities such as kangaroo and shark" and a "good choice of veggie meals") is "good value" and "consistently consistent, with flashes of greatness"; the artified décor and the noise level are not to all tastes. / **Sample dishes:** goat's cheese & spinach ciabatta; pork fillet with apple gravy; Bailey's & Malteser cheesecake. **Details:** at beginning of A37; 10 pm; D only, closed Mon & Sun; no Amex.

The Glass Boat £ 30 Ⓐ

Welsh Back BS1 4SB (0117) 929 0704

This "beautiful moored boat, with lovely waterside views" is a natural special-event location; the cooking does not quite match up, though some say it has "improved". / **Sample dishes:** crab ravioli with crustacean sauce; monkfish & scallops wrapped in pancetta; plum tart with hazelnuts. **Value tip:** set 2-crs L £10.95. **Details:** 11 pm; closed Sat L & Sun; no smoking area.

Harveys £ 55

12 Denmark St BS1 5DQ (0117) 927 5034

"The biggest wine list you've ever seen" is a dependable attraction at this restaurant in the famous sherry shippers' cellars, and there are many reports of "absolutely exceptional" cooking; it can be "hit and miss", though, and there are those who feel the place "survives on its name". / **Sample dishes:** potato & truffle salad with scallops; lamb with herb risotto; roast pineapple with ginger syrup. **Value tip:** set 2/3-crs L £14.95/£17.95. **Details:** 10.45 pm; closed Sat L & Sun.

Hope & Anchor £ 22 Ⓐ★

38 Jacobs Wells Rd (0117) 929 2987

"Unfortunately, it's becoming a legend for pub food in Bristol; "waiting for a seat is worth it", however, for the "interesting", "varied" and 'freshly prepared" menu (which includes "the biggest variety of ploughman's lunches ever"). / **Sample dishes:** deep-fried potato skins; whole trout stuffed with prawns; treacle sponge. **Details:** 1.5m from city centre; 9 pm; no credit cards; no booking.

Jameson's £ 33

30-32 Upper Maudlin St BS2 8DJ (0117) 927 6565

"Consistently good food" is just part of the attraction of this "good city-centre restaurant" – a "cosy" spot which some find "romantic". / **Sample dishes:** duck & chicken liver pâté; breast of guinea fowl; summer pudding with berry coulis. **Value tip:** set 2-crs L £7.50. **Details:** opp Royal Infirmary; 10.30 pm, Fri & Sat 11 pm; closed Sat L & Sun D.

Johns   **£ 23**

27 Midland Rd BS2 0JT   (0117) 955 0333

*"Quirky" spot, serving "Thai or Anglo/Thai" food "without fuss" in a
"friendly" atmosphere.* / ***Sample dishes:*** *crispy duck salad; monkfish in
Thai green curry sauce; chocolate & amaretto truffle torte.* ***Details:*** *nr Evening
Post building; 10 pm; closed Mon; no Amex.*

Markwick's   **£ 38**   ★★

43 Corn St BS1 1HT   (0117) 926 2658

*Stephen Markwick's "imaginative and clever" British cooking
(especially the "wonderful fish and seafood") wins many enthusiastic
endorsements for this "superb", "formal but friendly" restaurant;
it occupies a converted bank vault in the city's old merchant
quarter, and boasts a notably "good wine list".* / ***Sample dishes:*** *duck
confit salad with potato pancake; sea bass with caramelised red cabbage;
honeycomb parfait.* ***Value tip:*** *set 2/3-crs L £14.50/£17.50.* ***Details:*** *10 pm;
closed Mon, Sat L & Sun; smoking discouraged.*

Melbournes   **£ 26**

74 Park St BS1 5JX   (0117) 922 6996

*Despite its somewhat un-prepossessing and dated appearance, this
"pleasant" central French establishment is a "very popular" budget
option, and is "good for groups", on account of its "fair choice at
reasonable prices"; the ability to BYO is a key part of the appeal.*
/ ***Sample dishes:*** *avocado, salmon & pepper terrine; roast lamb with wild
mushroom stuffing; warm lemon cake.* ***Details:*** *nr University; 10.30 pm;
D only, ex Sun when L only.*

Mud Dock   **£ 27**   🄰

40 The Grove BS1 4RB   (0117) 934 9734

*"Laid-back" (yet "efficient") and always with "a good mix of people",
this "trendy", elevated riverside café (over a large cycling shop) is
enthusiastically supported as one of the better "medium-priced"
places in town; it's open all day, from "delicious" breakfasts onwards.*
/ ***Sample dishes:*** *tiger prawns in ginger & chilli sauce; spicy lamb sausages
& mash; chocolate pecan pie.* ***Details:*** *11 pm; closed Mon D;
no smoking area; Sat & Sun max booking 8.*

Over The Moon   **£ 23**   🄰

117 St George's Rd BS1 5UW   (0117) 927 2653

*This "top-of-the-range bistro" is "such a welcoming and friendly
place", and its modern British cooking offers "lots of fresh flavours";
"the only quibble is that the chairs are uncomfortable, but that's a
detail".* / ***Sample dishes:*** *Thai style curried salmon; baked goat's cheese
soufflé; chocolate & banana pancake.* ***Details:*** *nr Cathedral; 10.30 pm;
no Amex.*

Red Snapper   **£ 29**   ★

1 Chandos Rd BS6 6PG   (0117) 973 7999

*"It may be served at red Formica tables", but – by universal acclaim
– "the food is sharp and affordable, and service is good", at this
"lively" shop-conversion venture ("slightly off the main drag",
near Clifton); it boasts an "original" menu, majoring in fish.*
/ ***Sample dishes:*** *spiced mussels & cockles; skate wing with capers & fennel;
rhubarb & ginger crème brûlée.* ***Value tip:*** *set 2/3-crs L & Sun L £9/£12.*
Details: *on M32, follow signs to BRI Hospital then Redland; 10 pm; closed
Mon L & Sun D.*

The River Station   £ 32   A★
The Grove BS1 4RB   (0117) 914 4434
*Not just the "wonderful", "stimulating" setting – a "stylishly"
converted river police station with "nice views over the harbour" –
has made this "delightful" and "very relaxed" yearling into a real
success; the "very imaginative" modern British cooking offers "the
freshest ingredients, beautifully presented". / **Sample dishes:** scallops
with coriander sauce; duck with lentils & spiced clementines; panna cotta with
chestnut liqueur. **Value tip:** set 2/3-crs L in bar £10.50/£12.75 (Sun
L £12/£15). **Details:** nr St Mary's Redcliffe Church; 10.30 pm, Fri & Sat
11 pm; closed Sat L; no Amex; no smoking area.*

Rocinantes   £ 32   A★
85 Whiteladies Rd BS8 2NT   (0117) 973 4482
*It's "busy, sometimes hectic, but the food is always tasty, appetising
and good value" at this "lively" and "informal" Clifton hang-out
("half tapas-bar, half restaurant"); "good organic produce and
attention to the real taste of ingredients is the key to its success".
/ **Sample dishes:** scallops with pea & mint purée; sea bass with roast fennel
& garlic mash; chocolate marquise with summer berries. **Value tip:** set 2-crs
L & Sun L £10.95. **Details:** 10.30 pm.*

Thai Classic   £ 21   ★
37 Whiteladies Rd BS8 2NT   (0117) 973 8930
*"Absolutely fabulous" Thai cooking (offering "wonderful
combinations" of "delicate" flavours) and "attentive" service mean
this Clifton Thai lives up to its name. / **Sample dishes:** satay chicken
wings; deep-fried crispy duck; coconut pancakes. **Value tip:** set 2-crs L £5.50.
Details: 11.30 pm; no smoking area.*

Tico Tico   £ 27
24 Alma Vale Rd BS8 2HY   (0117) 923 8700
*Clifton spot praised for its well-realised, "interesting", "versatile
and flexible menu" ("from Spain to South America"). / **Sample
dishes:** sweet pea & lovage gazpacho; char-grilled monkfish with bacon
& spinach; cinnamon & raspberry shortcake. **Details:** off Whiteladies Road;
10 pm; closed Mon D & Sun; no Amex.*

BRITWELL SALOME, OXON   2–2D

The Goose   £ 36   ★
OX9 5LG   (01491) 612304
*"Excellent-quality produce" (much of it organic, as you would hope
with a chef who used to cook for the Prince of Wales) makes this
recently "gentrified" pub, on the fringe of the village, well worth trying
out; it's "not cheap", however, and not everyone leaves impressed.
/ **Sample dishes:** crab & ginger salad; venison with braised cabbage & lentils;
summer berry cheesecake. **Details:** M40 J6, nr Wellington; 9.30 pm; closed
Mon & Sun D; no Amex; no smoking.*

BROADHEMBURY, DEVON   2–4A

Drewe Arms   £ 33   A★
EX14 0NF   (01404) 841267
*A "consistently good quality fish menu" (plus "other local delights")
and a "great setting in the heart of a picturesque village" make this
"classically pretty" pub a top West Country choice. / **Sample
dishes:** seafood selection; whole Dover sole; bread pudding with whisky sauce.
Details: 5m from M5, J28, on A373 to Honiton; 10 pm; closed Sun D;
no smoking.*

BROADWAY, WORCS   2–1C

Lygon Arms   **£ 55**   Ⓐ
High St WR12 7DU   (01386) 852255
It's the "wonderful baronial feel" of the Savoy Group's famous
Elizabethan outpost in the Cotswolds which makes it a special place
– "expensive, but worth it"; the food may not be the main point,
but it's "very edible". / *Sample dishes:* red shallot tarte Tatin with foie gras;
roast venison with plum millefeuille; honey & apricot ravioli. *Value tip:* set 2/3-
crs L £21/£23 (Sun £27.50). *Details:* 9.15 pm; no smoking; children: 8+.
Accommodation: 65 rooms, from £175.

BROCKENHURST, HANTS   2–4C

Le Poussin   **£ 45**   ★
The Courtyard, Brookley Rd SO42 7RB   (01590) 623063
This "tiny restaurant serving first-rate traditional French food"
continues to please most reporters with its "restricted but innovative"
menu; the "elegant" dining room can lack atmosphere, though, and
there were a couple of reports this year of experiences which were
"in no sense special". / *Sample dishes:* salad of wood pigeon; venison, pork
& lamb in red wine sauce; passion fruit soufflé. *Details:* behind Bestsellers
Bookshop; 9.30 pm; closed Mon & Tue; no Amex; no smoking.

BROMFIELD, SHROPSHIRE   5–4A

Cookhouse   **£ 27**
SY8 2JR   (01584) 856565
"Bright" restaurant whose décor seems "surprisingly modern" in its
"traditional shell"; the "up-to-the-minute" cooking is "good-value" –
"even more so in the bistro". / *Sample dishes:* fish soup with croutons;
rack of lamb with roast vegetables; lemon tart. *Value tip:* set 3-crs Sun
L £10.50. *Details:* 2m N of Ludlow on A49 to Shrewsbury; 10 pm;
no smoking area.

BROOKWOOD, SURREY   3–3A

Moghul   **£ 24**
142 Connaught Rd GU24 0AS   (01483) 472610
"The service is sometimes slow, but the food is always excellent" say
fans of this unpretentious spot, who swear it delivers "the best Indian
cooking in Surrey". / *Sample dishes:* samosas; chicken tikka masala; ice
cream. *Details:* 5m from centre of Brookwood; 11.15 pm; D only, closed Mon.

BROOM HILL, S YORKS   5–2C

Bahn Nah   **£ 25**
19-21 Nile St S10 2PN   (0114) 268 4900
"Small" and "homely" Thai establishment whose "authentic" and
"tasty" cooking makes it a top local choice. / *Sample dishes:* Thai
fishcakes; red fish curry; banana in coconut milk. *Details:* off A57; 11 pm;
D only, closed Sun; no smoking.

BROUGHTY FERRY, DUNDEE   9–3D

South Kingennie House   **£ 21**   ★
South Kingennie DD5 3PA   (01382) 350562
"Imaginative" home-cooking (with "great vegetables" and an
"outstanding sweet trolley") is the stock-in-trade of this "dependable"
family-run restaurant, out in the countryside near Dundee. / *Sample
dishes:* warm salad of avocado & pigeon; Angus beef with smoked ham
& Madeira sauce; vanilla bavarois & citrus sauce. *Details:* from A92 take
B978-to Kellas, then road to Drumsturde; 8:45 pm; closed Mon & Sun D.

Buckland Manor   £ 61   A★

WR12 7LY (01386) 852626

"Very good, if pricey" Cotswold country house hotel, charmingly located in its own grounds, and offering high standards across the board. / **Sample dishes:** butternut squash risotto with pancetta; truffled chicken & parsnip dumplings; chocolate & coconut délice. **Value tip:** set 3-crs Sun L £23.50. **Details:** 2m SW from Broadway on B4632; 9 pm; jacket & tie; no smoking; children: 12+. **Accommodation:** 14 rooms, from £188.

Lamb at Buckland   £ 35

Lamb Ln SN7 8QN (01367) 870484

A *"very pleasant"*, *"away-from-it-all"* pub in a *"nice village"*, with *"excellent"* food, *"mainly Australian"* staff and *"good Oz wines to match"*. / **Sample dishes:** rabbit & guinea fowl terrine; veal escalope in Marsala sauce; hot raspberry brûlée. **Details:** 9.30 pm; no smoking. **Accommodation:** 4 rooms, from £37.50.

The Lamb   £ 35   A★

Sheep St OX18 4LR (01993) 823155

"All that a traditional pub should be"; this *"lovely, old"* Cotswolds pub/hotel/restaurant has a *"delightful"* setting, and receives high praise for its *"superb selection"* of *"imaginative"* food, and its *"noisy but friendly"* atmosphere. / **Sample dishes:** crab, smoked trout & avocado; rack of lamb with caramelised shallots; nougatine parfait with apricot compote. **Value tip:** set 2-crs Sun L £18.50. **Details:** 9 pm; D only, ex Sun open L & D; no Amex; no smoking. **Accommodation:** 15 rooms, from £95.

Fishes   £ 29

Market Pl PE31 8HE (01328) 738588

"Determinedly old-fashioned and unpretentious fresh fish restaurant", with *"dependable"* cooking, *"basic"* décor and *"nice"* staff. / **Sample dishes:** oysters baked with Stilton; monkfish with mussels in orange sauce; rhubarb meringue pie. **Value tip:** set 2/3-crs L £11.25/£12.75 (Sun £11.70/£14.75). **Details:** 9 pm, 9.30 pm Sat; closed Mon & Sun L; no smoking; need 5+ to book; children: not at D.

Hoste Arms   £ 28   A★

PE31 8HD (01328) 738777

Over the years, the *"flamboyant owner"* has *"transformed"* this country inn, on the village green, into a well-known destination (it's *"sometimes too popular for its own good"*); it offers *"a good menu, particularly fish"* in stylishly *"eccentric"* surroundings. / **Sample dishes:** salmon & chilli fishcake; crisp fried seabass with leek risotto; hot raspberry soufflé. **Details:** 6m W of Wells next-the-Sea; 9 pm; no Amex; no smoking area. **Accommodation:** 28 rooms, from £64.

St James   £ 35   ★

30 High St WD2 3DN (020) 8950 2480

Concerns persist that it's *"a bit overpriced"*, but the consensus is that this *"trendy modern restaurant in a pretty location"* is *"trying hard and ultimately succeeding in bringing 'London restaurant' food, service and ambience to the suburbs"*. / **Sample dishes:** carrot, coriander & coconut soup; sea bass with chive mash; Toblerone cheesecake. **Details:** opp St James Church; 9.30 pm; closed Sun; no smoking area.

Buxted Park   £ 34

TN22 4AY   (01825) 732711

*This "lovely country house", set in a deer park, continues to inspire mixed commentary; for some it's "perfect for special events", while others say it's "poor" in every respect. / **Sample dishes:** warm pigeon & lentil salad; Scotch beef with pine nuts & oyster mushrooms; white chocolate parfait. **Value tip:** set 3-crs L £14.95. **Details:** 10 pm; no smoking. **Accommodation:** 44 rooms, from £130.*

Browns   £ 30   Ⓐ

23 Trumpington St CB2 1QA   (01223) 461655

*"Not as good as it was or should be", but this large "buzzy" branch of the well-known English brasserie chain is still one of the few potential "good night out" places in this underprovided town. / **Sample dishes:** gravadlax; steak, mushroom & Guinness pie; lemon tart. **Value tip:** set 2-crs early eve £5. **Details:** opp Fitzwilliam Museum; 11.30 pm; no smoking area.*

Loch Fyne Oyster Bar   £ 28   new

31 Trumpington Street CB2 1QY   (01223) 362433

*It opened too recently to rate, but initial reports suggest that this seafood specialist (related to the famous Scottish establishment) might be just the kind of decent eatery the city so obviously needs. / **Sample dishes:** oysters with garlic & breadcrumbs; deep-fried scallops; sorbet. **Details:** opposite the Fitzwilliam Museum; 10 pm; no smoking in dining room.*

Maharaja   £ 17

9-13 Castle St CB3 0AH   (01223) 358399

*There's "always a great curry" to be had at this busy local Indian of long standing. / **Sample dishes:** chicken tikka pakora; lamb jalfrezi; lychees. **Details:** 11.45 pm; no Switch; children: 6+.*

Michels Brasserie   £ 33

21-24 Northampton St CB3 0AD   (01223) 353110

*The characterful, "friendly and efficient" original branch of this (generally undistinguished) bistro chain is worth knowing about in this under-provided city; its bistro-fare is "good if nothing special". / **Sample dishes:** mussels in lime & chilli sauce; roast lamb with onion marmalade; chocolate pot with cumin shortbread. **Value tip:** set 2/3-crs L £6.95/£8.45. **Details:** 10.30 pm; no smoking area.*

Midsummer House   £ 55   Ⓐ

Midsummer Common CB4 1HA   (01223) 369299

*Daniel Clifford – the latest chef at the grandest restaurant in town by far – has got some work to do; the place may have a "comfy ambience" – and a nice location between the common and the Cam – but the impression that the cooking is "overblown" and "overpriced" is going to take some shaking off. / **Sample dishes:** scallops with truffle vinaigrette; pigs trotter with sweetbreads & morels; hot apricot soufflé. **Value tip:** set 3-crs L £19.50. **Details:** facing University Boathouse; 9.45 pm; closed Mon, Sat L & Sun D; no jeans; no smoking.*

Sala Thong   £ 21

35 Newnham Rd CB3 9EY   (01223) 323178

*Popular oriental located near the Mill Pond; perhaps it's not remarkable, but it's "nice to find a place with decent Thai home-cooking in a town that's mainly Pizza Huts". / **Sample dishes:** mung bean toast with sweet chilli sauce; honey-roast duck with ginger pickle; coconut custard with jackfruit. **Value tip:** set 2-crs early eve £6.50. **Details:** 9.45 pm; closed Mon; no Amex & no Switch; no smoking.*

22 Chesterton Road   £ 34

22 Chesterton Rd CB4 3AX   (01223) 351880
*Agreeable, if cramped, dining room in an Edwardian house,
liked for its "imaginative" modern British cooking, and service which is
"neither too formal, nor too informal".* / **Sample dishes:** *brandade of
haddock; lamb with sultana & herb couscous; rhubarb tarte Tatin.*
Details: *9.30 pm; D only, closed Mon & Sun; no smoking during D;
children: 12+.*

Venue   £ 33   🅐

66 Regent St CB2 1DP   (01223) 367333
*Some mistake surely? – reporters speak of an "exceptional new lively
place", with "great food and service", and, "really good live classical
music and jazz"; this can't be the Cambridge we know and love!*
/ **Sample dishes:** *hot sea trout mousse; salmon steak with Japanese seaweed;
Cointreau strawberries.* **Value tip:** *set 2-crs L £9.50.* **Details:** *11 pm;
no Amex; no smoking area.*

CANONBIE, DUMFRIES & GALLOWAY   7–2D

Riverside Inn   £ 26   ★

DG14 0UX   (013873) 71295
*The "fish, shellfish, meat and game" dishes – "all home-produced"
and "simply cooked" to a turn – inspire unanimously good reports on
this small, 17th-century hostelry, run for a quarter of a century by a
husband-and-wife team.* / **Sample dishes:** *fish & shellfish soup; roast duck
with cherry & port sauce; date pudding with toffee sauce.* **Details:** *off A7, nr
border; 9 pm; no Amex; no smoking.* **Accommodation:** *7 rooms, from £55.*

CANTERBURY, KENT   3–3D

Café des Amis   £ 25   🅐

95 St Dunstan's St CT2 8AA   (01227) 464390
*"I always associate it with happiness and having fun"; it's hardly
surprising this "original" Mexican is "very busy at all times" – it offers
"satisfying" and "very good-value" food in an agreeably "hectic"
environment.* / **Sample dishes:** *salmon & prawns with roast tomatoes;
chicken in coriander & almond cream sauce; fruit with chocolate sauce, biscuits
& cream.* **Details:** *by Westgate Towers; 10 pm; no smoking area.*

CARDIFF, CITY OF CARDIFF   2–2A

The elegance of its shopping arcades may impress the
visitor to the Welsh capital, but that same visitor cannot
avoid being struck by the almost total absence of quality
eating from the centre of the city. That is not to say that the
most notable venture – the enormous complex comprising
La Brasserie, Champers and *Le Monde* – does not succeed in
its aims, just that they are not particularly lofty.

The striking redevelopment of the Waterfront has so far
spawned little in the way of a restaurant-scene. The city's
most convincing stab at a modern brasserie changed hands
this year – what was Scott's being taken over by *Wood's
Brasserie.*

Such other beacons of quality as exist (*Armless Dragon,
Cassoulet, Gallois y Cymru*) are dotted throughout the inner
suburbs, particularly Canton. A few miles out of town in
Pentrych (see also), the perhaps somewhat overblown
de Courcy's serves the business and conference market.

Armless Dragon £ 25 ★

97 Wyeverne Rd CF2 4BG (029) 2038 2357

"Difficult to find" – in a backstreet location near the university –
this *"friendly and cosy"* bistro of long standing is *"something special"*;
it offers *"interesting"*, *"traditional"* cooking, *"using only the best
quality ingredients"*, at *"good-value"* prices. / **Sample dishes:**
laverballs & mushrooms; Welsh lamb with garden herbs; lemon tart.
Value tip: set 2/3-crs L £7.90/£9.90. **Details:** 10.15 pm, Sat 10.30 pm;
closed Mon & Sun; no smoking in dining room.

La Brasserie £ 29 🅐

60 St Mary St CF1 1FE (029) 2037 2164

"Hearty fare in a lively atmosphere" is the highly successful format
at this, the largest part of Benigno Martinez's impressively scaled
restaurant 'complex' (which has 600 seats in total); you choose from
"high quality ingredients" (*"fish and steaks"* mostly) at the bar, which
are then *"simply cooked and served"*. / **Sample dishes:** king prawns;
venison with game sauce; lemon & ginger cheesecake. **Details:** midnight;
closed Sun; no trainers; no booking.

Le Cassoulet £ 39 ★

5 Romilly Cr, Canton CF1 9NP (029) 2022 1905

"True French provincial cooking with style" makes this pleasant,
long-serving establishment, in a smart suburb, one of the most
satisfactory choices in town. / **Sample dishes:** tuna carpaccio & quail's
eggs; lamb & spinach pie with parsnip purée; flambéed banana & pineapple.
Value tip: set 2/3-crs L £12.50/£15. **Details:** 10 pm; closed Mon & Sun.

Champers £ 25 🅐

62 St Mary St CF1 1FE (029) 2037 3363

Bodega-style sibling to La Brasserie whose similarly *"unfussy"*
approach – *"you choose it, they cook it"* – makes it a similarly
consistent success. / **Sample dishes:** marinated seafood salad; chicken
Mexicana; Spanish cheeses with biscuits. **Details:** midnight; closed Sun L;
children: 5+.

Gallois y Cymru £ 38 ★

6-8 Romilly Cr CF1 9NR (029) 2034 1264

This modish, *"most welcome"* yearling, run by a Franco-Welsh family,
is already *"always busy"*, on account of its *"imaginative modern
cooking"* and *"friendly"* service. / **Sample dishes:** beef carpaccio with
raclette cheese; cod with mustard mash & cockle gravy; chocolate fondant.
Value tip: set 2/3-crs L £8.95/£10.95. **Details:** 1.5m W of Cardiff Castle;
10.30 pm; closed Mon & Sun.

Happy Gathering £ 25 ★

233 Cowbridge Rd East CF11 9AL (029) 2039 7531

It's a touch *"impersonal"*, and service can belie the place's name,
but this place is *"popular with the Chinese community"* for a reason
– the food is *"very good indeed"*. / **Sample dishes:** barbecued spare ribs;
cashew nut chicken; Cantonese puddings. **Details:** 11.45 pm.

King Balti £ 22 ★

131 Albany Rd CF24 3NS (029) 2048 2890

"Lots of variety" – in cooking and customers – wins very high praise
from supporters of this *"Curry King"*, whose unusual atmosphere is
likened by some to a wine bar, by others to *"an American diner with
Bollywood posters"*. / **Sample dishes:** poppadoms & chutney; lamb balti;
ice cream. **Details:** off Newport road; 11.45 pm; D only; no smoking area.

Le Monde   **£ 30**   Ⓐ
62 St Mary St CF1 1FE (029) 2038 7376
*"Simple, fresh food, cooked simply" ("excellent meat and fish"),
served in stylish surroundings ensure that this first-floor restaurant
(the upmarket bit of the complex attached to La Brasserie) is
"very popular".* / **Sample dishes:** *spare ribs; sea bass in rock salt; chocolate
marquise.* **Details:** *midnight; closed Sun; no trainers; no booking; children:
10+.*

Wood's Brasserie   **£ 32**   ★
Pilotage Building, Stuart St CF10 5BW (029) 2049 2400
*"Marvellous" cooking, "imaginatively served" established quite a
reputation for this modern brasserie, when it was in Llantrisant;
let's hope they maintain standards at the new premises, in
"hyped and horrible" Cardiff Bay (on the site formerly occupied
by Scott's Brasserie).* / **Sample dishes:** *warm potato salad; lamb shank
with mash; chocolate fondant & pistachio ice cream.* **Details:** *in the
Inner Harbour; 10 pm; closed Mon & Sun.*

CARTERWAY HEADS, NORTHUMBERLAND   8–3B

Manor House   **£ 24**
DH8 9LX (01207) 255268
*Simply prepared fish and sticky toffee pudding are typical of the
sort of fare this dining pub, near the Derwent Reservoir, does well.*
/ **Sample dishes:** *smoked kippers; duck with chilli & coriander; fig & almond
cake.* **Details:** *A68 just past turn-off for Shotley Bridge; 9.30 pm;
no smoking area; children: 9+ at D.* **Accommodation:** *4 rooms, from £43.*

CARTMEL, CUMBRIA   7–4D

Uplands   **£ 36**   ★
Haggs Ln LA11 6HD (015395) 36248
*"Delightful, unfussy" traditional British cooking, from a chef who
formerly cooked at Cumbria's famous Miller Howe, helps win general
approval for this Lakeland hotel restaurant.* / **Sample dishes:** *hot
salmon soufflé; venison with blackcurrant & juniper sauce; peaches in
butterscotch sauce.* **Value tip:** *set 3-crs L £15.* **Details:** *follow signs to The
Grange (becomes Haggs Ln), turn left after 0.75m; 8pm; closed Mon; closed
Jan & Feb; no smoking; Sat no bookings; children: 8+ at D.*
Accommodation: *5 rooms, from £71.*

CARTMEL FELL, CUMBRIA   7–4D

Masons Arms   **£ 25**   Ⓐ★★
Strawberry Bank LA11 6NW (015395) 68486
*"Wonderful home-made food", "incredibly good beer" and "an
isolated pastoral location" in "fabulous countryside" is a heady brew,
and one which leads to universal satisfaction with this "unique"
"microbrewery"-cum-pub; it has fine Lakeland views.* / **Sample
dishes:** *French-style fish soup; Coachman's casserole; jam roly-poly.* **Details:** *W
from Bowland Bridge, off A5074, right then left at crossroads; 8.45 pm.*
Accommodation: *6 rooms, from £140 for 3 nights.*

CASTLETON, DERBYS   5–2C

George Hotel   **£ 20**
Castle St S33 8WG (01433) 620238
*"Good traditional northern home-cooking", from a "regularly changing
menu" is the special strength of this characterful pub/restaurant.*
/ **Sample dishes:** *duckling confit with hoisin sauce; steak stuffed with Stilton
wrapped in bacon; fresh strawberry shortbreads.* **Details:** *16m from Sheffield
along A625 to Peak District; 10 pm; no Amex.*

CAUNTON BECK, NOTTS 5–3D
Caunton Beck £ 30

Main St NG23 6AB (01636) 636793
*"Better than average" pub food and a "good wine and beer selection"
commend this "very welcoming" establishment to reporters; it's the
rural sibling of Lincoln's Wig & Mitre. / Sample dishes: leek & Stilton
soufflé; scallops, bacon & fennel tagliatelle; white chocolate biscuit cake. Value
tip: set 3-crs L £12.50. Details: 6m NW of Newark past British Sugar
Factory on A616; 11 pm.*

CHAGFORD, DEVON 1–3D
Gidleigh Park £ 72 ★★

TQ13 8HH (01647) 432367
*"Rolls-Royce" cooking – some consider it "the best outside London" –
wins high praise at this famous hotel "beautifully located" in
landscaped gardens on the fringe of Dartmoor (and rather curiously
styled in 'Stockbroker Tudor'); the general approach is "relaxed",
but a few find the style of the restaurant discordantly "precious".
/ Sample dishes: roast scallops with marinated aubergine; roast pigeon & foie
gras with Madeira; crème brûlée with caramelised pears. Value tip: set 2/3-crs
L £22/£30. Details: from Chagford, turn right at Lloyds, fork right, 2m to end
of lane; 9 pm; no Amex; no smoking; children: 7+. Accommodation: 15
rooms, from £365, incl D.*

22 Mill Street £ 38 ★

22 Mill St TQ13 8AW (01647) 432244
*"A restaurant that's got it right", in this "pretty market town";
it offers notably "good food at good prices", and "delightfully served".
/ Sample dishes: crab lasagne; sweetbreads & kidneys in shallot sauce;
raspberry soufflé. Value tip: set 2/3-crs L £13.95/£15.95. Details: 9 pm;
closed Mon L; no Amex; no smoking area; children: 14+. Accommodation: 2
rooms, from £45.*

CHAPELTOWN, S YORKS 5–2C
Greenhead House £ 40 𝔸★

84 Burncross Rd S35 1SF (0114) 246 9004
*With its air of "a family house", its "helpful" service and the
"delicious" results from a "high-quality", "seasonal" menu, this
"warm" and "elegant" establishment wins consistent support.
/ Sample dishes: timbale of smoked salmon & crab; blanquette of lamb;
chocolate crème brûlée. Value tip: set 2-crs L £10. Details: 1m from M1,
J35; 9 pm; closed Mon, Tue, Wed L, Sat L & Sun; no smoking; children: 5+.*

CHEESDEN, LANCS 5–1B
Nutter's £ 37 ★

Edenfield Rd OL12 7TY (01706) 650167
*TV chef Andrew Nutter "has turned an old pub into a wonderful
restaurant"; the atmosphere is "friendly" and the "interesting",
"new wave" cooking is "beautifully presented" and prepared
"with flair and finesse". / Sample dishes: crispy black pudding wontons;
duck with blueberry & mulled wine sauce; nutty chocolate torte. Value tip:
set 3-crs Sun L £19.95. Details: between Edenfield and Nordon on A680;
9.30 pm; closed Tue; closed first 2 weeks in Aug; no smoking.*

CHELTENHAM, GLOUCS 2–1C
Champignon Sauvage £ 48

24-26 Suffolk Rd GL50 2AQ (01242) 573449
*For its fans, this "long-standing favourite" delivers "delicious" Gallic
fare in "intimate" comfort; for somewhere that's a 'name' in the
foodie world, feedback is surprisingly thin, though, and there's the
odd report of "dull" results. / Sample dishes: scallops with pumpkin
purée; pork with black pudding & stuffed cabbage; fig tart with honey spiced
bread. Value tip: set 2-crs L & early eve £15.50. Details: on A40 to Oxford,
nr Boys' College; 9.15 pm; closed Mon & Sun; no smoking during D.*

Daffodil   £ 31   𝔸

18-20 Suffolk Parade GL50 2AE   (01242) 700055
"A wonderful conversion of a beautiful old cinema" provides the
"interesting setting" for this well-received newcomer – *"drinks in
the circle, dine in the stalls, the kitchen the screen"*; the *"brasserie
food"* is *"French"*, and *"filling"*. / **Sample dishes:** wild mushrooms on
toasted brioche; roast monkfish; toffee pudding. **Details:** 10.30 pm; closed
Sun; no smoking area.

Le Petit Blanc   £ 31

Queen's Hotel, Promenade GL50 1NN   (01242) 266800
Raymond Blanc's new town-centre brasserie may have *"quickly settled
in as a popular venue"*, but its *"poor"* ambience (with *"yukky"* décor
and *"tables which are too close together"*) have helped make it
"a disappointing transplant of a well-known name" for many people;
the modern French cooking can be *"very good"*, but consistency has
a way to go. / **Sample dishes:** crab cakes with green onion risotto; sautéed
calves' liver with lime jus; chocolate fondant with gingerbread.
Details: 10.30 pm; no smoking.

Ruby   £ 27

52 Suffolk Rd GL50 2AQ   (01242) 250909
"Better than average" Chinese, close to the city-centre, where staff
are *"accommodating and eager to please"*. / **Sample dishes:** aromatic
crispy duck; crispy shredded beef; lychees. **Details:** 11.30 pm;
no smoking area.

CHESTER, CHESHIRE   5–2B

Chester Grosvenor Hotel, Arkle   £ 61   ★

Eastgate CH1 1LT   (01244) 324024
Supporters of this very grand city-centre hotel dining room hail it as
"undoubtedly the best restaurant in the North West"; it's *"probably
the most expensive too"*, and, for a small but ever-present minority,
"good, but overrated". / **Sample dishes:** langoustine ravioli; Welsh beef
with braised celery; mocha tart with raspberries. **Value tip:** set 3-crs L £25.
Details: by Eastgate clock; 9.30 pm; closed Mon & Sun; jacket & tie;
no smoking. **Accommodation:** 85 rooms, from £160.

Francs   £ 23

14 Cuppin St CH1 2BN   (01244) 317952
"Usually enjoyable", this *"crowded"* bistro – *"French, friendly, and
relaxing"* – is a great success in this much visited, yet underprovided
city; it's generally thought to offer *"good food at reasonable prices"*,
but can be *"erratic"*. / **Sample dishes:** pecan, melon & Roquefort salad;
smoked rainbow trout with lemon butter sauce; almond & pear tart. **Value
tip:** set 3-crs L & early eve £6.95. **Details:** just off Bridge St; 11 pm;
no smoking.

CHICHESTER, W SUSSEX   3–4A

Comme Ça   £ 33   𝔸

67 Broyle Rd BO19 4BD   (01243) 788724
"Booking is essential" if you want to enjoy a *"relaxed"* and *"leisurely"*
meal – with some *"excellent"* French cooking – at this *"friendly"* and
"unpretentious" converted pub. / **Sample dishes:** crab & fish soup; Dover
sole with mushrooms & prawns; trio of sorbets. **Value tip:** set 2-crs L £14.75,
set 2-crs pre-th £15.20. **Details:** 0.5m N of city centre; 10.30 pm; closed Mon
& Sun D; no smoking area.

White Horse   £ 35
High St PO18 9HX   (01243) 535219
*New owners Charles and Nicola Burton still provide a "superb wine list" at this œnophiles' pub on the South Downs, even if under their new regime the number of bins has sunk to a paltry 500; the overhauled menu majors in game and seafood, and food is now available in the bar too. / **Sample dishes:** grilled pigeon breasts; wild mushroom risotto; honey, ginger & whisky bavarois. **Value tip:** set 2-crs Sun L £14. **Details:** 8m NW of Chichester on B2141; 10 pm; closed Sun D; no smoking area. **Accommodation:** 5 rooms, from £70.*

Griffins Head   £ 25
CT3 1PS   (01304) 840325
*"Carefully prepared" and "individual" fare made from "local produce" is served at this village pub, in a "fine medieval building". / **Sample dishes:** garlic mushrooms; chicken breast stuffed with Stilton & spinach; sticky toffee pudding. **Details:** 9.30 pm; closed Sun D; children: 10+.*

Sir Charles Napier   £ 35   𝔸★
Spriggs Alley OX9 4BX   (01494) 483011
*It's as "a great day-out destination from London" that this "cosy" and "trendy" pub/restaurant (complete with helipad) is best known; perhaps inevitably it's a touch "expensive", but most reporters praise its atmospheric "buzz", its "imaginative" modern British cooking and its "companionable" and "relaxed" approach. / **Sample dishes:** tomato risotto with Gruyère wafers; rabbit with hazelnut & Ricotta stuffing; strawberry crème brûlée. **Details:** M40 J6 into Chinnor, turn right at roundabout, up hill to Spriggs Alley; 10 pm; closed Mon & Sun D; no smoking area; children: 6+ at D.*

Chavignol   £ 49   ★★
7 Horsefair OX7 5AL   (01608) 644490
*Marcus Ashenford – who made his name at Lovells at Windrush Farm (now closed) – has done it again at this "very informal" (but "very ambitious") new operation, where a "skilful and enthusiastic young team" presents "superb ingredients with real flair and imagination". / **Sample dishes:** grilled scallops & ratatouille; lamb with mint hollandaise & kidneys; banana & pistachio parfait. **Value tip:** set 2/3-crs L £19/£25. **Details:** on main Banbury road; 9.30 pm; closed Mon & Sun; no smoking.*

Quails   £ 31
1 Bagshot Rd GU24 8BP   (01276) 858491
*"The room is not the best advert for the consistent cooking" at this "relaxed" family-run, town-centre restaurant; "sensible" prices for the "enjoyable" (if "standard") "quasi-continental fare" ensure "it's always full". / **Sample dishes:** char-grilled squid with rice noodles; sesame-crusted lamb with apricots & aubergines; calvados brioche & butter pudding. **Value tip:** set 2/3-crs set L £11.95/14.95, set 2/3-crs set D £15.95/£18.95. **Details:** 9.30 pm; closed Mon, Sat L & Sun.*

CLACHAN, ARGYLL & BUTE 9–3B

Loch Fyne Oyster Bar £ 29 A★★

PA26 8BL   (01499) 600236

*"The best seafood in Scotland", "amazing scenery" and an
"unpretentious" ("log cabin") atmosphere make it "worth a detour"
to this "fantastic" and "deservedly popular" establishment – the
inspiration for a mushrooming national chain; "remember to book".
/ Sample dishes: rock oysters; kiln-smoked salmon; homemade sweets.
Details: 10m E of Inveraray on A83; 8.30 pm; Nov-Mar D only;
no smoking area.*

CLAYGATE, SURREY 3–3A

Le Petit Pierrot £ 30 ★

4 The Parade KT10 0NU   (01372) 465105

*"A really good little village bistro", with an "imaginative" French menu
and "friendly" service. / Sample dishes: salad of scallops & smoked duck;
Dover sole with leek fondue; clafoutis of plums & grapes. Details: nr station;
9.30 pm; closed Sat L & Sun; children: 8+.*

CLEVEDON, AVON 2–2A

Junior Poon £ 31

16 Hill Rd BS21 7NZ   (01275) 341900

*Superior Chinese cooking – especially by the standards of the area –
and "very attentive but discreet" service make this upmarket oriental
by Clevedon Pier a top local choice. / Sample dishes: chicken with salt
& chilli; Peking crispy duck; toffee apple. Details: nr Clevedon Pier; 10.30 pm;
closed Sun; no jeans or trainers.*

CLITHEROE, LANCS 5–1B

Inn at Whitewell £ 34 A★★

Forest of Bowland BD7 3AT   (01200) 448222

*"A special place"; it's "worth the trek" to this "gem in the middle
of nowhere", not just for the "majestic setting with beautiful views"
(over the River Hodder, in the Forest of Bowland), but also for the
"traditional and delicious" nosh – some of "the best pub cooking in
the UK". / Sample dishes: braised baby squid; rack of Bowland lamb; bread
& butter pudding. Details: nr Bruwsholme Hall; 9.30 pm; bar meals only at L.
Accommodation: 15 rooms, from £78.*

CLYTHA, MONMOUTHSHIRE 2–2A

Clytha Arms £ 29 ★

NP7 9BW   (01873) 840206

*"Inviting" pub – with a "French country feel" – where "fresh local
produce" is used to produce a "fascinating range of dishes".
/ Sample dishes: bacon, laverbread & cockles; teriyaki fillet steak; raspberry
& chianti sorbet. Value tip: set 3-crs Sun L £13.95. Details: on old
Abergavenny Road; 9.30 pm; closed Mon D & Sun D; no smoking.
Accommodation: 4 rooms, from £50.*

COBHAM, SURREY 3–3A

La Capanna £ 36

48 High St KT11 3EF   (01932) 862121

*"Very popular" and "bustling" Italian in "a converted barn";
cooking which is "good if lacking finer touches" to some, is just
"a throwback to the '70s" for others. / Sample dishes: stuffed
aubergine; fillet steak with truffles; oranges in Grand Marnier. Value tip:
set 3-crs L £14.95. Details: 10.45 pm; closed Sat L.*

COCKERMOUTH, CUMBRIA   7–3C

Quince & Medlar   £ 22   A★
13 Castlegate CA13 9EU   (01900) 823579
*"Avoiding all the usual pitfalls of veggie food", the cooking at this
"famous" Lakeland spot offers "excellent flavours and textures";
the setting – in the panelled dining room of a Georgian house –
similarly eschews herbivorous cliché.* / **Sample dishes:** Lebanese pancake
with roasted red onion; mushroom & chestnut coulibiac; banana & honey ice
cream terrine. **Details:** next to Cockermouth Castle; 9.30 pm; D only, closed
Mon & Sun; no Amex & no Switch; no smoking; children: 5+.

COLCHESTER, ESSEX   3–2C

Warehouse   £ 23
12 Chapel St North CO2 7AT   (01206) 765656
*"Popular, busy bistro" – it can be "crowded" – located in a converted
town-centre chapel, offering a "consistent" and "well served"
brasserie menu.* / **Sample dishes:** smoked haddock Florentine; roast duck
breast with cassis sauce; vanilla & butterscotch millefeuilles. **Value tip:** set 2/3-
crs L & Sun L £6.95/£8.95. **Details:** 10 pm; closed Sun D; no smoking area.

COLERNE, WILTS   2–2B

Lucknam Park   £ 66   A
SN14 8AZ   (01225) 742777
*The "excellent" surroundings – a beautiful Georgian house at the end
of a mile-long drive – are the undoubted draw here; the modern
British cooking is "expensive" for what it is.* / **Sample dishes:** foie gras
salad with peach Tatin; spring lamb with garlic courgettes; chocolate fondant.
Value tip: set 3-crs Sun L £25. **Details:** 6m NE of Bath, 10 mins from M4
J17; 9.30 pm; D only, ex Sun open L & D; jacket & tie; no smoking; children:
12+ at D. **Accommodation:** 41 rooms, from £180.

COLSTON BASSET, NOTTS   5–3D

Martins Arms Inn   £ 39   A
School Ln NG12 3FD   (01949) 81361
*The "great surroundings" of this venerable and "cosy" pub, complete
with panelled dining room, help to make it a favoured destination;
results from the ambitious menu are "inconsistent".* / **Sample
dishes:** pickled trout & tomato compote; roast pork with parsnip purée; mocha
panna cotta. **Details:** 9.30 pm; closed Sun D; no Amex; children: 14+.

COMPTON, SURREY   3–3A

Withies   £ 34   A
Withies Ln GU3 1JA   (01483) 421158
*"Always a high standard of food and service" and a "special"
ambience make this smart hostelry a consistent recommendation;
summer visitors can also enjoy the garden.* / **Sample dishes:** fresh crab
with papaya; roast duckling with peach sauce; crème brûlée. **Details:** 10 pm;
closed Sun D.

CONGLETON, CHESHIRE   5–2B

Swettenham Arms   £ 23
CW12 2LF   (01477) 571284
*It's "worth going out of your way" for this village pub's "consistent"
and "high-quality" British grub, at "reasonable prices".* / **Sample
dishes:** mango & prawns; venison & juniper berry casserole; summer pudding.
Details: behind church; 9.30 pm; no smoking area.

CONSTANTINE, CORNWALL

Trengilly Wartha Inn £ 34 🅰★

Nancenoy TR11 5RP (01326) 340332

A "truly exceptional" pub restaurant whose "stylish" setting contributes to its "lovely atmosphere" (as do the "good wines and whiskies"); the Gallic cooking is "original", "innovative" and "tasty". / **Sample dishes:** scallop mousse on linguini; sea bass with olives & plum tomatoes; strawberry & rosemary sorbet. **Details:** 1m outside village; 9.30 pm; closed Sat L & Sun L; no smoking. **Accommodation:** 8 rooms, from £68.

CORK, CO CORK, EIRE

Ivory Tower IR £ 35 ★★

Exchange Buildings, 35 Princes St (021) 2274 665

Seamus O'Connell's "immensely creative" International/eclectic fare causes some to claim this restaurant as one of the "best in the British Isles"; according to your disposition, the atmosphere is "lovely and relaxed" or "rather irritatingly New Agey". / **Sample dishes:** nigiri sushi; blackened swordfish & banana ketchup; strawberry saffron. **Details:** 10 pm; no Amex & no Switch.

CORSE LAWN, GLOUCS

Corse Lawn Hotel £ 40 ★

GL19 4LZ (01452) 780771

This leafily-located "country house hotel, with bistro and restaurant" has a name for its "good food and flavours", and – notwithstanding a couple of reports this year of "uninspiring" performances – once again generally received a very positive overall press. / **Sample dishes:** char-grilled squid & rocket salad; veal with wild mushroom risotto; lemon tart & lemon ice cream. **Value tip:** set 2/3-crs L £14.95/£16.95 (Sun £17.95). **Details:** 5m SW of Tewkesbury on B4211; 9.30 pm; no smoking. **Accommodation:** 19 rooms, from £100.

COTEBROOK, CHESHIRE

Fox & Barrel £ 25

Forest Rd CW6 9DZ (01829) 760529

"Original" dishes – "imaginative, for a pub" – makes this "very friendly" spot a "good-value" choice. / **Sample dishes:** tuna & crab fishcake; stir-fried strips of pork tenderloin; ice cream. **Value tip:** set 3-crs Sun L £10.25. **Details:** on A49 NE of Tarporley; 9 pm; closed Mon D; no Amex; no smoking.

COXWOLD, N YORKS

Fauconberg Arms £ 23 🅰★

YO61 4AD (01347) 868214

"Excellent home-cooking" makes this "wonderfully situated" pub, in the Hambleton Hills north of York, a popular destination. / **Sample dishes:** salmon & roast sea trout mousse; chicken & mushroom millefeuille; chocolate marquise. **Details:** 8:30 pm; closed Mon D in winter; no Amex & no Switch. **Accommodation:** 4 rooms, from £55.

CREIGAU, MID GLAMORGAN

Caesars Arms £ 28

Cardiff Rd CF4 8NN (029) 2089 0486

An "excellent display of food" is a feature at this "very good pub/brasserie" where "fresh and tasty" dishes are "perfectly cooked" and served in a "pleasant atmosphere". / **Sample dishes:** Bajan fishcakes; fillet of beef Alicia; strawberry millefeuille. **Value tip:** set 2-crs L £5 (Sun £6.95). **Details:** 2m from M4, J34; 10.30 pm; closed Sun D.

The Bear £ 32 Ⓐ

High St NP8 1BW (01873) 810408

"Wonderful Welsh lamb" is the kind of trusty, traditional fare which makes this splendid, "rustic" coaching inn – on the marketplace – a classic "good Sunday lunch" destination; service can become overstretched. / **Sample dishes:** *scallops with bacon & leek risotto; Welsh lamb with sweet potato mash; char-grilled pineapple.* **Details:** *NW of Abergavenny on A40; 9.30 pm; closed Sun D; children: 7+.* **Accommodation:** *38 rooms, from £61.*

Nantyffin Cider Mill £ 31 Ⓐ★★

Brecon Rd NP8 1SG (01873) 810775

"Excellent local fare" (including "great game"), "imaginatively" cooked, combines with "good beers and wines", "charming" service and "unusual surroundings" to make eating here a "very enjoyable" experience. / **Sample dishes:** *smoked chicken & bacon ravioli; spinach & Ricotta tart with herb crumb topping; tiramisu.* **Details:** *on A40 between Brecon & Crickhowell; 9.30 pm; closed Mon; no smoking area.*

The Sun Inn £ 22 ★

LA8 8LA (01539) 821351

"Excellent local food, home-cooked" and served at keen prices helps ensure that this "gorgeous" village pub is usually "full of locals, walkers and visitors". / **Sample dishes:** *smoked & fresh salmon roulade; fillet of sea bass; sticky toffee pudding.* **Details:** *on B5284 between Kendal & Bowness-on-Windermere; 9 pm; no Amex; no smoking.*

The Punch Bowl £ 28 ★

LA8 8HR (01539) 568237

Eminent Lakes gastropub, where, despite the odd complaint that it is "relying on its reputation", most praise "metropolitan food at parochial prices", made from "first-rate ingredients". / **Sample dishes:** *tuna salad niçoise; breast of barbary duck; chocolate brownie.* **Value tip:** *set 2/3-crs set L £6.95/£8.95 (Sun £9.95/£11.95).* **Details:** *off A5074 towards Bowness on Windermere, turn right after Lyth Hotel; 8.45 pm; closed Mon in winter; no Amex; no smoking.* **Accommodation:** *3 rooms, from £57.50.*

Bear & Ragged Staff £ 30 ★

Appleton Rd OX2 9QH (01865) 862329

"Very good-quality pub grub"– with a Gallic spin – makes this 14th-century hostelry, leafily located just outside Oxford, a top local choice. / **Sample dishes:** *chicken satay; meatballs with herbed mash; chocolate fudge cake.* **Value tip:** *set 3-crs Sun L £6.95.* **Details:** *up Cumnor Hill, turn right at Vine Pub, then left after post office; 9.30 pm.*

Ostlers Close £ 37 ★

25 Bonnygate KY15 4BU (01334) 655574

The husband-and-wife team at this "small and intimate" Gallic restaurant produces "impeccable" results from "fresh, local ingredients", and at "reasonable prices" too. / **Sample dishes:** *seared scallops with asparagus; roast venison with wild mushroom sauce; lemon coconut tart & coconut ice cream.* **Details:** *9.30 pm; closed Mon, Wed L, Thu L & Sun; no smoking; children: 6+.*

The Peat Inn £ 45 A★★

KY15 5LH (01334) 840206

*For over a quarter of a century, "intense and precise fish and game cookery" (with "no concessions to fashion") and "the best-value wine list in the UK" have made David and Patricia Wilson's "elegantly simple" converted coaching inn a "haven of quality food, without pretentiousness". / **Sample dishes:** roast scallops with pea purée; lamb & duck cassoulet with flageolet beans; trio of caramel desserts. **Value tip:** set 3-crs L £19.50. **Details:** at junction of B940 & B941, SW of St Andrews; 9.30 pm; closed Mon & Sun. **Accommodation:** 8 rooms, from £135.*

DALTON, N YORKS 8–3B

Travellers Rest £ 30

DL11 7HU (01833) 621225

*"Another village pub turned into a small restaurant by a young couple"; it's an "attractive" place, whose Gallic patron offers an "imaginative" menu. / **Sample dishes:** grilled black pudding with smoked trout mousse; pan-fried magret of duck; apple tarte with cinnamon ice cream. **Details:** 8m N of Scotch Corner on A66; 9.30 pm; closed Sun; no Amex.*

DARTINGTON, DEVON 1–3D

Cott Inn £ 30 A★

TQ9 6HE (01803) 863777

*"Above-average food, served in a fine rural setting" makes this splendid and justifiably well-known pub (with its "roaring fires" in winter) a "tasteful" and "friendly" retreat — "if you can find a table, that is". / **Sample dishes:** warm duck salad; rack of lamb; chocolate mousse. **Details:** straight up hill from mini-roundabout by Cider Press Centre; 9.30 pm; no smoking. **Accommodation:** 6 rooms, from £65.*

DARTMOUTH, DEVON 1–4D

Carved Angel £ 55 ★

2 South Embankment TQ6 9BH (01803) 832465

*"Lovely food with inspired use of ingredients" (in particular "wonderful fresh fish, simply cooked") has long made this "unassuming", "brightly lit" harbourside dining room (with open kitchen) a famed destination; since the recent departure of one of the chef/patrons, however, there have been a concerning number of reports of "surprisingly ordinary" cooking. / **Sample dishes:** duck, pork & pistachio terrine; brill with sorrel & cucumber spaghetti; pineapple tarte Tatin. **Value tip:** set 2-crs L £22.50. **Details:** opp passenger ferry pontoon in Dartmouth; 9.30 pm; closed Mon & Sun D; no Amex; no smoking.*

DEDHAM, ESSEX 3–2C

Le Talbooth £ 42

Gun Hill CO7 6HP (01206) 323150

*This long-established Constable Country fixture, "beautifully sited on the river, in a medieval timber-frame house", is "well known internationally", so no one's surprised that its "good, if not extraordinary" cooking is a touch "pricey"; some, though, do find that an "unwelcoming" attitude contributes to a "disappointing" overall experience. / **Sample dishes:** foie gras terrine with figs; roast venison with mulled wine fruits; banana cheesecake. **Value tip:** set 2/3-crs set L £16.50/£19. **Details:** 5m N of Colchester on A12, take B1029 towards Dedham; 9.30 pm; closed Sun D in winter. **Accommodation:** 10 rooms, from £150.*

Darleys on the River   £ 37   A★

Darley Abbey Mill DE22 1DZ   (01332) 364987
*Especially if you can get "the view from the window seat across the
weir", this former mill is a "great" place to eat; the modern British
cooking is "gorgeous" – make sure you leave space for puddings,
as they're "a work of art".* / **Sample dishes:** *pan-fried asparagus;
tournedos of beef with Stilton rarebit; bittersweet chocolate tart.* **Value tip:**
set 2/3-crs set L & Sun L £12.50/£14.50. **Details:** *2m N of city centre by
River Derwent; 10 pm; closed Sun D; no smoking.*

DINGLE, CO KERRY, *EIRE*   10–4A

Beginish   IR £ 40   ★

Green St   (066) 915-1588
*"Fantastic fresh seafood" is the highlight of the "contemporary Irish
menu" served at this "friendly", "family-run" establishment, in a
Georgian terraced house.* / **Sample dishes:** *capers & horseradish cream;
crab claws with garlic butter; sticky toffee pudding.* **Details:** *10 pm; closed
Mon; closed Dec to mid-Mar; no Switch; no smoking.*

Doyle's Seafood Bar   IR £ 30   ★★

4 John St   (066) 915 1174
*"Great seafood" – "the best in Ireland cooked to perfection, straight
from the trawlers" – has won a huge reputation for this "totally
relaxed" townhouse restaurant; to date the 1998 change of hands
seems to have led to little in the way of diminished enthusiasm.*
/ **Sample dishes:** *crabcakes; West Coast seafood platter; ice cream,
chocolate delight.* **Details:** *9.30 pm; D only, closed Sun; closed Nov to mid-
Mar; no Switch; no smoking area.* **Accommodation:** *8 rooms, from IR £40.*

DISLEY, CHESHIRE   5–2B

Copperfield   £ 35

49-53 Buxton Old Rd SX12 2RW   (01663) 764333
*"Great food and a family atmosphere", supported by "friendly and
helpful service", make this village restaurant a "superb" local
stand-by.* / **Sample dishes:** *peach & prawn salad; crispy duck
with cherries; lemon meringue.* **Details:** *9.30 pm; closed Mon & Sun D;
no Amex & no Switch.*

DODDISCOMBSLEIGH, DEVON   1–3D

Nobody Inn   £ 23   A★★

EX6 7PS   (01647) 252394
*"Well and truly off the beaten track", it may be, but this "archetypal
country pub" in its "beautifully peaceful setting" is "worth getting lost
for"; it gets consistent and enthusiastic support for its "wonderful,
tasty grub" (including fifty "fabulous local cheeses") and its "array of
over a thousand wines and whiskies" – and all at "reasonable prices",
too!* / **Sample dishes:** *roasted salmon; chicken & ham in mustard sauce; hot
spiced bread pudding.* **Details:** *9 pm; closed Mon & Sun; no smoking area;
children: 14+.* **Accommodation:** *7 rooms, from £52.*

DORCHESTER, DORSET   2–4B

Mock Turtle   £ 25

34 High West St DT1 1UP   (01305) 264011
*This "expensive but reputable" establishment in a converted rectory
has "attentive" staff who deliver some "unexpectedly impressive"
Anglo-French cooking.* / **Sample dishes:** *Portland crab parcel; lamb cutlet
with chilli pepper salsa; crème brûlée with strawberries.* **Details:** *9.30 pm;
closed Mon L, Sat L & Sun; no smoking area.*

Fleur de Lys   £ 18   🄐
9 The High St OX10 7HH   (01865) 340502
*The ambience of this "village pub" – with its "wooden beams",
"real fire" and "nice, canalside location" – is its special strength;
that's not to decry the food, however, which is "simple" and
"well priced". / **Sample dishes:** mushrooms with garlic dip; peppered steak;
lemon tart. **Details:** opp Dorchester Abbey; 9.30 pm; in winter, no Sun D;
no Amex; no smoking area.*

DORKING, SURREY   3–3A

Partners   £ 41   🄐
2-4 West St RH4 1BL   (01306) 882826
*"Beautiful" and "heavily beamed", this "recently refurbished"
medieval building is a rare beast down Surrey way – it offers a
"romantic" environment in which to enjoy "a good choice of modern
British cuisine" that's not just "good to look at" but also "delicious to
eat". / **Sample dishes:** Cornish crab with guacamole & chilli; peppered
English lamb; apricot, hazelnut & cinnamon bavarois. **Value tip:** set 2-crs
L £14.50. **Details:** 10 pm; closed Sun; no smoking area.*

DUBLIN, CO DUBLIN, *EIRE*   10–3D

In keeping with its reputation as a 'good-time' destination,
the Irish capital has a thriving restaurant scene. It is one
which has been boosted by the city's booming economy
over the last few years.

A major difference from London – reflecting a history
which until recently involved more emigration than
immigration – is that ethnic restaurants are by-and-large
incidental to the city's appeal (not, as in London,
fundamental to it). Most restaurants of real note cook with
a style which in England would be called 'modern British',
with more traditional establishments being heavily
French-influenced.

Patrick Guilbaud is the restaurant which wears Dublin's
culinary crown as far as the Michelin men are concerned,
but reporters are more impressed with its rival, *Peacock Alley*. Mentioned in foodie despatches are
Jacob's Ladder, the out-on-a-limb *Thorntons* and the
excellent-value *Mermaid Café*. For an emphasis on
traditional grandeur rather than cutting-edge cuisine,
Le Coq Hardi is the place, or alternatively the less expensive
L'Ecrivain (though its current re-fit may change matters
somewhat).

As everywhere, reporters' favourites tend not to be places
where the emphasis is solely on the food. The very
atmospheric *La Stampa* is many people's top tip for a
Big Night Out, while (though the cooking is, in fact, good)
Roly's Bistro is fashionable Dublin's smart, everyday brasserie.
Hipsters with celebration in mind head to the über-trendy
Clarence Hotel.

Ballsbridge is the smartest of Dublin's inner-suburbs and has a number of fashionable establishments offering good quality. Temple Bar is the best known touristy area, but – just like London's Covent Garden – few of its addresses are worth remembering.

(UK readers who habitually rely on a Switch card should note that it cannot be used in the Republic.)

Clarence Hotel, Tea Rooms   IR £ 43   𝔸★★
6-8 Wellington Quay D2   (01) 670 7766
*"First-rate everything" wrings a string of superlatives from reporters for the "stylish", if vaguely sepulchral, dining room of this ultra-hip (U2-backed) hotel; there are "sublime" results to be had from the "exciting" menu, and enjoyment is aided by notably reasonable pricing. / Sample dishes: grilled beef salad; roast hake with aubergine & tomato; strawberry & vanilla meringue. **Details:** 10 pm; closed Sat L & Sun L; no Switch; no smoking area.*

Cooke's Café   IR £ 45   𝔸
12 South William Street D2   (01) 679 0536
*In-crowd Cal-Ital café, by the impressive Powerscourt Centre; results may be thought "mediocre", especially given the vertiginous prices; (upstairs, the Rhino Room – separate kitchen – wins full marks for effort on the décor front). / Value tip: stick to the set 2/3-crs L & D £14.50/£18. **Details:** 10 pm; no Switch; no smoking area.*

Le Coq Hardi   IR £ 60   𝔸
35 Pembroke Rd D4   (01) 668 9070
*John and Catherine Howard are much in evidence at their long-serving establishment, in a "beautiful" Ballsbridge Georgian house; the cooking, strongly rooted in the French classics, is "fabulous" for many, but the odd "let-down" is also noted. / Sample dishes: Clonakilty black & white pudding; Coq Hardi smoked haddock; crème brûlée. **Details:** nr Lansdowne Park; 10.30 pm; closed Sat L & Sun; no Switch.*

L'Ecrivain   IR £ 40   ★
109 Lower Baggot St D2   (01) 661 1919
*"A real winner"; chef-patron, Derry Clarke's modern Irish cooking "has maintained high standards" at this convivial establishment – a favoured business lunching venue; as we go to press, the place is about to emerge from a major expansion into a neighbouring building – let's hope the "consistent quality" emerges unscathed. / Sample dishes: prawns in provençale sauce; John Dory with chilli sauce; crème brûlée. Value tip: set 2/3-crs L £13.50/£16.50. **Details:** opp Bank of Ireland; 11 pm; closed Sat L & Sun; no Switch; no smoking area; children: welcome if well-behaved.*

Elephant & Castle   IR £ 31   𝔸
18 Temple Bar D2   (01) 679 3121
*"Totally unpretentious" (a rarity in Temple Bar), this "casual" diner's key strength is its "great", "relaxed" atmosphere; "efficient and friendly" staff serve "simple", "satisfying" staples. / Sample dishes: spicy chicken wings; sliced steak & ginger vinaigrette; banana split. **Details:** 11.30 pm; no Switch; no smoking area; no booking.*

Jacob's Ladder   IR £ 37   ★
4-5 Nassau Street D2   (01) 670 3865
*"Overlooking Trinity College's grounds", this rather serious first-floor venture is "as yet gloriously undiscovered"; supporters say it's "simply out on its own", thanks to its "imaginative use" of "excellent-quality ingredients". / Sample dishes: caramelized scallops; honeyed & peppered breast of duck; rhubarb & ginger soufflé. **Details:** 10 pm; closed Mon & Sun; no Switch; no smoking area.*

Juice   **IR £ 24**

73-83 South Great Georges St D2   (01) 475 7856
An "innovative" veggie menu, a "trendy" and "relaxed" vibe and
"welcoming" service win much praise for this "affordable" café/bar,
to the north of Temple Bar. / **Sample dishes:** stuffed vine leaves;
Thai chicken curry; raspberry & hazelnut torte. **Details:** opp Globe pub;
11.30 pm; no Switch; no smoking area.

The Lobster Pot   **IR £ 40**   ★

9 Ballsbridge Terrace D4   (01) 668 0025
Turn up without a reservation at the locked front door of this very
characterful, long-established Ballsbridge fixture and it may be some
time before they notice and let you in; it may be "pricey", but the fish
is "excellent". / **Sample dishes:** dressed crab; turbot; death by chocolate.
Details: 10.30 pm; closed Sat L & Sun; no Switch; no smoking area; children:
4+ after 8pm.

Mao   **IR £ 26**   ★

2-3 Chatham Rw D2   (01) 670 4899
"Interesting", "very reasonably priced", "Asian/fusion" cooking and
a "colourful", "bright and airy" style make this "funky" café, off
Grafton Street, a big hit. / **Sample dishes:** chilli squid; Indonesian special
fried rice; lime & cardamon cheesecake. **Details:** 11 pm; no Amex
& no Switch; no booking.

Mermaid Café   **IR £ 36**   ★★

69-70 Dame Street D2   (01) 670 8236
Fabulous, "tasty and different", cooking belies the almost Spartan
setting of this "wonderful" café-style restaurant, on the fringe of
Temple Bar; laid-back but professional service and an interesting wine
list complete the package. / **Sample dishes:** antipasti; aromatic seafood
casserole; ginger chocolate cake. **Details:** nr Olympia Theatre; 10.30 pm;
no Amex & no Switch; no smoking area.

101 Talbot Street   **IR £ 25**   🅰★

100-102 Talbot St D1   (01) 874 5011
"There's always something imaginative" on the "wholesome",
"very reasonably priced" Middle Eastern-inspired menu at this quirky
venture, a short step from O'Connell street. / **Sample dishes:** smoked
haddock & spinach pie; goat's cheese & polenta lasagna; poached pears with
shortbread. **Details:** nr Abbey; 11 pm; D only, closed Sun; no Switch;
no smoking.

Patrick Guilbaud   **IR £ 78**   ★

Merrion Hotel, 21 Upper Merrion St D2   (01) 676 4192
"Michelin-heaven"; "expertly judged" modern French cooking,
"matched by faultless service" can make the dining room of this
august hotel "a joy"; predictably it's punishingly "expensive", though,
and – despite the airy surroundings and the benefit of an outside
terrace – the atmosphere can seem rather "dead"; "2000-bin wine
list. / **Sample dishes:** lobster ravioli with curry oil; roast pigeon with Bunratty
mead; assiette gourmande aux chocolats. **Value tip:** set 2-crs L £22.
Details: opp government buildings; 10.15 pm; closed Mon & Sun; no Switch;
no smoking area.

Peacock Alley   **IR £ 67**   ★★

Fitzwilliam Hotel, 119 St Stephen's Grn D2   (01) 677 0708
"You leave poor but happy" from Conrad Gallagher's flagship venture,
now installed in the Fitzwilliam Hotel – our reporters top foodie rave
in the Irish capital; "truly creative" cooking is "prepared to perfection"
and "presented with panache". / **Sample dishes:** roasted scallops;
beef daube with basil mash; chocolate tart & cappuccino ice cream.
Details: 10.30 pm; no Switch; no smoking area; children: 12+.

Roly's Bistro
IR £ 34 A★★

7 Ballsbridge Terr D4 (01) 668 2611

"Brilliant", "really buzzy", and "bustling" bistro/brasserie "in prosperous Ballsbridge", which owes its enormous popularity to the "exceptional value" of its modern Irish cooking, and the fact that it "gets everything right without being smug about it". / Sample dishes: crispy duck spring roll; pan-fried Dublin Bay prawns with chilli; vanilla crème brûlée. Value tip: set 3-crs L £12.50. Details: nr American Embassy; 9.45 pm; no Switch; no smoking area.

La Stampa
IR £ 39 A

35 Dawson St D2 (01) 677 8611

"Enter via a deceptive 'someone's house' entrance, through a narrow hall, then, BANG, a cathedral-like dining room"; the "superb atmosphere" of this "buzzing" 19th-century ballroom makes it reporters' most popular Dublin venue; generally, it's a good all-rounder, but the odd "poor show" on the food front is not unknown. / Sample dishes: Ricotta with red pepper tapenade; spiced duck with noodles, coriander & spring onion; bitter chocolate, raspberry bavarois & raspberry ice cream. Value tip: set 2/3-crs early eve £14.50/£17.50. Details: off St Stephens Green; midnight; closed Sat L & Sun L; no Switch; no smoking.

Thorntons
IR £ 57 ★

1 Portobello Rd D8 (01) 454 9067

"A wonderful oasis of quality, flavour and style", this canal-side venture justifies the trek north of the city-centre to sample Kevin Thornton's "lovely blend of classical and modern" cooking; service, though, can be "rather overbearing". / Sample dishes: foie gras & scallops with cep sauce; roast suckling pig; iced nougat parfait & orange sauce. Value tip: set 3-crs Sun L £24. Details: 2m S of city centre; 11 pm; closed Mon, Tue L, Wed L, Thu L, Sat L & Sun; no Switch; no smoking.

Tosca
IR £ 28 A

20 Suffolk St D2 (01) 679 6744

"Good" and "inexpensive" tapas, "gracious" service and a "trendy", atmosphere help keep this central café, near Trinity College, very "busy". / Sample dishes: mushroom & Gorgonzola crostini; roast duck confit; sticky toffee pudding. Value tip: set 2-crs L £6.95. Details: N end of Grafton St; 11.30 pm; no Switch.

DUNDRUM, CO DOWN
10–2D

Bucks Head
£ 27 A

77-79 Main St BT33 0LU (01396) 751868

This "excellent village restaurant displays a touch of class with both food and wine" (which you might not guess, looking at it from the outside); a conservatory and a changing display of art for sale are among its attractions. / Sample dishes: cockles & mussels; steak & Guinness pie; bitter chocolate tower. Value tip: set 3-crs Sun L £12.50. Details: 3m N of Newcastle; 9 pm; Oct-Mar, closed Mon.

DUNGARVAN, CO WATERFORD, *EIRE*
10–4C

The Tannery
IR £ 33 A★

10 Quay St (058) 45420

This "airy" and "comfortable", "loft-style" restaurant, in a "disused tannery/warehouse", has an "owner/patron with bright ideas and talent"; reports are limited, but all speak of a "good all-round experience". / Sample dishes: marinated lamb salad; grilled sea-bream with peperonata; gratin of strawberries. Details: nr Old Library; 10 pm; closed Mon & Sun; no Switch; children: only until 8.30pm.

DUNKELD, PERTHS

9–3C

Kinnaird House £ 58 A★

Kinnaird Estate PH8 0LB (01796) 482440

"This must be the most understated luxury – food, wine and setting – in the whole of the UK", say supporters of this 'big house' set in a vast estate; it's a "pity about the cost, but the value is there". / **Sample dishes:** scallops wrapped in pancetta; roast loin of venison; cappuccino of Scottish strawberries. **Value tip:** set 2/3-crs set L £19.50/£24. **Details:** 8m NW of Dunfield, off A9 onto B898; 9.30 pm; during Jan & Feb, closed Mon, Tue, & Wed; no Amex & no Switch; jacket & tie; no smoking; children: 12+. **Accommodation:** 9 rooms, from £345.

DUNKINEELY, CO DONEGAL, *EIRE*

10–1B

Castle Murray House IR £ 40 A★

St John's Pt (073) 37022

"Lovely scenery", "very friendly" service and, not least, a talented "French chef/patron" have made this "beautiful" clifftop hotel a destination of note. / **Sample dishes:** grilled seafood brochettes; roast lamb in pepper sauce; lemon sorbet with vodka. **Details:** 1m along main road to Donegal; 9.30 pm; D only, ex Sun open L & D; no Amex & no Switch; no smoking area. **Accommodation:** 10 rooms, from IR £30.

DUNVEGAN, ISLE OF SKYE

9–2A

Three Chimneys £ 39 A★★

Colbost IV55 8ZT (01470) 511258

An "out-of-the-way" location that's well worth seeking out; Shirley and Eddie Spear's "converted crofter's cottage" delivers "excellent home-made food" ("very good seafood platters" being particularly recommended), washed down with selections from the "good wine list and range of malts". / **Sample dishes:** roast mallard with scallops; beef with mushroom & Madeira sauce; rhubarb compote & ginger ice cream. **Value tip:** set 2/3-crs L £11.95/£16.50. **Details:** 5m from Dunvegan Castle on B884 road to Glendale; 9.30 pm; closed Sun L, closed mid Jan-mid Feb; no smoking. **Accommodation:** 6 rooms, from £140.

DUNWICH, SUFFOLK

3–1D

The Ship £ 22 A★

IP17 3DT (01728) 648219

Thanks to its "perfect post-walk pub food" ("awesome fish and chips", in particular), it can be "hard to get a table" at this "cosy" establishment; "outstanding beer" and a "fresh sea breeze in the garden" complete the package. / **Sample dishes:** Camembert parcels; fish & chips; plum & coconut crumble with custard. **Details:** on coast 7m S of Southwold; 9.30 pm; no Amex; no smoking; no booking at L. **Accommodation:** 3 rooms, from £51.

DURHAM, CO DURHAM

8–3B

Bistro 21 £ 32 A★

Aykley Heads House DH1 5TS (0191) 384 4354

"The best restaurant in Durham", this "consistently lovely" offshoot of Newcastle's 21 Queen Street is justly popular for its "superb" and "very varied" modern British cooking (at "reasonable bistro prices"), its "beautifully converted farmhouse setting" and its "excellent wine list". / **Sample dishes:** field mushroom fritters; lamb cutlets & mint bérnaise; rhubarb & macaroon crumble. **Details:** nr Durham Trinity School; 10.45 pm; closed Sun; no smoking.

DUXFORD, CAMBS   3–1B
Duxford Lodge   £ 35   ★
Ickleton Rd CB2 4RU   (01223) 836444
*"Quiet competence" distinguishes this "expertly managed" hotel
near the aircraft museum; its restaurant offers "high-quality" and
"inventive" cooking "at reasonable prices"; "it can be busy at
weekends".* / **Sample dishes:** salad of smoked duck with mango salsa;
char-grilled sirloin steak with red onion sauce; bitter chocolate mousse.
Value tip: set 2/3-crs L £10/£14, set 3-crs Sun L £16.95.
Details: 9.30 pm; closed Sat L; no smoking area. **Accommodation:**
15 rooms, from £85.

EAST BARNET, LONDON   3–2B
Mims   £ 30
63 East Barnet Rd EN4 8RN   (020) 8449 2974
*The "adventurous", slightly wacky Anglo-French cooking at this
"ordinary-looking" Barnet spot is "variable" but "can be very good";
the décor ("plastic") and service ("slow" or "curt") do it few favours.*
/ **Sample dishes:** roast quail with herbed noodles; grilled black bream; pears
& almond tart. **Details:** between Cockfosters and High Barnet; 11 pm;
closed Mon & Sat L; no Amex & no Switch; no smoking area.

EAST BOLDON, TYNE & WEAR   8–2B
Forsters   £ 29   ★
2 St Bedes Station Rd NE36 0LE   (0191) 519 0929
*"Small" and "friendly" "husband-and-wife" outfit, where "excellent"
Anglo-French cooking is served in a "simple and elegant" style.*
/ **Sample dishes:** grilled king prawns with Thai sauce; roast duck in red wine
sauce; vanilla crème brûlée. **Details:** on A184 between Sunderland
& Newcastle; 9.30 pm; D only, closed Mon & Sun; no smoking; children: 7+.

EAST GRINSTEAD, W SUSSEX   3–4B
Gravetye Manor   £ 60   𝔸★
Vowels Ln RH19 4LJ   (01342) 810567
*This family-run Elizabethan manor house, set in "amazing" grounds
is claimed by some as "the best hotel and restaurant in south east
England"; it may be "a little old-fashioned" but is "always a delight",
thanks to its "fabulous" cooking and the "impeccable" general
standards.* / **Sample dishes:** feuilleté of English asparagus; saddle of rabbit
with Denhay ham; baked lemon soufflé pudding. **Value tip:** set 3-crs L £28.
Details: 2m outside Turner's Hill; 9.30 pm; no Amex or Diners; jacket & tie;
no smoking; children: babes in arms and children 7+. **Accommodation:** 18
rooms, from £175.

EAST LINTON, E LOTHIAN   9–4D
Drovers Inn   £ 30
5 Bridge St EH40 3AG   (01620) 860298
*"Careful preparation of a varied menu" can make this bistro-style
dining room behind a pub an "unexpected find"; "good seafood" is
particularly recommended.* / **Sample dishes:** smoked scallops with
horseradish; rabbit with caraway roast vegetables; brown sugar meringue with
fudge sauce. **Details:** by A1; 9.30 pm; no smoking area.

EAST WITTON, N YORKS   8–4B
Blue Lion   £ 32   𝔸★★
DL8 4SN   (01969) 624273
*The "marvellous stone-flags-and-log-fire atmosphere" sets the
scene at this "absolutely outstanding" pub, "beautifully located in the
Dales"; there's "excellent", "very imaginative" cooking to be had too
(which some feel is "better in the bar than in the restaurant").*
/ **Sample dishes:** gravadlax with caperberries; roast lamb with herb mash
& shallots; sultana crème caramel. **Details:** between Masham and Leyburn on
A6108; 9.30 pm; no Amex. **Accommodation:** 12 rooms, from £75.

A sprinkling of new openings raises the perennial hope that Auld Reekie's restaurant scene may finally match the expectations one has of the Scottish capital. Despite having a relative wealth of good, mid-range options, the city still, however, lacks a gastronomic standard-bearer. The most popular all-rounder is the *blue bar café* – a successful, modern-day brasserie any city would be happy to call its own, but not, perhaps, a hugely memorable destination.

Two of the biggest 'names' – the atmospheric *Witchery by the Castle* and the trendy-going-on-contrived, *Atrium* – are more notable for their atmosphere than their cooking, and the newly-opened *Tower* seems set to go the same way. The style and prices of the Balmoral's grand *Number One* limit its appeal mainly to expense-accounters. Top tips for those paying their own way must therefore be the New Town's *36 Restaurant* and Leith's *Vintners Rooms* (which have one of the most interesting settings of any UK city restaurant).

Mid-range places tend to be good and comfortable but in a rather dated, traditional idiom (such as *Café St-Honoré*, *Martin's* and *Winter Glen*). The contrast presented by the *blue bar café* and by upmarket deli-café *Valvona & Crolla* may account for what some might say is their disproportionate popularity.

Leith has become well-known as a going-out destination, and boasts a number of lively waterside bistros, such as *Fisher's*, *The Shore* and *Skippers*. Away from the waterfront, *Fitz(Henry)* is a commendable modern place in a converted warehouse

Thanks perhaps to the university and the number of younger visitors, there are a number of good less expensive places, many of them vegetarian, such as *Black Bo's*, *Hendersons* and the Indian *Kalpna*.

Ann Purna   £ 22   ★
44-45 St Patrick's Sq EH8 9ET   (0131) 662 1807
"Subtly flavoured, home-cooked veggie dishes" make this *"small, simply furnished"* spot one of the better Indians in town. / **Sample dishes:** deep-fried puri bread with chutney; aubergine Ann Purna; kulfi. **Value tip:** set 3-crs L £4.95. **Details:** 10.45 pm; closed Sat L & Sun L; no Amex & no Switch; no smoking; children: 10+.

The Atrium   £ 41
10 Cambridge St EH1 2ED   (0131) 228 8882
For most reporters, Edinburgh's most talked-about modern restaurant is a *"seductive"* venue, providing *"creative"* cooking in a *"fabulous"*, trendy setting; there are still many refuseniks, however, who deride *"pretentious cooking, glibly served in a designer bunker"*. / **Sample dishes:** seared scallops & crab salad; roast rump of lamb & garlic mash; vanilla panna cotta. **Value tip:** set 2-crs L £14. **Details:** by Usher Hall; 10.30 pm; closed Sat L & Sun.

Black Bo's   **£ 26**

57-61 Blackfriar's St EH1 1NB   (0131) 557 6136
"Candlelit veggie restaurant" (adjoining a busy bar), whose
"delicious food" and *"good prices"* appeal especially to the student
market. / *Sample dishes:* pistachio & tofu roulade; cashew & carrot balls
with smoked cheese; crêpes with cherries. *Details:* 10.30 pm; closed Sun L;
no Amex.

blue bar café   **£ 32**   ★★

10 Cambridge St EH1 2ED   (0131) 221 1222
"Imaginative, freshly prepared food with flair", and at *"terrific prices"*,
makes the Atrium's simpler, minimalist offshoot a much, much better
bet than its parent; it's *"noisy"*, though, and has *"hard chairs"* –
"a place to eat and run, rather than linger". (A Glasgow sibling
opened as we went to press, in Mitchell Ln, G1, tel 0141-204 2404.)
/ *Sample dishes:* salmon ballantine; mallard & black pudding; banana
& chocolate chip soufflé. *Value tip:* set 2/3-crs set L £9/£12. *Details:* by
Usher Hall; midnight, Sun & Mon 11 pm.

Le Café St-Honoré   **£ 34**   𝔸★

34 NW Thistle St Ln EH2 1EA   (0131) 226 2211
"A French brasserie using Scottish ingredients", tucked away
(quite romantically) in the New Town; it offers a *"quality menu
and excellent service"* and is a favoured business lunching venue.
/ *Sample dishes:* squid, scallops & chorizo; lamb with garlic confit & spinach;
crème brûlée. *Details:* 10 pm; closed Sat L & Sun - closed 2 weeks Easter,
1 week October; no smoking in dining room.

La Cuisine d'Odile   **£ 13**   ★

13 Randolph Cr EH3 7TT   (0131) 225 5685
"French home cooking with flair and intelligence" makes the cafe
in the basement of the Institut Français a good spot for a light lunch
(especially on a sunny day when you can sit on the terrace);
BYO – small corkage charge. / *Sample dishes:* green split pea soup;
smoked haddock with red pepper coulis; choc'Odile. *Details:* L only; closed
Mon & Sun.

Daniel's   **£ 22**   ★

88 Commercial St EH6 6LX   (0131) 553 5933
"Great Alsatian food" wins enthusiastic backing for Daniel Vencker's
"extremely personal" venture – a simple, but tastefully decorated
café/restaurant. / *Sample dishes:* Alsacienne pizza; Fisherman's Wharf
casserole; bread & butter pudding. *Value tip:* set 2/3-crs set L £4.95/£5.95.
Details: 10 pm; no Amex; no smoking area.

The Dial   **£ 28**   𝔸★

44 George IV Br EH1 1EJ   (0131) 225 7179
"Personal service from the owner" and a *"minimalist, cool, relaxed
interior"* are among the features which make this quirky Old Town
basement notable; that's not to detract from the menu *"which
changes daily to use the freshest produce available"*, to excellent
effect. / *Sample dishes:* wild mushrooms; fillet of Aberdeen Angus with
Camembert glaze; honey & Glayva parfait. *Value tip:* set 3-crs L £7.95, set 3-
crs early eve £9. *Details:* 11 pm.

Dubh Prais   **£ 31**   ★

123b High St EH1 1SG   (0131) 557 5732
"Tiny", cosily dated basement, off the Royal Mile, offering a *"special"*
spin on traditional Scottish grub. / *Sample dishes:* West Coast broth;
Aberdeen Angus beef with pickled walnuts; white peach cheesecake.
Value tip: set 2/3-crs L £7.50/£9.50. *Details:* opp Holiday Inn Crowne Plaza
Hotel; 10.30 pm; closed Mon, Sat L & Sun.

Fisher's Bistro　　　　　　　　**£ 30**　　　Ａ★

1 The Shore EH6 6QW (0131) 554 5666
"Uncomplicated" and *"welcoming"* seafood bistro near the Leith
waterfront, with a *"fun"* and *"relaxed"* atmosphere; it generally
serves the *"freshest fish"* (though the odd *"amateurish"* off-night is
also reported). / **Sample dishes:** fishcakes with lemon & chive mayonnaise;
roast fillet of halibut; Grand Marnier torte. **Details:** opp Malmaison Hotel;
10.30 pm.

(Fitz) Henry　　　　　　　　**£ 37**　　　Ａ★

19 Shore Pl EH6 6SW (0131) 555 6625
"Very good", *"creative"* cooking (*"especially fish"*) and *"an
eccentrically loveable mein host"* makes this *"funky"* Leith
warehouse-conversion an *"exciting"* choice for many reporters.
/ **Sample dishes:** rabbit confit with cocoa purée; roast lamb with chick peas
& spinach; crème caramel & lavender tuile. **Value tip:** set 2/3-crs L £12/£16.
Details: 10 pm, Fri & Sat 10.30 pm; closed Sun.

Henderson's　　　　　　　　**£ 16**　　　★

94 Hanover St EH2 1DR (0131) 225 2131
"Good food, reasonably priced and convenient for Princes Street" is a
formula which has made this *"excellent"* self-service basement veggie
(with characterful, if *"passé"*, '70s-style décor) a popular stand-by for
more than three decades. / **Sample dishes:** lentil & apricot soup; wild
mushrooms with nuts & basil; dried fruits with ginger. **Value tip:** set 2-crs
L £3.95. **Details:** 10.30 pm; closed Sun except during Festival;
no smoking area.

Indian Cavalry Club　　　　　　**£ 23**

3 Atholl Pl EH3 8HP (0131) 228 3282
"Colonial-style" Indian, providing a smart, yet *"fun"* environment,
and popular for informal business lunches; many approve of the
"jolly good" food, though no one pretends it's cutting-edge stuff.
/ **Sample dishes:** chicken pakora; curried mushrooms in coconut milk;
kulfi. **Details:** between Caledonian Hotel & Haymarket Station; 11.30 pm;
no smoking area.

Indigo (yard)　　　　　　　　**£ 28**

7 Charlotte Ln EH2 4QZ (0131) 220 5603
With its *"trendy and unusual"* design, this lively bar/restaurant is a
'scene' as much as it is a place to eat, and it can get *"very noisy"*;
culinarily speaking, breakfast/brunch is the time to visit. / **Sample
dishes:** moules marinière; beef in peppercorn sauce with straw potatoes;
banoffi crumble. **Value tip:** set 3-crs D £15. **Details:** just off Queensferry St;
10 pm; no smoking area; children: 12+.

Kalpna　　　　　　　　　　**£ 22**　　　★★

2-3 St Patrick Sq EH8 9EZ (0131) 667 9890
"Taking traditional curries into a different realm" – the *"unusual"*,
"beautifully cooked and presented" vegetarian cooking at this
unpretentious spot near the University makes it the most popular
Indian in town. / **Sample dishes:** lentil & basmati rice pancake; mixed Thali;
pistachio kulfi. **Details:** 10.30 pm; closed Sat L & Sun; no Amex & no Switch;
no smoking.

Khushi's　　　　　　　　　　**£ 16**　　　★

16 Drummond St EH8 9TX (0131) 556 8996
"Family-run", *"down-to-earth"* Indian canteen of over 50 years'
standing, popular with students from the nearby university; it offers
"tasty and satisfying" dishes at bargain-basement prices (aided by the
BYO policy). / **Sample dishes:** vegetable pakora; lamb bhuna; kulfi.
Details: 9 pm; closed Sun; no credit cards.

Martins   **£ 41**   ★
70 Rose St, North Ln EH2 3DX   (0131) 225 3106
*"Everything a trendy London restaurant is not", Gay & Martin Irons's
"hidden-away" New Town fixture offers "fantastic food all round",
with an emphasis on the organic (and some of the "best cheeses in
Edinburgh"); service is "very attentive", but the atmosphere –
generally seen as "relaxed" and "inviting" – strikes some as a touch
"funereal".* / **Sample dishes:** *mussel, fennel & red pepper risotto; pan-fried
halibut with herbed couscous; Scottish & Irish cheeses.* **Details:** *between
Frederick St & Castle St; 10 pm; closed Mon & Sun; closed 4 weeks at
Christmas; no smoking; children: 7+.*

Number One   **£ 53**   ★
The Balmoral Hotel, 1 Princes St EH2 2EQ   (0131) 557 6727
*Despite a local reputation almost justifying the name, this hotel
basement generates surprisingly little survey feedback (due, perhaps,
to the rather flat ambience); a good-value set menu makes lunch the
best time to hazard a trip.* / **Sample dishes:** *duck foie gras & confit
terrine; Dover sole with langoustines, scallops & oysters; mango & papaya with
white chocolate sorbet.* **Value tip:** *set 2/3-crs L £16.95/£19.95.*
Details: *above Waverley Station; 10 pm, Thu–Sat 10.30 pm; closed Sat L &
Sun L; no smoking area.* **Accommodation:** *189 rooms, from £215.*

Passepartout   **£ 21**   Ⓐ
24 Deanhaugh St EH4 1LY   (0131) 332 4476
*There's "a good experience all round" to be had in this "intimate,
warm and welcoming" basement bistro, designed "in the style of a
railway booking office and carriage"; simple cooking is "well cooked
and presented", and there's a "good range of reasonably priced
wines".* / **Sample dishes:** *chorizo & red onion tart; salmon in filo pastry;
chocolate & ginger cheesecake.* **Details:** *10 pm; D only; no Amex; no smoking;
children: 14+.*

Pâtisserie Florentin   **£ 10**
8 St Giles St EH1 1PT   (0131) 225 6267
*These twin cafés (this original near the Castle, and the Stockbridge
branch at 5 NW Circus Pl) are the discerning burgher's top choice
for coffee and a bun; the original also offers late-night sustenance;
no alcohol.* / **Sample dishes:** *soup of the day; jacket potato with chilli
& cheese; pastries.* **Details:** *11 pm, Fri-Sat 1 am; no credit cards;
no smoking area; no booking.*

Le Petit Paris   **£ 21**   Ⓐ
38-40 Grassmarket EH1 2JU   (0131) 226 2442
*"A true taste of French cooking in the heart of the Scottish capital";
this "welcoming" and "straight-forward" bistro – with its "hustle and
bustle" environment – offers "uncomplicated" dishes at "reasonable"
prices.* / **Sample dishes:** *garlic snails; French black pudding in calvados
sauce; crêpes.* **Details:** *bottom of Edinburgh Castle; 11 pm.*

Sept   **£ 22**   Ⓐ
7 Old Fishmarket Cl EH1 1RW   (0131) 225 5428
*With its "great location", hidden away down an Old Town alley,
this atmospheric bistro offers simple cooking at "good-value prices".*
/ **Sample dishes:** *smoked venison; Salmon fillet; banana crêpes.*
Value tip: *set 2/3-crs set L £5/£6.* **Details:** *10.30 pm, Fri 11.30 pm;
no smoking area.*

The Shore   **£ 29**   Ⓐ
3-4 The Shore EH6 6QW   (0131) 553 5080
*Though there is "good food and service" at this Leith bar-restaurant
near the waterfront, the "lovely" atmosphere is perhaps the most
important ingredient in ensuring it's often "busy".* / **Sample
dishes:** *grilled garlic shrimps; grilled sea bass with pesto; plum & almond tart.*
Value tip: *set 3-crs L £14.25.* **Details:** *10 pm; no smoking in dining room.*

Skippers £ 29 A★

1a Dock Pl EH6 6UY (0131) 554 1018

*There are only words of praise for this "quirky" bistro near the
waterfront – not only does it have "great atmosphere", but it offers
"wonderful fresh fish" at "unbelievably reasonable prices".
/ **Sample dishes:** Skippers' fishcakes; Dover sole with smoked salmon
butter; pear & almond flan. **Details:** 10 pm; closed Sun.*

Stac Polly £ 34

29-33 Dublin St EH3 6NL (0131) 556 2231

*"Scottish-kitsch" ("strictly for the Burberry-wearing classes")
New Town fixture, whose traditional-with-a-twist cooking is known
for its "good value for money" if not, perhaps, for more cutting-edge
qualities; there's another, less grand branch at 8-10 Grindlay St
(tel 229 5405). / **Sample dishes:** haggis filo pastry parcels; Scottish salmon
mousse; bramble & Mascarpone crème brûlée. **Details:** 10.30 pm; closed Sun
L; no smoking area.*

Susies £ 16

51-53 West Nicholson St EH8 9DB (0131) 667 8729

*"Healthy" and "filling" veggie fare at "very reasonable prices" is
served at this studenty café, by the University; it's licensed, but you
can BYO. / **Sample dishes:** spinach & chick pea soup; moussaka with
Greek salad; pear frangipane flan. **Details:** nr Museum of Scotland; 9 pm;
closed Sun; no credit cards; no smoking at L; need large group to book.*

36 Restaurant £ 38 A★

36 Great King St EH3 6QH (0131) 556 3636

*An "elegant" Georgian setting and "exciting modern interior" provide
a "sophisticated" location for some "culinary masterpieces", at this
New Town dining room – arguably the highpoint of gastronomy in the
Scottish capital. / **Sample dishes:** sweetcorn & sorrel soup; chicken with
olive & thyme polenta; passion fruit syllabub. **Value tip:** set 2/3-crs L & Sun L
£16.50/£19.50. **Details:** 10 pm; closed Sat L; no smoking.
Accommodation: 15 rooms, from £245.*

Tinelli's £ 22 ★

139 Easter Rd EH7 5QA (0131) 652 1932

*"Traditional Italian", popular – mainly with locals, thanks to its
obscure location – for its quality cooking and "warm and friendly"
service. / **Sample dishes:** bruschetta with melted Dolcelatte; veal & Parma
ham in marsala wine sauce; zabaglione. **Details:** 11 pm; closed Sun;
no Switch.*

The Tower £ 33 A

Museum of Scotland, Chambers St EH1 1JF (0131) 225 3003

*A "knockout location overlooking Edinburgh Castle" has made the
Atrium's new sibling, atop the Museum of Scotland, instantly notable;
the place is "still bedding in", and while many pronounce it "a class
act", offering "imaginative" modern British cooking and an
"excellent" wine list, others say it "should be better". / **Sample
dishes:** duck liver with toasted brioche; pork fillets with apricot & spinach;
lemon tart with ginger & lime sorbet. **Value tip:** set 2-crs early eve £12.
Details: 11 pm; no smoking.*

Valvona & Crolla £ 27 ★

19 Elm Row EH7 4AA (0131) 556 6066

*"Real southern Italian food, with top ingredients not mucked about
with" makes it "well worth the inevitable queue" to lunch in the rear
café of what fans consider "the best Italian deli outside Italy"; sceptics
admit the place is good, but think it a mite over-egged (though no one
disputes the brilliant bargain of being able to choose any wine from
their "amazing selection" with £3 corkage). / **Sample dishes:** antipasti;
fried fresh squid, prawns & white fish; panna cotta. **Details:** at top of Leith
Walk, 500m from the Playhouse Theatre; 5 pm; closed Sun; no smoking.*

Vintners Rooms £ 38 A★

The Vaults, 87 Giles St EH6 6BZ (0131) 554 6767

*One of the UK's more interesting restaurant settings (a 17th-century wine warehouse with impressive plasterwork) is only one element of the package offered by this Leith favourite (located some way from the waterfront); the "unusual and very good" cooking is "generously portioned" and "reasonably priced". / **Sample dishes:** scallops with rhubarb; venison in bitter chocolate sauce; prune, almond & armagnac tart. **Value tip:** set 2/3-crs L £11/£14.50. **Details:** 10.30 pm; closed Sun; closed first 2 weeks in Jan; no smoking in dining room.*

The Waterfront £ 28 A

1c Dock Pl EH6 6LU (0131) 554 7427

*With its "lovely ambience, especially in the conservatory" and "extensive and modestly priced" wine list, this "brilliantly located" Leith wine bar is a "reliable" choice, serving a "good range of seafood dishes". / **Sample dishes:** Catalan-style monkfish; roast sea bass with scallops; vanilla cheesecake with raspberries. **Details:** 9.30 pm; no smoking area; children: 5+.*

The Witchery by the Castle £ 47 A

352 Castlehill EH1 2NF (0131) 225 5613

*With its "Gothic movie" setting, this "extraordinary" spot, in the heart of historic Edinburgh, has long been the city's most impressive restaurant venue; the more you succumb to the place's "very romantic" charms, the more forgiving you are likely to be of cooking which some find "pretentious", "fussy" and "overpriced". / **Sample dishes:** whisky cured salmon with capers; fillet of Aberdeen Angus beef; pistachio ice cream parfait. **Value tip:** set 2-crs L & early eve £9.95. **Details:** next to Whisky Heritage Centre; 11.30 pm. **Accommodation:** 2 rooms, from £195.*

ELY, CAMBS 3–1B

Old Fire Engine House £ 30

25 St Mary's St CB7 4ER (01353) 662582

*Perhaps inevitably, after over 30 years, the Jarman's "comfortable" and "warm" restaurant – famous for its "traditional English cooking" – seems to be dating; it is undoubtedly a "homely and useful place", but while die-hard fans proclaim the food "superb", there are also many who find it "very ordinary" nowadays. / **Sample dishes:** seasonal vegetable soup; steak & kidney pie; syllabub. **Details:** next to Cathedral; 9 pm; closed Sun D; no Amex; no smoking area.*

EMSWORTH, HANTS 2–4D

36 on the Quay £ 46 ★

47 South St PO10 7EG (01243) 375592

*This smartly decorated establishment doesn't just benefit from a "charming seaside location" – it's a "very good all-rounder" (if "very expensive"), and offers "memorable" modern British cooking. / **Sample dishes:** salmon & tomato salad; sea bass with black olive mash; lemon parfait with strawberries. **Value tip:** set 2/3-crs L £16.50/£19.50. **Details:** 10 pm; closed Mon L, Sat L & Sun; no smoking in dining room.*

EPWORTH, N LINCS 5–2D

Epworth Tap £ 28

DN9 1EU (01427) 873333

*A "small", "rustic" and "hospitable" wine bar offering "exceptional" wines from an "extensive" list, to accompany fare that's "simple", but "well cooked and tasty"; "fish and game are very good". / **Sample dishes:** parsnip & pear soup; venison casserole with star anise; pannetone bread & butter pudding. **Details:** 3m from M180 Junction; 9 pm; D only, open Wed-Sat only; no Amex; no smoking.*

ESHER, SURREY
3–3A

Good Earth
£ 36   ★

14-18 High St KT10 9RT   (01372) 462489

"Consistent" and *"efficient"* Chinese, which may now be rather long in the tooth, but remains *"classy"* and *"shows attention to detail"*; it's *"not cheap"*, but it is still *"worth it"*. / **Sample dishes:** spring rolls; Mandarin chicken; toffee banana. **Details:** 11 pm.

ETON, WINDSOR
3–3A

Eton Wine Bar
£ 32

82-83 High St SL4 6AF   (01753) 855182

"Reasonably priced food in a pleasant atmosphere" and *"helpful service"* compensate for the *"discomfort of the church pew seating"* at this useful, if not hugely ambitious, spot. / **Sample dishes:** tomato & artichoke tart; red mullet with sun-dried tomato mash; poached pears with praline. **Details:** 5 mins walk from Windsor Castle; 10.30 pm, Fri & Sat 11 pm.

EVERSHOT, DORSET
2–4B

Summer Lodge
£ 48   A★

Summer Lodge DT2 0JR   (01935) 83424

"It's worth the hundred mile drive each way", says at least one devotee of this *"lovely"*, *"relaxing"* country house hotel (with a *"beautiful walled garden"*) in the heart of Hardy country; the *"superb"* cooking *"never fails to delight"*, and staff *"go out of their way to help"*. / **Sample dishes:** pan-fried scallops; pink-roast Dorset lamb; honey-roasted pears. **Value tip:** set 3-crs L £13.75 (Sun £19.75). **Details:** 12m NW of Dorchester on A37; 9 pm, Fri-Sat 9.30 pm; jacket; no smoking in dining room; children: 7+ at D. **Accommodation:** 17 rooms, from £165.

EVESHAM, WORCS
2–1C

Riverside
£ 26   A★

The Parks, Offenham Rd WR11 5JP   (01386) 446200

An *"idyllic"* spot, enjoying *"gorgeous view of the Avon"*; it wins praise both for its *"discreet but attentive"* service, and for its *"beautifully prepared and presented"*, modern British cooking. / **Sample dishes:** Parmesan risotto with pancetta; char-grilled duck with garlic mash; raspberry & strawberry tartlet. **Details:** 9 pm; closed Mon L & Sun; no Amex; no smoking. **Accommodation:** 7 rooms, from £80.

EXETER, DEVON
1–3D

Double Locks Pub
£ 22   A★

Canal Banks, Alphington EX2 6LT   (01392) 256947

A *"very peaceful setting"* and a *"wide-ranging"* menu ensure a *"brilliant local reputation"* for this canal-side pub, near the centre of town. / **Sample dishes:** soup of the day; feta cheese & spinach pie; carrot cake. **Details:** through Marsh Barton industrial estate, follow dead-end track over bridges to end of towpath; 10.30 pm; no Amex; children: welcome, except in bar.

FALMOUTH, CORNWALL
1–4B

Pennypots
£ 44   ★★

Maenporth Beach TR11 5HN   (01326) 250251

"Glorious", *"fresh"* fish, *"stunningly presented"*, and a *"spectacular"* view *"overlooking a small bay"*, make this *"formal"* seaside restaurant a destination deserving its reputation. / **Sample dishes:** roast crab & smoked salmon with melon; beef with wild mushrooms & Madeira jus; bread & butter pudding. **Details:** 3m from Falmouth; 9.30 pm; D only, closed Sun & Mon, closed for 4 weeks in winter; no smoking before 10 pm.

Read's　　　　　　　　　　　　　　　　£ 37
Mummery Court ME13 0EE (01795) 535344
*Despite its "dreadful" exterior, most reporters still find it worth
braving this "eccentric" venture in its "unfortunate building"
(a former supermarket) on account of the "very good" English
cooking; there were, however, a couple of disappointments this year.
/ **Sample dishes:** omelette Arnold Bennett; turbot with onion mash & shrimps;
passion fruit soufflé. **Details:** 2.5m SW of Faversham, by A2 & Brogdale Road;
9.30 pm; closed Mon & Sun.*

General Tarleton　　　　　　　　　　　£ 31　　　★
Boroughbridge Rd HG5 0PZ (01423) 340284
*The "top-notch bar food" – "worth the detour from the A1" –
is marginally preferred to that in the "comfortable" dining room
of this roadside inn; there's a "good choice of specials", using
"fresh local produce", and service is "knowledgeable". / **Sample
dishes:** crispy duck salad with lardons; roast halibut fillet; chocolate marquise.
Value tip: set 3-crs Sun L £17.50. **Details:** 9.30 pm; Mon-Sat closed L, Sun
closed D; no jeans; no smoking. **Accommodation:** 14 rooms, from £60.*

Three Main Street　　　　　　　　　　£ 35　　　★
3 Main St SA65 9HG (01348) 874275
*"Excellent cooking" making "nice use of local ingredients" wins
consistent praise for this "attractive" town-centre Georgian house;
many also praise the "relaxed" atmosphere and the "attention to
detail from people who really care", but there are those who say
there's "no fun" to be had at a place which "is trying a bit too hard
to be a 'serious' restaurant". / **Sample dishes:** sea bass with pink
peppercorns; roast pigeon with celeriac remoulade; sweet goat's cheese tart
with plums. **Details:** 9 pm; closed Mon & Sun; no credit cards; no smoking.
Accommodation: 3 rooms, from £60.*

The Griffin Inn　　　　　　　　　　　£ 30
TN22 3SS (01825) 722890
*"Very good pub grub" in a "delightful olde-world atmosphere" – and
"good beer", too – make this "attractively located" spot a "popular"
destination, especially on a sunny day. / **Sample dishes:** crab & saffron
ravioli; guinea fowl with butternut squash risotto; almond, lemon & Ricotta cake.
Details: off A272; 9.30 pm; closed Sun D except May-Sep; no smoking area.
Accommodation: 8 rooms, from £65.*

Flitwick Manor　　　　　　　　　　　£ 53　　　Ⓐ
Church Rd MK45 1AE (01525) 712242
*There's some "surprisingly good food" to be had at "one of the UK's
lesser-known country house hotels"; its setting, though – in a lovely
small manor house – is much of the attraction. / **Sample dishes:**
pan-fried sea scallops; medallions of Angus beef; hot strawberry jam soufflé.
Details: from M1, first left within village; 9.30 pm; no smoking; children: 5+.
Accommodation: 17 rooms, from £135.*

Crannog £ 30 🇦

Town Pier PH33 7NG (01397) 705589

"A beautiful location overlooking Loch Linnhe" is the undoubted strength of this *"friendly"* establishment in a converted smokehouse; most find it *"one of the best seafood restaurants"*, too, though there are also dissenters who think it *"mediocre"*. / **Sample dishes:** *langoustines in wild garlic butter; scallops in saffron & dill cream; Crannog cream heather cake.* **Details:** *10 pm; no smoking area.*

Inverlochy Castle £ 58 🇦

Torlundy PH33 6SN (01397) 702177

"Everything is of the best", say reports on this baronially splendid fortress, in the shadow of Ben Nevis; cooking is in grandly traditional style, with prices to match. / **Sample dishes:** *foie gras with smoked apple purée; grilled turbot with scallop mousse; mango & lime parfait.* **Details:** *off A82; 9.15 pm; closed Jan-mid Feb; jacket & tie; no smoking; children: 12+.* **Accommodation:** *17 rooms, from £250.*

Chequers £ 30 ★

SG8 7SR (01763) 208369

This *"friendly"* and *"pleasant"* village pub is *"well known"* (to generations of Cambridge students, anyway) and offers *"imaginative"* cooking, using *"fresh"* ingredients, including lots of fish. / **Sample dishes:** *Jerusalem artichoke soup; Moroccan beef tagine; rhubarb crumble.* **Details:** *on B1368 between Royston & Cambridge; 10 pm; no smoking area.*

The Fox & Goose £ 32 🇦★

IP21 5PB (01379) 586247

"All the better for being in such an unlikely place" (*"in the middle of rural Suffolk"*), this very *"jolly"* and *"atmospheric"* old inn provides *"really fresh"* and quite *"eclectic"* cooking. / **Sample dishes:** *smoked salmon with crispy bacon; Scotch entrecôte with peppercorn sauce; sticky toffee pudding.* **Value tip:** *set 2/3-crs L £9.50/£12.50 (Sun £13.50).* **Details:** *9.30 pm; closed Mon & Tue; no Amex; no smoking.*

Bottle and Glass £ 34

HP17 8TY (01296) 748488

"Very pleasant" and rambling thatched pub/restaurant, specialising in fish and seafood. / **Sample dishes:** *moules marinière; Normandy seafood & lobster sauce; sticky toffee pudding.* **Details:** *on A418 between Thame & Aylesbury; 9.30 pm; closed Sun D.*

Glasgow remains the UK's most vital and interesting restaurant city outside of London. The magnificent Art Deco *Rogano's* – one of the few restaurants in the UK which has what might be described as a real history – stands as a symbol of a long history of dining out. Further attractions include other distinguished traditional-style places (*The Buttery*, *City Merchant*), quirky institutions (*Café Gandolfi*, *Stravaigin*, *Two Fat Ladies*), ambitious and competent modern British restaurants (*Yes!*, *78 St Vincent's*) and decent ethnics (see comments on Indians below, and also *Amber Regent* and the *Thai Fountain*). It seems very appropriate that the city was the cradle for the UK's trendy, fast-expanding townhouse hotel chain, Malmaison, which began at *One Devonshire Gardens* – still undoubtedly the grandest place in town.

Indian restaurants are a particular strength, with *Ashoka*, *Mother India*, *Mr Singh's India*, *Killermont Polo Club* and *The Spice of Life* among the leading participants in a vibrant scene.

Glasgow is one of the few cities outside London where the restaurant-scene is fast-changing enough that there is always some hot new place which the locals are chattering about. *Gamba* was the newcomer which caught most attention from reporters this year.

Visitors benefit from the compactness of the area in which many establishments are found. Glasgow's grid-patterned city centre has long been a going-out destination, and many of the top places are to be found there. The West End – a smart inner suburb near the University – is the other key area. Its cute Ashton Lane is home to a famous and much-cherished, if perhaps now somewhat dated, institution, the *Ubiquitous Chip*.

Air Organic £ 31 ★
36 Kelvingrove G3 7SA   (0141) 564 5200
"Good quality, and attention to detail" are helping to make this wackily designed organic specialist *"a new favourite"*; its *"extensive but very fresh menu"* (which includes some *"good sushi"*) is *"interesting, without being tricksy"*. / **Sample dishes:** *vegetable tempura; beef fillet with wild mushrooms; passion fruit sorbet.* **Details:** *11 pm; no smoking area.*

Amber Regent £ 29 ★
50 West Regent St G2 2QZ   (0141) 331 1655
Smart, city-centre oriental offering *"authentic"* *Chinese cooking of* *"consistent"* *quality.* / **Sample dishes:** *hot & sour soup; beef in mandarin sauce; banana fritter.* **Value tip:** *half-price main courses Mon & Tue and Wed-Sat L.* **Details:** *500m from Central Station; 11 pm; closed Sun.*

Ashoka   **£ 26**   A★

19 Ashton Ln G12 8SJ   (0800) 454817

*"It's difficult to go wrong" with this popular local chain of Indians, which wins praise for "fantastic" and "unusual" dishes and "good humoured" and "well informed" staff – "you need to book, even during the week"; we've only listed one of the busier branches (confusingly, the original, at 108 Elderslie St, tel 0141-221 1761, is not run by the group that own the rest of the chain). / **Sample dishes:** mushroom pakoras; chicken tikka masala; orange & lemon sorbet. **Details:** behind Hillhead underground station; midnight; closed Sun L.*

Babbity Bowster   **£ 28**   A

16-18 Blackfriar's St G1 1PE   (0141) 552 5055

*"Good-quality fare for a pub", "good value", "good beer", "good wine", "good art on the walls", "good with friends on a Sunday afternoon"... there are few 'cons' attached to this celebrated Merchant City pub, which occupies a fine Adam-style building; (see also Schottische). / **Sample dishes:** fish soup; roast monkfish with mushrooms & lardons; pear & almond tart. **Details:** 9.30 pm; closed Sat L & Sun D.*

The Belfry   **£ 25**   ★

652 Argyle St G3 8UF   (0141) 221 0630

*"Good-value" food from "an imaginative menu" using "mainly Scottish ingredients", together with "well priced" wines, make a consistent success of this "very cosy" spot, in the basement of The Buttery (see also). / **Sample dishes:** seared scallops with fettuccine; beef & foie gras with shallot purée; hazelnut tart with poached pears. **Value tip:** set 2/3-crs L £12.95/£14.95. **Details:** M8 J19, down St Vincent St, under Kingston Bridge; 10.30 pm; closed Sat L & Sun.*

Buttery   **£ 47**   ★

652 Argyle St G3 8UF   (0141) 221 8188

*A location convenient for the SECC and a comfortable, panelled interior make this clubby institution a particular business favourite; there was surprisingly little feedback on it this year, but such as we received was positive. / **Sample dishes:** cauliflower soup with Roquefort; Scottish beef with porcini; chocolate pancakes with mint cream. **Value tip:** set 2/3-crs L £14.95/£16.95. **Details:** M8, J19, down St Vincent St, under Kingston Bridge; 10.30 pm; closed Sat L & Sun; no smoking area.*

The Cabin   **£ 30**   A★

996-998 Dumbarton Rd G14 9NJ   (0141) 569 1036

*This "camp" distant-West End oddity is a restaurant "like no other"; it offers "a fantastic night out, guaranteed" – "when the fat lady sings", it does not mean that your dinner is at an end; rather surprisingly, the food is "out of this world", and you can BYO for fairly modest corkage. / **Sample dishes:** crayfish soup with mussels; roast venison with pink grapefruit; soufflé with poached fruit. **Value tip:** set 2/3-crs L £10/£12. **Details:** close to Clyde Tunnel (N side); 10 pm; Fri-Sat 8 pm; closed Mon & Sun.*

Café Gandolfi   **£ 25**   A★

64 Albion St G1 1NY   (0141) 552 6813

*"An old Glasgow favourite, for good reason" – this "lively" Merchant City café/restaurant, with its distinctive woody décor, provides a "warm and perfect environment" in which to enjoy some "robust" cooking. / **Sample dishes:** Scottish fish stew; smoked venison with gratin dauphinois; lemon tart. **Details:** nr Tron Theatre; 11.30 pm; no Amex; no smoking area.*

Café India £ 22 ★

171 North St G3 7DA (0141) 248 3818

*Some 'café' – this 450-seater is generally lauded for its good-value Indian cooking, especially from the buffet. / **Sample dishes:** butterfly prawns; garlic chilli chicken; almond kulfi. **Details:** nr Charing Cross, next to Mitchell Library; midnight; no smoking area.*

City Merchant £ 31 A★

97-99 Candleriggs G1 1NP (0141) 553 1577

*"Busy – and no wonder", this no-nonsense Merchant City institution packs 'em in, thanks to its "beautiful" food; fish and seafood from the blackboard menu is particularly recommended. / **Sample dishes:** scallops with couscous & chilli; venison with black pudding mousse; crannachan ice cream. **Value tip:** set 3-crs L & early eve £12.75. **Details:** 11 pm; closed Sun L; no smoking area; children: 6+.*

Crème de la Crème £ 28

1071 Argyle St G3 8LZ (0141) 221 3222

*This "Indian restaurant in an old cinema" (in a slightly grotty location) is a somewhat 'different' venue which fans say "combines Glasgow humour with a celebratory atmosphere"; a good-value buffet is a special attraction. / **Sample dishes:** vegetable samosa; garlic & chilli chicken; kulfi. **Details:** nr Scottish Exhibition Centre; 11 pm; closed Sun L; no smoking area.*

Cul de Sac £ 33

44 Ashton Ln G12 8SJ (0141) 334 4749

*De luxe diner (under the same ownership as the nearby Puppet Theatre), offering a "simple menu, with innovative ideas for pasta, crêpes and so on", in comfortable surroundings. / **Sample dishes:** chicken livers & parsnips in port jus; salmon fillet with Thai cream sauce; caramel & banana cheesecake. **Value tip:** set 2/3-crs set L £7.95/£9.95. **Details:** 11 pm, Fri-Sat midnight.*

Gamba £ 36

225a West George St G2 2ND (0141) 572 0899

*"Fish is king" at this "stylish" new Milngavie seafood restaurant, which numbers "friendly" staff and a "first-class wine list" among its supporting attractions. / **Sample dishes:** halibut with crème fraîche; baked sea bass with grilled red peppers; pear & pistachio cheesecake. **Value tip:** set 2/3-crs L & early eve £10.95/£13.95. **Details:** 10.30 pm; closed Sun; children: 14+.*

The Inn on the Green £ 29 A

25 Greenhead St, Glasgow Green G40 1ES (0141) 554 0165

*A "friendly pianist" and a "lady singing the blues" (both of whom "take requests") contribute to the "chummy" atmosphere of this "lively" and "happy" basement; the Scottish cooking is "good" too, "especially for veggies". / **Sample dishes:** 'designer' haggis; monkfish tempura; 'cholesterol cocktail' (chocolate mousse). **Value tip:** set 2-crs L & early eve £5.95 (Sun £11.95). **Details:** 1m E of city centre on London Rd; 9.30 pm. **Accommodation:** 18 rooms, from £65.*

Kama Sutra £ 25 A

331 Sauchiehall St G2 3HW (0141) 332 0055

*"Designer", "upmarket" Indian, with "comfortable" and amusingly OTT premises opposite the Centre for Contemporary Art; the "imaginative", varied menu wins mostly praise, but is rather beside the point. / **Sample dishes:** vegetable pakora; chicken korma; chocolate fudge cake. **Details:** midnight; closed Sun L.*

Killermont Polo Club £ 25 A ★

2022 Maryhill Rd G20 0AB (0141) 946 5412

"Country house comfort and outstanding Indian food" ("totally unlike any other curry I have had") combine with "helpful" service to make this "fabulous", "light and airy" spot a very superior all-rounder; indeed, it comes "complete with resident polo team". / **Sample dishes:** tandoori king prawns; stuffed chicken with orange & saffron gravy; labe-mashook kulfi. **Details:** nr Maryhill station; 10.30 pm; closed Sun L; jacket & tie; no smoking area.

Mitchell's £ 27

157 North St G3 7DA (0141) 204 4312

"Chef/patron Angus Boyd knows what he's doing" say fans of his "small, cosy and unpretentious" bistro; at the broadly similar West End offshoot (35 Ashton Ln, tel 339 2220), dishes are prepared "in full view"; you can BYO for modest cost. / **Sample dishes:** Scottish salmon Caesar salad; fillet of beef with wild mushroom sauce; homemade gingerbread. **Value tip:** set 2/3-crs early eve £8.95/£10.95. **Details:** nr Charing Cross; 10.30 pm; closed Sat L & Sun; children: 12+.

Mother India £ 28 A ★★

28 Westminster Ter G3 7RU (0141) 221 1663

"There are many modern Indian restaurants in Glasgow, but this is the best" – reporters unanimously hail its "great curries" (both "traditional and innovative"), its "happy" staff and its "lovely, homely atmosphere"; "remember to BYO". / **Sample dishes:** aubergine pakora; ginger jeera chicken; kulfi. **Value tip:** set 3-crs L £6.95, set 2-crs early eve £7.95. **Details:** beside Kelvingrove Hotel; Sun-Thu 11 pm, Fri-Sat 11.30 pm; closed Sun L; no Amex.

Mr Singh's India £ 23 A ★

149 Elderslie St G3 7JR (0141) 204 0186

"Quality every time" and "superb service" from "handsome waiters in kilts and turbans" means "you have to book" for this "relaxing and comfortable" modern Indian restaurant, near Kelvingrove Park. / **Sample dishes:** chicken korma; chicken masala; ice cream. **Value tip:** set 3-crs L £6.95. **Details:** Charing Cross corner, next to art galleries; 10.30 pm.

Nairns ✳ £ 40

13 Woodside Cres G3 7UP (0141) 353 0707

"Trading on Nick Nairn's reputation", this townhouse-restaurant yearling, near Kelvingrove Park, became famous overnight; the feeling that it's "a rip-off" is now, however, overwhelming – a brush with TV celebrity offering insufficient compensation for "uninteresting", "badly-cooked", "poor-quality" food, served by "surly", "pushy" and "uninformed" staff. / **Sample dishes:** salmon with avocado & tomato salsa; chicken with spring onion mash; cherry clafoutis. **Value tip:** set 2/3 crs L £13.50/£17 (Sun £18.50). **Details:** nr Charing Cross; 10 pm; no smoking during D; children: 10+ at D. **Accommodation:** 4 rooms, from £90.

Oblomovs £ 20 A ★

372-374 Great Western Rd G4 9HT (0141) 339 9177

"Excellent Eastern European food" is not an oxymoron – well, not if reports on this Bohemian and "interesting" West End bistro are to be believed, at any rate. / **Sample dishes:** blinis (potato cakes); Hungarian goulash; Hungarian cheesecake. **Value tip:** set 2/3-crs early eve £5.50/£7.50. **Details:** 11.45 pm; children: only allowed before 5 pm.

One Devonshire Gardens £ 53   A★

I Devonshire Gardens G12 0UX (0141) 339 2001

This "very elegant" restaurant, in a fashionable Georgian townhouse-hotel, enjoys a "deserved reputation" for its "fantastic" cooking and "individual service"; it's undoubtedly the poshest dining room in town and, perhaps inevitably, some find it a touch "stuffy". / **Sample dishes:** *crispy duck & watercress salad; Aberdeen Angus with béarnaise sauce; apple & cinnamon soufflé.* **Value tip:** *set 2-crs L £21.* **Details:** *1.5m after leaving J17 from M8; 9.45 pm; closed Sat L; no Switch; no smoking.* **Accommodation:** *27 rooms, from £130.*

Papingo £ 32

104 Bath St G2 2EN (0141) 332 6678

The "quality and value" of the "tasty" Franco-Scottish cooking on offer at this "lively" but "well spaced" basement make it a reliable choice, if perhaps a slightly characterless one. / **Sample dishes:** *Pecorino salad with pears; Highland venison with spring cabbage & bacon; chocolate pudding with ginger Mascarpone.* **Details:** *10.30 pm; closed Sun L.*

Parmigiana £ 34

447 Great Western Rd G12 8HH (0141) 334 0686

"Consistently reliable" and "professional" traditional Italian, on the city centre's western fringe; "specials" come particularly recommended. / **Sample dishes:** *red pepper terrine with anchovy dressing; chicken stuffed with spinach & Mortadella; apple & calvados crème brûlée.* **Value tip:** *set 3-crs D £8.60.* **Details:** *at Kelvinbridge underground station; 11 pm; closed Sun.*

Puppet Theatre £ 45   A

II Ruthven Ln G12 9BG (0141) 339 8444

A "sensual, satisfying experience, offering total enjoyment" is how many see this "magical" and "intimate" series of rooms, and the "imaginative" Scottish cooking they offer; some find that "no one seemed to be pulling any strings", though, and they say that the place is "living on an unearned 'in-crowd' reputation". / **Sample dishes:** *smoked fish cannelloni; roast guinea fowl with carrot & celery confit; iced whisky & oatmeal parfait.* **Value tip:** *set 2/3-crs L £12.95/£14.50.* **Details:** *nr Ashton Ln; 10.30 pm; closed Mon & Sat L; no smoking area; children: 12+.*

Rogano £ 45   A

II Exchange Pl G1 3AN (0141) 248 4055

A "very special Art Deco interior" (replicating rooms from the Clyde-built Queen Mary), "relaxed service" and "a high quality seafood and Scottish menu" make this Glasgow "favourite" a "fantastic" choice for a night out (albeit a "very expensive" one). / Sample dishes: *scallops with peaches & bacon; monkfish with roast capsicums; crème brûlée.* **Value tip:** *set 3-crs L & Sun L £16.50; cheaper Café Rogano in basement.* **Details:** *off Buchanan St, opp Borders Books; 10 pm; no smoking before 10 pm.*

Sarti's £ 24   A★

121 Bath St G2 2SZ (0141) 204 0440

"Very busy" and "very friendly", this "Italian institution" ("combining delicatessen, café & restaurant") is, for one exile at least, "the only place to make me feel nostalgic for Glasgow"; the cooking is "basic" but "excellent" ("especially pizzas"). / **Sample dishes:** *antipasti; spinach & Ricotta pizza; crème caramel.* **Details:** *11 pm; no smoking area; no booking at L.*

Schottische £ 26 🄰

16-18 Blackfriar's St G1 1PE (0141) 552 7774
"Farmhouse-style restaurant" on the first floor of the Merchant City's
Babbity Bowster (see also) that offers *"fine Scottish produce prepared
à la française"*. / **Sample dishes:** haggis, neeps & tatties; seasonal
fish stew; steamed Scottish fruit dumpling. **Value tip:** set 2-crs L £7.50.
Details: 10.15 pm; closed Sat L & Sun D; no Switch. **Accommodation:** 6
rooms, from £65.

78 St Vincent £ 33 🄰★

78 St Vincent's St G2 5UB (0141) 221 7710
"Smart" but *"relaxed"* city-centre brasserie – in a very lofty
converted banking hall – where an *"interesting mixture"* of
"great-value" dishes is offered from a *"regularly changing menu"*.
/ **Sample dishes:** smoked salmon & peppered strawberries; scallops with
pea purée; honey parfait with caramelised figs. **Value tip:** set 2/3-crs
L £10.95/£13.95, set 2-crs early eve £9.95. **Details:** 10.30 pm, Fri & Sat
10.45 pm; closed Sun L; no smoking area.

The Spice of Life £ 23 🄰★

1293 Argyle St G3 8TL (0141) 334 0678
This upmarket Ashoka group outlet, with its Gaudi-esque décor, is a
place to *"make a night of it"*; fans say its Indian cooking offers some
"exquisite flavours". / **Sample dishes:** pakora; karahi lamb; gulab jamon.
Value tip: set 3-crs L £5.95. **Details:** midnight; closed Sat L & Sun L;
no smoking area.

Stravaigin £ 33 ★

28 Gibson St G12 8NX (0141) 334 2665
The *"broad and imaginative"* menu (*"Glasgow's most innovative"*,
say fans) is the key feature at this relaxed and simply decorated
establishment, near the University; some wonder whether it's *"resting
on its laurels"*, but most praise *"menu combinations that are unusual
and work well"*. / **Details:** 11 pm; closed Sun L; no smoking before 10 pm.

Thai Fountain £ 30 ★

2 Woodside Cr G3 7UL . (0141) 332 1599
Thanks to its *"exquisite"*, *"unusual"* and *"immaculately presented"*
cooking, this smartish Charing Cross Thai is arguably *"the best in
Scotland"* – in the absence, it must be said of much competition –
and is *"good for business meetings"*. / **Sample dishes:** chicken parcels;
green chicken curry; bananas in coconut milk. **Details:** in Charing Cross area,
by Clydesdale Bank; 11 pm; closed Sun; children: 7+.

Thirteenth Note £ 21

50-60 Kings St G1 5QT (0141) 553 1638
"Why are there not more vegan pubs?"; perhaps this one – with its
"fresh, tasty and cheap" grub and its *"lively"* (read studenty)
atmosphere – can set a trend. / **Sample dishes:** vegan sushi; red curry;
vegan cheesecake. **Details:** just off Argyle St at Trongate clock tower;
10.30 pm; no Amex; children: 18+ after 7 pm.

The Tron Bar £ 25 🄰

63 Trongate G1 5HB (0141) 552 8587
Many a trendy Glaswegian's hang-out of choice, this local favourite
(within the Tron Theatre) serves some dependable, modish cooking.
/ **Sample dishes:** smoked haddock rarebit; caramelised pork salad; citrus
sorbet & poached fruit. **Value tip:** set 2-crs early eve £8.95. **Details:**
on Trongate, by Glasgow Cross in heart of Merchant City; 11 pm; closed Sun
D if theatre is closed; no smoking area.

Two Fat Ladies £ 35 𝔸★

88 Dumbarton Rd G11 6NX (0141) 339 1944

*"Wonderful, wonderful fish dishes", "superbly cooked, from excellent ingredients", (and "great puds" too) win a dedicated following for this "tiny" but "cheery" dining room, despite its out-on-a-limb location; it's unrelated to the TV duo (which it pre-dated). / **Sample dishes:** leek, mussel & saffron broth; baked sea bass with teriyaki sauce; baked lime tart with vanilla cream. **Details:** 10 pm; closed Mon, Tue-Thu L & Sun L; no Amex.*

Ubiquitous Chip £ 43 𝔸

12 Ashton Ln G12 8SJ (0141) 334 5007

*With its "unique", "funky" setting and "bustling yet relaxed" atmosphere, this local hero is still many people's top choice for "a great night out"; the "inventive" Scottish cooking (supported by a huge and "intriguing" wine list) also has its fans, but it's "very expensive", and, for many, what was "once novel" now seems a wee bit "contrived" or "lazy". / **Sample dishes:** guinea fowl terrine; Darjeeling tea smoked salmon; raspberry parfait & amaretto zabaglione. **Value tip:** set 3-crs Sun L £16.60. **Details:** directly behind Hillhead underground; 11 pm.*

Yes! £ 41 𝔸★

22 West Nile St G1 2PW (0141) 221 8044

*"Wonderfully prepared" modern British cooking, and "excellent service" continue to win strong approval for this "relaxed" and "stylish" city-centre basement. / **Sample dishes:** haggis, neeps & tattie cake; rack of lamb with raisin mustard; baked cappuccino pudding. **Value tip:** set 2/3-crs set L £13.95/£16.95. **Details:** 10.30 pm; closed Sun.*

GLENCULLEN, CO DUBLIN, *EIRE* 10–3D

Johnny Foxes Pub IR £ 31 𝔸★

(01) 295 5647

*"The best place for a real Irish experience and meal", this "traditional (genuine) Irish pub" – "famous for seafood" – serves up "fresh", "high-quality" grub in a "buzzing", "down-to-earth" environment; it can get as "busy as hell". / **Sample dishes:** wild mussels; salmon steak; Bailey's cheesecake. **Details:** off N11, in Wicklow Hills; 10 pm; closed Sun L; no Amex; children: 18+ after 7 pm.*

GOREY VILLAGE, JERSEY

Jersey Pottery Restaurant £ 34 𝔸★

JE3 9EP (01534) 851119

*"Simple but most effective preparation of fresh seafood, in a beautiful setting" ensures that this "very pleasant, airy restaurant" is "busy" ("even if it's not cheap"). / **Sample dishes:** pan-fried scallops with butter sauce; Jersey lobster salad; torte of summer berries. **Details:** signposted from St Helier; L only, closed Sun; no smoking area.*

Village Bistro £ 32 𝔸★

Main Rd JE3 9EP (01534) 853429

*"Lively" and "very friendly" little bistro, in a converted chapel; it offers "consistently excellent" results from an "interesting" menu. / **Sample dishes:** king prawn & mushroom risotto; duck confit with haricot beans; chocolate fondant. **Value tip:** set 3-crs L £12.50 (Sun £14.50). **Details:** signposted from St Helier, next to Post Office; 10 pm; closed Mon.*

GORING-ON-THAMES, BERKS 2–2D
Leatherne Bottel £ 40   🄰

Bridleway RG8 OHS (01491) 872667
*An "idyllic" setting is the undisputed attraction of this Thameside
venture, whose "somewhat eclectic" ("pretentious") style makes for
what is otherwise a rather love-it-or-hate-it experience; the "mainly
Pacific/Med fusion" cooking is "rather expensive". / **Sample
dishes:** chicken livers with nasturtium jelly; hake with sweet ginger & white
bean cassoulet; seasonal fruits with strawberries & ice cream. **Details:** 0.5m
outside Goring-on-Thames on B4009; 9 pm; closed Sun D; children: 8+.*

GRAMPOUND, CORNWALL 1–4B
Eastern Promise £ 29

1 Moor View TR2 4RT (01726) 883033
*An "unlikely place to find a Chinese restaurant", but the cooking is of
a "high standard" and "they try to make you feel special (unusual in
Cornwall)". / **Sample dishes:** steamed king prawns in shell with garlic sauce;
crispy aromatic duck; fresh fruit platter. **Details:** between Truro & St Austell on
A390; 10 pm; D only ex Wed open L & D; no smoking area; children: 3+.*

GRANGE MOOR, W YORKS 5–1C
Kaye Arms £ 26

29 Wakefield Rd WS4 4BG (01924) 848385
*"Surprisingly imaginative and tasty food" is part of the formula
which makes this "old pub turned into a restaurant" a "very popular"
choice. / **Sample dishes:** oyster mushroom & bacon salad; roast rack of
lamb; trio of sweets. **Details:** 7m W of Wakefield on A642; 9.30 pm;
no Amex; no smoking area; children: not at D.*

GRASMERE, CUMBRIA 7–3D
Michael's Nook £ 58   🄰★

LA22 9RP (015394) 35496
*"Light and imaginative" French cooking ("simple but tastefully
presented") combines with "outstanding personal service" and an
"excellent wine list" to make this "beautifully located" country house
hotel restaurant a "very special place". / **Sample dishes:** langoustine
croustillant; quail galette with foie gras; chocolate and orange fondant.
Details: A591 Grasmere – turn right at Swan hotel; 9 pm; jacket & tie;
no smoking; children: 7+. **Accommodation:** 14 rooms, from £135, incl D.*

White Moss House £ 34   ★

Rydal Water LA22 9SE (015394) 35295
*"Consistently high standards over many years" win raves from
regulars at this "small", traditional Lakeland restaurant, for whom
"exceptional dishes (if from a limited choice)" and a position
"overlooking Rydal Water" make for "a total experience"; there
are those who find the cooking "overrated" and the setting too
"tightly packed". / **Sample dishes:** redfish soufflé; crispy roast mallard;
sticky toffee pudding with pecan sauce. **Details:** N end of Rydal Water, on
A591; 8 pm; D only, closed Sun; closed Dec to Feb; no Amex; no smoking;
children: no toddlers. **Accommodation:** 8 rooms, from £83, incl D.*

GREAT DUNMOW, ESSEX 3–2C
Starr £ 35

Market Pl CM6 1AX (01371) 874321
*This "beamed village inn" attracts quite a lot of comment, and
supporters particularly applaud its "vast choice of main courses";
service can be "patronising", though, and some feel that this is
a place which "tries to be upmarket, but fails". / **Sample dishes:**
pan-fried scallops with bacon; rack of lamb with rosemary & garlic; syrup
pudding with custard. **Value tip:** set 2-crs L £11. **Details:** to J8 M11,
then 7m E on A120; 9.30 pm; closed Sun D; no jeans; no smoking.
Accommodation: 8 rooms, from £90.*

Harry's Place £ 68 ★

17 High St NG31 8JS (01476) 561780

"Michelin star-standard cooking in a family cottage dining room" comes as a bit of a surprise at, and ensures a more-than-local following for, this ambitious modern British restaurant; it only has ten seats! / **Sample dishes:** seared king scallops; loin of venison; apple & calvados soufflé. **Details:** on B1174 N of Grantham; 9 pm; closed Mon & Sun; no Amex & no Switch; no smoking; children: 5+.

Anupan Restaurant £ 21

85 Church St WR14 2AE (01684) 573814

Some *"good quality"* Indian cooking makes this restaurant overlooking Great Malvern Priory *"popular with theatre-goers and actors"*; some find it *"a bit pricey"*, for a curry house, but *"this is hardly an area in which you are spoilt for choice"*. / **Sample dishes:** onion bhaji; chicken tikka masala; Indian sweets. **Value tip:** set 3-crs Sun L £8. **Details:** midnight; no smoking area.

Le Manoir aux Quat' Saisons £ 99 🄰★

Church Rd OX44 7PD (01844) 278881

It's not just the *"sheer artistry"* of Raymond Blanc's *"complex and subtle"* modern French cuisine which makes a visit to this *"five stars all round"* destination *"seventh heaven"* for most reporters – the *"lovely"* manor house setting and *"unrivalled"* service also play their part; needless to say, however, it's all *"very, very expensive"*, and the number of those who find the place *"a bit of a let-down"* is too large for them to be dismissed as cranks. / **Sample dishes:** langoustine macaroni & truffle jus; roast Barbary duck with tamarind sauce; pistachio soufflé with chocolate sorbet. **Value tip:** set 3-crs L £32. **Details:** off J7 M40 coming from London, A329 to Great Milton; 10.15 pm; no smoking; booking: max 8. **Accommodation:** 32 rooms, from £230.

Falkland Arms £ 23 🄰★

The Green OX7 4DB (01608) 683653

It's *"worth a visit for the building alone"*, but this *"exceptional country pub"* is also worth seeking out for its *"great home-cooking, served in generous portions"*. / **Sample dishes:** pork & mushrooms in Stilton cream; honey-glazed lamb; sticky toffee pudding. **Details:** A361 between Banbury & Chipping Norton; 11 pm; no smoking; children: 14+. **Accommodation:** 5 rooms, from £65.

White Hart £ 32 🄰★

CO9 4HJ (01787) 237250

"A London-standard restaurant with local atmosphere and local prices" should be popular anywhere – all the more so in a rural pub with a *"cosy"* setting in a 15th-century building (with *"stone floors"* and a *"big, open fire"*), *"real ales"* and *"excellent wines"*. / **Sample dishes:** goat's cheese with spiced figs; roast monkfish with haricots & tomato tart; pineapple polenta cake. **Value tip:** set 2/3-crs L £8.50/£12.25. **Details:** between Haverhill & Braintree; 10 pm; no smoking.

Café de Paris   **£ 32**

35 Castle St GU1 3UQ   (01483) 534896

*This town-centre restaurant-cum-brasserie is "very popular" locally;
at best it serves "authentic French cooking in generous portions",
but misfires are not unknown. / **Sample dishes:** French onion soup;
Marseillaise fish & seafood stew; pear tart. **Details:** 11 pm; closed Sun.*

Cambio   **£ 35**

10 Chapel St GU1 3UH   (01483) 577702

*"Slightly expensive, but high-quality" modern Italian, in "an old
beamed building" ("with very steep stairs"), on the fringe of the town.
/ **Sample dishes:** spaghetti with sun-dried tomatoes; fillet steak with
mushrooms; tiramisu. **Value tip:** set 2-crs L £9.50. **Details:** 10.30 pm, Fri
& Sat 11 pm; closed Sun; no smoking; children: not encouraged.*

La Potinière   **£ 43**   ★★

Main St EH31 2AA   (01620) 843214

*"Marvellous" and "memorable"; "like the best kind of French
provincial restaurant", David and Hilary Brown's famous rural fixture
provides an "unchanging formula" – "great personal attention",
"superlative" Scottish-French food and "a wonderful wine list"; the
set dinner menu is served at a single sitting. / **Sample dishes:** crispy
salmon with sauce vierge; honey-roast venison with roast vegetables; lemon
surprise pudding. **Value tip:** set 3-crs L & Sun L £21.50. **Details:** 17m E of
Edinburgh; 8 pm; closed Sun-Thu D, Fri L & Sat L; no credit cards; no smoking.*

Horn of Plenty   **£ 48**   𝔸★★

PL19 8JD   (01822) 832528

*"Beautiful views of the Tamar Valley" add extra lustre to this
"top-rate" establishment – a "welcoming, relaxed and elegant"
environment in which to enjoy Peter Gorton's "memorable"
modern British cooking; the wide-ranging wine list is a further plus.
/ **Sample dishes:** lemon sole tempura; sautéed beef in brandy sauce; apple
& blackcurrant crumble. **Value tip:** set 2-crs L £18.50, set 3-crs Mon D ('Pot
luck') £23.50. **Details:** 3m W of Tavistock on A390; 9 pm; closed Mon L;
no smoking; children: 13+. **Accommodation:** 8 rooms, from £115.*

Waterside Bistro   **£ 28**   𝔸

1-5 Nungate EH41 4BE   (01620) 825674

*A great waterside location makes this "friendly", well-established and
atmospheric bistro-restaurant particularly "good for lunch on a sunny
day"; it serves "good, plain food" in "large portions". / **Sample
dishes:** deep-fried haggis in whisky sauce; chicken à la maison; chocolate
& rum mousse. **Details:** 17m E of Edinburgh, on A1; 10 pm.*

Design House   **£ 31**

Dean Cl HX3 5AZ   (01422) 383242

*Support waned somewhat this year for this minimalist,
"London-comes-to-Halifax" mill-conversion; for fans, it still offers
"excellent" value, but it strikes others as "uninspiring". / **Sample
dishes:** leek & potato soup; pot roast pheasant; baked jasmine custard. **Value
tip:** set 2/3-crs L £10.95/£14.95. **Details:** 0.5m from Halifax, towards Ceeps;
10 pm; closed Mon D, Sat L & Sun D.*

HAMBLETON, RUTLAND   5–4D

Hambleton Hall   **£ 62**   𝔸★★
Hambleton LE15 8TH   (01572) 756991
"Classic, classy country house cooking" and *"unusually friendly"*
but *"truly professional"* service combine to make it a *"glorious
experience"* to visit Tim Hart's *"outstanding"* hotel, on a peninsula
surrounded by Rutland Water; yes, it's *"very expensive"*, but almost
everyone agrees that it's *"worth it"*. / **Sample dishes:** poached tails of
langoustine; gallatine of quail, Florentine ravioli; pavé of white & dark chocolate.
Value tip: set 2-crs L £19.50, Sun 3-crs L £35. **Details:** 3m E of Oakham;
9.30 pm; no smoking. **Accommodation:** 15 rooms, from £170.

HARBORNE, W MIDLANDS   5–4C

California Pizza Factory   **£ 21**
42-44 High St B17 9NE   (0121) 428 2636
"Casual and friendly" Harborne spot, *"enjoyable for both adults
and kids"*; *"great"* pizzas with *"unusual toppings"*. / **Sample
dishes:** Chinese chicken salad; barbecue pizza; New York cheesecake. **Value
tip:** set 3-crs early eve £6.95. **Details:** 10.45 pm; no Amex.

HARLECH, GWYNEDD   4–2C

Castle Cottage   **£ 30**   ★
Pen Llech LL46 2YL   (01766) 780479
This *"small hotel of character"* is tipped as *"the best restaurant in
Gwynedd"* by its fans; it's a *"cosy"*, almost *"clubby"* spot, whose
cooking makes *"gorgeous use of home-grown herbs"*. / **Sample
dishes:** grilled asparagus; roast herbed lamb; lemon posset & raspberries.
Details: nr castle; 9 pm; D only; no Amex; no smoking. **Accommodation:** 6
rooms, from £33.

HARPENDEN, HERTS   3–2A

Chef Peking   **£ 26**   ★
5-6 Church Green AL5 2TP   (01582) 769358
"Always full and bustling", this *"reliable"*, *"classic Chinese, with a
modern twist"* wins a unanimous thumbs-up. / **Sample dishes:** spring
rolls; crispy duck; toffee apple. **Details:** just off High Rd; 10.45 pm; no Switch;
no smoking area.

HARROGATE, N YORKS   5–1C

Bettys   **£ 27**   𝔸
1 Parliament St HG1 2QU   (01423) 502746
"Everyone's cup of tea!"; this *"absolute institution"* is, for many,
"the ultimate café/restaurant", thanks to its *"leisurely and relaxed"*
atmosphere and *"irresistible tea and cakes"*; it's *"pricey"*, though,
and *"queues are a problem"*. / **Sample dishes:** Yorkshire rarebit; bacon
rosti with Raclette cheese; Swiss chocolate torte. **Details:** 9 pm; no Amex
& no M/c; no smoking area; no booking.

Drum & Monkey   **£ 27**   𝔸★★
5 Montpellier Gardens HG1 2TF   (01423) 502650
"First class in every way"; *"amazingly fresh fish in a charming setting"*
has made a big name for this, *"the only real quality restaurant in
town"*, which is housed in a *"tastefully refurbished"* Victorian bar;
thanks to it's *"reliable"* value, it can get *"noisy"* and *"very crowded"* –
it's *"advisable to book"*. / **Sample dishes:** queen scallops in garlic butter;
sea bass with lime & coriander; treacle tart. **Details:** 10.15 pm; closed Sun;
no Amex.

Garden Room £ 23 ★

Harlow Carr Bot. Gdns, Crag Ln HG3 1QB   (01425) 505604

This "large, light room", overlooking the Botanical Gardens, is a "pleasant" spot – "especially at lunchtime"; its "traditional cooking with an edge" "never disappoints". / **Sample dishes:** rabbit terrine, Toulouse sausage & juniper jam; honey-glazed breast of duck; dark chocolate torte. **Details:** closed Sun D; no smoking.

Villu Toots £ 32 𝔸

Balmoral Hotel, Franklin Mount HG1 5EJ   (01423) 705805

This "shiny, minimalist" newcomer achieves only modest commentary as yet; comments to date, though, are unanimous that it offers "great style" and "warm and efficient" service, not to mention "imaginative" and "well executed" British cooking. / **Sample dishes:** salmon fishcakes; coq au vin; lemon tart. **Details:** just off King's Rd; 10 pm. **Accommodation:** 20 rooms, from £84.

HASLEMERE, SURREY 3–4A

Little Gem £ 30 ★

23-27 Lower St GU27 2NY   (01428) 651462

Some think it's "a shame about the name", but "superb-value set menus", an "impressive wine list" and "friendly, professional service" win consistent support for this informal modern British newcomer (which has taken over the site formerly called Fleur de Sel). / **Sample dishes:** potato & rocket soup; rack of lamb with red wine sauce; hot chocolate pudding. **Value tip:** set 2-crs L & Sun L £8.50. **Details:** on High Pavement of Lower St; 10.30 pm; closed Mon, Sat L & Sun D.

HASTINGS, E SUSSEX 3–4C

The Mermaid Café £ 19 ★★

2 Rock-a-Nore Rd TN34 3DW   (01424) 438100

"The best fish and chips in the south" and a "unique site looking towards the nets and fishing boats" win consistent praise for this "incredible-value" seaside café. / **Sample dishes:** chicken salad; plaice & chips; spotted dick & custard. **Details:** centre of old town; 7.30 pm; no credit cards; no booking.

HATFIELD PEVEREL, ESSEX 3–2C

Blue Strawberry £ 30 ★

The Street CM3 2DW   (01245) 381333

A beamed cottage "in the middle of nowhere" may seem an unlikely setting for a modern bistro, but this "relaxing" and "classy" joint proves it can be done; it's "very busy", thanks to "consistently good" cooking, "reasonably priced" wines and "friendly" service. / **Sample dishes:** Malaysian chicken; turbot with garlic & herb rosti; vanilla & raspberry gratin. **Details:** 3m E of Chelmsford; 10 pm; closed Sun D.

HAWORTH, W YORKS 5–1C

Weavers £ 26 ★

15 West Ln BD22 8DU   (01535) 643822

It may look "just like an average tourist trap" – in a row of old cottages, by a museum – but this surprisingly "cosy" and "convivial" spot offers "professional and remarkably original cooking", and has done so "consistently for many years". / **Sample dishes:** aubergine & roast vegetable soufflé; Yorkshire lamb with minted gravy; school pudding & custard. **Details:** 1.5m W on B6142 from A629 close to Parsonage; 9 pm; D only, closed Mon & Sun; no smoking. **Accommodation:** 3 rooms, from £75.

HAY ON WYE, POWYS   2–1A
The Pavement   £ 28
The Pavement HR3 5BU   (01497) 821932
"You are made to feel at home" at this *"value-for-money"* café-like
place – a useful spot to know about in a thin area; one regular tips
the ambience as *"good at weekends, poor midweek"*. / *Sample
dishes:* deep-fried cockles with salsa; roast rack of lamb; glazed lemon tart.
Details: by town clock; 9.30 pm; closed Mon & Tue; no Amex or Diners.

HAYFIELD, DERBYS   5–2C
Waltzing Weasel   £ 30   ★
New Mills Rd SK22 1BT   (01663) 743402
"Superb pub food" – traditional British fare is served in both bar and
restaurant – is praised by the few who stumbled over this country inn
on the edge of the Peak District; it also has a *"view to die for"*.
/ *Sample dishes:* St Bradon roast; duck & pheasant casserole; summer
pudding. *Details:* 9 pm; no smoking; children: 5+. **Accommodation:** 8
rooms, from £68.

HENLEY-ON-THAMES, OXON   2–2D
Villa Marina   £ 26
18 Thameside RG9 1BH   (01491) 575262
Perhaps surprisingly, this simple, *"very pleasant local Italian"* –
near the Bridge – is the only place of any gastronomic note in this
picturebook Thames Valley town; it's *"very popular"*. / *Sample
dishes:* goat's cheese salad; fillet of beef in wine sauce; tiramisu. *Details:*
opp Angel pub, nr Bridge; 10.30 pm.

HEREFORD, HEREFORD & WORCS   2–1B
Café at All Saints   £ 16
All Saints Church, High St HR4 9AA   (01432) 370415
"Brilliant wholefood in a well designed church café" is *"a much
better formula than it sounds"*; the place is *"ideal for a light lunch"*,
but it's also available for *"occasional pre-booked evening meals"*.
/ *Sample dishes:* butter bean broth; aubergine & tomato quiche; lemon tart.
Details: nr Cathedral; L only, closed Sun; no smoking; no booking; children: 6+.

HETTON, N YORKS   5–1B
The Angel   £ 39   Ⓐ★★
BD23 6LT   (01756) 730263
A location in a *"remote part of the Dales"* does nothing to diminish
the deserved renown of this *"friendly but slick"* *"gourmet pub"* whose
"consistent excellence" is all the more impressive given the numbers
served; *"both bar and the restaurant"* offer *"absolutely superlative"*
cooking (with an emphasis on fish), and a *"superb wine list"*.
/ *Sample dishes:* Yorkshire blue cheese soufflé; roast duckling with rhubarb
& juniper; melting chocolate pudding. **Value tip:** set 2/3-crs early-eve
£13.50/£16.50, set 3-crs Sun L £19.75. *Details:* 5m N of Skipton off B6265
at Rylstone; 9.30 pm; closed Sun D; no smoking area.

HEXHAM, NORTHUMBERLAND   8–2A
The Hadrian Hotel at Wall   £ 23
Wall Village NE46 4EE   (01434) 681232
"A memorable surprise", say some of those who have stumbled upon
this small hotel, outside Hexham; *"good-value"* dishes of *"local
produce"* (complete with *"an impressive cheeseboard"*) are the order
of the day. / *Sample dishes:* Swiss mushroom tart; sole in wine & cream
sauce; sticky toffee pudding. *Details:* 3m out of Hexham on 6079 (for
Hadrian's Wall toward Acomb & Chollerford); 9 pm; no Amex & no Switch;
no smoking. **Accommodation:** 6 rooms, from £49.

HEYDON, CAMBS
King William IV £ 27 ★

Chishill Rd SG8 8PW   (01763) 838773
This "small, friendly pub, tucked up a steep lane" offers a "good
selection" of "well cooked" food ("including many veggie dishes") in
"ample portions"; "good beer" and "superb puddings" too.
/ *Sample dishes:* crispy whitebait with columns of grained bread;
char-grilled lamb steak; chocolate shell. *Details:* take A505 from M11 J10;
10 pm; no Amex; no smoking area.

HINTLESHAM, SUFFOLK
Hintlesham Hall £ 46 ★

IP8 3NS   (01473) 652334
"Great when you want to impress", this "rather old-fashioned"
country house hotel, famous for its association with Mr Robert
Carrier, offers interesting modern British cooking at "good-value"
prices; some do find the dining room a touch "cavernous".
/ *Sample dishes:* scallops with deep-fried salsify; lamb with roast vegetables
& goat's cheese; pineapple tart with black pepper ice cream. *Value tip:*
set 3-crs L £19.99. *Details:* 4m W of Ipswich on A1071; 9.30 pm; closed Sat
L; jacket & tie; no smoking; no booking; children: 12+. *Accommodation:* 33
rooms, from £115.

HINTON CHARTERHOUSE, BATH & NE SOMERSET
Homewood Park £ 60 ★

BA3 6BB   (01225) 723731
"Exceptional meals with perfect service" are often praised at this
imposing Georgian house near Bath; many find that "prices are too
steep", though, and some find the dining room "lacks ambience".
/ *Sample dishes:* spinach ravioli; roast squab pigeon; fluffy chocolate soufflé.
Value tip: set 3-crs L £19.50 (Sun £22.50). *Details:* 6m from Bath on A36
to Warminster; 9.30 pm; no smoking. *Accommodation:* 19 rooms,
from £135.

HISTON, CAMBS
Phoenix £ 23 ★

20 The Green CB4 4JA   (01223) 233766
"Standard Chinese fare, impeccably cooked" makes this village
restaurant a worthwhile destination; "order off the Chinese menu if
you can". / *Sample dishes:* spring rolls; crispy duck; toffee apple. *Value
tip:* set 2-crs L £6.50. *Details:* 10.30 pm; no Amex; no smoking area.

HOCKLEY HEATH, W MIDLANDS
Nuthurst Grange £ 42 Ⓐ

Nuthurst Grange Ln B94 5NL   (01564) 783972
"An elegant ambience and good food" and service which "makes
every effort" ensure that this country house hotel dining room is a
better-than-average choice for a special occasion. / *Sample
dishes:* duck & Chinese spice confit; poached salmon salad; iced orange and
lemon parfait. *Details:* J4 off M42, A3400; 9.30 pm; no smoking area.
Accommodation: 15 rooms, from £145.

HOLT, NORFOLK
Yetman's £ 42 Ⓐ★

37 Norwich Rd NR25 6SA   (01296) 713320
Thanks to its "excellent modern British cuisine" and "brilliant"
service, this "wonderful", "cosy" haven – the product of an
"enthusiastic husband and wife team" – is "deservedly building a
strong following"; an "excellent, moderately priced wine list" is a
further attraction. / *Sample dishes:* Louisiana crab cakes; char-grilled pork
with balsamic vinegar; whitecurrant fool. *Details:* on A148, 20m N of
Norwich; 9.30 pm; D only, ex Sun open L & D; no smoking area.

HORNCASTLE, LINCS 6–3A

Magpies £ 28

71-75 East St LN9 6AA (01507) 527004

"Certainly the best, original place in a twenty mile radius", say fans of the *"excellent, freshly cooked, real food"* at this *"popular"* small, family-run establishment; even supporters say it's been a bit *"erratic"* though, of late. / **Sample dishes:** roast scallops with parsley coulis; Lincolnshire beef with béarnaise sauce; lemon tart. **Value tip:** set 3-crs Sun L £12.50. **Details:** 10 pm; D only, ex Sun when L only, closed Mon; no Amex; no smoking.

HORNDON ON THE HILL, ESSEX 3–3C

The Bell Inn £ 29

High Rd SS17 8LD (01375) 642463

"Good food with a good wine list at reasonable prices" make it worth remembering this family-run pub/restaurant. / **Sample dishes:** Thai chicken broth; roast sea bass & pancetta; tart of figs. **Details:** 10 pm; no smoking. **Accommodation:** 15 rooms, from £40.

HORTON, NORTHANTS 2–3D

French Partridge £ 36 ★

NN7 2AP (01604) 870033

"Utterly reliable" local restaurant, which has been *"consistently good for 25 years"*; it's a *"friendly"* place, but *"don't be late – Mrs Partridge can be very unforgiving"*. / **Sample dishes:** Morecambe Bay potted shrimps; venison with gin & juniper sauce; panna cotta & mango. **Details:** on B526, between Newport Pagnell & Northampton; 9 pm; D only, closed Mon & Sun; no credit cards; no smoking; children: not encouraged.

HOUGHTON CONQUEST, BEDS 3–2A

Knife & Cleaver £ 32 ★

The Grove MK45 3LA (01234) 740387

"Value-for-money", quality dishes and *"professional"* service make this restaurant-cum-tavern a *"popular"* local choice. / **Sample dishes:** crab & lobster cake; calves' liver on bacon & onion mash; chocolate tart with fresh raspberries. **Value tip:** set 2/3-crs L £11.95/£13.95. **Details:** 9.30 pm; closed Sat L & Sun D; no smoking. **Accommodation:** 9 rooms, from £49.

HOYLAKE, MERSEYSIDE 5–2A

Linos £ 26

122 Market St CH47 3BH (0151) 632 1408

This *"small, exceptionally friendly"* French restaurant, in the centre of the village, gets a great press for its *"imaginative"* starters, *"satisfying"* main courses and *"dramatic desserts"*. / **Sample dishes:** Mozzarella wrapped in Parma ham; veal escalopes with ginger & onions; apricot parfait. **Details:** 9.45 pm; closed Mon & Sun.

HUDDERSFIELD, W YORKS 5–1C

Bradley's £ 30

84 Fitzwilliam St HD1 5BB (01484) 516773

"Very good all round", this *"recently extended"* city-centre spot offers modern British cooking *"with imagination and skill"*; lunch and early-evening set menus are particularly praised, and jazz evenings are a feature. / **Sample dishes:** chicken Waldorf salad; roast lamb & cherry tomatoes; chocolate & coffee bean mousse. **Value tip:** set 3-crs D Mon-Fri (& pre-th Sat) £14.50. **Details:** 10 pm; closed Mon D, Sat L & Sun; no Amex; no smoking area.

Cerutti's   £ 27

10 Nelson St HU1 1XE   (01482) 328501
*The "careful, quite imaginative cooking" is "worth a detour", say
fans of this fish restaurant which is "excellent" for the area. / **Sample
dishes:** avocado, scallop & bacon salad; halibut stuffed with cheese; assiette of
desserts. **Value tip:** set 3-crs L & D £15. **Details:** follow signs to fruit market;
9.30 pm; closed Sat L & Sun; no Amex.*

Hitchcocks   £ 14   ★

1 Bishop Ln HU1 1PA   (01482) 320233
*"Totally unlike any other restaurant I know" – an eat-all-you-can,
buffet-style vegetarian (one sitting only) which only opens if enough
bookings are received, and where the menu (Italian, Indian, etc) is
decided upon by the early bookers for the night; "budgety and
studentville", it may be, but value-merchants say results are
"invariably wonderful". / **Sample dishes:** tomato bruschetta; spaghetti
carbonara; pecan pie. **Details:** on corner with High St (follow signs to Old
Town); no credit cards.*

Pheasant   £ 32   ★

PE18 0RE   (01832) 710241
*"Top-notch food", "many great wines by the glass" and a
"warm welcome" are among the attractions which make this
thatched gastropub (from the same stable as the better known
Three Horseshoes at Madingley) a palpable hit. / **Sample
dishes:** spinach & Ricotta ravioli; red mullet with saffron mussel soup;
jam roly-poly & custard. **Details:** 10 pm; no smoking area.*

The Mediterranean   £ 20

328 Ley St IG1 4AF   (020) 8478 1174
*In a thin area, this "Spanish à la carte, Greek or Moroccan"
restaurant, in a residential part of the town, makes a "good value
for money" choice. / **Sample dishes:** kleftiko; steak in black olive sauce;
strawberry gâteau. **Value tip:** set 3-crs L & D £9. **Details:** between Ilford
Station & Green Gate; 11 pm; closed Sat L & Sun; no Amex.*

The Box Tree   £ 40   ★★

35-37 Church St LS29 9DR   (01943) 608484
*Thanks to Thierry LePrêtre-Granet's "consistently outstanding"
modern French cooking, it can be "difficult to get a table" at this
"comfortable" establishment – one of the North's longest-established
gastronomic destinations; some find service slightly "severe". / **Sample
dishes:** scallops with fruit chutney; lamb with sweetbreads in provençale sauce;
hot raspberry soufflé. **Details:** on A65 close to town centre; 9.30 pm; closed
Mon & Sun D; no smoking.*

George Hotel   £ 47   𝔸 ★

Quay St PO41 0PE   (01983) 760331
*Though there is the odd complaint of "ordinary" results, this well-
known hotel wins general praise for its "excellent location" (with fine
views over the harbour), its "lovely atmosphere" and its "very good"
modern British cooking. / **Sample dishes:** poached oysters with chive
butter; calves' liver & veal with béarnaise sauce; passion fruit tart. **Details:**
nr harbour; 10 pm; D only, closed Mon & Sun; children: 8+.
Accommodation: 17 rooms, from £130.*

IVINGHOE, BUCKS

Kings Head   £ 47   ★

Station Rd LU7 9EB   (01296) 668388

A "pleasant village location", "excellent food" and "first-class service"
help make this well-known and "popular French restaurant", in a
former pub, a "consistently reliable" choice. / **Sample dishes:** salmon
soufflé with avocado; roast duck with sage & onion stuffing; syllabub.
Value tip: set 3-crs L £13.95. **Details:** 3m N of Tring on B489 to Dunstable;
9.30 pm; closed Sun D; jacket & tie; no smoking in dining room.

IXWORTH, SUFFOLK
3–1C

Theobalds   £ 40

68 High St IP31 2HJ   (01359) 231707

With its "beamed setting", this "well established" "village restaurant",
in a charming 17th-century house, wins praise for its "seasonal menu,
using local produce"; it's "especially good on game". / **Sample
dishes:** twice-baked cheese soufflé; pan-fried calves' liver; lemon & lime tart
with lemon sorbet. **Value tip:** set 2-crs L £13.90, set 3-crs Sun L £17.95.
Details: on A143 to Diss, 7m from Bury St Edmunds; 9.15 pm; closed Mon,
Sat L & Sun D; no Amex; no smoking in dining room; children: 8+.

JEVINGTON, E SUSSEX
3–4B

Hungry Monk   £ 36   𝔸★

BN26 5QF   (01323) 482178

"Sumptuous" décor and a "very unusual location in converted
Elizabethan cottages" help make this "cosy", "crowded" place a top
"romantic" choice; "delicious" cooking is found by most reporters,
too, but a few say it's "just OK". / **Sample dishes:** mussel & shallot tart;
lamb with rosti & redcurrant sauce; banoffi pie. **Details:** 5m W of Eastbourne;
10 pm; D only, ex Sun open L & D; no Amex; no smoking in dining room;
children: 5+.

KENDAL, CUMBRIA
7–4D

The Moon   £ 29

129 Highgate LA9 4EN   (01539) 729254

Some have "never been disappointed" by the "unusual" blackboard
menu, "with a good choice of English meat dishes and veggie
options", at this "reasonably priced" spot. / **Sample dishes:** goat's
cheese on carrot & courgette rosti; swordfish with wild mushroom ragoût;
cardamon chocolate heaven. **Details:** opp Brewery Arts Centre; 10 pm; closed
Mon, Tue L, Thu L & Sat L; no Amex; no smoking.

KENILWORTH, WARKS
5–4C

Bosquet   £ 38   ★

97a Warwick Rd CV8 1HP   (01926) 852463

The location may only be "a house on a high street", but the
"truly French" cooking at this "friendly" family-run establishment is
of "very high quality", and there is "good attention paid to the
little things". / **Sample dishes:** sweetbreads in pastry with truffle sauce;
venison with juniper berries; lemon tart & passion fruit sorbet.
Details: 9.15 pm; closed Mon & Sun.

Simpsons   £ 39

101-103 Warwick Rd CV8 1HL   (01926) 864567

Highly popular, modern town-centre bistro, praised for its
"imaginative menus" and "very attentive service"; there is the odd
complaint of "hit-or-miss" realisation. / **Sample dishes:** pea, ham & mint
soup; roast cod with basil cream; apricot & almond tart. **Value tip:** set 2-crs
L £10. **Details:** 10 pm; closed Sat L & Sun; no smoking area.

KILCHRENAN BY TAYNUILT, ARGYLL & BUTE   9–3B

Taychreggan   £ 40   𝔸★

PA35 1HQ   (01866) 833211

"Unbeatable for peace and tranquillity", this *"wonderfully relaxed but exceptional hotel restaurant"* is a *"great romantic escape"*; it offers *"exceptional loch views"* and some *"superb"* cooking, *"especially seafood"*. / **Sample dishes:** roast Oban Bay scallops; Highland venison; forest fruits & Drambuie millefeuille. **Value tip:** set 3-crs L £19.95. **Details:** 7m from Taynuilt on B845; 8.45 pm; no smoking; children: 14+. **Accommodation:** 19 rooms, from £52.

KILLARNEY, CO KERRY, *EIRE*   10–4A

Gaby's   IR £ 42   ★

27 High St   (064) 32519

"In high season, book early for the best seafood in Killarney" – it's *"incredible"*, as is the happy discovery that the *"Guinness seems to go with everything from the lobster to the fish bake"*. / **Sample dishes:** cassolette of prawns & monkfish; fresh salmon salad; pear & apple tarte Tatin. **Details:** 10m from local airport; 10 pm; D only, closed Sun; closed mid Feb-mid Mar; no Switch.

KING'S CLIFFE, NORTHANTS   6–4A

King's Cliffe House Restaurant   £ 33   ★

31 West St   PE8 6XB   (01780) 470172

"Small, intimate and quiet" restaurant, with *"excellent food and service"* and an *"interesting, reasonably priced wine list"*; note the very restricted opening times. / **Sample dishes:** plate of mixed fish; spinach tartlet & hollandaise; sticky toffee pudding with apricots. **Details:** 4m W of A1, close to A47; 9 pm; D only, open Wed-Sat only; no credit cards; no smoking area.

KINGS LYNN, NORFOLK   6–4B

Rococo   £ 37   𝔸★

11 Saturday Marketplace   PE30 5DQ   (01553) 771483

Nick and Anne Anderson's *"elegant"*, *"small and individual"* 17th-century cottage, provides a *"lovely setting"* for a meal; *"good modern British cooking using local ingredients"* is *"served with charm"*. / **Sample dishes:** baked goat's cheese on pommes Anna; roast lamb with celeriac fondant & rosemary jus; champagne mousse & raspberries. **Value tip:** set 2/3-crs set L £12.50/£14.50. **Details:** in Old Town, opp St Margaret's Church; 10 pm; closed Mon L & Sun; no smoking area.

KINGUSSIE, HIGHLAND   9–2C

The Cross   £ 45   ★

Tweed Mill Brae, Ardbroilach Rd   PH21 1TC   (01540) 661166

"An oasis in a culinary desert"; this *"welcoming"* converted tweed mill offers *"delicate and delicious"* Scottish cooking in a *"relaxing"* setting. / **Sample dishes:** pan-fried scallops; venison with redcurrants & port; raspberry shortbread. **Details:** head uphill on Ardbroilach Rd, turn left into private drive after traffic lights; 8.30 pm; D only, closed Tue; no Amex; no smoking; children: 8+. **Accommodation:** 9 rooms, from £95, incl D.

KINSALE, CO CORK, *EIRE*   10–4B

The Man Friday   IR £ 32   ★

Scilly   (021) 772260

"Nothing is too much trouble" for this *"friendly"* spot, overlooking the harbour – it *"combines a maritime outlook with excellent seafood"*. / **Sample dishes:** crab au gratin; grilled fillet of turbot; passion fruit mousse. **Details:** 10.30 pm; D only, closed Sun; no Switch; no smoking area.

KIRKBY LONSDALE, CUMBRIA 7–4D

Snooty Fox Hotel £ 24 A★

Main St LA6 2AH (01524) 271308

"With its log fires and olde worlde ambience", this "elegant" hostelry in the centre of a picturesque town is arguably "best in winter"; it consistently offers "sophisticated" food – "not your usual pub fayre" – "of good quality and well presented". / **Sample dishes:** *deep-fried crispy duck pancake; scallops with spinach & brandy cream; Lancashire apple cheesecake.* **Details:** *just off A65 - 6m from M6 J36; 10 pm; no smoking in dining room.* **Accommodation:** *9 rooms, from £50.*

KNUTSFORD, CHESHIRE 5–2B

La Belle Epoque £ 30

King St WA16 6DT (01565) 633060

This splendid "art nouveau listed building" offers "inconsistent" brasserie cooking and sometimes "perfunctory" service; it remains "one of the best stand-bys in an area not overly well endowed with gastronomic opportunities", but it could do better. / **Sample dishes:** *carrot & coriander samosas; grilled gammon steak; baked strawberry cheesecake.* **Value tip:** *set 2/3-crs L £5.95/£6.95.* **Details:** *1.5m from M6 J19; 10 pm; closed Sun; no smoking area; children: 9+.* **Accommodation:** *6 rooms, from £55.*

Dick Willetts £ 29 ★

Toft Hotel, Toft Rd WA16 9EH (01565) 634443

Is this, as fans claim, "the best vegetarian restaurant in the North West"?; reports rave about its "inventive and very fresh" dishes ("using only organic ingredients") and the atmosphere which "feels as if you personally have been invited to dinner"; note the very restricted opening. / **Sample dishes:** *sweet & sour aubergine caponata; pasta with garden herbs & vegetables; mulled fruit salad.* **Details:** *on main A50 between Stoke & Warrington; 9.30 pm; open only Fri D & Sat D; no smoking; children: not permitted.* **Accommodation:** *12 rooms, from £70.*

KYLESKU, HIGHLAND 9–1B

Kylesku Hotel £ 23 ★

IV27 4HW (01971) 502231

"Stunning langoustines straight from the sea" can make a visit to this very simple hotel bar-restaurant, set amidst stunning scenery, a "fantastic" experience. / **Sample dishes:** *mussels with lobster sauce; grilled Ardvar salmon with lobster sauce; crème brûlée.* **Details:** *on A894, S of Durness, N of Ullapool; 8.30 pm; no Amex; no smoking.* **Accommodation:** *8 rooms, from £50.*

LANCASTER, LANCS 5–1A

Sultan of Lancaster £ 14 A★

Brock St LA1 1UU (01524) 61188

"Non-alcoholic, but overall an excellent eating experience", this "converted church" (now "with Islamic interior design") offers "fresh" Pakistani cooking in an interesting setting. / **Sample dishes:** *houmous with sesame oil; shish kebab; Ras malai (cream cheese balls).* **Details:** *in Town Hall Centre; 11 pm; D only; no Amex.*

LANGAR, NOTTS 5–3D

Langar Hall £ 29

NG13 9HG (01949) 860559

Welcoming Georgian house, which makes a "charmingly eccentric" choice for a reasonably priced English meal. / **Sample dishes:** *cheese soufflé; turbot with red wine sauce; summer pudding.* **Value tip:** *set 2/3-crs L £7.50/£10.* **Details:** *9.30 pm, Sat 10 pm, Sun 8.30 pm; no smoking area.* **Accommodation:** *10 rooms, from £100.*

LANGHO, LANCS   5–1B
Northcote Manor   £ 49   ★

Northcote Rd BB6 8BE   (01254) 240555

*"Superb" and "imaginative" English cooking ("with some of the best
puds anywhere") wins applause for this grand Ribble Valley country
house, with its "friendly and welcoming" atmosphere. / **Sample
dishes:** hot-smoked salmon with oysters; duck with mulled pears & onion jam;
Eccles cake with spiced cream. **Value tip:** set 3-crs L & Sun L £16.
Details: M6, J31, follow signs for Skipton & Clitheroe, turn left onto A59,
follow for 8m; 9.30 pm; closed Sat L; no smoking. **Accommodation:** 14
rooms, from £110.*

LANGTON GREEN, KENT   3–4B
The Hare   £ 27   🄰★

Langton Rd TN3 0JA   (01892) 862419

*"Open fire in winter – great outdoors in summer"; this
"well-appointed" pub provides a "lovely setting" in which to enjoy
some "more-than-averagely interesting" cooking at a "reasonable
price" (and in "good portions" too). / **Sample dishes:** chicken & oyster
mushroom pancake; chicken & mushrooms wrapped in bacon; sticky toffee
pudding. **Details:** on A264, E Grinstead Rd; 9.30 pm.*

LAPWORTH, WARKS   5–4C
The Boot   £ 29   🄰★

Old Warwick Rd B94 6JU   (01564) 782464

*"A great treat for a pub meal", this "fun" and "noisy" canal-side
tavern – a popular day-out destination from Brum – offers a
"good range" of "imaginative" dishes. / **Sample dishes:** salmon & tuna
sashimi; duck with spring onion & Parmesan mash; banana, coconut & rum
sponge. **Details:** 10 pm.*

LAVENHAM, SUFFOLK   3–1C
Great House   £ 34   🄰★

Market Pl CO10 9QZ   (01787) 247431

*"Great attention to detail" is the hallmark of this "medieval house
on the market square", which provides a "superb" setting for a meal;
"cuisine bourgeoise at its best" – "from snacks to full meals" – is
served by "very friendly" staff. / **Sample dishes:** tuna carpaccio; lamb
provençale; brioche & butter pudding. **Value tip:** set 2-crs L £9.95.
Details: take Market Lane from High St, follow directions to Guildhall;
9.30 pm; Oct-May, closed Sun L & Mon; no smoking in dining room.
Accommodation: 5 rooms, from £70.*

LEEDS, W YORKS   5–1C

Leeds is no traditional restaurant centre, but the economic
vitality of the last few years has brought with it something of
a restaurant boom. The city now vies with Manchester as
the restaurant capital of northern England. Despite having a
number of quality establishments, though, it has some way
to go before it matches the diversity of the larger city.

Though the affluent suburbs have long had some places of
modest note, visitors will probably find all they need within
walking distance of the railway station. The younger, trendier
places, such as the seminal *Art's Bar*, tend to be in the
Exchange Quarter (around the Corn Exchange). Most of the
more upmarket new establishments (*Leodi's, Pool Court at 42*)
are in recent warehouse-conversions, around the canal, and
have locations which are intriguing, but not (at least in our
view) especially charming.

For atmosphere, we prefer *Darbar*, a striking Indian, very centrally located, or the timeless setting of *Whitelocks Luncheonette*. For sheer value, don't miss the vegetarian Indian *Hansa* or the Italian-with-a-twist delights of Headingley's *Salvo's*.

Amigos   £ 17   Ⓐ

70 Abbey Rd LS5 3JG   (0113) 228 3737
*This "lively restaurant run by Spanish people" is widely praised for its "authentic" tapas and a "good choice of Spanish wines", and its "small" Headingley premises are "packed in the evenings". / **Sample dishes:** pepper salad; tomato ragoût with chicken; Spanish custard. **Details:** on A65; 11 pm; no Amex.*

Art's Bar ✳   £ 22   Ⓐ

42 Call Ln LS1 6DT   (0113) 243 8243
*"Exciting tapas-style food" and "good main meals" help maintain the success of this "chilled" café/bar (whose opening, in 1994, was one of the first shots in the battle to trendify the Exchange Quarter). / **Sample dishes:** goat's cheese crostini; char-grilled lamb steak; citrus fudge tart. **Details:** 11 pm; no Amex.*

Bibis ✳   £ 32   Ⓐ★

Minerva House, 16 Greek St LS1 5RU   (0113) 243 0905
*The "loud", "bustling", "non-relaxing" atmosphere is the key selling point of this big, brassy and "very busy" city-centre Italian; "the food is good", though. / **Sample dishes:** monkfish & courgette tempura; chicken stuffed with smoked Mozzarella; zabaglione. **Details:** just off Park Row; 11.30 pm.*

Brasserie Forty Four   £ 27   ★

44 The Calls LS2 7EW   (0113) 234 3232
*"Better value than Pool Court" (with which it shares a kitchen), this large brasserie offers consistently "imaginative and tasty" modern British cooking in a "modern-style" setting; some have found the atmosphere rather flat – perhaps that will be put right by the recent revamp. / **Sample dishes:** Turkish spiced aubergines; hot-smoked cod with saffron mash; chocolate & walnut brownies. **Value tip:** set 2-crs set L £9.75. **Details:** 10.30 pm, Fri & Sat 11 pm; closed Sat L & Sun.*

Bryan's   £ 18   ★

9 Weetwood Ln LS16 5LT   (0113) 278 5679
*"Very busy" Headingley spot, offering "the ultimate traditional fish and chips experience", fuelled by "vats of industrial-strength tea". / **Sample dishes:** Thai fishcakes; haddock & chips; sponge pudding & custard. **Details:** nr Headingley Cricket Ground; Sun 7.30pm; no Amex; no smoking.*

Darbar   £ 25   Ⓐ★

16-17 Kirkgate LS1 6BY   (0113) 246 0381
*"Very good" Indian food makes this a surprisingly "authentic" find in the heart of Leeds, and, after the drab entrance, the "superb", ornately decorated first-floor dining room comes as a real surprise. / **Sample dishes:** mulligatawny soup; chicken biryani; kulfi. **Details:** behind Marks & Spencer; midnight; closed Sun.*

Flying Pizza   £ 28   Ⓐ

60a Street Ln LS8 2DQ   (0113) 266 6501
*"North Leeds's trendy place" where "ladies-who-lunch meet the business set"; "bright", "cheerful" and "atmospheric", this Italian "all-rounder" is "always packed", thanks – in part at least – to its "excellent pizzas and good value". / **Sample dishes:** salad; cannelloni; chocolate mousse. **Value tip:** set 2-crs L & pre-th. £8.95. **Details:** just off A61, 3m N of city centre; 11.30 pm; no smoking area; no booking at D.*

Fuji Hiro £ 16 ★
45 Wade Ln LS2 8NJ   (0113) 243 9184
*"Unique" hereabouts, this "diner-style" restaurant serves "fantastically fresh Japanese cuisine" (including, but not only, "fast food noodles") in "unpretentious" surroundings. / **Sample dishes:** leek & sweet pepper kebabs; chicken & soba noodles; no puddings. **Details:** Merrian centre; 10 pm; no credit cards; no smoking.*

Hansa £ 19 ★★
72-74 North St LS2 7PN   (0113) 244 4408
*"Vegetarian, home-cooked Gujerati Indian cooking" – from an all-female team who "care" – certainly makes this a "curry house with a difference"; "excellent" food and the "very relaxed and professional" atmosphere win it a huge local following. / **Sample dishes:** vegetable patra; vegetable curry; Gajjar (carrot cake). **Details:** 200 yds from Grand Theatre; 11 pm; closed Sun D; no Amex; no smoking area.*

Leodis £ 33 Ⓐ
Victoria Mill, Sovereign St LS1 4BJ   (0113) 242 1010
*With its impressive canal-side premises, this "popular", "modern Franco-British brasserie" benefits from a "lively" atmosphere; the food is "hearty", but the service, though generally "friendly and efficient", can seem a touch "ambivalent". / **Sample dishes:** black pudding, bacon & poached eggs; salmon with rosti spinach & béarnaise sauce; fudge nut candy cake. **Value tip:** set 3-crs L & early eve £14.95. **Details:** nr City Hilton Hotel; 10 pm, Fri & Sat 11 pm; closed Sat L & Sun.*

Lucky Dragon £ 28 ★
Templar Ln LS2 7LP   (0113) 245 0520
*As a "half-oriental" clientèle suggests, this large Chinatown basement (with its "ordinary but genuine" ambience) serves some "marvellous" food, particularly dim sum. / **Sample dishes:** prawn wrapped in rice paper; fillet steak Cantonese style; ice cream. **Details:** midnight.*

Maxi's £ 29
6 Bingley St LS3 1LX   (0113) 244 0552
*"Good food and service" makes this rather cavernous place "the best Chinese ever" to its perhaps slightly over-enthusiastic fans. / **Sample dishes:** Peking spare ribs; Cantonese sizzling beef steak; banana fritter. **Details:** beyond Westgate; 11.30 pm.*

Pool Court at 42 £ 48 ★
42 The Calls LS2 7EW   (0113) 244 4242
*"Best-quality raw materials cooked with imagination" make this "fashionably located docksider" a foodie destination of some note; the setting is "a touch clinical", however, and "patronising" service has "ruined" some meals. / **Sample dishes:** lobster consommé & spiced crab dumplings; Welsh lamb with celeriac dauphinoise; baked amaretto cheesecake. **Value tip:** set 2/3-crs L £14.50/£19. **Details:** 10 pm, Fri & Sat 10.30 pm; closed Sat L & Sun; children: no babies.*

Rascasse £ 39
Canal Wharf, Water Ln LS11 5BB   (0113) 244 6611
*What's gone wrong at this promising canalside warehouse-conversion?; some do still vaunt the virtues of Simon Gueller's "fine, unfussy" modern French cuisine, but the overwhelming impression amongst reporters is that this "barn" of a place is becoming irredeemably "overpriced", "snooty" and "pretentious". / **Sample dishes:** saffron risotto; cod with tomato fondue; pineapple & black pepper tarte Tatin. **Value tip:** set 2/3-crs L & early eve £13.50/£17. **Details:** behind Granary Wharf off road from M621 J3; 10 pm, Fri & Sat 10.30 pm; closed Sat L & Sun.*

Sala Thai   £ 24

Oakbank 13-17, Shaw Ln LS6 4DH   (0113) 278 8400

*This Headingley Thai attracts much comment; it's unusually mixed,
though – cooking that's hailed as "fresh" and "pungent" by some is
dismissed as "generic" by others, and there are quite a few gripes of
"slow" service. / **Sample dishes:** beef satay; stir-fried beef with chilli
& onions; Thai custard. **Details:** just off Otley Rd, nr Arndale Centre;
10.30 pm; closed Sun; no smoking area.*

Salvo's   £ 23   ★★

115 Otley Rd, Headingley LS6 3PX   (0113) 275 5017

*Its huge fan club "just can't get enough" of this "lively", "family-run"
Headingley Italian – an "all-round enjoyable experience" which has
demonstrated "amazing consistency over 20 years"; the highlight is
"innovative" Italian food "of top quality" ("with oriental influences
from the proprietor, who travels"); no booking. / **Sample dishes:**
whole crab thermidor; Mediterranean seafood stew; chocolate whisky cake.
Details: 2m N of university on A660; 10.45 pm, Fri & Sat 11 pm; closed Sun;
no smoking area; no booking.*

Sous le Nez en Ville   £ 24

Quebec House, Quebec St LS1 2HA   (0113) 244 0108

*This wine bar/restaurant "may not be Leeds's trendiest", but it's
very central, "very lively", and its 'early bird' menu (till 7.30pm)
attracts many favourable mentions. / **Sample dishes:** crispy duck
& cabbage spring roll; sea bass with crab pesto; iced white chocolate pâté.
Details: 100 yds from City Square; 10 pm; closed Sun.*

Whitelocks Luncheonette   £ 18   𝔸★

Turk's Head Yard, off Briggate LS7 6H3   (0113) 245 3950

*"One of the last great city-centre pubs, with food to match"; imagine
a restaurant visit in an Ealing Comedy, and you have something of the
atmosphere of the dining room here. / **Sample dishes:** Yorkshire pudding
& gravy; steak & potato pie; jam roly-poly & custard. **Value tip:** set 3-crs Sun
L £7.95. **Details:** nr Marks & Spencer; 8 pm, Fri-Sat 7 pm, Sun 2 pm; closed
Sun D.*

LEICESTER, LEICS   5–4D

Bobby's   £ 17   ★

154 Belgrave Rd LE4 5AD   (0116) 266 0106

*"Family-run and friendly" Indian 'dive' whose "freshly cooked veggie
fare" provides lots of "amazing flavours"; service can be chronically
slow and not every dish is a hit, but rock-bottom prices help disarm
criticism. / **Sample dishes:** deep-fried puri bread; Gujarati curry; carrot
halwa. **Details:** 10.30 pm; closed Mon; no Amex & no Switch; no smoking.*

Case   £ 32   𝔸

4-6 Hotel St LE1 5AW   (0116) 251 7675

*"A really Londonish restaurant in the provinces!", say fans of this
atmospheric factory-conversion venture in St Martins, which serves
some "imaginative" modern British dishes. / **Sample dishes:** tomato
& Mozzarella terrine; smoked haddock ravioli & leeks; chocolate orange torte.
Details: close to cathedral; 10.30 pm; closed Sun; no smoking area.*

Curry Fever   £ 25   ★

139 Belgrave Rd LE4 6AS   (0116) 266 2941

*A "small, friendly restaurant serving quality Indian food"; it's
"a bit different from the rest", in this curry capital, and "worth a
visit". / **Sample dishes:** cumin chicken; chicken masala; kulfi. **Details:** 0.5m
from city centre; 11.30 pm; closed Mon.*

Friends Tandoori   **£ 25**   ★
41-43 Belgrave Rd LE4 6AR (0116) 266 8809
*An "opulent" location – certainly by the standards of the city's famous
'Golden Mile' – offering superior and "well balanced" cooking; service
seems surprisingly erratic for such an apparently professional outfit.
/ **Sample dishes:** garlic chicken kebab; tandoori beef salad; kulfi. **Details:**
off Inner Ring; 11.30 pm; no smoking in dining room.*

LEMSFORD, HERTS   3–2B
Auberge du Lac   **£ 52**   𝔸
Brocket Hall AL8 7XG (01707) 368888
*They are "trying very hard" at this year-old operation, which enjoys
a "lovely location", by the lake in the grounds of Brocket Hall (you can
eat outside in summer); service is "very attentive" and "friendly", the
modern British cooking is of solid quality, and there's an interesting
selection of "fine wines by the glass". / **Sample dishes:** lobster & scallop
salad; baked leg of lamb, mash & caramelised onion; apricot soufflé & apple
sorbet. **Value tip:** set 2-crs L £18.50 (Sun 3-crs £25). **Details:** on B653,
towards Harpenden; 10.30 pm; closed Mon & Sun D; no jeans.*

LEWDOWN, DEVON   1–3C
Lewtrenchard Manor   **£ 41**   𝔸★
EX20 4PN (01566) 783256
*This "wonderful" Elizabethan house with its "superb setting in
glorious countryside" offers "imaginative cooking" and "friendly
service"; "sadly, it seems to be a less and less well-kept secret!"
/ **Sample dishes:** ham & parsley terrine with asparagus; roast beef with red
wine risotto; caramelised rice pudding with mango. **Details:** 9 pm; jacket;
no smoking; children: 8+. **Accommodation:** 9 rooms, from £110.*

LICHFIELD, STAFFS   5–4C
Thrales   **£ 27**
40-44 Tamworth St WS13 6JJ (01543) 255091
*A "half-timbered, town-centre restaurant" that generally offers
"good-value" Gallic cooking and an "enjoyable" night out; some feel
it "doesn't quite live up to its promise", but it's undoubtedly one of
the better places in a thinly provided area. / **Sample dishes:** fresh
sardines in lime & garlic sauce; roast lamb noisettes; chocolate & crème de
menthe parfait. **Value tip:** set 2/3-crs set L £9.50/£10.50, set 3-crs D £11.95.
Details: on corner of Backcester Ln, at start of one-way system coming into
Lichfield; 9.30 pm; closed Sun D.*

LIFTON, DEVON   1–3C
Arundell Arms   **£ 45**
Fore St PL16 0AA (01566) 784666
*The "fish is caught in the grounds" of this "'classic' country hotel"
(owned by an angler of note, and with 20 miles of the River Tamar at
guests' disposal); it delivers "very good" straightforward cooking in an
ambience some find rather "stuffy". / **Sample dishes:** red mullet
& saffron fritters; Gressingham duckling with blueberry compote; passion fruit
mousse. **Value tip:** set 2/3-crs L £16/£20. **Details:** 0.5m off A30, Lifton
Down exit; 9.30 pm; no smoking. **Accommodation:** 28 rooms, from £110.*

LINCOLN, LINCS   6–3A
Browns Pie Shop   **£ 24**   ★
33 Steep Hill LN2 1LU (01522) 527330
*"The ultimate pie experience"; "good, home-cooked food" (game is
the speciality) leads many to make a pilgrimage to this intimate,
no-frills spot; it has a "great location, near the cathedral". / **Sample
dishes:** Stilton choux buns & port sauce; venison with raspberries & whisky;
melon parfait & ginger lime sauce. **Value tip:** set 2-crs pre-th £5.95.
Details: nr cathedral; 10 pm; no smoking area.*

Jew's House   £ 33   A★

15 The Strait LN2 IJD (01522) 524851

*"Great French cooking" in the setting of "one of the oldest buildings in Lincoln" makes this "friendly" place well worth seeking out – "recorded music from Joni Mitchell et al" only enhances the "intimate" atmosphere. / **Sample dishes:** scallops with crispy leeks; duck with kumquats; tarte Tatin. **Value tip:** set 2/3-crs L £5/7.50. **Details:** bottom of hill from Cathedral; 9.30 pm; closed Mon & Sun; no smoking.*

The Wig & Mitre   £ 34   ★

30 Steep Hill LN2 ITL (01522) 535190

*It may be somewhat less characterful in its "sympathetically restored" new premises, near the Cathedral, but this town-centre tavern is still "the local to die for", offering "an excellent choice of good food" (all day, from breakfast onwards) in a "friendly" and "relaxed" setting. / **Sample dishes:** smoked salmon with herb couscous; roast duck with buttered spinach; chocolate brownies & honeycomb ice cream. **Details:** top of hill between cathedral and castle; 11 pm.*

LINLITHGOW, W LOTHIAN   9–4C

Champany Inn   £ 60

EH49 7LU (01506) 834532

*For some, top-quality Aberdeen Angus beef and a heavyweight wine list served in these rural 16th-century buildings is nothing short of "perfection"; the prices, however, give little away. / **Sample dishes:** hot-smoked salmon; char-grilled Aberdeen Angus Beef; cheesecake. **Value tip:** set 2-crs set L £16.75. **Details:** 2m NE of Linlithgow on junction of A904 & A803; 10 pm; closed Sat L & Sun; jacket & tie; children: 8+. **Accommodation:** 16 rooms, from £95.*

LITTLE SHELFORD, CAMBS   3–1B

Sycamore House   £ 31

1 Church St CB2 5HG (01223) 843396

*A "small, family-run restaurant", which offers "good value" from its adventurous set menus. / **Sample dishes:** mushroom & hazelnut soup; roast pork with tamarind & apple; rhubarb & Muscat trifle. **Details:** 1.5m from M11, J11; 9 pm; D only, closed Mon & Sun; no Amex; no smoking; children: 12+.*

LIVERPOOL, MERSEYSIDE   5–2A

Casa Italia   £ 19

40 Stanley St L1 6AL (0151) 227 5774

*"The warmth of true Italian style" and some "authentic cooking" make this "relaxed" and "chatty" central trattoria one of the better bets in town. / **Sample dishes:** antipasti; spaghetti carbonara; tiramisu. **Details:** 10 pm; closed Sun; no Amex; need 8+ to book.*

Everyman Bistro   £ 14   A★

5-9 Hope St L1 9BH (0151) 708 9545

*A "huge range of top-quality food", with "inspired use of seasonal ingredients", makes David Scott's "self-service bistro, in the popular wine bar beneath the Everyman Theatre" a "consistently good" choice – "I took my children in the 1970s, now I take my grandchildren"; "lovely puds" get special commendation. / **Sample dishes:** Thai chicken & noodle soup; beef with wild mushrooms; stawberry curd tartlet. **Details:** ground floor of Everyman Theatre; midnight; closed Sun; no Amex; no smoking area; booking sometimes restricted.*

Far East   £ 19   ★
27-35 Berry St L1 9DF   (0151) 709 3141
An "astonishing array of dishes" is just part of the formula which
makes this "huge" and "consistently good" spot (located over an
oriental supermarket) "the best in Liverpool's Chinatown".
*/ **Sample dishes:** crispy duck; fillet steak Cantonese style; banana fritters.*
***Details:** by church on Berry St; 11.15 pm; no smoking area.*

Left Bank   £ 32   ★
1 Church Rd L15 9EA   (0151) 734 5040
"Ring a month in advance" if you want to ensure your table at this
local "favourite" – a "very small and intimate restaurant", with
"an excellent chef, a very friendly proprietor and a decent wine list";
*service, though, can be "slow". / **Sample dishes:** quail meringue; fillet*
*steak with pesto & vegetable stew; tiramisu. **Value tip:** set 3-crs L £6.95.*
***Details:** off Penny Lane; 10 pm; closed Mon L & Sat L.*

Not Sushi   £ 22
Imperial Court, Exchange St East L2 3PH   (0151) 236 0643
"Something new", for the 'Pool'; this welcoming oriental noodle
bar/restaurant wins consistent praise for its "fresh", "generous" and
"creative" fare (with "good veggie and vegan options"), though its
*surroundings are too "minimalist" for some tastes. / **Sample***
***dishes:** seafood tempura; chilli seafood ramen; fruit dumplings. **Value tip:** set*
*3-crs L £6.95. **Details:** nr Town Hall; 9.45 pm; closed Sun; no Amex;*
no smoking.

Que Pasa Cantina   £ 20   🅐
94-96 Lark Ln L17 8UU   (0151) 727 0006
The "cheap and yummy Mexican food" is better than you might
expect at this "noisy" and "lively" venture, which is recommended
*"especially for groups". / **Sample dishes:** nachos; chicken fajitas; assiette of*
*chocolate desserts. **Details:** nr Sefton Park; 11 pm; no smoking area.*

Tai Pan   £ 21
WH Lung Building, Gt Howard St L5 9TX   (0151) 207 3888
Large Chinese, above an oriental cash-and-carry; the food can be
"excellent" and the place is "very popular with the local Chinese
*population". / **Sample dishes:** Peking duck; fried lamb in garlic sauce; ice*
*cream. **Value tip:** set 2/3-crs L £5.45/£8.45. **Details:** 11.30 pm.*

Ziba   £ 33   ★
15 Berry St L1 9DF   (0151) 708 8870
"Some of the best cuisine Liverpool has to offer" is served at this
trendy Chinatown-fringe venture, where an "enlightened owner"
serves some "excellent" modern British grub and offers a "super
*wine list". / **Sample dishes:** roast scallops & lobster Roscoff salad; loin of*
*lamb, tomato & courgette tart; banana bread. **Details:** on the edge of*
Chinatown; 10 pm; closed Sun; no smoking area.

Zorbas   £ 19
1 Leece St L1 2TR   (0151) 709 0190
"Consistent" budget Greek, where fans find "lots of character";
*it's licensed, but those in the know BYO. / **Sample dishes:** Greek salad*
*with calamari; lamb kebab; caramel flan. **Details:** top of Bold St; 11.30 pm;*
D only, closed Sun; no credit cards.

LLANDEGLA, DENBIGHSHIRE 5–3A

Bodidris Hall Hotel £ 39 🄰★★
LL11 3AL (01978) 790434
*"A view of the lakes and snow-capped hills" is but one of the joys of
dining at this medieval manor house "run by an enthusiastic foodie";
"six superb courses, meticulously presented and served" from an
"imaginative" menu make a dinner-time visit (and, almost inevitably,
a stay) here truly memorable. / **Sample dishes:** langoustine & saffron
soup; chicken ragoût with cabbage & chestnuts; chocolate teardrop. **Value
tip:** set 3-crs L & Sun L £16. **Details:** on A5104 from Wrexham; 9.15 pm;
jacket & tie; no smoking; children: 18+ on Sat. **Accommodation:** 9 rooms,
from £96.*

LLANDEILO, CARMARTHEN 4–4C

Cawdor Arms £ 29 🄰★
Rhosmaen St SA19 6EN (01558) 823500
*You get some "surprisingly good food" (using "really excellent local
produce") in the "tasteful surroundings" of this charming "market
town hotel" – both in the "intimate" restaurant and at the bar.
/ **Sample dishes:** lamb & marjoram brioche; char-grilled duck with rosemary
jus; elderflower & honey tart. **Value tip:** set 2/3-crs L £11.50/£13.50.
Details: NE of Carmarthen, adjacent to A40 on main street; 9 pm;
no smoking. **Accommodation:** 17 rooms, from £60.*

LLANDEWI SKIRRID, MONMOUTHSHIRE 2–1A

Walnut Tree £ 43 ★★
NP7 8AW (01873) 852797
*Arguably "the most utterly confident simple cooking in the UK"
(never mind Wales!) – where Italian flair is "married to perfection"
with local ingredients – has created a huge reputation for Franco
Taruschio's "casual" and "unpretentious" pub, out "in the wilds"
of Monmouthshire; it's rather "squashed", though, and can get
"overcrowded" and "noisy". / **Sample dishes:** spring vegetable risotto;
roast cod with caponata; Toulouse chestnut pudding. **Details:** 3m NE of
Abergavenny on B4521; 10.15 pm; closed Mon & Sun; no credit cards.*

LLANDRILLO, DENBIGHSHIRE 4–2D

Tyddyn Llan £ 33 🄰★
LL21 0ST (01490) 440264
*"Nothing is too much trouble" for the owners of this "warm and
comfortable" Georgian shooting lodge in the Vale of Edeyrnion;
the cooking is "exceptionally good". / **Sample dishes:** black pudding
& spring onion pancake; pigeon with roast parsnip purée; gingerbread soufflé.
Value tip: set 3-crs Sun L £15.50. **Details:** on B4401 between Corwen and
Bala; 9.30 pm; closed Mon L; no smoking. **Accommodation:** 10 rooms,
from £153.*

LLANDUDNO, CONWY 4–1D

Richards £ 32 🄰★
7 Church Walks LL30 2HD (01492) 877924
*"Great food in a town where you might never expect to find a
good eatery"; Richard's "wonderful home-cooking" is well above the
standard usually associated with that description (and the "wine and
cheese are excellent"); "romantic" and "intimate" cellar premises
complete the package. / **Sample dishes:** grilled goat's cheese with plums;
skate stuffed with spinach & crab; toffee apple cheesecake. **Details:** nr pier;
11 pm; D only.*

LLANFIHANGEL NANT MELAN, POWYS 2–1A

Red Lion £ 24 ★

LD8 2TN (01544) 350220

"Good food in a traditional and welcoming setting" makes this
unassuming *"drover's inn nestling, on the main road, in the Hills
of Radnor"* rightly popular; the lamb, in particular, is *"exceptional"*,
and everything is *"well cooked and presented"*. / **Sample dishes:** fresh
& smoked venison terrine; salmon with wild garlic; Welsh berry pudding.
Details: off A44 between Cross Gates & New Radnor; 9 pm; closed Sun L (&
Tue D, Sep-Jun); no Amex; no smoking area. **Accommodation:** 3 rooms,
from £40.

LLANGAMMARCH WELLS, POWYS 4–4D

Lake Country House £ 41 ★

LD4 4BS (01591) 620202

An Edwardian mansion, set in 50 acres of parkland, which
maintains its domestic ambience; it comes *"highly recommended"*
for its *"good food"*, *"very pleasant service"* and *"superb wine list"*.
/ **Sample dishes:** leek & potato velouté with smoked haddock; rabbit stuffed
with brioche & herbs; chocolate tart with cinnamon cream. **Value tip:** set 3-crs
L £17.50. **Details:** off A483 at Garth; 9 pm; jacket & tie; no smoking;
children: 7+. **Accommodation:** 19 rooms, from £120.

LLANGOLLEN, DENBIGHSHIRE 5–3A

Bryn Howel Hotel £ 34 🅰★

LL20 7UW (01978) 860331

For those of a more traditional bent, this scenically-located hotel
dining room – with its fine views – offers *"perfect food in perfect
surroundings"*. / **Sample dishes:** deep-fried Pen Carreg cheese; Welsh lamb
with organic leek mousse; rich chocolate terrine. **Value tip:** set 3-crs Sun
L £14.50. **Details:** on A539 towards Ruabon; 9 pm; no smoking.
Accommodation: 36 rooms, from £95.

LLANTRISANT, RHONDDA CYNON TAFF 2–1A

La Trattoria £ 29

11 Talbot Rd, Talbot Green CF72 8AF (01443) 223399

A *"nice little Italian, considering it's in the middle of nowhere"*,
offering cooking *"like Mama's"*, and a hospitable atmosphere.
/ **Sample dishes:** fish & shellfish soup with garlic toast; tortelloni with wild
mushroom sauce; amaretto ice cream. **Value tip:** set 2-crs L £6.50.
Details: nr M4 J34; 9.30 pm; closed Sun.

LLANWDDYN, POWYS 4–2D

Lake Vyrnwy Hotel £ 35 🅰★

Lake Vyrnwy SY10 0LY (01691) 870692

This Victorian pile was built to house the engineers who built the
huge reservoir it overlooks, but a *"beautiful location"* is not this dining
room's only strength – its *"interesting"* cooking and *"considerate"*
service are also commended. / **Sample dishes:** potted Stilton with walnut
bread; duck confit with braised red cabbage; port & claret jelly. **Value tip:**
set 3-crs L & Sun L £18.95. **Details:** on B4393 at SE end of Lake Vyrnwy;
9.15 pm; no jeans; no smoking. **Accommodation:** 35 rooms, from £99.

LLYSWEN, POWYS 2–1A

Griffin Inn £ 27 ★

LD3 0UR (01874) 754241

This *"pretty, rural pub"* – *"with its log fires, an ideal location for a
romantic weekend"* – offers an *"eclectic"* menu of a *"consistently
high standard"*. / **Sample dishes:** hot-smoked salmon; slow-roast Welsh
lamb; whimberry crumble. **Details:** on A470; 9 pm; closed Sun D;
no smoking area. **Accommodation:** 9 rooms, from £70.

Llangoed Hall   £ 51   🅐★

LD3 0YP   (01874) 754525

*"A classic country house hotel", in "stunning surroundings" and "without pretensions", where the standards of the "inventive" cooking "never fail". / **Sample dishes:** cappuccino of shellfish; cannon of Welsh lamb; chocolate fondant. **Value tip:** set 2/3-crs L £17/£20 (Sun 3-crs £23.50). **Details:** 11m NW of Brecon on A470; 9.30 pm; jacket & tie; no smoking; children: 8+. **Accommodation:** 23 rooms, from £185.*

LOCH LOMOND, W DUNBARTON   9–4B

Cameron House   £ 60   🅐

G83 8QZ   (01389) 755565

*It's the "pampering luxury", the "magnificence" and the "view" which are the highlights of a visit to this grand lochside hotel; the traditional cooking is lauded by some, but not all reporters. / **Sample dishes:** roast langoustine with crab risotto; roast stuffed quail with port jus; passion fruit soufflé. **Value tip:** set 2/3-crs L £17.50/£21. **Details:** M8, cross over Erskine Bridge to A82, take roundabout to Crianlarich; 9.45 pm; closed Sat L & Sun L; jacket & tie; no smoking; children: 14+. **Accommodation:** 96 rooms, from £185.*

LOCKINGTON, E RIDING, YORKS   6–1A

Rockingham Arms   £ 37   ★

52 Front St   YO25 9SH   (01430) 810607

*"Fab", "tucked away" pub-conversion, offering "excellent" modern British fare in a "peaceful" setting. / **Sample dishes:** cumin-cured salmon; saffron roast cod with Gruyère mash; caramelised pineapple. **Details:** between Beverly & Driffield; 9.30 pm; D only, closed Mon & Sun; no Amex. **Accommodation:** 3 rooms, from £110.*

LOCKSBOTTOM, KENT   3–3B

Chapter One   £ 35   ★

Farnborough Common   BR6 8NF   (01689) 854848

*"The West End comes to Kent" at this "beacon in an otherwise culinarily deserted area"; some question the degree of "local hype" it receives, but most praise the "varied and interesting" menu, "in the style of Gary Rhodes". / **Sample dishes:** baked goat's cheese; roast haddock with seafood risotto; chocolate soufflé with marmalade sorbet. **Value tip:** set 3-crs Sun L £16. **Details:** 2m E of Bromley on A21; 10.30 pm.*

LONG CRENDON, BUCKS   2–2D

Angel Inn   £ 35

Bicester Rd   HP18 9EE   (01844) 208268

*"Tastefully restored" old hostelry, proclaimed a "great find" on account of its "reliable" "bistro" cooking and "friendly and informal service". / **Sample dishes:** moules marinière; oriental red snapper; blackberry crème brûlée. **Value tip:** set 2/3-crs set L £12.95/£14.95. **Details:** 2m NW of Thame, off B4011; 10 pm; closed Sun D; no Amex; no smoking area. **Accommodation:** 3 rooms, from £65.*

Mole & Chicken   £ 31   🅐

Easington   HP18 9EY   (01844) 208387

*The road climbs steeply (from Long Crendon) to reach this "picturesque", "cosy" and "comfortable" country pub, near the top of the hill; the modern British cooking is "fresh", good value and "dependable". / **Sample dishes:** mushrooms stuffed with spinach & cheese; char-grilled lamb fillet stuffed with mint; winter berry cheesecake. **Details:** nr Chandions Hotel; 9.45 pm.*

LONG MELFORD, SUFFOLK 3–1C

Chimneys £ 39 Ⓐ

Hall St CO10 9JR (01787) 379806

"Particularly outstanding for a special occasion, say, around Christmas", this "wonderful" restaurant in a "beautiful village" is the sort of place where you enjoy "the chef's own canâpés next to a roaring fire". / **Sample dishes:** Scottish smoked salmon; braised lamb shank; passion fruit bavarois. **Details:** 9.30 pm; closed Sun D; no Amex & no Switch.

LONGRIDGE, LANCS 5–1B

Heathcote's £ 46

104-106 Higher Rd PR3 3SY (01772) 784969

Reporters' satisfaction with the "naff-cottagey" flagship of the North West's leading chef-entrepreneur plummeted across the board this year; the theory that the sometimes "zingy" cooking "only excels when Paul Heathcote is in the kitchen" (and not off empire-building) may explain the number of "exceedingly expensive and deeply disappointing" experiences. / **Sample dishes:** black pudding; roast breast of duck; bread & butter pudding. **Value tip:** set 3-crs L & Sun L £22.50. **Details:** follow signs for Jeffrey Hill; 9.30 pm; closed Mon, Tue-Thu L & Sat L; no smoking.

LOUGHBOROUGH, LEICS 5–3D

Cactus Café £ 18

16a High St LE11 2PY (01509) 214585

"The best Mexican restaurant in Leicestershire by a mile" – is there any competition? – earns consistent praise for its "generous", "tasty" and "inexpensive" dishes, and for its "lively" atmosphere. / **Sample dishes:** cheese nacjos; chicken burritos; death by chocolate. **Details:** 10 pm; D only, closed Sun; no Amex.

LOUGHTON, ESSEX 3–2B

Ne'als Basserie £ 32

241 High Rd IG10 1AD (020) 8508 3443

"A real trier in an area that's a desert for good places", where the chef/patron dishes up "generous portions" of "imaginative" and "well presented" modern British fare to a "lively" crowd of "appreciative" diners. / **Sample dishes:** onion tarte Tatin; stuffed ballottine of chicken; pear sablé. **Value tip:** set 2/3-crs Sun L £12.50/£15.50. **Details:** 10 pm; closed Mon & Sun D; no Amex.

LOWER BEEDING, W SUSSEX 3–4A

Jeremy's at the Crabtree £ 34 Ⓐ★

Brighton Rd RH13 6PT (01403) 891257

It may be "difficult to locate", but this atmospheric "restaurant annex to a pub" justifies the effort with some "first-class food". / **Sample dishes:** seared tuna steak; roast duck magret; coconut, chocolate & banana tartlet. **Value tip:** set 3-crs menu Mon-Thu £12.50. **Details:** 2m N of Cowfold on A281 to Horsham; 10 pm; closed Sun D; no smoking area.

LOWER PEOVER, CHESHIRE 5–2B

Bells of Peover £ 34

The Cobbles WA16 9PZ (01565) 722269

A "lovely old pub in the heart of the Cheshire countryside", offering "warm and welcoming service and excellent pub food"; for the restaurant, "book well in advance". / **Sample dishes:** smoked salmon with lime dressing; steak with port wine sauce; crème brûlée. **Value tip:** set 3-crs Sun L £15.95. **Details:** opp St Oswald's church; 9 pm; children: 14+ in bar.

LOWER SLAUGHTER, GLOUCS 2–1C

Lower Slaughter Manor £ 72 A★

GL54 2HP (01451) 820456

"Wonderful food in a lovely Cotswold setting" wins consistent praise
for this elegant hotel dining room, on the edge of a charming village,
where Dominic Blake has presided over the stoves for a year now.
/ **Sample dishes:** smoked salmon with capers; duck with parsnip & chestnut
purée; roast pineapple with lemon grass ice cream. **Value tip:** set 3-crs Sun
L £22.50. **Details:** 9.30 pm; no smoking; children: 10+.
Accommodation: 16 rooms, from £150.

LUDLOW, SHROPSHIRE 5–4A

Merchant House £ 38 A★★

Lower Corve St SY8 1DU (01584) 875438

*"We've toyed with the idea of moving to Shropshire so we could
eat there weekly"*; Shaun Hill's *"simply perfect"* cooking –
"supremely confident and unshowy", and using *"excellent fresh
produce"* – draws discerning diners back *"again and again"* to this
"idiosyncratic", *"take-us-as-we-are"* gourmet *"mecca"*. / **Sample
dishes:** calf's sweetbreads with potato & olive cake; turbot with dill crème
fraîche; chocolate Pithiviers. **Details:** 9 pm; closed Mon & Sun; no Amex
& no Switch; no smoking in dining room.

Oaks Restaurant £ 34 ★★

17 Corve St SY8 1DA (01584) 872325

*Could Ken Adams's "cosy", "family-run" restaurant be the "very best
in the West"?* – fans say it's *"unfairly overlooked"* due to the stellar
local competition; the modern British cooking, using *"local and
organic produce"*, is *"interesting"* and *"memorable"*, and a *"personal
touch"* is always evident in the *"formal but not fussy"* dining room.
/ **Sample dishes:** caramelised shallot tart with foie gras; roast turbot with
langoustines & girolles; panna cotta with iced strawberry & mint soup.
Details: below Feathers Hotel; 9.30 pm; D only, closed Mon & Sun; no Amex;
no smoking; Sat D max booking 6; children: 10+.

LUTON, BEDS 3–2A

Man Ho £ 21

72 Dunstable Rd LU1 1EH (01582) 723366

"Quality and variety, with value" make this consistent Chinese a
useful place to know about in a culinary desert. / **Sample dishes:** bang
bang chicken; spicy chicken; ice cream. **Value tip:** set 3-crs L £5.50, 3-crs early
eve £6.95. **Details:** in town centre; 10.30 pm.

LYDGATE, GREATER MANCHESTER 5–2B

White Hart £ 30 A

51 Stockport Rd OL4 4JJ (01457) 872566

*The ground-floor "pub/brasserie" here is praised just as much as the
"consistently good" restaurant upstairs; the latter is "not too formal,
but still special", and its "varied" menus "punch well above their
weight".* / **Sample dishes:** roast squab with black pudding; lamb with risotto
Milanese; chocolate marquise & peppered strawberries. **Value tip:** set 2/3-crs
L £9/£11.50 (Sun £11.50/£13.50). **Details:** on A6050; 9.30 pm;
no smoking area. **Accommodation:** 5 rooms, from £70.

LYMINGTON, HANTS 2–4C

The Old Bank House £ 31

68 High St SO41 9AL (01590) 671128

"Guaranteed good food", of diverse inspiration, wins consistent
support for this *"friendly"* and *"busy"* wine bar-cum-restaurant.
/ **Sample dishes:** seared scallops & bacon salad; smoked duck breast with
honey & mustard; chocolate pot. **Value tip:** set 2-crs L £7.95.
Details: 10 pm; closed Sat L & Sun.

Three Horseshoes   **£ 30**   ★
CB3 8AB   (01954) 210221
*You often find "wonderful" cooking, with strong Mediterranean
and Thai influences (not to mention "superlative wines by the glass")
at this pretty village pub near Cambridge (which has a "lovely
conservatory"); the "bar food is the same as the restaurant, but you
can't book". / **Sample dishes:** gnocchi with mussels & crab; roast beef with
white onion risotto; spiced plums. **Value tip:** set 3-crs Sun L £19.95.
Details: 2m W of Cambridge, off A14 or M11, J13; 9.30 pm, Fri & Sat
10 pm; closed Sun D; no smoking area.*

Five Horseshoes   **£ 29**   𝔸
RG9 6EX   (01491) 641282
*Charming Chilterns pub (10 minutes' drive from Henley) offering
"good-sized portions of well flavoured food" (there's bar food, a
restaurant, and, in the summer, a BBQ); it's always "busy", so
arrive early. / **Sample dishes:** wild duck & smoked bacon terrine; seafood
in cream & orange sauce; double chocolate mousse cake. **Value tip:** set 3-crs
Sun L £14.95. **Details:** on B481, between Nettlebed & Watlington; 10 pm;
no Amex.*

Croque en Bouche   **£ 53**   ★★
221 Wells Rd WR14 4HF   (01684) 565612
*Marion Jones's "beautiful" modern British cooking and Robin J's
"amazingly comprehensive and good-value" wine list help make
their "idiosyncratic" establishment one of the UK's finest; its shop-
conversion premises may have no special charm, but, for many
"this is the perfect restaurant – serious about food, but not
oppressive". / **Sample dishes:** crab croustade; Cotswold spring lamb;
apricot tart. **Details:** 2m S of Gt Malvern on A449; 9.30 pm; D only,
open only Thu-Sat; no Amex; no smoking; max booking 6.*

MANCHESTER, GREATER MANCHESTER   5–2B

Boosted by the demands of the largest student population
of any city in Europe, Manchester boasts a thriving café-bar
scene and an impressive variety of interesting, inexpensive
places to eat. Unlike any other UK city, there is even a
'Gay Village' – a square half-mile devoted to going out,
and whose appeal extends far beyond the gay world.

Fans of the major ethnic cuisines are very well catered for.
The *Yang Sing*, now restored to its old home, is probably
the country's best known Chinese restaurant. Chinatown
(to the east of Portland Street) offers a range of further
possibilities, and there's much for fans of the subcontinent in
Rusholme's 'street of a thousand curries' (a half-mile stretch
of Wilmslow Road).

The city-centre still falls down, though, in its provision of more ambitious non-ethnic places. There are no 'landmark' restaurants, no real 'institutions' and few mid-range places with any real style. None of the large, modern British ventures of the past few years (such as *Simply Heathcotes* or *Mash & Air*) could be pronounced an unambiguous success. There are some interesting developments, though – among newcomers, the ambitious year-old *Lincoln* has made a good start on the cooking front. The 'gangster-Baroque' style of the *Reform* confirms Manchester's traditional strength in 'clubbing', and the creation of environments to go with it (though the place's culinary attractions are less certain). Amongst more established restaurants, the small and idiosyncratic *Market* is very highly thought of.

Those not wishing to eat ethnically or in trendy joints may consider heading out of town. Gary Rhodes has newly set up camp by Old Trafford. West Didsbury is a restaurant concentration of some note, with the excellent *Lime Tree* and a good veggie, *Green's*, now joined by the former top city-centre Thai *Chiang Rai*. For an old-style dinner on expenses, *Moss Nook* (see Moss Nook) and *Etrop Grange* (Manchester Airport) are also worth considering.

Atlas £ 22 ἓ

376 Deansgate M3 4LY   (0161) 834 2124
*Stylishly incorporated into a converted railway arch, by Deansgate station, this trendy all-day café-bar is hailed by some for serving "the best healthy casual food in town"; it has a pleasant rear terrace. / **Sample dishes:** soup of the day; tortellini & sun-dried tomato pesto; chocolate bread & butter pudding. **Details:** next to G-MEX Metrolink stop; 8pm; closed Sat D & Sun D; no Amex; no booking.*

Barça ✳ £ 29

Catalan Sq M3 4WD   (0161) 839 7099
*It's as a trendy drinking place and "a great place to eat outside in summer" that this celebrity-backed spot – set into converted Castlefields railway arches – is best known; the food, though, could be worse, both in the bar and the first-floor dining room. / **Sample dishes:** squid & chorizo with pak choi; lamb with black pudding & beetroot; spiced apple crème brûlée. **Details:** 11 pm; closed Sun D.*

Brasserie St Pierre £ 44 ἓ

57/63 Princess St M2 4EQ   (0161) 228 0231
*"Great surroundings", "attentive service", a "super wine list" and sometimes "excellent" cuisine win high praise for this atmospheric city centre all-rounder. / **Sample dishes:** onion galette with foie gras; roast monkfish with curried mussels; nougat glacé. **Details:** 10.30 pm; closed Mon D, Sat L & Sun.*

Cachumba £ 25 ★

220 Burton Rd M20 2LW   (0161) 445 2479
*A "wonderful mixture of Asian and African dishes" ("full of fresh herbs and spices") is carving out a name for this "tiny" West Didsbury spot where the "haphazard service and low-key décor are part of the charm"; BYO – no corkage. / **Sample dishes:** Sri Lankan spiced lentils; red coconut chicken curry; sticky toffee pudding. **Details:** M56 towards Leeds, turn left at hospital; 9.30 pm; closed Sun; no credit cards.*

Chiang Rai £ 21

1st Floor, 762 Wilmslow Rd M20 2DR (0161) 448 2277

What was an "outstanding Thai restaurant in Chinatown" has now succumbed to Didsbury's suburban charms; performance has been very mixed over the transition, so it's not yet clear whether the formerly "fabulous" performance can be re-created. / **Sample dishes:** *spicy fishcakes; sweet & sour chicken; toffee fruit.* **Details:** *10.30 pm; closed Mon, Sat L & Sun L; no smoking area.*

Darbar £ 17 ★

65-67 Wilmslow Rd M14 5TB (0161) 224 4392

"Massively popular" Rusholme subcontinental whose "well priced" cooking receives credible nominations for "the most accomplished food in the 'curry mile'". / **Sample dishes:** *chicken tikka; Kahari lamb; kulfi.* **Details:** *midnight; no Amex; no smoking area.*

Dimitri's £ 25 𝔸

1 Campfield Ave Arcade, Tonman St M3 4FN (0161) 839 3319

It's the "fantastic atmosphere, especially in summer" which makes this "busy", "bustling" and "laid-back" spot, in an arcade off Deansgate, such a popular rendezvous; the meze and other Greek fare are of solidly "good" quality. / **Sample dishes:** *Loukanika pork sausages; char-grilled lamb kebab; Greek yoghurt & honey.* **Details:** *11.30 pm.*

Est Est Est £ 27

5 Ridgefield M2 6EG (0161) 833 9400

A "simple, solid and reliable" chain-outlet, offering "fairly authentic" ("run-of-the-mill", some say) Italian cooking and a "nice atmosphere"; it's a "good places with families". / **Sample dishes:** *Caesar salad; penne arrabbiata; tiramisu.* **Details:** *nr House of Fraser; 11 pm; no smoking area; Fri & Sat need 8+ to book.*

Great Kathmandu £ 17 ★

140 Burton Rd, West Didsbury M20 1JQ (0161) 445 2145

"Excellent Nepalese food" that's "fresh and tasty every time" – and "at reasonable prices" – ensures continued huge popularity for this small, "busy" and "cramped" family-run spot, in West Didsbury. / **Sample dishes:** *chilli chicken; Nepalese masala; kulfi.* **Value tip:** *set 3-crs L £5.90.* **Details:** *midnight.*

Green's £ 23 𝔸★★

43 Lapwing Ln M20 2NT (0161) 434 4259

"Simple, excellent combinations of the freshest ingredients, wonderfully presented" win a disproportionately large fan club for this "trendy, small and intimate" BYO veggie café in West Didsbury; "good service and good value" complete a winning package. / **Sample dishes:** *baked goat's cheese in sesame seeds; mushrooms, leeks & tomatoes in filo pastry; chocolate & Tia Maria pie.* **Value tip:** *set 2-crs L £5 (Sun £8.50), set 3-crs pre-th & Sun & Mon D £10.* **Details:** *4m S of city centre; 10.30 pm; closed Mon L, Sat L & Sun L; no Amex.*

The Greenhouse £ 15 ★

331 Great Western St M14 4AN (0161) 224 0730

There's "a vast choice of dishes" and "every one's a winner!" at this "great veggie haven" – a quirky, cosy dining room in a Rusholme end-terrace; "friendly, personal service" and "a good range of organic wines" are further attractions. / **Sample dishes:** *deep-fried avocado with garlic mayonnaise; Stilton and vegetable bake; chocolate & coffee mousse.* **Details:** *at junction of Great Western St & Herald Grove; 11 pm; no Amex; no smoking.*

The Grinch £ 22 Ⓐ

5-7 Chapel Walks, off Cross St M2 IHN (0161) 907 3210
"Funky décor and food" make this *"very mellow"* central café-wine
bar a favourite young-at-heart choice. / **Sample dishes:** tiger prawns
& oriental noodles; Mediterranean couscous paella; lemon cheesecake.
Details: 10.30 pm.

The Lime Tree £ 29 Ⓐ★★

8 Lapwing Ln M20 2WS (0161) 445 1217
"An exceptional and varied menu" is just part of the *"trusty"*
formula which explains why many people go back and back to
this *"appealing"* and *"unstuffy"* modern British brasserie, in
West Didsbury – Manchester's best all-rounder by far; it's *"always
buzzing"*, and the din is too much for some. / **Sample dishes:** scallops
with sweet chilli dressing; roast lamb with ratatouille & garlic mash; iced
tiramisu parfait. **Value tip:** set 2-crs L & early eve £9.95, set 3-crs Sun
L £12.95. **Details:** nr Withington Hospital; 10.30 pm; closed Mon L & Sat L;
no smoking area.

The Lincoln £ 43 ★

I Lincoln Sq M2 5LN (0161) 834 9000
As you'd expect from an ex-Lime Tree chef, there's some
"exceptional modern cooking" to be had at this *"friendly and
first-class"* newcomer; stylish premises, off Deansgate, and good-value
set menus are further attractions. / **Sample dishes:** scallops; roast lamb;
raspberry shortbread. **Value tip:** set 2/3-crs L & early eve £12.50/£14.95.
Details: closed Sat L & Sun D.

Little Yang Sing £ 28 ★★

17 George St MI 4HE (0161) 228 7722
"First-class" cooking makes this *"very small"*, *"brightly lit"* Chinese –
on the Yang Sing's original site, and still under the same ownership –
"very popular". / **Sample dishes:** steamed scallops in garlic; spiced lamb
with Peking sauce; custard dumpling. **Value tip:** set 3-crs L £8.95.
Details: I I pm.

Malmaison Hotel £ 34 Ⓐ

Piccadilly MI 3AQ (0161) 278 1000
"Trendy", *"sophisticated"* city-centre brasserie attached to this
designer-hotel; its *"tasty"* and *"wholesome"* cooking wins consistent
support. / **Sample dishes:** Caesar salad; steak frites; crème brûlée.
Value tip: set 2/3-crs L £9.50/£12.50. **Details:** nr Piccadilly Station;
I I pm. **Accommodation:** 112 rooms, from £75.

The Market £ 41 Ⓐ★★

104 High St M4 IHQ (0161) 834 3743
*"The thought that goes into the menu is marvellous and those
puddings, wow!"* – *"fresh produce"*, *"well cooked"*, and delivered at
a very reasonable price, wins unanimous support for this *"homely"*
and *"friendly"* city-centre spot, where much of the crockery and
décor dates from the '40s. / **Sample dishes:** smoked haddock ravioli;
peppered fillet of beef with red wine gravy; walnut meringues & caramel sauce.
Details: 9.30 pm; D only, open Wed-Sat only.

Mash & Air (Air) £ 39

40 Chorlton St MI 3HW (0161) 661 1111
The more ambitious top-floor restaurant above Mash (see below)
affords a *"stark"* and cavernous setting in which to savour cooking
which many find *"precious"*, *"over-complicated"* and *"overpriced"*;
unremarkably, it's sometimes rather *"quiet"*. / **Details:** next to Chorlton
St Coach Station; I I pm; D only, closed Sun.

Mash & Air (Mash) £ 35
40 Chorlton St M1 3HW (0161) 661 1111
Enthusiasm for this style-driven microbrewery/restaurant is wearing thin; a few people still think it's "cool", but far too many reporters find "both the employees and the décor exceptionally pretentious", and the pattern of commentary on the cooking is broadly similar. / **Details:** *next to Chorlton St Coach Station; 11 pm, Thu-Sat midnight; closed Sun.*

Metropolitan £ 22 A★
2 Lapwing Ln M20 2WS (0161) 374 9559
Thanks to its "good all-round quality", it's no surprise that this "reasonably priced" Withington gastropub is "very busy"; even so, "easy armchairs", an "open fire" and "waitress service" contribute to an "unrushed" atmosphere. / **Sample dishes:** *chicken liver pâté; sausages with spring onion mash; sticky toffee pudding.* **Details:** *nr Withington Hospital; 9.30 pm; no smoking area.*

Metz £ 24 A
2 Canal St M1 3PJ (0161) 237 9852
In spite of self-promotion as a 'gay space', this "warm" and "friendly" spot by the canal (with a pontoon for summer drinking) attracts a "mixed clientèle", and general praise for its "unusual" and inexpensive eastern European food. / **Sample dishes:** *pork meatballs; mint coated roast lamb; dark chocolate sponge.* **Details:** *10 pm.*

Nico Central £ 38
Mount St M60 2DS (0161) 236 6488
A "very poor relation" of the Nico-branded empire where the cooking is "a pity" and the service too often "gormless"; it's a shame that this pretty dining room (within the landmark Midland hotel) can only really be recommended for its "good-value set lunch". / **Sample dishes:** *smoked eel, black pudding & poached egg salad; duck confit with thyme potatoes & olives; chocolate pudding & coconut ice cream.* **Value tip:** *set 2/3-crs L £10.50/£13.50.* **Details:** *11 pm.*

Pearl City £ 27 ★
33 George St M1 4PH (0161) 228 7683
"In the heart of Chinatown", this sprawling emporium offers "a real taste of China" and is "always bursting with diners, Chinese and English"; it offers "reliably good food", including "excellent dim sum", from an "overwhelming" menu. / **Sample dishes:** *chicken & sweetcorn soup; fillet steak Cantonese style; coconut pudding.* **Details:** *2 am, Fri & Sat 3 am, Sun 11 pm.*

Reform £ 38 A
Spring Gardens, King St M2 4ST (0161) 839 9966
Its "decadent" and "romantic" setting has made this new venture in an extravagantly remodelled Victorian club an instant hit with the "trendy urban cream of Manchester"; not everyone likes its style though ("dreadful"), and the "pricey" modern British cooking is "inconsistent". / **Sample dishes:** *pan-fried goose liver; red mullet with sea urchin sauce; goblet of chaud froid red fruit.* **Value tip:** *set 2/3-crs L & early eve £12.95/£16.95.* **Details:** *11 pm.*

Rhodes & Co £ 31
Waters Reach M17 1WS (0161) 868 1900
Initial feedback is mixed on Gary R's homage to his heros, a stone's throw from Old Trafford – a protochain now also with a branch in Edinburgh (and with more promised); fans report the "excellent meals" one would expect from the Gazza of gastronomy, though others have found so-so cooking and slack service in a "rather stark" building. / **Sample dishes:** *smoked haddock with Welsh rarebit; salmon fishcakes with lemon & butter sauce; sticky toffee pudding.* **Value tip:** *set 2-crs L £11.50.* **Details:** *next to Quality Hotel; 9.45 pm; closed Sat L & Sun L.*

Royal Orchid £ 22

36 Charlotte St M1 4FD (0161) 236 5183
"Very dependable" central Thai; even those who admit its *"good standards"* can find the atmosphere *"boring"*, and service can be *"slow"*. / **Sample dishes:** beef & pork satay; Siamese fried chicken; ice cream. **Details:** nr Piccadilly Gardens; 11.30 pm; closed Sun.

Shere Khan £ 18

52 Wilmslow Rd M14 5TQ (0161) 256 2624
This *"bright, brash and brassy"* establishment *"certainly stands out in the Rusholme curry mile"*; it probably is *"one of this curry capital's better restaurants"*, but there's a feeling that *"it seems to be resting on its laurels"*. / **Sample dishes:** onion bhajia; chicken tikka masala; kulfi. **Details:** midnight.

Shezan £ 20 ★

119 Wilmslow Rd M14 5AN (0161) 224 3116
Large, *"consistently good"* Rusholme Indian, complete with endearingly glitzy décor; BYO. / **Sample dishes:** lamb shish kebab; karahi chicken; homemade kulfi. **Details:** midnight; no smoking area.

Siam Orchid £ 22 ★

54 Portland St M1 4QU (0161) 236 1388
An *"excellent BYO Thai"*, behind Piccadilly station, offering a *"wide range"* of *"tasty"* dishes; *"service can be slow but the staff are charming"*. / **Sample dishes:** beef & pork satay; Siamese fried chicken; ice cream. **Details:** 11.30 pm; closed Sun D.

Simply Heathcotes £ 36

Jackson Row, Deansgate M2 5WD (0161) 835 3536
It's *"Manchester's best"*, say the many fans of this modish, central brasserie, who are inspired by *"intriguing combinations of well prepared Lancashire produce"*; complaints of *"unpredictable"* quality are numerous, though, as are references to *"brusque"* service and a setting which is too *"warehouse-like"*. / **Sample dishes:** crab & avocado salad with sweet chilli; roast duck with sweet pea purée; peach melba soufflé. **Value tip:** set 2/3-crs L & pre-th £10.50/£12.50. **Details:** nr Opera House; 11 pm, Sun 9 pm.

Tampopo £ 17 ★

16 Albert Sq M2 5PF (0161) 819 1966
"Ultra-minimalist", *"very utilitarian"* noodle *"canteen"* in a cellar off Albert Square, which offers *"generous"* portions of *"tasty"* and *"enjoyable"* SE Asian fare (including a *"good variety of veggie dishes"*) to a *"casual, young"* crowd. / **Sample dishes:** vegetable tempura; chicken ramen; kulfi. **Details:** in front of town hall; 11 pm; no Amex; no smoking; children: 7+.

Tandoori Kitchen £ 14 ★

131-133 Wilmslow Rd M14 5AW (0161) 224 2329
"Excellent food in inauspicious surrounding, and very cheap" – this *"old favourite"* of a quarter of a century's standing is, for many, still *"the best unlicensed curry house in Rusholme's golden mile"*. / **Sample dishes:** mixed tandoori platter; Poodina lamb; ice cream & fruit. **Details:** midnight; no smoking area.

That Café £ 30 𝔸

1031 Stockport Rd M19 2TB (0161) 432 4672
"Imaginative cooking at good prices" seems to be surviving the changes of ownership at this welcoming, if grottily located Levenshulme shop-conversion. / **Sample dishes:** pigeon & beetroot ballottine; roast cod with saffron seafood risotto; white chocolate & strawberry ripple parfait. **Value tip:** set 2-crs early eve & Sun L £9.95. **Details:** on A6 between Manchester & Stockport; 10.30 pm; closed Mon, Sat L & Sun D; no Amex.

Yang Sing £ 32 ★★

34 Princess St M1 4JY (0161) 236 2200

*"The best Chinese in the North West!", "... in Europe!", "... in the world!" – fans are not shy in their claims for the culinary pride of Manchester; even while displaced from its normal Chinatown premises by a fire – it returned to base in September '99 – it remained the best-known oriental restaurant in the UK, and rightly so given its "superb and imaginative" cooking and overall "attention to detail". / **Sample dishes:** cuttlefish cake; ostrich casserole; fresh fruit platter. **Details:** close to city art gallery; 11 pm.*

MANNINGTREE, ESSEX 3–2C

Stour Bay Café £ 24 ★

39-43 High St CO11 1AH (01206) 396687

*"Not a café, but a very good bistro-type place", praised for its carefully prepared, modern British cooking. / **Sample dishes:** spiced salad of duck breast; pan-fried cod with creamed onions; strawberries & mango with Mascarpone. **Value tip:** set 2/3-crs L £8.50/£10. **Details:** 9.30 pm; closed Mon, Sat L & Sun.*

MARKET HARBOROUGH, LEICS 5–4D

Han's £ 22

29 St Mary's Rd LE16 7DS (01858) 462 288

*Better than average food and "excellent" service make it worth remembering this upmarket Chinese, near the town square. / **Sample dishes:** crispy aromatic duck; beef in black bean sauce; toffee banana. **Details:** nr town centre; 11 pm; closed Sun.*

MARLOW, BUCKS 3–3A

Compleat Angler £ 55

Marlow Br SL7 1RG (01628) 484444

*"The best view of the river you'll find" presumably explains how this famous Thameside hotel/restaurant gets away with offering "predictable" cooking at "sky-high" prices; breakfast, lunch ("in spring and summer") and tea are the meals most warmly applauded. / **Sample dishes:** pan-fried goose liver & olives; sea bass with saffron risotto & cockles; sticky toffee pudding. **Value tip:** set 2/3-crs L £17.50/£21.50 (but Sun £33.50). **Details:** 10 pm; no jeans; no smoking area. **Accommodation:** 65 rooms, from £175.*

MARSTON TRUSSELL, LEICS 5–4D

The Sun Inn £ 28

Main Street LE16 9TY (01858) 465531

*The French owners of this hostelry not far from Market Harborough are applauded by local fans for their "market-directed menu" of "fresh" fare; the setting also wins approval for its "traditional and warm" style. / **Sample dishes:** leek & potato soup; duck in red wine sauce; profiteroles. **Value tip:** set 3-crs Sun L £12.95. **Details:** 3.5m from Market Harborough; 9.30 pm. **Accommodation:** 20 rooms, from £69.*

MASHAM, N YORKS 8–4B

Floodlite £ 29 ★

7 Silver St HG4 4DX (01765) 689000

*"Excellent game" and other straightforward fare make this small Dales town restaurant a place worth seeking out; "they need to work on the atmosphere", though. / **Sample dishes:** moules marinière; roast saddle of venison; blackberry & apple bread & butter pudding. **Details:** 9 pm; closed Mon & Tue L-Thu L; no Switch; no smoking area.*

MELBOURN, CAMBS
Pink Geranium   £ 50   3–1B
                                                              A★
25 Station Rd SG8 6DX   (01763) 260215
*This "thatched house converted into a restaurant" ("a gem in the
gastronomic desert of Hertfordshire") has a "beautiful" location,
and – "despite the celebrity-status of the owner" (TV chef
Steven Saunders) – "maintains high standards"; the modern British
cooking is "sometimes brilliant", if perhaps on the pricey side.
/ Sample dishes: char-griddled foie gras; roast black-legged chicken;
hot caramelised strawberry Tatin. Value tip: set 2/3-crs L £14/£17.
Details: off A10 from Royston to Cambridge, 2nd exit (opp church); 10 pm;
closed Mon & Sun; jacket; no smoking; children: not permitted.*

MELBOURNE, DERBYS
Bay Tree   £ 39   5–3C
4 Potter St DE73 1DW   (01332) 863358
*Though some feel that the approach to modern British cooking is
a little "old-fashioned", this former 17th-century town-centre
coaching inn is still a "reliable" "favourite" for most reporters.
/ Sample dishes: baked figs stuffed with goat's cheese; English lamb with herb
crust; lemon jelly & passion fruit sauce. Value tip: set 3-crs Sun L £17.50.
Details: 9.45 pm; closed Mon; no smoking area; children: not encouraged.*

MELKSHAM, WILTS
Toxique   £ 40   2–2C
                                                              A★
SN12 7AY   (01225) 702129
*"Exotique" – and to some "érotique" – this "quirkily converted
farmhouse" is far from being your typical provincial eatery; the
whole approach may be "unusual and eccentric", but the eclectic
cooking consistently impresses. / Sample dishes: goat's cheese tart with
red peppers; pan-fried cod with lime & noodles; apricot tart. Details: on back
road to Laycock, 1m from Melksham; 10 pm; D only; open Wed-Sat only;
no smoking. Accommodation: 5 rooms, from £160, incl D.*

MELLOR, LANCS
Shajan   £ 21   5–1B
                                                              ★
Longsight Rd, Clayton-le-Dale BB1 9EX   (01254) 813640
*It may have a "strange location" – in a Dales village outside
Blackburn – but fans proclaim "consistently great food" at this
Bangladeshi bar/restaurant, where "the owner Mr Ali and his son are
always very welcoming". / Sample dishes: fish kebab; chicken Shajan;
mango sorbet. Details: 8m E of Preston on A59; 11.30 pm; no smoking area.*

MELMERBY, CUMBRIA
Village Bakery   £ 23   8–3A
                                                              ★
CA10 1HE   (01768) 881515
*An "organic bakery" with a difference, offering "delicious" breads,
cakes, cheeses and salads; "proper Cumbrian breakfasts" are a
further attraction. / Sample dishes: fresh marinated Hawkshead trout;
Old English pork casserole; lemon tart with blackcurrant sauce. Details: 10m
NE of Penrith on A686; L only; no Amex; no smoking.*

MERTHYR TYDFIL, MERTHYR TYDFIL
Nant Ddu Lodge   £ 29   4–4D
                                                              A
Brecon Rd CF48 2HY   (01685) 379111
*The "romantic", "away-from-it-all", riverside setting isn't all there is
to say about this family-run Georgian hunting lodge, with its
"wood fires and friendly staff"; there are also good reports, both
on the restaurant grub and on the "large selection" of bar dishes.
/ Sample dishes: mackerel with warm potato salad; roast hake with mango
& lime salsa; char-grilled bananas & toffee cream. Details: 6m N of Merthyr
on A470; 9.30 pm; closed Sun D; no smoking; max booking 8.
Accommodation: 22 rooms, from £69.50.*

MIDDLESBOROUGH, MIDDLESBOROUGH   8–3C
Purple Onion   **£ 32**
80 Corporation Rd TS1 2RF   (01642) 222250
*"Relaxed and convivial", "French-style" bistro; it's useful in a thin
area, but mixed commentary supports those who say it's "average".
/ Sample dishes: scallops with saffron & coriander dressing; San Franciscan
bouillabaisse; hot chocolate & chilli sponge. Details: by law courts & Odeon
cinema; no Amex.*

MILTON KEYNES, MILTON KEYNES   3–2A
Jaipur   **£ 25**   Ⓐ★
502 Eldergate MK9 1LR   (01908) 669796
*It's especially worth seeking out the "banquet evenings" at this
eminent subcontinental – "presided over by the ever-attentive
Mr Ahad", though the "extensive menu" of "quality", "freshly spiced"
dishes justifies a visit at any time. / Sample dishes: prawn purée;
pistachio chicken korma; pineapple delight. Value tip: set 3-crs Sun L £9.95.
Details: next to railway station; 11.30 pm; no smoking area.*

MORETON-IN-MARSH, GLOUCS   2–1C
Marsh Goose   **£ 35**
High St GL56 0AX   (01608) 653500
*This "smart" and prettily located Cotswold village restaurant has
quite a reputation for its "inventive and delicious" English cooking;
it's "in danger of slipping quite seriously", though, with reports of
"so-so" food, and continued gripes about "disinterested" and
"unfriendly" service. / Sample dishes: veal & pigeon terrine; seared blue fin
tuna; iced yoghurt & honey terrine. Details: 9.30 pm; closed Mon & Sun D;
no smoking area.*

MORPETH, NORTHUMBERLAND   8–2B
Linden Hall Hotel   **£ 39**   Ⓐ
NE65 8XF   (01670) 516611
*"A great welcome", "log fires" and "beautiful china and silver"
help make a visit to this picturesque country house hotel a "special"
experience; the "good-value" Anglo/French cooking does not let the
side down. / Sample dishes: game & lamb terrine; grilled fillet of beef;
dark chocolate truffle torte. Value tip: set 3-crs L & Sun L £17.95.
Details: off A1 on A697 between Longhorsley and Long Framlington; 9.45 pm;
no jeans; no smoking; children: 10+. Accommodation: 50 rooms, from £125.*

MORSTON, NORFOLK   6–3C
Morston Hall   **£ 43**   Ⓐ★
Main Coast Rd NR27 7AA   (01263) 741041
*This "small hotel" (occupying a house dating back to the
17th century), is "set in lovely gardens on the North Norfolk coast";
its dining room offers some "brilliant" cuisine from a "very wide-
ranging set price menu", "personal attention" and an "excellent wine
list". / Sample dishes: morel risotto; char-grilled beef with bubble & squeak;
raspberry brûlée. Value tip: set 3-crs Sun L £20. Details: between Blakeney
& Wells; 8 pm; D only, ex Sun open L & D; no smoking during D.
Accommodation: 6 rooms, from £190, incl D.*

MOSS NOOK, GREATER MANCHESTER   5–2B
Moss Nook   **£ 46**   ★
Ringway Rd M22 5WD   (0161) 437 4778
*"The décor may resemble a brothel" (or "a Victorian gin palace"),
but there's no doubting the quality of the "traditional" French cooking
at this long-established ("dated") restaurant, near Ringway Airport;
service can be "overbearing". / Sample dishes: king prawns wrapped in
salmon; rack of lamb with tomato & rosemary sauce; chocolate medley.
Value tip: set 3-crs L £18.50. Details: on B5166, 1m from Manchester
airport; 9.30 pm; closed Mon, Sat L & Sun; no jeans; children: 11+.*

Beetle & Wedge £ 45 🄰★

Ferry Ln OX10 9JF (01491) 651381

It's not only the "perfect setting on the banks of the river" which makes this "elegant" and "welcoming" restaurant with rooms one of the best places in the Thames Valley – the modern British cooking is "consistently good, and reasonably priced"; in the boathouse, a less ambitious grills menu is served. / **Sample dishes:** aubergine & Mozzarella gratin; calves' liver & bacon; plum tart with custard. **Details:** on A329 between Streatley & Wallingord, turn into Ferry Lane at crossroads; 9.45 pm. **Accommodation:** 10 rooms, from £135.

Black Bull £ 36 🄰★

DL10 6QJ (01325) 377289

The "lovely atmosphere, in a former Pullman railway carriage" helps make a visit to this long-established pub and restaurant something of an occasion; that's not to overlook the "consistently good" results from the "long traditional menu" (with fish the speciality), and the "dedication" of the staff. / **Sample dishes:** spinach & Cheddar soufflé; salmon & asparagus with hollandaise; crème brûlée. **Value tip:** set 3-crs L £14.95. **Details:** 1m S of Scotch Corner; 10.15 pm; closed Sun; children: 7+.

Pandora Inn £ 25 🄰★

Restronguet Creek TR11 5ST (01326) 372678

Despite its "grade A" waterfront location, the cooking in this terrific thatched medieval pub is "much better than the let's-rely-on-the-ambience variety", and "the local fish is out of this world". / **Sample dishes:** crab & smoked salmon salad; John Dory with herb & prawn sauce; chocolate meringue roulade. **Details:** signposted off A390, between Truro & Falmouth; 9.30 pm; no smoking.

White Hart £ 29 ★

11 High St C06 4JF (01206) 263382

"An excellent mix of French and British" cooking – from a Roux brothers protégé – makes this former 15th-century public house a top local destination. / **Sample dishes:** gravadlax & horseradish crème; roast beef with seed mustard & white wine sauce; chocolate crème brûlée & raspberries. **Details:** between Colchester & Sudbury; 9.30 pm. **Accommodation:** 6 rooms, from £69.50.

Goff's £ 44 🄰★

Langwith Mill House NG20 9JF (01623) 744538

This "converted mill, off the beaten track", with its "country house" atmosphere, is the "number one venue locally"; the modern British cooking is "beautifully cooked and presented", and service is "homely". / **Sample dishes:** seafood terrine; roast escalope of Welsh veal; almond meringue with chocolate mousse. **Value tip:** set 2-crs L £12.50. **Details:** 9.30 pm; no smoking.

NEW MILTON, HANTS   2–4C
Chewton Glen   **£ 57**   A
Christchurch Rd BH25 6QS   (01425) 275341
For its fans, this "opulent" country house hotel, on the fringe of the
New Forest, offers "reliably good food, using fresh local ingredients";
the consistency of praise one would expect at this price-level is,
however, notable by its absence. **Sample dishes:** *celeriac soup with*
Stilton; pan-fried veal with spinach & ham ravioli; sweet blinis with blackberry
caviar. **Value tip:** *set 2/3-crs L £13.50/£18.50 (Sun £27.50).*
Details: *between New Milton & Highcliffe on A337; 9.30 pm; closed Mon L;*
jacket at D; no smoking; children: 7+. **Accommodation:** *53 rooms,*
from £230.

NEWBURY, BERKS   2–2D
Dew Pond   **£ 37**   ★
Old Burghclere RG20 9LH   (01635) 278408
Though the "lovely setting" (in view of 'Watership Down') and the
charming, "family-run atmosphere" make this "secluded" restaurant
worth seeking out, its key appeal is its "excellent" cooking, and
"good wines". / **Sample dishes:** *crab with spiced tomato sorbet; venison*
with creamed wild mushrooms; assiette of chocolate. **Details:** *6m S of*
Newbury, off A34; 10 pm; D only, closed Mon & Sun; no smoking area;
children: 5+.

NEWCASTLE UPON TYNE, TYNE & WEAR   8–2B

The going-out heart of Newcastle is to be found in the old
docks, the Quayside – an area utterly transformed over the
past few years. It is home to the North East's most notable
gastronomic destination, *21 Queen Street* – a modern British
venture whose success has spawned a series of 'diffusion'
outlets in nearby towns (but which, paradoxically, is set to
move from the address that it has made famous). There are
also a couple of notable Indians (*Leela's, Vujon*).

The hill leading up from the Quayside to the town centre is
the location for a number of good, slightly quirky places. In
the centre of town, *Barn Again* is a great favourite as an
informal venue.

A short taxi-ride from town, and leafily located in Jesmond
Dene, the *Fisherman's Lodge* enjoys a particularly picturesque
situation.

Barn Again Bistro ✳   **£ 30**   A★
21a Leazes Park Rd NE1 4PF   (0191) 230 3338
With its "casual, relaxed and busy" atmosphere and "helpful" staff,
this "fabulous", "quirky" barn-conversion is one the most popular
places in town for a top night out; a "refreshingly unusual menu"
(do they really serve "Brown Ale risotto?") is part of the winning
package. / **Sample dishes:** *Spanish octopus & chorizo salad; roast lamb with*
sweet potato tagine; Spice Island ginger cake. **Details:** *nr St James's Park*
football ground; 10 pm; closed Mon, Sat L & Sun.

Courtney's   **£ 40**
5-7 The Side NE1 3JE   (0191) 232 5537
A "very small and cosy", "traditional-style" restaurant on the
Quayside; opinion divides between the majority who say it's an
"atmospheric" place which is "good on all counts", and the minority
who find it "bland" and "ordinary". / **Sample dishes:** *salmon & avocado*
tartlet; marinated lamb chop; chocolate & amaretto parfait. **Value tip:** *set*
2/3-crs set L £14.95/£16.95. **Details:** *beneath Tyne Bridge; 10 pm; closed Sat*
L & Sun.

Da Vincis   £ 27   Ⓐ

Osborne Rd NE2 2IN   (0191) 281 5284

A "lively, buzzy local Italian" – attached to an hotel, but "deserving
to be separately considered" – whose "large menu" proposes
"consistently good" food; "great staff" contribute to a "lovely
atmosphere". / **Sample dishes:** avocado & lobster; chicken cappuccino;
tiramisu. **Value tip:** set 3-crs £10.25. **Details:** 10.30 pm.

Dragon House ❊   £ 23

30-32 Stowell St NEI 4XQ   (0191) 232 0868

"Stylish, friendly and elegant" spot, worth seeking out in
"Newcastle's China Town"; "good veggie choice and quality" is among
the attractions. / **Sample dishes:** chicken & sweetcorn soup; king prawns in
chilli & black bean sauce; ice cream. **Value tip:** set 2/3-crs L £5.50/£7.25.
Details: 11 pm; no Amex.

Fisherman's Lodge   £ 42

Jesmond Dene NE7 7BQ   (0191) 281 3281

"A delightful rural setting in the heart of the city" (in the leafy
Jesmond Dene river valley) helps make this "rather formal"
restaurant a classic "special occasion" destination; traditional cooking
which is "unbeatable" for some ("exceptional" fish, in particular)
seems a little "run-of-the-mill" to others. / **Sample dishes:** shellfish
tempura with soy sauce; poached lemon sole topped with lobster; mango
brûlée. **Value tip:** set 3-crs L £17.80. **Details:** 2m from city centre on A1058,
follow signposts to (and in) Jesmond Dene; 10.45 pm; closed Sat L & Sun;
no smoking; children: 8+.

Fox Talbot ❊   £ 23   Ⓐ

46 Dean St NEI IPG   (0191) 230 2229

"Useful", "small, café-style" operation, above the Quayside, offering
an "amazing variety" of "imaginative" ("wacky") and well presented
dishes in a "lively" and "cosmopolitan" atmosphere. / **Sample
dishes:** pan-fried kangaroo; roast sea bass; buttermilk pancakes. **Value
tip:** set 2-crs L £4.87. **Details:** nr Theatre Royal; 11 pm; no booking 8pm-
9pm.

Francesca's   £ 17   Ⓐ ★

Manor House Rd NE2 2NE   (0191) 281 6586

"Traditional" and "clichéed" it may look, but this "buzzing" ristorante
and pizza parlour "must be doing something right" – "from 6.30
every night, there's a queue at the door"; the "gorgeous garlic
prawns" receive a particular thumbs-up. / **Sample dishes:** king prawns
in garlic; capricciosa pizza; tiramisu. **Details:** 9 pm; closed Sun; no Amex;
no booking.

King Neptune ❀   £ 26

34-36 Stowell St NEI 4XQ   (0191) 261 6657

Above-average cooking ("superb seafood", in particular), "attentive
and personal" service and a "very relaxed" atmosphere help to make
this an "excellent Cantonese restaurant". / **Sample dishes:** spare ribs
with garlic & spicy salt; sliced beef in Szechuan black pepper sauce; toffee
apple. **Value tip:** set 3-crs L & Sun L £6.50. **Details:** 10.45 pm.

Leela's   £ 30   ★

20 Dean St NEI IPG   (0191) 230 1261

"A revelation"; reporters heap praise on the "aromatic, fragrant, and
delightful" cooking (offering much to interest veggies) at this "totally
excellent", family-run South Indian, near the Quayside. / **Sample
dishes:** lamb in almond sauce; rice & lentil pancake with coconut chutney;
payasm (Indian vermicelli sweet). **Value tip:** set 3-crs L £9.95.
Details: 11.30 pm; closed Sun; no Switch.

Magpie Room   £ 36   ★

St James's Pk Football Ground NE1 4ST   (0191) 201 8439
*A "real find" – the "magnificent top-floor dining room at Newcastle
United's football ground" provides a "very civilised" environment for
"an excellent meal, with professional service"; there's a "terrific view
over the ground, so it's always sold out on match days". / **Sample
dishes:** smoked haddock risotto; pan-fried cod with mussel & asparagus broth;
pear & almond crumble. **Value tip:** set 2/3-crs L £10.50/£13.
Details: 10.30 pm; closed Mon, Sat L & Sun D; shirt & tie; no smoking;
children: not encouraged.*

Metropolitan ✳   £ 27

35 Grey St NE1 6EE   (0191) 230 2306
*"Smart", "hi-tech" modern European café/restaurant, which inspires
an impressive amount of commentary, especially regarding its "fun",
"snazzy" style; even some fans acknowledge the occasional "off-day",
however, and a fair number of sceptics discern a "lazy" and
"pretentious" approach. / **Sample dishes:** seared tuna & red onion
salad; spiced duck confit with black bean salsa; white chocolate & raspberry
cheesecake. **Value tip:** set 2-crs L £8.95. **Details:** nr Theatre Royal;
10.45 pm; closed Sun; no smoking area.*

Sachins   £ 25   ★

Sachins NE1 3SG   (0191) 261 9035
*The "subtle and spicy tastes" of its "consistent", "high quality"
cooking makes this large and "busy" Indian reporters' top curry
house in town; the décor may not be to all tastes, but the service is
usually "friendly" and "slick". / **Sample dishes:** Sachins tandoori platter;
butter chicken; kulfi. **Details:** behind Central Station; 11.15 pm; closed Sun.*

21 Queen Street ✳   £ 40   ★★

21 Queen St, Princes Wharf NE1 3UG   (0191) 222 0755
*"Superbly cooked" food from an "interesting and varied" modern
French menu ensures that, in the evenings at least, this "friendly and
innovative" (if rather "bare") Quayside "haven" – long the hottest
place in town – is "always full"; NB as we go to press, chef/patron
Terry Laybourne is looking to move to new premises. / **Sample
dishes:** sauté of scallops & artichokes; braised rabbit & fresh pasta; caramel
soufflé. **Details:** 10.30 pm; closed Sat L & Sun.*

Valley Junction   £ 22   𝔸

Old Jesmond Stn, Archbold Terr NE2 1DB   (0191) 281 6397
*A converted railway carriage provides an "unusual" setting for this
"friendly and hospitable" spot; "it's more like a restaurant that
happens to be Indian than a traditional Indian restaurant".
/ **Sample dishes:** varke prawns; pistachio beef curry; gulab jamon.
Details: nr Civic Centre, off Sandyford Rd; 11.30 pm; closed Mon;
no smoking area.*

Vujon   £ 29   ★

29 Queen St NE1 3UG   (0191) 221 0601
*Located just off the busy Quayside, this "elegant" and "top-class"
Indian delivers "unexpected recipes" and some "subtle cooking".
/ **Sample dishes:** kebabs, tikka & pakoras; lamb korma & pilau rice; Indian
milk sweet. **Details:** 11 pm; closed Sun L.*

NEWPORT, NEWPORT   2–2A

Junction 28   £ 25   𝔸

Station Approach NP1 9LD   (01633) 891891
*Unpromisingly named, it may be, but this "busy" restaurant in a
converted railway station offers a "wide" and "reasonably priced"
menu; "outrageously friendly" service wins special praise.
/ **Sample dishes:** pigeon breast on creamed cabbage; monkfish with shrimp
mousse in filo pastry; lemon tart. **Details:** J8 M4, towards Caerphilly; 9.30 pm;
closed Sun D; no Amex.*

Cook & Barker   £ 31   ★
LA65 9JY   (01665) 575234

"Tasty food in a very pleasant, informal setting" helps ensure that this village pub-restaurant is *"often very crowded"*. / **Sample dishes:** crispy marinated duck; beef in Stilton sauce; Belgian chocolate truffle. **Details:** 12m N of Morpeth, just off A1; 8.30 pm; no smoking area. **Accommodation:** 4 rooms, from £70.

Hundred House   £ 34   𝔸
Bridgnorth Rd   TF11 9EE   (01952) 730353

"Lovely", characterful, *"family-run"* pub, set in pretty gardens; it serves an *"imaginative menu"*. / **Sample dishes:** smoked haddock with deep-fried leeks; lamb with braised fennel; vanilla crème brûlée. **Details:** on A442 between Bridgnorth & Telford; 9.30 pm. **Accommodation:** 10 rooms, from £95.

Adlards   £ 49
79 Upper Giles St NR2 1AB   (01603) 633522

David Adlard's restaurant *"delightfully situated in 'olde' Norwich"* offers *"an oasis in a food desert"*, and fans say it's *"worth the often interminable wait"* for his *"wonderful"* food; too many reports find the cooking *"poor, for a Michelin star winner"*, however, *"though the prices are certainly high enough!"* / **Sample dishes:** scallops with apple & ginger purée; lamb with roast shallots; Grand Marnier soufflé. **Value tip:** set 3-crs L £15. **Details:** nr Roman Catholic Cathedral; 10.30 pm; closed Mon L & Sun; no smoking during D.

By Appointment   £ 35   𝔸
27-29 St George's St NR3 1AB   (01603) 630730

Quality cooking and a *"strong wine list"* at a *"reasonable price"* help make this *"intimate"*, *"richly decorated"* spot (which is *"filled with antiques"*) *"a wonderful dining experience"* for some reporters. / **Sample dishes:** red snapper with scallops & curried prawns; lamb stuffed with apricot & pistachio; white chocolate parfait. **Details:** from St George's St, turn into Colegate then 1st right into courtyard; 9.30 pm; D only, closed Mon & Sun; no Amex; no smoking in dining room; children: 12+.

Siam Bangkok   £ 26
8 Orford Hill NR1 3QD   (01603) 617817

"Very relaxed" city-centre spot, strongly approved locally for *"the best choice of fish and seafood"*, and *"excellent vegetarian Thai cooking"*. / **Sample dishes:** chicken satay; chicken curry; ice cream. **Value tip:** set 3-crs L £8.95. **Details:** nr Timber Hill; 10.30 pm; closed Mon L & Sun L.

Tatlers   £ 29   ★
21 Tombland NR3 1RF   (01603) 766670

"Charming and friendly service, a relaxed atmosphere and first-rate food" make this intimate English spot – just yards from the Cathedral – an all-round success. / **Sample dishes:** haddock with spinach & Emmental; roast lamb with ratatouille; lemon tart. **Value tip:** set 3-crs L £12.50. **Details:** nr Cathedral; 10 pm; closed Sun; no Switch.

The Tree House   £ 18
14-16 Dove St NR21 1DE   (01603) 403448

Service is *"slow"*, and even some supporters say the ambience is *"not good"*, but this *"bright"* café is unanimously praised for its *"very tasty"*, *"non-stodge"* veggie fare; *"every community should have one"*. / **Sample dishes:** carrot & coriander soup; kidney beans & broccoli in chilli & garlic sauce; chocolate banana cake. **Details:** 9 pm; closed Mon D, Tue D, Wed D & Sun; no credit cards; no smoking; no booking at L.

Bees Make Honey   £ 29
12 Alfreton Rd NG7 3NG   (0115) 978 0109
*This small establishment may have a "greasy spoon ambience",
but it boasts a devoted fan club, who laud its "interesting" cooking;
even some of those who say it's "excellent", agree it's "not cheap",
given the comfort level, and some find service "appalling". /* **Sample
dishes:** *avocado with grilled Haloumi; Spanish seafood & shellfish stew; white
chocolate cheesecake.* **Details:** *10.15 pm; D only, closed Mon & Sun;
no credit cards.*

La Boheme   £ 31   A
Barker Gate, Lace Market NG1 1JU   (0115) 912 7771
*A "tasteful" setting and "super" food (with an Eastern European
twist) is already winning fans for this "stylish" city-centre yearling
bar/restaurant; live jazz is a feature. /* **Sample dishes:** *twice-baked
cheese soufflé; grilled salmon with chorizo salad; glazed lemon tart.* **Value
tip:** *set 3-crs Sun L £15.95.* **Details:** *11 pm; closed Sun D; children: not
encouraged.*

Hart's   £ 34   A★
Standard Court, Park Row NG1 6GN   (0115) 911 0666
*With its "attractive 1990's interior", "very happening" atmosphere,
and "dynamic" modern British cooking, this "polished", city-centre
yearling wins unusually consistent praise, and is the kind of "classy"
venture which would be welcome anywhere. /* **Sample dishes:** *grilled
squid in lemon oil; quail with asparagus & spring cabbage; Hart's fruit salad.*
Details: *nr castle; 10.30 pm Mon-Sat, Sun 9 pm.*

The Indian   £ 22   ★
5 & 7 Bentinck Rd NG7 4AA   (0115) 942 4922
*"Curry as you think it should be" makes this "stylish" and "friendly"
spot "highly recommended". /* **Sample dishes:** *garlic & mushroom balti;
chicken tikka masala; kulfi.* **Details:** *2m from centre, off A610; 10.30 pm;
closed Mon & Sun; closed 2 weeks in Aug & 1 week in Dec; no smoking area.*

Merchants   £ 36
29-31 High Pavement, Lace Market NG1 1HS   (0115) 958 9898
*Did the receipt of a Michelin 'bib gourmand' go to the head of this
year-old, city-centre venture?; some still find a brilliant all-round
experience, but there are too many reports which suggest that a
place which "used to be excellent", now offers "overpriced" and
"unadventurous" food, and "neglectful'" service. /* **Sample dishes:** *roast
chicken ravioli; Aberdeen beef with bacon & wild mushrooms; apple tart with
calvados & sultanas.* **Value tip:** *set 2-crs L £10.* **Details:** *10.30 pm; closed
Sat L & Sun D.*

Pretty Orchid   £ 22
12 Pepper Street NG1 2GH   (0115) 958 8344
*"Copious and flavoursome" Thai cooking that's "interesting" and
"well presented" wins wide support for this city-centre oriental;
its setting and level of service are less of an attraction. /* **Sample
dishes:** *pork satay; kung po chicken; papaya sorbet.* **Details:** *behind
Marks & Spencer; 11 pm; closed Sun.*

Saagar   £ 34
473 Mansfield Rd NG5 2DR   (0115) 962 2014
*Some inconsistency mars reports on this central Indian, but for its
fans it's the "best in town", with "great chef's specials" particularly
commended. /* **Sample dishes:** *chicken pakora; king prawn with mustard
seed & peppers; banana split.* **Details:** *1.5m from city centre; midnight; closed
Sun L; no smoking area; children: 6 mos.*

Sonny's £ 33

3 Carlton St NG1 1NL (0115) 947 3041

This "stylish" and "easy-going" modern restaurant attracts much commentary, pleasing most reporters with its "interesting", "beautifully presented" modern British menus; the setting can seem a touch "sterile", though, and a number think it currently "over-rated", especially in the light of its previous high standards. / **Sample dishes:** fish soup with rouille & Gruyère; duck with mango & coriander salsa; sticky toffee pudding. **Value tip:** set 2/3-crs L £10 (not Sun)/£13.95. **Details:** nr Victoria Centre; 10.30 pm, Fri & Sat 11 pm.

ODIHAM, HANTS 2–3D

The Grapevine £ 33 A★

121 High St RG29 1LA (01256) 701122

"Really good food at extremely reasonable prices" is part of the formula that makes this "beautifully located", "intimate" and "friendly" bistro into "a local gem". / **Sample dishes:** pan-fried scallop and bacon salad; roast lamb with sweet potato rosti; dark chocolate and lime tart. **Value tip:** set 2-crs L £8.95, set 3-crs early eve £14.95. **Details:** follow signs for Odiham from M3, J5; 10 pm; closed Sat L & Sun.

OLDHAM, GREATER MANCHESTER 5–2B

HoHo's £ 27

57-59 High St, Lees OL4 3BN (0161) 620 9500

"Set in a small village", this "very bright" Chinese restaurant, with its "Mediterranean décor", is something of a novelty and, though it's "a little pricier than Chinatown" it provides "good food and good fun". / **Sample dishes:** seafood teriyaki; Szechuan chilli beef; toffee banana. **Value tip:** set 3-crs L £7.95. **Details:** follow signs from M62, J20; 10 pm; closed Mon L-Wed L.

ONGAR, ESSEX 3–2B

Smiths Brasserie £ 33

Fyfield Rd CM5 0AL (01277) 365578

"Busy" and "bubbly" town-centre bistro which majors in "very good fish dishes"; "smart", "friendly" and "efficient" staff win particular praise. / **Sample dishes:** cocktail of crab & prawn in croustade cases; grilled scallops in white wine & mushroom sauce; roast pineapple & butterscotch sauce. **Value tip:** set 3-crs L £13.50. **Details:** turn left off A414 towards Fyfield; 10.30 pm; closed Mon; no Amex; children: 12+.

ORFORD, SUFFOLK 3–1D

Butley Oysters £ 24 ★

Market Hill IP12 2LH (01394) 450277

"No atmosphere, but it doesn't seem to matter" – "outstanding fish" and "wonderfully fresh seafood" are what this "brilliant, basic café" is all about. / **Sample dishes:** smoked oysters; grilled Dover sole; rum cake with cream. **Details:** 10m E of Woodbridge; 9 pm; no Amex; no smoking.

ORPINGTON, KENT 3–3B

Xian £ 21 ★

324 High St BR6 0NG (01689) 871881

"You must book for this very busy Chinese", praised for its "fabulous food and service"; some say it's "the best I've been to". / **Sample dishes:** sesame prawn toast; crispy aromatic duck; toffee apples. **Details:** 11 pm; closed Sun L; closed first week of Aug.

OSWESTRY, SHROPSHIRE   5–3A

Sebastians   **£ 33**   ★
45 Willow St SY11 1AQ   (01691) 655444
*"Consistently high-quality French food, well presented" helps make
this dining room in a 16th-century house "very popular". / Sample
dishes: fish & shellfish soup with saffron; duck in blackcurrant sauce;
strawberry meringue. Details: nr town centre, follow directions to Selattyn;
9.45 pm; closed Mon & Sun; no smoking. Accommodation: 4 rooms,
from £45.*

The Walls   **£ 28**   𝔸
Welsh Walls SY11 1AW   (01691) 670970
*An "exceptional venue", say fans of this atmospheric "converted
schoolhouse" (which has the "welcome feature of lots of space
between the tables"); new management have maintained the
"consistently good" (if fairly straightforward) culinary standards.
/ Sample dishes: potted smoked fish & prawns; pork belly with beans; lemon
tart with fromage frais. Details: from town centre, take Cross Street, fork right
then first left; 9.30 pm, Fri & Sat 10 pm; closed Sun D.*

OVINGTON, HANTS   2–3D

Bush   **£ 27**   𝔸
SO24 0RE   (01962) 732764
*With its "open fires in winter, and tables by the river in summer",
it's difficult to beat the "simply exquisite" setting of this "superb rural
pub"; the menu doesn't aim to set the world on fire, but wins very
consistent approval. / Sample dishes: crab cakes with chilli peanut dressing;
calves' liver with blackcurrant jus; blueberry bread & butter pudding.
Details: just off A31 between Winchester & Alresford; 9.30 pm; closed Sun D.*

OXFORD, OXON   2–2D

Oxford may lack any great restaurants – those in search of a
gastronomic 'high' head for *Le Manoir aux Quat' Saisons*
(Great Milton) – but for those looking to eat well without
spending too much money this is arguably the best city
outside London in England.

The Manoir's younger sibling, *Le Petit Blanc* – a large,
metropolitan-style modern brasserie – is by far the most
talked-about place in town, if not one which deserves star
billing. The top ethnics are a more reliable attraction, with
Al Shami, *Bangkok House* and *Chaing Mai*, in particular,
very convenient for the centre.

As you might hope in the city which claims the greatest
concentration of listed buildings in the country, there are
a number of restaurants with real charm and atmosphere,
including *Cherwell Boat House*, the *Lemon Tree* and the
Old Parsonage.

Al Shami   **£ 22**   ★★
25 Walton Cr OX1 2JG   (01865) 310066
*"Lebanese food at its best" (with "great meze and pastries") makes it
worth booking ahead for this "authentic", "friendly" and very popular
establishment, in a quiet Jericho street. / Sample dishes: Armenian
sausages; fish kebabs; Lebanese desserts. Details: 11.45 pm; no Amex.*

Aziz   £ 27   ★★

228-230 Cowley Rd OX4 IUH   (01865) 794945

"It's hard to beat this Indian gem" – an East Oxford curry house
that's a "quantum leap ahead" of its local competition; it's not just
the "reasonably priced" cooking which is "of consistently high
standards" – the service is "friendly" and the setting "attractive".
/ Sample dishes: fishcake with green chillies; lamb razalla with yoghurt;
curdled milk with nuts. Details: 10.45 pm; no smoking area.

Bangkok House   £ 20   Ⓐ★

42a High Bridge St OX1 2EP   (01865) 200705

"Interesting" central Thai restaurant which is "very popular, and
worth visiting", thanks to its "delicious, spicy food", "charming"
service and "unusual" décor. / Sample dishes: mixed Thai starters; green
chicken curry; sticky rice with mango. Details: 10.45 pm; closed Mon;
no smoking area.

Browns   £ 30   Ⓐ

5-11 Woodstock Rd OX2 6HA   (01865) 319655

"Happy memories" keep nostalgics coming back to this "classic
Oxford dining experience", the original of the UK's leading English
brasserie chain; "it has deteriorated since the take-over" (by Bass),
however, and though the "buzz and animation" remain, service is
now of the "pack 'em in, sling 'em out" school and the cooking
often "poor". / Sample dishes: gravadlax; steak, mushroom & Guinness pie;
lemon tart. Value tip: set 2-crs early eve £5. Details: 11.30 pm;
no smoking area; no booking at D.

Chaing Mai   £ 29   ★★

130a High St OX1 4DH   (01865) 202233

"Superb", "authentic" and "beautifully presented" Thai dishes,
together with "attentive" service and a location in a "marvellous old
building", off the High, make this central oriental well worth seeking
out; it may be "an odd combination of Tudor England and SE Asia",
but it works! / Sample dishes: spiced Thai chicken; steamed fish with Thai
herbs & plums; exotic ice creams. Details: nr Carfax; 10.45 pm;
no smoking area.

Cherwell Boat House   £ 27   Ⓐ★

Bardwell Rd OX2 6ST   (01865) 552746

"Especially on a summer evening", this "beautifully located" but
"Spartan" riversider offers a "lovely" experience; the "tiny menu,
picking the freshest local ingredients" is widely approved, as is
"the most interesting and best-value wine list for miles around".
/ Sample dishes: smoked ostrich with green beans; Gressingham duck with
plum sauce; tiramisu. Details: 1m N of St Giles, by Dragon School playing
fields; 10 pm; closed Mon & Sun D; no smoking.

Elizabeth's   £ 37

82 St Aldates OX1 1RA   (01865) 242230

This intimate city-centre stalwart (est 1966) hasn't tried to move with
the times, much to the satisfaction of devotees of the classic French
approach – "when the menu's this good you know why it hasn't
changed"; for some, however, the approach is "so traditional it verges
on kitsch". / Sample dishes: smoked fish pâté; salmon in white wine sauce;
raspberry sorbet. Value tip: set 3-crs L & Sun L £16. Details: 11 pm; closed
Mon.

Fishers   £ 32   ★

36-37 St Clements OX4 1AB   (01865) 243003

"Excellent fish and seafood" – "a wide range, cooked simply, and
presented in an unpretentious way" – have made quite a name for
this "cheerful" and "bustling" bistro. / Sample dishes: Dublin Bay
prawns in garlic butter; baked sea bass with ginger; sticky date pudding.
Value tip: set 2-crs L £10.50. Details: by Magdalen Bridge; 10.30 pm; closed
Mon L; no Amex; no smoking area.

Gees   **£ 38**   Ⓐ

61 Banbury Rd OX2 6PE   (01865) 553540
A "wonderfully romantic" Victorian conservatory setting makes quite
a "favourite" of this atmospheric restaurant; after a "dull" patch,
the food appears to be improving. / **Sample dishes:** crab & avocado
salad with shrimp dressing; lamb shank confit with glazed shallots; steamed
marmalade sponge. **Value tip:** set 2/3-crs L £7.50/£9.75. **Details:** 11 pm.

The Lemon Tree   **£ 35**   Ⓐ

268 Woodstock Rd OX2 7NW   (01865) 311936
Even fans who praise the "beautifully presented Mediterranean
cooking" at this airy and "exceptionally attractive" establishment,
located in a large north Oxford villa, admit it's "fairly expensive"
for what it is; to the many doubters, though, this place just offers
"very disappointing food in a lovely setting". / **Sample dishes:**
aubergine & goat's cheese; pork stuffed with sage & Mozzarella; pineapple
tarte Tatin. **Details:** 1.5m N of city centre; 11 pm.

Luna Caprese   **£ 28**   ★

4 North Parade OX2 6XL   (01865) 554812
"Eternally welcoming" (since 1962), mega-kitsch north Oxford side
street spot, offering "huge portions of very fresh Italian cooking";
"listen to the waiter's recommendations". / **Sample dishes:** grilled
sardines; veal & scallops in lemon sauce; tiramisu. **Details:** 11 pm;
no smoking area.

The Old Parsonage   **£ 36**   Ⓐ

1 Banbury Rd OX2 6NN   (01865) 310210
It's the "informal" and "serene" setting – an impressive medieval
townhouse a few minutes from the centre of town – which makes
this the kind of place which is a "very good choice for taking relatives
to lunch"; the modern British cooking plays a supporting rôle.
/ **Sample dishes:** spinach & Parmesan soufflé; duck with honey teriyaki sauce;
chocolate tart. **Details:** 0.5m N of city centre; 11 pm. **Accommodation:** 30
rooms, from £125.

Le Petit Blanc   **£ 32**

71-72 Walton St OX2 6AG   (01865) 510999
Raymond Blanc's "buzzy" modern Gallic brasserie in Jericho may be
"hot", "cramped" and "noisy", but for its many fans it's a "cheerful"
and "efficient" spot (and "child-friendly", too); sadly, only a couple of
years after opening, it's already "resting on its laurels" – those in
search of "great value" must go for the "very tasty" set lunch.
/ **Sample dishes:** Morteaux sausage & lentil salad; rabbit with mustard farci;
chocolate feuilleté. **Value tip:** set 2-crs L & pre-th £12.50.
Details: 10.45 pm; no smoking area.

Shimla Pinks   **£ 27**   Ⓐ

16 Turl St OX1 3DH   (01865) 244944
In its "zany" conversion of an old building near Jesus College, this
year-old branch of the expanding national chain offers a "refreshingly
different approach to an old Indian theme" and "pleasant" service;
some say the "amazing buffet" is "better than the à la carte".
/ **Sample dishes:** spiced prawns in breadcrumbs; chicken stuffed with
pomegranates; Indian rice & milk dessert. **Details:** nr Exeter & Lincoln
colleges; 10.30 pm; no smoking area.

Thai Orchid   **£ 24**

58a St Clements St OX4 1AH   (01865) 798044
"Ornately decorated" Thai restaurant that offers an "extensive",
"good-value" choice – the buffet lunch menu is especially
recommended. / **Sample dishes:** beef satay; green chicken curry; chocolate
spiced with rum. **Value tip:** set 3-crs L £8.95. **Details:** nr Headington Park;
11 pm; closed Sat L & Sun L.

Seafood Restaurant   £ 51

Riverside PL28 8BY   (01841) 532700

*To visit TV-chef Rick Stein's "unpretentious" harbourside fixture –
famed for its "classically simple" seafood menu – promises
"a real adventure", and, for many, "he really delivers"; there is,
though, a powerful undertow of dissatisfaction, however, with what
too many see as "outrageous prices" for a "conveyor-belt approach",
and an experience which "does not live up to the hype". / **Sample
dishes:** grilled shellfish; turbot with hollandaise sauce; panna cotta with
rhubarb. **Value tip:** set 3-crs L £29.50. **Details:** 10 pm; closed Sun; no Amex;
no smoking in dining room; children: 3+. **Accommodation:** 13 rooms,
from £80.*

Country Elephant   £ 34

New St GL6 6XH   (01452) 813564

*An "adventurous" menu (you might find "snails AND tripe"),
usually cooked to "good" effect, makes it worth trying this "small",
"quiet country restaurant". / **Sample dishes:** Hereford snails with Pernod;
monkfish escalopes with leek risotto; lemon & lime posset. **Value tip:** set 2/3-
crs Sun L £15/£18. **Details:** 5m W of Cheltenham; 10 pm; closed Mon
& Sun; no smoking.*

Yorke Arms   £ 34   𝔸★

Ramsgill HG3 5RL   (01423) 755423

*"An exceptionally good restaurant in a pub in the middle of nowhere";
it has a "beautiful" location, and offers a "lovely" range of "good"
British fare (especially game) in "cosy" surroundings. / **Sample
dishes:** crispy duck with roasted fennel; calves' liver, black pudding & sweet
potato mash; honey madeleine & saffron pears. **Details:** 4m W of Pately
Bridge; 8.45pm; closed Sun D; no smoking; max booking 6.*
***Accommodation:** 13 rooms, from £65.*

Vine House   £ 36   ★

100 High St NN12 7NA   (01327) 811267

*A "fixed menu, using fresh, local produce, and served in a
charming and intimate dining room" wins praise for Julie and Marcus
Springett's pleasant 17th-century village house. / **Sample
dishes:** salmon mousse; steak & kidney pie; bread pudding. **Details:** 2m S of
Towcester just off A5; 9.15 pm; closed Mon-Wed L, Sat L & Sun; no Amex
& no Switch; no smoking. **Accommodation:** 6 rooms, from £69.*

Churchill Arms   £ 26   ★

GL55 6XH   (01386) 594000

*This "typical pub in a small, very beautiful Cotswold village" has
been "rejuvenated by the owners of the well-known Marsh Goose
(at Moreton-in-Marsh)"; you'd "better get there early" if you want to
enjoy the "imaginative" cooking, though – "there's no booking, and it
can get crowded". / **Sample dishes:** chicken livers & aubergine purée;
red snapper with carrot fondue; sticky toffee pudding. **Details:** on Fosse Way;
9 pm; no Amex; no booking. **Accommodation:** 4 rooms, from £60.*

PENSHURST, KENT   3–3B

Spotted Dog   £ 24   Ⓐ

Smarts Hill TN11 8EP   (01892) 870253

This "charming old pub", with its "open fires" and "terraced garden"
– and "good, traditional English food" too – is especially praised as a
summer destination, "when you can sit outside". / **Sample
dishes:** prawns in garlic butter; swordfish marinated in chilli & citrus;
strawberry meringue cream. **Details:** 9.15 pm; closed Mon D.

PENTRYCH, CITY OF CARDIFF   2–2A

De Courcey's   £ 38

Tyla Morris Ave CF4 8QN   (029) 2089 2232

Purpose built neo-Georgian banqueting complex, a fair drive from
central Cardiff, best suited to business and 'big nights out'; it attracts
limited but positive commentary. / **Sample dishes:** warm pigeon salad
with cranberries; peppered monkfish with cucumber mash; hot passion fruit
soufflé. **Value tip:** set 3-crs Sun L £15.95. **Details:** M4 J32, 2m E of
Llantrisant on A4119; 10 pm; D only, ex Sun when L only, closed Mon.

PERTH, PERTH & KINROSS   9–3C

Let's Eat   £ 31   ★

77-79 Kinnoull St PH1 5EZ   (01738) 643377

"Welcoming", "bric à brac-filled" bistro, offering "super" modern
Scottish cooking (using "wonderful, fresh produce") and "genuinely
good" service. / **Sample dishes:** roast scallops with sweet chilli dressing;
seared halibut with lobster & pesto butter; bread & butter pudding.
Details: opp North Inch Park; 9.45 pm; closed Mon & Sun; no smoking area.

PINNER, LONDON   3–3A

La Giralda   £ 24   Ⓐ

66-68 Pinner Green HA5 2AB   (020) 8868 3429

A "Spanish restaurant which has stood the test of time" – even fans
of this "old favourite" admit it "can be a bit variable", but no one
doubts it's a "friendly" and "bustling" spot. / **Sample dishes:** garlic
mushrooms; poached halibut; crème brûlée. **Details:** A404 to Cuckoo Hill
Junction; 10 pm; closed Mon & Sun D.

PLYMOUTH, DEVON   1–3C

Chez Nous   £ 47   ★

13 Frankfort Gate PL1 1QA   (01752) 266793

"Excellent cooking, using fresh local produce" makes this very Gallic
bistro worth knowing about it, and not just because it's in this under-
provided town; to say that its "downtown Plymouth" location is "poor"
is to understate its total hideousness. / **Sample dishes:** scallops with
ginger; bouillabaisse; chocolate mousse. **Details:** 10.30 pm; closed Mon, Sat
L & Sun.

The China Garden   £ 29

17/19 Perrys Cross PL1 2SW   (01752) 664472

"Pity about the surroundings", but you get some "excellently cooked"
Cantonese dishes at this chow house "in an unprepossessing part of
town". / **Sample dishes:** spare ribs; beef with chilli; toffee apple.
Details: 11.15 pm; closed Sun; casual; no booking.

Veggie Perrins   £ 17

97 Mayflower St PL1 1SD   (01752) 252888

A "city-centre veggie" that's "unusual (well, unusual for Devon)",
and some even claim is "the best Indian in the south west"; "the
owner has anticipated the usual puns by putting them on the menu".
/ **Sample dishes:** samosas; roast vegetables in oriental spices; no puddings.
Value tip: set 2-crs L £3.50. **Details:** nr Copthorne; 9.30 pm; closed Sun;
no Amex; no smoking.

The Wet Wok   £ 25
West Hoe Rd PL1 3   (01752) 664456
"Get a window seat", if you can, to get the best out of this
"excellently located" Chinese restaurant, overlooking the Sound;
it's a *"friendly"* place, whose *"authentic"* cooking is *"good,
but pricey"*. / **Sample dishes:** *sesame prawns; chicken in black bean
sauce; lemon sorbet.* **Details:** *11.30 pm.*

PONTELAND, NORTHUMBERLAND   8–2B

Café 21   £ 30   ★
35 The Broadway, Darras Hall NA20 9PW   (01661) 820357
*In spite of the place's rather unlikely location – a converted dockside
warehouse "in a housing estate close to Newcastle Airport" – this
"informal and friendly" venture is a worthy offshoot of Newcastle's
21 Queen Street; its "modern bistro-style cooking" displays "sound
brasserie techniques".* / **Sample dishes:** *goat's cheese ravioli; confit of duck
& roast potatoes; chocolate-filled meringue.* **Details:** *from A1, 1m past
Newcastle Airport; 10 pm; D only, closed Mon & Sun.*

POOLE-IN-WHARFEDALE, W YORKS   5–1C

Monkmans   £ 29   Ⓐ
Poole Bank, New Rd LS21 1EH   (0113) 284 1105
*This "trendy" restaurant is held by its fans to offer a "beautiful menu,
top service and a very upbeat environment"; it disappoints some,
though, for reasons which include "rude service" and "lack of menu
variety".* / **Sample dishes:** *won ton soup with spring onion dumplings; seared
white tuna with papaya salad; iced passion fruit soufflé.* **Value tip:** *set 3-crs
Sun L £14.50.* **Details:** *5m from Leeds, on road to Otley; 10 pm; closed Mon
L & Sat L; no Amex; no smoking area.* **Accommodation:** *6 rooms, from £70.*

PORT APPIN, ARGYLL & BUTE   9–3B

Pier House Hotel   £ 28   ★
PA38 4DE   (01631) 730302
*"Fabulous fish" still makes it "worth the drive" to this "relaxed" spot,
"superbly located" by where the ferry leaves for Lismore Island; but is
there a "loss of atmosphere" since its recent change of ownership?*
/ **Sample dishes:** *moules marinière; seafood platter; brandy baskets with fresh
fruit.* **Details:** *just off A828 by pier; 9.30 pm; no Amex; no smoking area.*
Accommodation: *12 rooms, from £70.*

PORT ISAAC, CORNWALL   1–3B

Port Gaverne Hotel   £ 29   ★
PL29 3SQ   (01208) 880244
*The dining room of this 17th-century inn, which has been under the
same ownership for the last three decades, wins unanimous praise
for its "excellent local fish" dishes.* / **Sample dishes:** *crab soup;
fish & shellfish in lemon butter; dark chocolate tart.* **Details:** *N of Port Isaac
on coast road (B3314); 9.30 pm; no smoking; children: 7+.*
Accommodation: *17 rooms, from £51.*

PORTAFERRY, CO DOWN   10–2D

Portaferry Hotel   £ 31   Ⓐ★
10 The Strand BT22 1PE   (012477) 28231
*"Excellent scallops and soda bread", typify the "superb" provisions
at this ferry-side hotel, which "overlooks Strangford Lough".* / **Sample
dishes:** *duck & pistachio terrine; seared scallops with bacon & garlic; raspberry
parfait.* **Details:** *9 pm.* **Accommodation:** *14 rooms, from £90.*

Harbour Lights £ 35 ★
SA62 5BL (01348) 831549
"A fabulous quayside hut", offering "fresh, unfussy food" which makes "excellent use of local produce"; "a limited choice but carefully considered". / Sample dishes: laverbread & spinach with bacon & cockles; Dover sole with parsley butter; blackcurrant & raspberry sorbet. Details: 7.5m NE of St Davids; 9.30 pm; open only Thu-Sat D; no Amex; no smoking area.

Portmeirion Hotel £ 43 Ⓐ★
LL48 6ER (01766) 770000
The "wonderful" and "unique setting" – at the centre of Sir Clough Williams-Ellis's fantasy Mediterranean village – ensures a visit here is a memorable experience (and very "romantic" too); travellers also come away with fond recollections of the "traditional but inventive" cooking and the "very good" service. / Sample dishes: poached eggs with Parma ham; salmon with leek & fennel fondue; glazed lemon tartlet. Value tip: set 3-crs L £10.50 (Sun £14.50). Details: off A487 at Minffordd; 9.30 pm; closed Mon L; no smoking. Accommodation: 39 rooms, from £100.

Crown Hotel £ 27
North Cr DG9 8SX (01776) 810261
"Local produce and seafood, well cooked and presented" is the forte of this charming harbourside pub and restaurant. / Sample dishes: scallops wrapped in bacon; Dublin Bay prawns; fruit crannachan. Value tip: set 3-crs D £14.90. Details: 10 pm; no smoking area. Accommodation: 12 rooms, from £72.

Ramore Wine Bar £ 32 ★★
The Harbour BT56 8D3 (01265) 824313
It isn't always clear whether reporters are talking about the first-floor restaurant (with wine bar downstairs) or the new bistro a few doors away, which all bear the 'Ramore' name; it doesn't really matter, though, as they're all "stylish" places, offering "reliably superb" fish and seafood. / Sample dishes: smoked chicken & blue cheese; grilled fillet of halibut with parsley mash; Grand Marnier soufflé. Details: 10 pm; D only, closed Mon & Sun; no Amex; children: 12+.

White House £ 34
New Rd SK10 4DG (01625) 829376
It's "fairly posh" – what else would you expect in this most chichi of north western villages? – but, thanks to its "lovely" surroundings and its rather trendy and generally successful cooking, this is a "very popular" pub/restaurant. / Sample dishes: sweet potato crisps & smoked chicken; crispy duck with roast orchard fruits; treacle pudding with apples. Value tip: set 3-crs L & Sun L £13.50. Details: 10 pm; closed Mon L & Sun D. Accommodation: 11 rooms, from £70.

PRESTON, LANCS

Heathcote's Brasserie £ 29 ★ 5–1A

23 Winckley Sq PR1 3JJ (01772) 252732

"Top-quality cooking, with fresh local ingredients" wins quite a
following for this modish, *"smart, town-centre eatery"* (located some
three miles from Heathcote's Longridge flagship); gripes include some
"uninspiring" meals, and the thought that the *"lunchtime ambience is
better than the evening's"*. / **Sample dishes:** black pudding hash with
Lancashire cheese; braised pork with spring mash; spiced peach soup.
Value tip: set 2/3-crs L & D £10.50/£12.50. **Details:** nr railway station;
10.30 pm; closed Sun.

PRESTWOOD, BUCKS 3–2A

Polecat £ 24

170 Wycombe Rd HB16 0HJ (01494) 862253

"Some imaginative new dishes, as well as trusty favourites" and a
"good wine list" make this *"charming pub and garden"* a *"great"*
destination for a number of reporters. / **Sample dishes:** baked
mushrooms with Welsh rarebit; venison with dandelion, nettle & mushroom
risotto; meringues with caramel sauce. **Details:** 9 pm; closed Sun D;
no credit cards; no smoking; children: not in dining room.

RAMSBOTTOM, GREATER MANCHESTER 5–1B

Village Restaurant £ 29

BL0 9HT (01706) 825070

Fans still hail the *"organic food, superbly sourced and presented"*,
served by *"people who obviously care"* at this intimate dining room
over a delicatessen and wine merchants; there are doubters, though,
who rail against a place that's *"gone downhill"*. / **Sample
dishes:** Caesar salad; breast of Goosenargh duckling; Ricotta cheesecake.
Details: nr M66 J1; 9.30 pm; closed Mon, Tue D & Sun D; no Amex;
no smoking.

REDMILE, LEICS 5–3D

The Peacock Inn £ 27

Church Corner NG13 0GA (01949) 842554

Recently expanded country inn which enjoys a *"lovely setting in
a valley"*, near Belvoir Castle (with some *"nice walks nearby"*);
a *"French catering team"* produces *"good"*, *"cheap and cheerful"*
results. / **Sample dishes:** Brie & grilled pepper gâteau; monkfish wrapped in
smoked salmon & celeriac mash; caramelised hazelnut parfait.
Details: Grantham exit from A52, then follow signs; 9.30 pm; no Amex;
no smoking. **Accommodation:** 8 rooms, from £90.

REIGATE, SURREY 3–3B

La Barbe £ 35

71 Bell St RH2 7AN (01737) 241966

"Honest" cooking and a *"decent wine list"*, served *"with Gallic charm
and flair"*, ensure you *"need to book well in advance"* for this popular
bistro; it's *"a bit pricey"* though, and some find the cooking *"very
calorific"* and rather *"over-complicated"*. / **Sample dishes:** snails in garlic
butter; lamb casserole with provençale tomatoes; raspberry & vanilla bavarois.
Details: nr Safeway; 9.45 pm; closed Sat L & Sun; no smoking area.

Dining Room £ 38 ★

59a High St RH2 9AE (01737) 226650

"TV chef Tony Tobin turns out a very good menu" – *"you can taste
every ingredient"* – at this much commented-upon, modern British
town-centre spot, housed in a series of *"small"* and *"cramped"*
rooms. / **Sample dishes:** crab cakes with coriander & lime pesto; roast lamb
with aubergine & tomato confit; tipsy rhubarb trifle. **Value tip:** set 2/3-crs
L £10/£13.50 (but Sun £25). **Details:** 10 pm; closed Sat L & Sun; no smoking.

Fairyhill   £ 41   A★★
SA3 1BS   (01792) 390139
"Excellent everything" typifies reports on the top-class, but relatively informal dining room at this small but celebrated hotel, whose Gower Peninsula location is reached through a maze of lanes; the "imaginative" but direct cuisine makes "best use of local produce", and regularly achieves "exceptional" results.
/ **Sample dishes:** scrambled eggs with cockles; loin & sausage of Welsh lamb with leeks & celery; apple & tarragon tart. **Value tip:** set 2-crs L £14.50. **Details:** off B4295; 9 pm; no smoking; children: 8+. **Accommodation:** 8 rooms, from £110.

Juboraj   £ 25   ★
11 Heol-y-deri CF14 6HA   (029) 2062 8894
"A real gem in suburban Cardiff"; its "distinctive and well prepared" cooking made it reporters' nomination as "the best of many Indian restaurants in the area". / **Sample dishes:** king prawn butterfly; coriander chicken; sticky toffee pudding. **Details:** in centre of village; 11 pm; closed Sun; no smoking area; no booking.

Burnt Chair   £ 37   A★
5 Duke St TW9 1HP   (020) 8940 9488
This "very small" but characterful spot wins unanimous praise for its "excellent" and "unusual" modern British cooking, and the "owner's knowledge of wines" adds "fun" to many an œnophile's visit.
/ **Sample dishes:** tomato & orange soup; spice-charred wild beef with thyme jam; apple & honey tarte Tatin. **Value tip:** set 2-crs D £15. **Details:** nr Richmond Theatre; 11 pm; D only, closed Sun; no Amex; no smoking before 10 pm; children: "love them".

Old Vicarage   £ 58   ★
Church Rd S12 3XW   (0114) 247 5814
For most reporters, this "beautifully restored Victorian vicarage" has it all – "fresh ingredients, an extensive cellar, stunning presentation and an imaginative menu"; those who report disappointment cite "slow" or "self-satisfied" service as the chief culprit. / **Sample dishes:** smoked salmon rosti with mango salad; duck confit sausage & lentil casserole; baked chocolate pudding & custard. **Value tip:** set 3-crs L & Sun L £30. **Details:** 10 pm; closed Mon & Sun D; no smoking.

Michels   £ 46   ★
GU23 6AQ   (01483) 224777
"Precise" French cooking is the undisputed attraction of this grandly housed establishment; some say the ambience is "perfect for a gastronomic diner" – perhaps that's the same as saying it can be "rather dull". / **Sample dishes:** duck foie gras with port jelly; pan-fried red sea bream with braised fennel; almond milk mousse. **Value tip:** set 2-crs L £14, set 3-crs D £23. **Details:** 9 pm; closed Mon, Sat L & Sun D; no smoking.

ROMALDKIRK, CO DURHAM

The Rose & Crown £ 32 Ⓐ

DL12 9GB   (01833) 650213

"A beautiful pub in a beautiful area" – near the High Force waterfall
– whose "creative and well presented" cooking wins it wide but not
unanimous support. / **Sample dishes:** casserole of scallops & monkfish
tails; roast lamb with potato & wild mushroom broth; steamed chocolate
& prune pudding. **Value tip:** set 3-crs Sun L £13.50. **Details:** 6m NW of
Barnard Castle on B6277; 9 pm; closed Mon-Sat L & Sun D; no Amex;
no smoking; children: 6+. **Accommodation:** 12 rooms, from £82.

ROMSEY, HANTS

2–3D

Old Manor House £ 37 ★

21 Palmerston St SO51 8GF   (01794) 517353

The food and wine are "hard to fault" at this tiny, long-established
Italian, which offers "unusual meals with excellent ingredients"
("wild boar and New Forest mushrooms", for example); some discern
a rather "stuffy" attitude. / **Sample dishes:** wild mushroom risotto; venison
escalope; sponge pudding & custard. **Details:** 9.30 pm; closed Mon & Sun D.

ROTHWELL, NORTHANTS

5–4D

The Thai Garden £ 26 ★

3 Market Hill NN14 6EP   (01536) 712345

"Consistent" oriental, where "knowledgeable staff" serve
"delicate and tasty" cooking that "doesn't pander too much to
English stereotypes of Thai cooking". / **Sample dishes:** Pander chicken;
chilli king prawns; Thai custard. **Details:** 10.45 pm; no smoking area.

ROWDE, WILTS

2–2C

George & Dragon £ 33 Ⓐ★

High St SN10 2PN   (01380) 723053

"We eat here monthly, and over eight years I've had one poor meal",
is the kind of report which indicates why this is one of the West
Country's top gastropubs; "superb, fresh fish dishes" and a "great
wine list" are highlights. / **Sample dishes:** cheese soufflé; deep-fried squid
with lemon & parsley; chocolate St Emilion. **Value tip:** set 2/3-crs
L £8.50/£10. **Details:** 10 pm; closed Mon & Sun; no Amex; no smoking.

RYE, E SUSSEX

3–4C

Landgate Bistro £ 24 ★

5-6 Landgate TN31 7LH   (01797) 222829

Consistency ("over 20 years") is the hallmark of this well-known
bistro, which offers "English food, using the best local fish and fowl",
cooked "in a conventional way" and "served in a pleasant
atmosphere". / **Sample dishes:** salmon & salt cod fishcakes; noisettes of
lamb with mint & tomato sauce; summer pudding. **Details:** 9.30 pm; D only,
closed Mon.

SALTAIRE, W YORKS

5–1C

Salts Diner £ 16 Ⓐ★

Salts Mill BD18 3LB   (01274) 530533

There's "plenty to watch all around you" at this "fun, bright
restaurant", which offers "good food and good value"; "escape on a
Sunday to art, music, the papers and some tasty cooking". / **Sample
dishes:** roast courgette & lentil soup; salmon & haddock fishcakes; sticky toffee
pudding. **Details:** 2m from Bradford on A650; 5 pm; L only; no Amex;
no smoking area.

SANDGATE, KENT   3–4D
La Terrasse   £ 44   ★★
Sandgate Hotel CT20 3DY (01303) 220444
*"If only all seaside hotels were like this"; this "little piece of France"
offers "impeccably balanced" food, "caringly served" in "pleasant
surroundings"; "space is limited", however, to the extent that some
reporters are "concerned that the place is becoming too popular".*
/ **Sample dishes:** *lobster ravioli; roast turbot; bitter chocolate mousse.*
Value tip: *set 3-crs L & D £20.50.* **Details:** *on A259 (main coastal road);
9.30 pm; closed Mon & Sun D; no shorts; no smoking in dining room;
booking: max 8.* **Accommodation:** *15 rooms, from £51.*

SANDIWAY, CHESHIRE   5–2B
Nunsmere Hall   £ 54
Tarporley Rd CW8 2ES (01606) 889100
*"Immaculate presentation" characterises the Anglo/French cooking at
this smart country house hotel, on the fringe of Delamere Forest.*
/ **Sample dishes:** *seared scallops with black pudding; Dover sole with
cauliflower purée; rich banana pastries.* **Value tip:** *set 3-crs Sun L £22.50.*
Details: *off A49, 4m SW of Northwich; 10 pm; no jeans; no smoking;
children: 12+ at D.* **Accommodation:** *36 rooms, from £105.*

SAWLEY, LANCS   5–1B
Spread Eagle   £ 26   𝔸★★
BB7 4NH (01200) 441202
*It's "always a pleasure" to visit this increasingly well-known pub
(under the same ownership as Crosthwaite's Punch Bowl), and not
just because of its "very attractive location" (overlooking "the River
Hodder and rolling hills"); the English cooking may be "simple",
but it's "excellent value" and "beautifully presented", and service is
"professional".* / **Sample dishes:** *red onion tart; duck with five spice; lemon
crème brûlée.* **Value tip:** *set 2/3-crs L £7.95/£9.50 (Sun £9.95/£11.95).*
Details: *NE of Clitheroe, off A59; 9 pm; closed 2 weeks in Nov; no smoking.*
Accommodation: *10 rooms, from £55.*

SAWSTON, CAMBS   3–1B
Jade Fountain   £ 22
42-46 High St CB2 4BG (01223) 836100
*"Consistently the best Chinese in the area", offering Szechuan
dishes which are well prepared, spicy and imaginatively presented.*
/ **Sample dishes:** *crispy duck; Szechuan king prawns; toffee banana.*
Details: *1m from M11, J10; 9.30 pm.*

SEAFORD, E SUSSEX   3–4B
Quincy's   £ 36
42 High St BN25 1PL (01323) 895490
*"Accomplished" modern British cooking comes in a style that seems
very "contemporary" in this seaside town.* / **Sample dishes:** *roast
pumpkin soup; pheasant with mushrooms & smoked sausage; steamed syrup
sponge with custard.* **Details:** *10 pm; closed Mon, Tue–Sat D only, closed Sun
D; no Switch; no smoking area.*

SEAVIEW, ISLE OF WIGHT   2–4D
Seaview Hotel   £ 30   𝔸
High St PO34 5EX (01983) 612711
*A "great location" is just part of the draw of this charming waterfront
hotel, whose vaguely nautical dining room offers a "wide-ranging"
menu of "fresh" English cooking.* / **Sample dishes:** *hot crab ramekin;
sea bass in champagne sauce; 'îles flottantes' with praline.* **Value tip:** *set 3-crs
Sun L £13.95.* **Details:** *9.30 pm; closed Sun D except on Bank Holidays;
no smoking area; children: 5+.* **Accommodation:** *16 rooms, from £90.*

SHANAGARRY, CO CORK, *EIRE*

10–4B

Ballymaloe Hotel

IR £ 46   A★★

(021) 652531

"The stuff of dreams"; Rory O'Connell's "wonderful food" – "the freshness is obvious" – is some of the best in the British Isles and it's "simply served" in the dining room of the Allen family's "unpretentious", "friendly" and "relaxed" country hotel; "breakfast is a banquet". / **Sample dishes:** avocado & tomato gazpacho; roast pork with Bramley apple sauce; farmhouse cheeses. **Value tip:** set 3-crs L £16.50 (Sun £19.50). **Details:** 9.30 pm; no Switch; no smoking; children: 4+. **Accommodation:** 32 rooms, from IR £65.

SHEFFIELD, S YORKS

5–2C

Kashmir Curry Centre

£ 11   ★

123 Spital Hill S4 7LD   (0114) 272 6253

"Fantastic spices, fresh ingredients and amazingly good value" is a package which wins much praise for this "cheap and cheerful" but "very basic" curry house. / **Sample dishes:** onion bhaji; chicken tikka; kulfi. **Details:** midnight; no credit cards; no smoking area.

Milano

£ 39

Archer Rd S8 OLA   (0114) 235 3080

This stylish new modern British (not Italian) establishment is off to a flying start in a number of people's books; they're "very concerned to make customers comfortable" (and some can find the concern "overbearing"). / **Sample dishes:** clams & cockles masala; braised shoulder of lamb with Moroccan sauce; gooseberry & rhubarb crumble. **Value tip:** set 2/3-crs pre-th £10.95/£12.95. **Details:** 10 pm; closed Sun D; no Amex; no smoking.

Nirmals

£ 22   ★★

189-193 Glossop Rd S10 2GW   (0114) 272 4054

"Consistent, exquisite flavours" (with some "excellent vegetarian dishes") distinguish Mrs Nirmal Gupta's "different" Indian cooking, and her long-established restaurant has a devoted following; the "authoritative" patronne is usually in evidence, and she and her staff are "anxious to please". / **Sample dishes:** swordfish; lamb bhuna; kulfi. **Details:** nr West St; midnight; Fri & Sat 1 am; closed Sun L; no smoking area.

Nonnas

£ 29

539-541 Eccleshall Rd S11 8PR   (0114) 268 6166

"Traditional Italian food" that's a cut above the norm, served in an "unpretentious" environment, wins support for this "bistro-style" spot; some feel it's "slightly pricey" for what it is. / **Sample dishes:** halibut & Ricotta parcels; chicken with rocket pesto; panna cotta with amaretto sauce. **Details:** 9.45 pm; no Amex.

Smiths of Sheffield

£ 35   A

34 Sandygate Rd S10 5RY   (0114) 266 6096

"Enthusiastic competence" is the hallmark of this "friendly" and "relaxed" bar/restaurant, whose modern British cooking is "reliably good". / **Sample dishes:** tartlet of vegetables, eggs & ham; rack of lamb with provençale vegetables; dark chocolate fondant & caramel ice cream. **Details:** off A57; 9.30 pm; D only, closed Mon & Sun; no smoking.

Zing Vaa

£ 22

55 The Moor S1 4PF   (0114) 275 6633

"Reliable" Chinese of long standing, praised by its fans for its "range and quality – at very reasonable cost". / **Sample dishes:** spicy tofu; beef with honey & pepper sauce; fritters. **Value tip:** set 3-crs L £5.50 (Sun £9.50). **Details:** 11.30 pm; no smoking area.

SHELLEY, W YORKS   5–2C
Three Acres   £ 31   𝔸★
Roydhouse HD8 8LR   (01484) 602606
*This isn't just a "good real ale pub"; it's a "great and child-friendly"
inn which is "highly respected" for its "marvellous sandwiches" and
for the "imaginative" twist it puts on "standard" dishes ("fish is the
speciality"). / **Sample dishes:** duck sausage with puy lentils; Dover sole in
ginger butter with samphire; caramelised rice pudding with roast figs. **Value
tip:** set 3-crs L & Sun L £15.95. **Details:** nr Emley Moor television transmitter;
9.45 pm; closed Sat L. **Accommodation:** 20 rooms, from £60.*

SHEPPERTON, SURREY   3–3A
Edwinns   £ 31
Church Rd TW17 9JT   (01932) 223543
*Pleasant modern British restaurant, with conservatory, in a
Thames-side village; it's especially commended for its "good-value
set meals", and often busy. / **Sample dishes:** duck & mango salad;
char-grilled beef with oyster mushrooms; sticky toffee pudding. **Details:**
opp church & Anchor Hotel, just outside village; 10.15 pm, Fri-Sat 10.45 pm;
closed Sat L & Sun D; no jeans; no smoking area.*

SHINFIELD, BERKS   2–2D
L'Ortolan   £ 80
The Old Vicarage, Church Ln RG2 9BY   (0118) 988 3783
*John Burton-Race's "stuffy" converted vicarage – long a foodie
destination of note – gives an impression of decline; "disgraceful"
service ("arrogant", "haphazard" and "uncaring") is at the root of
too many unhappy reports, and the food is "not as good as it was".
/ **Sample dishes:** tortellini with ginger & coriander; fillet of roast veal;
chocolate pyramid with pistachio biscuits. **Value tip:** set 3-crs L £28, set 3-crs
D Tue-Fri £44. **Details:** signposted off A33 to Basingstoke from M4 J11;
10 pm; closed Mon & Sun D.*

SHREWSBURY, SHROPSHIRE   5–3A
Cromwells Hotel   £ 27
11 Dogpole SY1 7EN   (01743) 361440
*"Probably the best value in town" is to be had at this "busy" (and
sometimes "smoky") wine bar/restaurant. / **Sample dishes:** potato
pancakes with chicken livers; wild rabbit & field mushrooms; banana & toffee
millefeuille. **Details:** 10 pm; no smoking. **Accommodation:** 7 rooms,
from £45.*

SLAUGHAM, W SUSSEX   3–4B
Chequers   £ 32   𝔸★
RH17 6AQ   (01444) 400239
*You're "always made welcome" at this "excellent coaching inn and
restaurant", which offers a "good selection of meat, fish and veggie
dishes" in "ample" portions; it has a "beautiful location" too.
/ **Sample dishes:** fresh marinated anchovies; Thai-style cod with noodles;
cheddar & biscuits. **Details:** opp church; 8.30 pm; closed Sun D; no smoking;
children: not permitted. **Accommodation:** 5 rooms, from £80.*

SNAPE, SUFFOLK   3–1D
The Crown Inn   £ 30   𝔸
Main St IP17 1SL   (01728) 688324
*"A cosy place with cut-above cooking" – this "charming" pub is a
"friendly" establishment whose strengths include "fish, game, glorious
puds" and "good beer". / **Sample dishes:** smoked goose breast; monkfish
& scallops; orange & chocolate torte. **Details:** nr Maltings; 9 pm; no Amex;
children: 14+. **Accommodation:** 3 rooms, from £50.*

Bull Inn £ 29
High St RG4 6UP (0118) 969 3901
*This "olde worlde pub" in a "beautiful location", not far from
the Thames, is "always busy"; the attractions are "good-value,
large portions and a good atmosphere".* / **Sample dishes:** *crab cakes
with lemon grass sauce; braised lamb with garlic mash; 'kitchen sink' pudding.*
Details: *9 pm; no smoking area; no booking.* **Accommodation:** *7 rooms,
from £70.*

The French Horn £ 60 A★
RG4 6TN (0118) 969 2204
*"Excellent food, served in elegant and spacious surroundings"
makes this charming riverside restaurant one of the Thames Valley's
best; some think the menu "overpriced", but a more typical view is
that "in winter, the spit-roasted duck is irresistible – in summer,
drinks by the river are".* / **Sample dishes:** *langoustines; roast veal;
selection of cheeses.* **Value tip:** *set 2-crs L £21.* **Details:** *M4, J8 or J9,
then A4; 9.30 pm; jacket & tie.* **Accommodation:** *20 rooms, from £100.*

Madhu's Brilliant £ 24 ★
39 South Rd UB1 1SW (020) 8574 1897
*"Always as brilliant as its name", say fans of this "very reasonably
priced" Southall curry house a couple of minutes from the BR station;
it's a step-sibling to the original Brilliant, and some say it's similarly
"overrated".* / **Sample dishes:** *butter chicken; Methi chicken; kulfi.*
Details: *nr railway station; 11.30 pm; closed Tue, Sat L & Sun L.*

Pipe of Port £ 21 A★
84 High St SS1 1JN (01702) 614606
*"Absolute consistency over many years" wins admirers for this
"old-fashioned", "down-to-earth" British restaurant, which offers
a "welcome oasis" in this unprepossessing town.* / **Sample
dishes:** *smoked salmon & crab pillows; chicken & chestnut pie; lemon
meringue pie.* **Details:** *at junction with Tylers Ave; 10.30 pm; closed Sun.*

L'Auberge Bistro £ 23
1b Sea Bank Rd PR9 0EW (01704) 530671
*"An excellent choice of carefully prepared dishes at reasonable
prices" and "helpful" service win unanimous support for this small
and "intimate" spot.* / **Sample dishes:** *seafood in filo pastry; monkfish with
lime & Parma ham; chocolate marquise.* **Details:** *10.30 pm.*

Warehouse Brasserie £ 30
30 West St PR8 0DP (01704) 544662
*"Good-value early evening meals" and lunches are particularly
praised at this "friendly" local, which makes a "stylish" choice for
the area.* / **Sample dishes:** *cajun-spiced tiger prawns; Moroccan lamb tagine;
sticky toffee pudding.* **Value tip:** *set 2/3-crs early eve £8.95/£10.95.*
Details: *10.15 pm.*

SOUTHWOLD, SUFFOLK

3–1D

The Crown

£ 32

A★

High St IP18 6DP (01502) 722275

"The overall experience" is "consistently wonderful" at this "very jolly" Adnams-owned inn – a "glorious location" to enjoy "wonderful fresh seafood" and a "superb-value wine list"; if you intend to eat in the bar (which many prefer), "make sure you get a seat an hour beforehand". / **Sample dishes:** goat's cheese & rocket salad; braised lemon sole; steamed chocolate pudding. **Value tip:** set 2-crs L £14.50. **Details:** 9.30 pm; no smoking. **Accommodation:** 12 rooms, from £68.

The Swan

£ 30

A

The Market Pl IP18 6EG (01502) 722186

Though not quite as celebrated as The Crown, this second Adnams hotel is similarly part of the Southwold landscape, and it has some "lovely" old fashioned rooms; some dependable cooking and "good wines" are among the attractions. / **Sample dishes:** lobster bisque; roast lamb with honey & brown sugar crust; sticky toffee & date pudding. **Value tip:** set 2/3-crs L & Sun L £16/£18. **Details:** 9.30 pm; closed L, Oct-Christmas; no jeans or shorts; no smoking; children: 5+. **Accommodation:** 95 rooms, from £98.

SOWERBY BRIDGE, W YORKS

5–1C

Java

£ 22

Wharf St HX6 2AF (01422) 831654

"Indonesian food at its best, and in the heart of Yorkshire" makes it "a treat" to visit this "authentically decorated" and highly popular spot. / **Sample dishes:** Indonesian chicken soup; beef with chilli, ginger & soy sauce; homemade ice cream. **Details:** 11 pm; no smoking.

SPARSHOLT, HANTS

2–3D

Plough Inn

£ 28

SA21 2NW (01962) 776 353

"Friendly" and "characterful" village boozer, whose "excellent" and varied menu of modern British, "restaurant-type" food receives a good number of plaudits. / **Sample dishes:** goat's cheese, avocado & tomato salad; beef with stir-fried vegetables; Baked Alaska. **Details:** take Stockbridge Rd from Winchester, after 1.5m turn left to Sparsholt; no Amex; no smoking.

SPEEN, BUCKS

3–2A

Old Plow

£ 39

HP27 OP2 (01494) 488300

This "lovely" old Chiltern inn is home to a "good bistro and restaurant"; it's a shame that sometimes "school-marmish" service and a tendency to "overprice" can take the edge off the experience. / **Sample dishes:** lobster & seafood bisque; grilled sea bass; lemon brûlée tartlet. **Details:** 20 mins from M40 J4; 8.45 pm; closed Mon & Sun D and last 3 weeks in August; no smoking.

ST ANDREWS, FIFE

9–3D

Vine Leaf Garden

£ 30

★

131 South St KY16 9UN (01334) 477497

"Exceptional Scottish produce" handled in an "imaginative" way (including "gourmet vegetarian and seafood" options) combines with "friendly and informative" service and a "comfortable setting" to make this "small" establishment a unanimously popular selection. / **Sample dishes:** fresh mango, carrot & cardamon soup; wood pigeon & duck with black cherries; caramelised clotted cream rice pudding. **Details:** 9.30 pm; closed Mon & Sun; no smoking.

ST IVES, CORNWALL

Fodders £ 30 ★

Norway Ln TR26 ILZ (01736) 794204

"Great" meals from *"inspiring"* menus (especially *"tremendous fish"*)
help make a visit here an ideal complement to visiting the nearby
Tate. / **Sample dishes:** grilled goat's cheese; fillet of John Dory; chocolate tart
with Grand Marnier Sauce. **Details:** 300 metres from Tate Gallery; 8.30 pm;
closed Mon & Sun; no Amex; no smoking.

ST LEONARDS, SUSSEX
3—4C

Rosers £ 38 ★

64 Eversfield Place TN37 6DB (01424) 712218

"Gerald Roser does not 'play safe'", but it's *"love at first bite"* for
reporters who have sampled the *"ambitious"* and *"highly innovative"*
French cooking – using the *"highest-quality ingredients, superbly
prepared"* – at his *"small, family-run restaurant"*. / **Sample
dishes:** pike soufflé; roast guinea fowl with shallot confit; caramelised lime
crème. **Value tip:** set 3-crs set L £19.95. **Details:** opp Hastings Pier; 10 pm;
closed Mon, Sat L & Sun; smoking discouraged.

ST MARGARET'S HOPE, ORKNEY

The Creel £ 36 𝔸★

Front Rd KW17 2SL (01856) 831311

"Top notch" fish and seafood, simply prepared, has made a name for
this unpretentious, far-flung island restaurant. / **Sample dishes:** crab
soup; halibut with spinach & haricot beans; lemon & rhubarb tart. **Details:**
off A961, S from main town, 13m across Churchill barriers on Seafront;
9.30 pm; D only; closed Jan-Mar; no Amex & no Switch; no smoking.
Accommodation: 3 rooms, from £60.

ST MARGARETS AT CLIFFE, KENT
3—3D

Walletts Court £ 51 𝔸★

Westcliffe CT15 6EW (01304) 852424

"Traditional English country hotel and restaurant", scenically
located at the top of a cliff; it offers *"wonderfully fresh"* cooking and
"impeccable" service. / **Sample dishes:** chicken & goat's cheese mousse;
sea bass en papillotte with steamed leeks; plum pudding. **Value tip:** set 3-crs
L £27.50. **Details:** on B2058 towards Deal, 3m NE of Dover; 9 pm;
no smoking. **Accommodation:** 16 rooms, from £75.

ST MAWES, CORNWALL
1—4B

Hotel Tresanton £ 43

Lower Castle Road TR2 5DR (01326) 270055

Forte scion Olga Polizzi's rural designer-hotel generates a mixed press;
many laud its fine cooking, relaxed attitude and sophistication; others
decry this *"Sloane Square-on-Sea"*, where the *"outlook is the only
redeeming feature"*. / **Sample dishes:** prosciutto, Parmesan & rocket
salad; Cornish sea bass with ratatouille; chocolate & passion fruit mousse.
Details: on the way up to St Mawes Castle; 9.45 pm; D only; no smoking
during dinner. **Accommodation:** 28 rooms, from £160.

ST SAVIOUR, JERSEY

Longueville Manor £ 53 𝔸

Longueville Rd JE2 7WF (01534) 25501

This beautiful country house is generally reckoned the Channel
Islands' top place; reports are complimentary, but speak more of
satisfaction than ecstasy. / **Sample dishes:** herb noodle salad with
seared tuna; calves' liver with mango & mint chutney; banana crème brûlée.
Value tip: set 2/3-crs set L £18/£22. **Details:** from St Helier take A3 towards
Gorey; 9.30 pm; no smoking area. **Accommodation:** 32 rooms, from £195.

STADDLEBRIDGE, N YORKS   8–4C

McCoys at the Tontine   £ 39   A ★
DL6 3JB   (01609) 882671
"Superbly cooked and presented food" ("with an accent on fish")
ensures that the ground-floor bistro of the McCoy brothers' eccentric,
Gothic-style hotel, on the fringe of the North Yorks Moors, is always
"bustling"; upstairs, there's a quieter restaurant. / **Sample dishes:**
duck confit & chicken tortellini; pan-fried sea bass; blackcurrant Bakewell.
Value tip: set 2/3-crs early eve £17/£21. **Details:** junction of A19 & A172;
10 pm; bistro open all week, restaurant open Fri D & Sat D only.
Accommodation: 6 rooms, from £90.

STAITHES, N YORKS   8–3C

Endeavour   £ 30   ★
1 High St TS13 5BH   (01947) 840825
"Superb fresh seafood", "wonderfully prepared and imaginatively
presented", is the menu highlight at this "low-key" and "not too
expensive" spot, near the quay. / **Sample dishes:** lovage & apple soup;
sea trout with orange & thyme; crème brûlée with raspberries. **Details:** 10m
N of Whitby; 9 pm; no credit cards; no smoking. **Accommodation:** 3 rooms,
from £42.

STAMFORD, LINCS   6–4A

The George Hotel   £ 45   A
71 St Martins PE9 2LB   (01780) 750750
"Unique", "solid and traditional" coaching inn, at the heart of this
fine Georgian town, which undoubtedly offers a "stunning" setting;
the pricey, "solid and traditional" fare is often praised too, but
off-days and incidents of amateurish service are not as rare as one
might hope. / **Sample dishes:** goat's cheese in a filo parcel; rump of lamb;
Stilton. **Value tip:** set 2-crs L £14.50. **Details:** off A1, 14m N of
Peterborough, onto B1081; 11 pm; jacket & tie. **Accommodation:** 47 rooms,
from £103.

STANTON, SUFFOLK   3–1C

Leaping Hare Café   £ 29   A ★
Wyken Vineyards IP31 2DW   (01359) 250287
"It's an experience to eat in this beautiful barn", which offers
"unusual", "good" and "fresh" Anglo-American cooking, washed
down with "pleasing wine from their own vineyard". / **Sample
dishes:** Gressingham duck terrine; Norfolk lamb with new potatoes
& rosemary gravy; lemon posset with walnut muffins. **Details:** 9m NE of Bury
St Edmunds; follow tourist signs off A143; 9 pm; closed Mon, Tue, Wed D, Thu
D & Sun D; no Amex; no smoking.

STAPLEFORD, LEICS   5–3D

Stapleford Park   £ 53   A
LE14 2EF   (01572) 787522
This is undoubtedly a "very pretty country house", and even those
who say that "for the price, food and service are not up to the mark"
admit it's a "great place" – one couple particularly appreciated their
"order taken from the Jacuzzi". / **Sample dishes:** sardine & potato
terrine; peppered venison with sloe gin sauce; dark chocolate & praline tart.
Value tip: set 3-crs Sun L £25. **Details:** 4m from Melton Mowbray on B676;
9.30 pm, 10.30 pm Fri & Sat; jacket & tie; no smoking; children: 5+.
Accommodation: 51 rooms, from £165.

STARBOTTON, N YORKS　　　　　　　　8–4B
Fox & Hounds　　　　　　　　　　**£ 19**
BD23 5HY　(01756) 760269
A "walkers' pub", whose "big menu" offers "lots of choice" of "fresh" and "tasty" dishes; "good veggie selection" and "friendly" service too. / **Sample dishes:** blue cheese soufflé; chicken & leek crumble; lemon ice box pie. **Details:** on B6160 N of Kettlewell; 9 pm; closed Mon D (all day Mon in winter); no Amex; no smoking area; no booking. **Accommodation:** 2 rooms, from £25.

STEETON, N YORKS　　　　　　　　5–1C
Aagrah　　　　　　　　　　　　**£ 23**
York Rd　LS24 8EG　(01937) 530888
"A converted village school, complete with tented ceiling" makes a rather unusual setting for this "authentic" and "consistently good" Indian restaurant. / **Sample dishes:** mixed tandoori platter; Hydrabadi chicken & lemon rice; kulfi. **Details:** 7m S of York on A64; 11.30 pm; D only; no smoking area.

STOCKCROSS, BERKS　　　　　　　　2–2D
Vineyard at Stockcross　　　　　**£ 57**　　★
RG20 8JU　(01635) 528770
This nakedly ambitious yearling – conceived as one (rich) man's homage to the Napa Valley – is already claimed by one or two reporters to "rival Blanc's Manoir (at Great Milton)"; culinary consistency is certainly impressive, but on the service and ambience fronts, there's still a way to go. / **Sample dishes:** Scottish salmon & oysters in truffle oil; Goosnargh duckling with port wine jus; assiette of chocolate. **Value tip:** set 2/3-crs L £15/£20. **Details:** from M4 J13, take A34 towards Newbury; 10 pm; no smoking. **Accommodation:** 33 rooms, from £185.

STOKE BRUERNE, NORTHANTS　　　　2–1D
Bruerne's Lock　　　　　　　　　**£ 33**　　🄰★
5 The Canalside　NN12 7SB　(01604) 863654
"Exceptional food", "excellent" service and a "lovely location" combine to put standards at this canal-side establishment "up with the best London restaurants" of a similar price. / **Sample dishes:** mussel and red onion tart; tuna with tomato & basil coulis; custard tart & nutmeg ice cream. **Details:** 0.5m off A508 between Northampton & Milton Keynes; 9.45 pm; closed Mon, Sat L & Sun D; no smoking in dining room.

STOKE BY NAYLAND, SUFFOLK　　　　3–2C
Angel Inn　　　　　　　　　　　**£ 26**
CO6 4SA　(01206) 263245
"A wide range of interesting dishes" of "local-sourced food at competitive prices" make this "old pub", "a long-time favourite" for a fair number of reporters. / **Sample dishes:** fishcakes with remoulade sauce; honey-glazed roast lamb; dark chocolate ganache. **Details:** 5m W of A12; 9 pm; no smoking area; children: 14+. **Accommodation:** 6 rooms, from £61.

STOKE HOLY CROSS, NORFOLK　　　　6–4C
Wildebeest　　　　　　　　　　**£ 29**　　★
Norwich Rd　NR14 8QJ　(01508) 492497
Tables which are "old trees, literally" and an owner "just the right side of eccentric" make this "converted pub" quite an experience; imaginative cooking at reasonable prices contributes to the "all-round fun". / **Sample dishes:** duck confit with pickled plums; smoked bacon with spring onion mash; almond & amaretto parfait. **Value tip:** set 2-crs L £9.95 (Sun £11.95). **Details:** turn left at Dunston Hall, left at T-junction; 10 pm; no smoking area.

STOKE ROW, HENLEY-ON-THAMES, OXON 2–2D
The Crooked Billet £ 33

Newlands Ln RG9 5PU (01491) 681048
Cooking with a fair amount of "flair" wins praise for this "good", rustic pub/restaurant, in the heart of the Chilterns. / **Sample dishes:** crab & monkfish cake; pink-roast venison; fudge & chocolate cheesecake. **Value tip:** set 2-crs L £10, set 3-crs Sun L £14.95. **Details:** on A4130; 10 pm; no Amex & no Switch.

STON EASTON, SOMERSET 2–3B
Ston Easton Park £ 57 A

BA3 4DF (01761) 241631
This "elegant" Palladian country house is certainly impressive, but the staff are "naturals at putting people at ease in this grand location"; the traditional cooking perhaps plays something of a supporting rôle (though "good-value lunches" are much approved). / **Sample dishes:** tartlet of calves' sweetbreads; char-grilled Dover sole with asparagus; treacle & lemon tartlet. **Value tip:** set 2/3-crs L £11/£16 (Sun £26). **Details:** 11m SW of Bath on A39; 9.30 pm, 10 pm Fri & Sat; jacket & tie; no smoking; children: 7+. **Accommodation:** 21 rooms, from £185.

STONEHAVEN, ABERDEEN 9–3D
Lairhillock Inn £ 35 A★

Netherley AB39 3QS (01569) 730001
This "old-fashioned coaching inn wins strong support as the place to eat around Aberdeen; if offers exceptional-value food using local produce". / **Sample dishes:** seafood crêpes; chicken écossaise; sticky toffee pudding. **Value tip:** set L & Sun L £12.95. **Details:** 7m S of Aberdeen; 9.30 pm.

STORRINGTON, W SUSSEX 3–4A
Fleur de Sel £ 45 A★

Manley's Hill RH20 4BT (01903) 742331
New owners of this well-established site – long known as Manley's – have continued its tradition of "beautifully cooked" Gallic fare; the dining room is nowadays thought a touch more "charming", but "amateurish" service needs attention. / **Sample dishes:** scallops & prawns with ginger; roast Gressingham duck with honey & ginger; crème brûlée with armagnac prunes. **Value tip:** set 2/3-crs L £12.50/£16.50 (Sun £16.50/£20.50). **Details:** 9.30 pm; closed Mon, Sat L & Sun D.

STOURBRIDGE, WORCS 5–4B
French Connection £ 32 A★

3 Coventry St DY8 1EP (01384) 390940
"Just like a village restaurant in Provence", and full of "joie de vivre", this "lively" restaurant offers "France on your doorstep" – "authentic" flavours from "innovative" and "frequently changing" menus. / **Sample dishes:** moules marinière; boeuf bourguinonne; tarte au citron. **Value tip:** set 3-crs L £9.95, set 3-crs pre-th £11.95. **Details:** 9.30 pm; closed Mon, Tue D, Thu D & Sun; no smoking area.

STRATFORD UPON AVON, WARKS 2–1C
Desports £ 32

13-14 Meer St CV37 6QB (01789) 269304
A newcomer to watch; even those who say they need either to "change the menu more frequently" or to "sort out the service" admit this brightly decorated spot, with its interesting Asian-influenced dishes, is "very promising". / **Sample dishes:** forest mushroom risotto; seared scallops with sweet tomato risotto; chocolate & cardamon pudding. **Value tip:** set 2/3-crs L £10.50/£14. **Details:** nr marketplace; 11 pm; closed all January; no smoking area.

Lambs £ 26

12 Sheep St CV37 6EF (01789) 292554
"Given the rush for pre-theatre meals, the results are surprisingly good" at this characterful and handily located French restaurant.
/ **Sample dishes:** crispy duck & watercress salad; roast chicken & mango in lime butter; sticky toffee pudding. **Value tip:** set L & early eve £9.
Details: nr Royal Shakespeare Theatre; 11 pm; no Amex.

Opposition £ 29

13 Sheep St CV37 6EF (01789) 269980
"Consistently high standards of cheap but interesting food" help make this *"satisfying-all-round"* wine bar our reporters' most popular choice in town, particularly as *"a very good place for pre-theatre suppers"*.
/ **Sample dishes:** trio of salmon; curried chicken & banana in lime butter; strawberry shortcake. **Details:** nr Royal Shakespeare Theatre; 11 pm; no Amex.

STROUD, GLOUCS 2–2B

The George £ 22

New Market GL6 0RF (01453) 833228
A *"varied menu, freshly cooked"*, *"excellent beer"* and a *"warm atmosphere"* are among the reasons to seek out this beamed Cotswold pub. / **Sample dishes:** chicken & leek pancake; chicken piri piri; caramelised rice pudding. **Details:** 9 pm; no smoking area; children: 14+.

STUCKTON, HANTS 2–3C

Three Lions £ 39 ★★

Stuckton Rd SP6 2HF (01425) 652489
"Star-quality food, without pomp" – the *"superb execution"* of Michael Womersley's *"traditional"* but *"imaginative"* menu makes this small and *"very welcoming"* pub-conversion, on the fringe of the New Forest, a special place; *"it's rare amongst prestigious restaurants in serving a good real ale"*. / **Sample dishes:** wild mushroom salad; sea bass & chicory in red wine sauce; hot chocolate pudding. **Value tip:** set 2-crs L £13.50. **Details:** 1m E of Fordingbridge off B3078; 9.30 pm; closed Mon & Sun D; no Amex; no smoking. **Accommodation:** 3 rooms, from £70.

STURMINSTER NEWTON, DORSET 2–3B

Plumber Manor £ 30 𝔸

DT10 2AF (01258) 472507
It's the *"beautiful old house"* and *"very friendly"* service which are the special attractions of this family-run hotel and restaurant; that said, the *"fish, game and beef"* are generally *"dependable"*, and there's a *"brilliant"* wine list. / **Sample dishes:** goat's cheese with roast peppers; pork stuffed with apricots in rosemary jus; chocolate truffle torte. **Details:** off A357 at Sturminster Newton towards Hazelbury Bryan, 2m on left-hand side; 9.30 pm; D only, except Sun when L only; closed Feb; bookings only. **Accommodation:** 16 rooms, from £95.

SUDBURY, SUFFOLK 3–1C

Red Onion Bistro £ 20 ★

57 Ballingdon St CO10 6DA (01787) 376777
A *"small bistro of the gingham table-cloth variety"* that's *"packed every night"*, thanks to its unshowy and *"great value for money"* cooking, and its *"reasonably priced regional wine list"*; there's a *"lovely garden for eating out in summer"*. / **Sample dishes:** fish soup; confit of duck; brown bread ice cream. **Value tip:** set 2/3-crs set L £6.25/£8.25. **Details:** on A131; 9.30 pm; closed Sun; no Amex.

SUNDERLAND, TYNE & WEAR 8–2C

Brasserie 21 £ 32 A★

Wylam Wharf, Low St SR1 2AD (0191) 567 6594
*"Excellent food and service at this newest addition to the
21 Queen Street (Newcastle) group"* is the unanimous theme of
commentary on this brasserie yearling, which benefits from a
"great setting" – in a converted warehouse – *"overlooking the river
and the quay"*. / **Sample dishes:** Shanghai seafood risotto; seafood mixed
grill; chocolate & mocha tart. **Details:** 10.30 pm; closed Sun.

throwingstones £ 29

National Glass Centre, Liberty Way SR6 0GL (0191) 565 3939
"An interesting location, with a museum attached" – the (as you
might hope, thoroughly glazed) restaurant of the National Glass
Centre provides a *"minimalist"*, *"bright"* and *"funky"* venue for a
meal; modern British cooking comes at *"good-value"* prices.
/ **Sample dishes:** spaghetti with mussels & cockles; roast duck with peppered
duck livers; lemon tart with crème fraîche. **Details:** A19 to Sunderland, follow
sign to National Glass Centre; 9.30 pm; L only, ex Fri & Sat when L & D; no
smoking at L.

SUTTON COLDFIELD, W MIDLANDS 5–4C

New Hall £ 53 A

Walmey Rd B76 1QX (0121) 378 2442
The *"wonderful setting"* – the oldest moated manor house in
England, and only eight miles from Brum city centre – is clearly the
most obvious attraction here; however, the *"creative"* menu also wins
praise (with *"smoked salmon from their own smokery"* particularly
approved). / **Sample dishes:** lobster & salmon terrine; fillet of brill; poached
peach. **Value tip:** set 3-crs L £12.50. **Details:** M6 J5, take A452, turn right
onto B4148, follow until 1m after Walmley village; 10 pm; closed Sat L;
no smoking; children: 8+. **Accommodation:** 60 rooms, from £160.

SWANAGE, DORSET 2–4C

Cauldron £ 31 ★

5 High St BH19 2LN (01929) 422671
An *"excellent fish menu, well cooked and presented"* and a *"short
but well chosen wine list"* make this *"personal"* establishment,
run by a husband-and-wife team, a *"reliable and consistent"* choice.
/ **Sample dishes:** seared king scallops; lamb with wild mushrooms & couscous;
Irish coffee crème brûlée. **Details:** lower end of High St, opp Old Quay; 9.15
pm; closed Mon, Tue L & Wed L; closed 2 weeks in Nov & Jan.

SWANSEA, CITY OF SWANSEA 1–1D

L'Amuse £ 29 A★

93 Newton Rd, Mumbles SA3 4BN (01792) 366006
"Imaginative French cooking" and *"enthusiastic, young French staff"*
make this *"French country-style"* bistro (recently relocated) a top local
choice; it's something of a shock, though, to discover that the lady
chef is, in fact, Welsh! / **Sample dishes:** onion tart with Parma ham; duck
confit with turnip gratin; frozen orange meringue. **Value tip:** set 2/3-crs
L £10.95/£13.95. **Details:** right at Mumbles mini-roundabout, top of hill on
left; 9.30 pm; closed Mon D & Sun D.

La Braseria £ 26 A

28 Wind St SA1 1DZ (01792) 469683
"Good atmosphere" and generous portions of hearty, *"plain"* cooking
create a *"very popular"* formula at this large and *"always busy"*,
"Spanish-style" restaurant; you choose your meal at the bar, and
it is delivered to your table. / **Sample dishes:** stuffed mushrooms;
crispy honeyed duck; tiramisu. **Value tip:** set 2-crs L £6.75.
Details: 11.30 pm; closed Sun; need 6+ to book; children: 6+.

Indigo £ 25 ★

Salubrious Place, 56 Wind St SA1 1EG (01792) 463466
You can get to this place through the 'No Sign Bar', but it seems a shame to miss the front door approach – via the magnificently named 'Salubrious Passage'; thus transported, you will find one of Swansea's best stabs at a trendy modern joint, with an "enjoyable atmosphere" and a "delicious" tapas and meze menu. / **Sample dishes:** *tuna with red pepper & olives; pancetta wrapped chicken with tarragon; cappuccino mousse.* **Value tip:** *set 2-crs set L £5.50.* **Details:** *11 pm; closed Sat & Sun.*

Patricks £ 27 ★

638 Mumbles Rd SA3 4EA (01792) 360199
"Recently enlarged but still homely", this family-run bistro, which looks out over Swansea bay from the Mumbles, is "not the cheapest", but its cooking is of "good quality". / **Sample dishes:** *roast calamari; grilled turbot with prawns; poppy seed & vanilla parfait.* **Details:** *in Mumbles, 1m before pier; 9.50 pm; closed Sun D; no Amex.*

SWINTON, BERWICKSHIRE 8–1A
Wheatsheaf Inn £ 28 ★

Main St TD11 3JJ (01890) 860257
This "intimate restaurant within a pub" serves up some "beautifully prepared" cooking, including "salmon from the nearby Tweed" and some "first-class puds"; bar food is also much approved. / **Sample dishes:** *pigeon & oyster mushroom sausage; roast venison with spiced redcurrant sauce; iced praline soufflé.* **Details:** *opp Village Green; 9.15 pm; closed Mon & Sun D; no Amex; no smoking.* **Accommodation:** *7 rooms, from £76.*

TALSARNAU, GWYNEDD 4–2C
Maes y Neuadd £ 31 ★

LL47 6YA (01766) 780200
"Good five-course set dinners" are hardly the norm in the "gastronomic desert" of the surrounding area, making this small, "reliable" and beautifully situated family-run hotel all the more worth knowing about. / **Sample dishes:** *air-dried beef with pickles; salt marsh lamb with wild mushrooms; Welsh honey cake.* **Value tip:** *set 2/3-crs L £11.75/£13.75 (Sun £14.95).* **Details:** *3m N of Harlech off B4573; 9 pm; no smoking.* **Accommodation:** *16 rooms, from £127, incl D.*

TAPLOW, BERKS 3–3A
Waldo's at Cliveden £ 75 Ⓐ

SL6 0JF (01628) 668561
"In splendour you sit, but the food is far from splendid"; eating in the basement dining room of the Astors' grandiose palazzo being "pampered" by "amazing flunkies" may "make you feel like you're in a movie", but (just as you might fear) the "grand and heavy" cooking is "only average, considering the prices". / **Sample dishes:** *pig's trotters & truffle salad; vanilla roast monkfish & foie gras; blackberry & Chambord soufflé.* **Details:** *M4 J7 then follow National Trust signs; 9.30 pm; D only, closed Mon & Sun; jacket & tie; no smoking.* **Accommodation:** *38 rooms, from £290.*

TAUNTON, SOMERSET 2–3A
Brazz £ 25 ★

Castle Bow TA1 1NF (01823) 252000
"Food that makes you want to lick the plate clean" at "reasonable prices" has made this bright but "relaxed" and "informal" modern British brasserie, adjoining the venerable Castle Hotel, a "happy arrival"; "haphazard service is the only drawback". / **Sample dishes:** *crab & saffron tart; char-grilled pork with greengage chutney; cider jelly.* **Details:** *10.30 pm.*

The Castle Hotel   **£ 36**   ★

Castle Green TA1 1NF   (01823) 272671

Phil Vickery had been cooking some of "the best English food in the UK" at this celebrated, but some think "cold", landmark hotel dining room; sadly he quit in the summer of '99, so we've reduced what would have been a two-star rating to a single star – let's hope that new man Richard Guest proves us to have been too cautious!
/ **Sample dishes:** *oven-dried tomato & rosemary soup; roast cod with herb mash & chicory; baked egg custard tart.* **Details:** *9 pm; no smoking.* **Accommodation:** *44 rooms, from £139.*

TAYVALLICH, ARGYLL   9–4B

Tayvallich Inn   **£ 27**   ★

PA31 8PL   (01546) 870282

"Seafood second to none" and a "scenic" setting help ensure that this small bar gets "very busy during the tourist season". / **Sample dishes:** *prawn salad with lime mayonnaise; pan-fried scallops with parsley & lemon; chocolate bread & butter pudding.* **Details:** *signposted off canal; 9 pm; closed Fri L & Sat L (& Mon Nov-Easter); no Amex; no smoking area.*

THAME, OXON   2–2D

Old Trout   **£ 37**

29-30 Lower High St OX9 2AA   (01844) 212146

Its name is an injustice – this thatched cottage-conversion can be "great for fish", and it has a "pleasant" atmosphere. / **Sample dishes:** *shredded duck with hoisin sauce; English lamb rump steak; chocolate & hazelnut torte.* **Details:** *off High St; 10 pm; closed Sun; no Amex.* **Accommodation:** *7 rooms, from £75.*

THORNBURY, GLOUCS   2–2B

Thornbury Castle   **£ 53**   Ⓐ

Castle St BS35 1HH   (01454) 281182

"The sumptuous luxury of the interior and the pretty gardens" are the star features at this baronially splendid Tudor landmark; the modern British cooking, though generally approved, generates less excitement. / **Sample dishes:** *scallops with basil polenta; beef with mushrooms, marrow & foie gras; florentines with apricot compote.* **Value tip:** *set 2/3-crs L £16.50/£17.50.* **Details:** *nr M4/M5 intersection; 9.30 pm, 10 pm Sat; jacket & tie; no smoking in dining room.* **Accommodation:** *20 rooms, from £120.*

THORNHAM, NORFOLK   6–3B

Lifeboat Inn   **£ 26**

PE36 6LT   (01485) 512236

This "quaint" pub "overlooks the Marshes" and has a "lovely, cosy fire"; it offers "simple but well-cooked" fare, including "good mussels and fish". / **Sample dishes:** *goat's cheese & pear salad; baked brill; ginger & pecan bread & butter pudding.* **Details:** *20m from Kings Lynn on A149; 9.30 pm; no Amex.* **Accommodation:** *12 rooms, from £74.*

THORPE LANGTON, LEICS   5–4D

Bakers Arms   **£ 28**

Main St LE16 7TS   (01858) 545201

An agreeable "typical English country pub atmosphere" and "varied menu" make it worth knowing about this "relaxed" hostelry. / **Sample dishes:** *tomato & basil soup; steak with Stilton crust; chocolate & blueberry fudgecake.* **Details:** *9.30 pm; closed Mon, Tue L-Fri L & Sun D; children: 12+.*

THREE COCKS, POWYS 2–1A

Three Cocks £ 36 ★

LD3 0SL (01497) 847215

"Homely" former coaching inn, in a tiny village outside the Brecon Beacons National Park, where a Belgian chef cooks up some *"excellent"* and *"reasonably priced"* dishes; there's an *"excellent beer list"* too. / **Sample dishes:** Ardennes ham; guinea fowl; iced nougatine & raspberry sauce. **Details:** on A438, 4m from Hay on Wye; 9 pm; closed Tue & Sun L; no Amex. **Accommodation:** 7 rooms, from £67.

TILE HILL, W MIDLANDS 5–4C

Rupali £ 27 ★

337 Tile Hill Ln CV4 9DU (024) 7642 2500

"Superb" and *"always packed"*, this *"brilliant curry house"* offers a *"large and unusual"* menu (*"including healthy and veggie choices"*) and an *"authentic ambience"* – *"if you can get a table"*, that is. / **Sample dishes:** shish kebab; sylheti chicken; Ras malai (cream cheese balls). **Details:** off A45, follow signs to Tile Hill; 10.30 pm; no smoking area.

TONBRIDGE, KENT 3–3B

Bottle House £ 27

Coldharbour Rd TN11 8ET (01892) 870306

"Large portions" of *"high-quality"* *"home-cooking"* make this 14th-century country inn a popular destination. / **Sample dishes:** deep-fried sesame coated Brie; beef Wellington & wild mushroom sauce; chocolate velvet. **Details:** leaving Penshurst SW on B2188 turn right on Smarts Hill; 9.30 pm; no Amex; no smoking area.

TOTLEY, S YORKS 5–2C

The Cricket Inn £ 26

Penny Ln S17 3AZ (0114) 236 5256

An *"amazing range of dishes"* – *"from Thai to Italian"* – helps make this *"justifiably popular"* spot an inn with a difference; the food is all *"well cooked and presented"*, but an *"authentic pub atmosphere"* is maintained. / **Sample dishes:** smoked salmon & pumpernickel bread; warm chicken salad, pine nuts & Parma ham; blueberry crème brûlée. **Details:** off A625; 8.45 pm; closed Sun D; children: only allowed in dining area.

TREBURLEY, CORNWALL 1–3C

Springer Spaniel £ 23 ★

PL15 9NS (01579) 370424

A *"marvellous, welcoming pub in a part of Cornwall where good food is hard to find"*; it offers *"consistently good"* and *"creative"* fare, in surroundings with *"no musak and plenty of space"*. / **Sample dishes:** mushrooms in bacon & brandy sauce; smoked duck breast with pear & ginger chutney; fresh fruit pavlova. **Details:** 4m S of Launceston on A388; 9 pm; no Amex or Diners; no smoking before 10 pm.

TRING, HERTS 3–2A

Jubraj £ 25

53a High St HP23 5AG (01442) 825368

"Very accommodating" tandoori restaurant, which is the locals' favourite on account of its *"excellent"* food. / **Sample dishes:** prawn purée; chicken tikka masala; honey pot ice cream. **Details:** inside main car park; 11.45 pm; no smoking area.

TROON, S AYRSHIRE 9–4B
The Oyster Bar £ 31 ★

The Harbour, Harbour Rd KA10 6DH (01292) 319339

"For all sea-foodies", this converted mill, overlooking the harbour
is "known throughout Scotland and beyond", and tipped by most
reporters as one of "the best" places. / **Sample dishes:** seared scallops;
sea bass with Parmesan & basil crust; summer berries & syrup. **Details:**
follow signs for Sea Cat Ferry Terminal, past shipyard; 9.45 pm; closed Mon
& Sun L; no Amex.

TROUTBECK, CUMBRIA 7–3D
Queen's Head £ 26 🄰★

LA23 1PW (01539) 432174

"Arrive early or you'll not get a seat" at this "dramatically located",
"warm and friendly" Elizabethan pub, which overlooks fine Lakeland
scenery; "great food at reasonable prices" means it can be "a little
overcrowded". / **Sample dishes:** Stilton, Ricotta & red onion pudding;
venison with braised lentils; butterscotch & banana ice pie. **Details:** A592, on
Kirkstone Pass; 9 pm; D only; no Amex; no smoking area.
Accommodation: 9 rooms, from £60.

TUNBRIDGE WELLS, KENT 3–4B
Hotel du Vin et Bistro £ 38

Crescent Rd TN1 2LY (01892) 526455

"Good, honest bistro food" served in a "comfortable" setting is
the general tenor of reports on this year-old member of an emerging
chain; maintaining consistency is the great 'chain challenge', however,
and it's not yet entirely clear whether this one's up to it. / **Sample
dishes:** ham hock terrine & brioche; pork with sage & onion risotto; chocolate
& pecan tart. **Value tip:** set 3-crs Sun L £22.50. **Details:** 9.30 pm.
Accommodation: 25 rooms, from £75.

Thackeray's House £ 44

85 London Rd TN1 1EA (01892) 511921

It's easier to recommend the "imaginative and sustaining" fare in
the downstairs wine bar of this elegant building (where the writer
once resided) than the "cramped" restaurant upstairs; the latter is
"much more expensive", and some, citing "service that is both slow
and rude", report nothing less than "disaster". / **Sample
dishes:** monkfish ceviche with tempura; duck with Szechuan pepper &
orange sauce; chocolate & cherry block. **Value tip:** set 2-crs L £13.50.
Details: 10 pm; closed Mon & Sun D; no Amex; no smoking area.

TURNBERRY, AYRSHIRE 7–1A
Turnberry Hotel £ 50 🄰

KA26 9LT (01655) 331000

"Excellent" standards all round win support for this "superb" golfing
hotel (which boasts two world-class courses and a great sea view);
its traditional-style cooking is perhaps a touch "expensive" for what
it is. / **Sample dishes:** roast tomato & red pepper soup; chicken & salmon
roulade with lime sauce; berries with champagne ice crystals. **Details:** A77,
2m after Kirkswald turn right, then right again after 0.5m; 9.30 pm.
Accommodation: 132 rooms, from £270.

TURNERS HILL, W SUSSEX 3–4B
Alexander House £ 50 🄰

East Street RH10 4QD (01342) 714914

This "beautifully furnished" country house hotel, in extensive grounds,
has a "superb ambience"; it also offers a "high standard" of cooking
and "first-class service". / **Sample dishes:** roasted ballatine of rabbit; fillet
of turbot; banana soufflé. **Details:** off the M23 Junction 10, follow signs to
E.Grinstead and Turner's Hill, on the B2110; 9.30 pm; jacket, no jeans;
no smoking; children: 7. **Accommodation:** 15 rooms, from ££155.

Olde Dog & Partridge   **£ 25**   ★

High St   DE13 9LS   (01283) 813030

You don't often get "absolutely excellent cooking" (with the "emphasis on game") at a carvery, but reports on the "innovative" food at this "cheerful" spot behind a "long-established, half-timbered pub/hotel" are consistently upbeat; there's also a relatively new brasserie. / *Sample dishes:* Dovedale cheese soufflé; Stilton coated beef fillet; pear Tatin. *Value tip:* set 2/3-crs L £6.95/£7.95. *Details:* N of Burton-on-Trent on A444; 11 pm; closed Sun L; no smoking area. *Accommodation:* 20 rooms, from £60.

Altnaharrie Inn   **£ 81**   𝔸★★

IV26 2SS   (01854) 633230

"As near to perfection as you could ever hope to find"; a visit to Gunn Eriksen and Fred Brown's isolated converted drovers' inn (accessed by boat from Ullapool across Loch Broom) may be "expensive", but it offers a "unique experience" – "brilliantly composed and perfectly balanced" cooking, served in a setting which is "very tranquil, very personal and very special". / *Sample dishes:* lobster ravioli; turbot with truffles; baked pineapple pastry. *Details:* by private launch from Ullapool; 8 pm; D only, closed Nov-Easter; no smoking; children: 8+. *Accommodation:* 8 rooms, from £165, incl D.

Ceilidh Place   **£ 29**   𝔸

14 West Argyle St   IV26 2TY   (01854) 612103

Not only "a great place to shelter from the rain and the midges", this café appended to a folk music venue (with hotel, bookshops, gallery and so on) makes a "reliable" choice for its "decent portions of wholesome, tasty and well-prepared food" – mainly fish and a good selection of veggie dishes. / *Sample dishes:* haggis; provençale fish stew; chocolate roulade. *Details:* 55m NW of Inverness on A835; 9 pm; no smoking; need 10+ to book. *Accommodation:* 13 rooms, from £70.

Sharrow Bay   **£ 55**   𝔸★★

CA10 2LZ   (01768) 486301

"Heaven on earth"; for its many (fairly mature) devotees, the "best country hotel in England" – "stuffed with furniture, expertise and many years of love" – is "the essence of perfection"; "beautiful food", "exquisite surroundings" and "stunning views of the lake" – "expect to spend several hours over an unforgettable meal". / *Sample dishes:* stuffed pigs trotter with pease pudding; guinea fowl with mushroom & herb ravioli; Old English Regency syllabub. *Details:* on Pooley Bridge Rd towards Howtown; 8 pm; no Amex; jacket & tie; no smoking; children: 13+. *Accommodation:* 28 rooms, from £290, incl D.

Bay Horse   **£ 38**   𝔸★

Canal Foot   LA12 9EL   (01229) 583972

A "magical" setting (a converted pub with "great views overlooking Morecambe Bay") and "beautifully prepared and presented" cooking combine to make this an "outstanding" hotel restaurant; "take a window seat for an ever-changing panorama". / *Sample dishes:* tomato & apricot soup; salmon with ginger & lime butter; brown sugar meringue. *Value tip:* set 3-crs L £16.75. *Details:* after Canal Foot sign, turn left and pass Glaxo factory; 7.30 pm; closed Mon L & Sun L; no Amex; no smoking; children: 12+. *Accommodation:* 7 rooms, from £65, incl D.

Lords of the Manor   £ 60   A★

GL54 2JD   (01451) 820243

"Formal, but not stuffy", chic country house hotel which provides all the elements of a *"real experience"* – *"truly excellent"* service, an *"outstanding, olde worlde setting"* and *"top class"* modern British cooking that comes *"beautifully presented"*. / **Sample dishes:** red mullet, scallop & tomato fondue; roast lamb with flageolet bean purée; rhubarb & champagne jelly. **Value tip:** set 2/3-crs L £11.95/£15.95 (Sun £21). **Details:** 2m W of Stow on the Wold; 9.30 pm; no denim or trainers; no smoking; children: 7+. **Accommodation:** 27 rooms, from £138.

Lake Isle   £ 32   A

16 High St East LE15 9PZ   (01572) 822951

"Delicious food served in an unfussy atmosphere" and an *"excellent cellar"* makes this homely, atmospheric hotel dining room (in a charming Rutland town) a good choice for an informal but *"memorable"* meal. / **Sample dishes:** gazpacho; char-grilled lamb with minted hollandaise; banana & coconut tart. **Details:** 9.30 pm; closed Mon L; no Switch. **Accommodation:** 12 rooms, from £65.

Manor House Walkington   £ 33

Northland HU17 8RT   (01482) 881645

Rather *"old-fashioned"* establishment, in a Victorian house peacefully situated in the Wolds, offering *"rich"* and *"substantial"* fare. / **Sample dishes:** tomato & goat's cheese tart; duck with curried puy lentils; brown bread ice cream with apricots. **Details:** towards Bishop Burton, pass Beverley Racecourse, 2nd left, first right; 9.15 pm; D only, closed Sun; no Amex; children: 6+. **Accommodation:** 7 rooms, from £75.

Bishopstrow House   £ 48   A

BA12 9HH   (01985) 212312

Better reports this year on meals at this *"gloriously"* located and luxuriously equipped Georgian house – *"delicious"* dishes and *"faultless"* service is the tenor of most commentary. / **Sample dishes:** warm salad of wood pigeon; salmon & roast scallops on Thai risotto; sticky toffee pudding & clotted cream. **Details:** on Boreham Rd; 9 pm; no smoking. **Accommodation:** 31 rooms, from £170.

Old Beams   £ 50   A★

Leek Rd ST10 3HW   (01538) 308254

"Consistent quality standards applied to an excellent choice of menus" have made this *"charming and comfortable"* 18th-century building a great asset in an area without much in the way of gastronomic competition. / **Sample dishes:** langoustine & scallop ragoût; roast grouse with foie gras parfait; mango crème brûlée. **Value tip:** set 2/3-crs L £16.95/£22. **Details:** on A523 between Leek & Ashbourne; 9.30 pm; closed Mon, Tue L, Sat L & Sun D; no smoking. **Accommodation:** 5 rooms, from £75.

WATH-IN-NIDDERDALE, N YORKS

Sportsman's Arms £ 29 ★

HG3 5PP   (01423) 711306

*They're a taciturn lot in Yorkshire, presumably why reporters wasted no actual words this year in describing WHY they like this popular, attractive stone inn on the fringe of the North York Moors preferring to let their ratings speak for themselves. / **Sample dishes:** smoked salmon with rosti potatoes; lamb with spinach croquettes; summer pudding.* **Details:** take Wath road from Pateley Bridge; 9 pm; no Amex; no smoking. **Accommodation:** 13 rooms, from £60.

WELLS-NEXT-THE-SEA, NORFOLK
6-3C

Moorings £ 32 Ⓐ★

6 Freeman St NR23 1BA   (01328) 710949

*"Tiny and squashed", but "delightful" seaside fish and seafood specialist, not far from the water, which is "very popular" thanks to its "extensive, varied and interesting" menu. / **Sample dishes:** pan-fried scallops with Parma ham; fillet of wild seabass; tarte au citron.* **Details:** nr harbour; 9 pm; D only, ex Sun when L only; no Amex; no smoking.

WEST BRIDGFORD, NOTTS
5-3D

New Oriental Pearl £ 22

42-44 Bridgford Rd NG2 6AP   (0115) 945 5048

*Consistent Chinese, close to the town centre, offering a "good range of standard dishes, well presented and served". / **Sample dishes:** crispy duck; sizzling beef satay; toffee banana.* **Details:** 0.25m from cricket ground; 11 pm; no smoking area.

WEST BYFLEET, SURREY
3-3A

Chu Chin Chow £ 25

63 Old Woking Rd KT14 6LF   (01932) 349581

*"Cheerful" Chinese with quite a local following, thanks to its "nice surroundings" and "yummy" food. / **Sample dishes:** sesame prawns; sizzling beef; ginger ice cream.* **Details:** opp Waitrose; 10.30 pm.

WESTERHAM, KENT
3-3B

Tulsi £ 26

20 London Rd TN16 1BD   (01959) 563397

*"Inventive Indian cooking, reasonably priced" helps make this distinctive bar/restaurant, with its "modern décor", worth remembering. / **Sample dishes:** chicken tikka; chicken rogan josh; kulfi.* **Details:** 11.30 pm.

WETHERSFIELD, ESSEX
3-2C

Dicken's £ 34 ★

The Green CM7 4BS   (01371) 850723

*It occupies a "super building" and has "friendly" and "diligent" service, yet many reporters still find this "village green" restaurant has "absolutely no atmosphere"; a shame, as the chef is "talented" and cooks some "wonderful" dishes. / **Sample dishes:** saffron risotto with roasted peppers; grilled seabass on caper mash with leek fondue; chocolate tart with peppermint cream. **Value tip:** set 2/3-crs L £9.75/£13.* **Details:** 9.30 pm; closed Mon, Tue & Sun D; no Amex.

WEYBRIDGE, SURREY
3-3A

Colony £ 27

3 Balfour Rd KT13 8HE   (01932) 842766

*This place is not just "more upmarket than most Chineses"– it offers "quality" food, and the "long-standing staff" are "always friendly". / **Sample dishes:** mushroom satay; chicken in yellow bean sauce; toffee apple.* **Details:** on A317 nr M25; 10.30 pm; no Switch.

Hack & Spade   £ 24

DL11 7JL   (01748) 823721

"This local pub is more like a restaurant nowadays", but it still offers "interesting food with value and quality" in a "friendly" atmosphere. / Sample dishes: goat's cheese, black pudding & chutney; sole fillet stuffed with crab; iced banana parfait & brandy snaps. Details: 4m N of Richmond; 9 pm; closed Mon D & Sun D; closed 2 weeks in Jan; no Amex; no smoking area.

Magpie   £ 19   ★

14 Pier Rd YO21 3PU   (01947) 602058

"Fish and chip heaven"; the "freshly cooked" fare and "down-to-earth" ambience of this very well-known, "posh" seaside chippie have a wide-ranging appeal – "you often have to queue to get in" (sometimes "even if you've booked"!). / Sample dishes: potted salmon & prawns; cod & chips; hazlenut meringue. Details: opp Fish Market; 9 pm; closed for 4 weeks in Jan; no Amex; no smoking.

Trenchers   £ 21

New Quay Rd YO21 1DH   (01947) 603212

"The traditional feast of the poor Briton, done to a T" and "very friendly" service win unanimous praise for this harbourside fish and chip restaurant. / Sample dishes: seafood starter; cod & chips; sticky toffee pudding. Details: opp railway station, nr marina; 9 pm; closed mid Nov-mid March; no smoking area; need 7+ to book.

The White Horse & Griffin   £ 27   🅰★

Church St YO22 4AE   (01947) 604857

"Excellent", mainly fish cooking can help make dinner at this "small", candlelit "hotel bistro" a "rich, romantic and memorable" experience. / Sample dishes: scallops with mango salsa; fillet of cod stuffed with cheese & mustard; chocolate & orange bread & butter pudding. Details: centre of old town, on Abbey side of river; 9.30 pm; no Amex. Accommodation: 11 rooms, from £50.

The Crown at Whitebrook   £ 38   🅰★

NP5 4TX   (01600) 860254

It may be "hidden away", but reporters are unanimous that this "Wye Valley country inn" should be sought out for its "well presented and tasty cooking", its "excellent wine list" and its "very attentive service". / Sample dishes: Welsh goat's cheese tart; rack of lamb with faggots; cappuccino ice cream. Value tip: set 2-crs L & Sun L £15.95. Details: 2m W of A466, 5m S of Monmouth; 9 pm; to non-residents, closed 2 weeks in Jan and Aug. Accommodation: 10 rooms, from £56.

Whitstable Oyster Fishery Company   £ 32   🅰★

Horsebridge Beach CT5 1BU   (01227) 276856

This "lovely" seaside favourite with its "basic", but "wonderfully quirky" premises "within sight and smell of the sea" (yet "only 90 minutes from London") risks becoming a victim of its own success; even to some fans, the "reliably excellent", "no-frills" seafood increasingly seems "a bit pricey", and sterner critics feel that "staff attitudes have become arrogant and complacent". / Sample dishes: Scottish moules marinière; grilled Dover sole; raspberries with Jersey cream. Details: off A299; 9 pm; closed Mon & Sun D in winter. Accommodation: 30 rooms, from £40.

WINCHESTER, HANTS   2–3D
Hotel du Vin et Bistro   £ 38   A★
14 Southgate St TN1 2LY   (01962) 841414
*"Four generations agreed it was a hit!"; this "classy" but "relaxed"
modern British bistro (now with siblings in Tunbridge Wells and
Bristol) has widespread appeal; most also hail the "reliable and
innovative food", but for an implacable band of critics, it's all "hype",
and the cooking is "bland". / **Sample dishes:** ham hock terrine & brioche;
pork with sage & onion risotto; chocolate & pecan tart. **Value tip:** set 3-crs
Sun L £22.50. **Details:** 9.45 pm. **Accommodation:** 23 rooms, from £89.*

Old Chesil Rectory   £ 45   ★
1 Chesil St SO23 OHU   (01962) 851555
*The "gloomy", if "charming" and "homely", surroundings of this
Tudor building (now under new management) offer an unusual setting
for some wonderful, "rich" cooking so "go very hungry". / **Sample
dishes:** crispy duck & black pudding salad; braised lamb with haricot bean
purée; fallen chocolate soufflé. **Value tip:** set 2-crs L £15. **Details:** 9.15 pm,
Sat 9.45 pm; closed Mon & Sun; no Amex; no smoking area.*

Wykeham Arms   £ 30   A★
75 Kingsgate St SO23 9PE   (01962) 853834
*An absolutely "wonderful old pub" – between the Cathedral and the
College; how nice to find a place so "full of history" offering reliably
"good and simple" food, and a wine list "of which the Savoy would
not be ashamed". / **Sample dishes:** caramelised onion & goat's cheese
tartlet; roast duck with noodles & bitter orange sauce; chocolate cappuccino
mousse. **Details:** next to College; 8.45 pm; closed Sun; no smoking area;
booking: max 8; children: 14+. **Accommodation:** 13 rooms, from £79.50.*

WINDERMERE, CUMBRIA   7–3D
Jerichos   £ 34   ★
Birch St LA23 1EG   (015394) 42522
*"Completely unexpected, for Windermere", this "charming" and
"informal" new place ("decorated on a shoestring") offers a real
culinary experience, and is "good value" too, "especially the wines".
/ **Sample dishes:** steamed mussels in white wine; lamb with kidneys & chilli
roast vegetables; lavender & vanilla crème brûlée. **Details:** 9.30 pm; D only,
closed Mon; no Amex; no smoking; children: 12+.*

WINKLEIGH, DEVON   1–2D
Pophams   £ 33   A★
Castle St EX19 8HQ   (01837) 83767
*"A tiny restaurant, serving only lunch, but a really excellent
experience"; this "eccentric" 10-seater offers a "lovingly prepared"
menu, "described in minute detail", and always using "fresh local
produce"; BYO. / **Sample dishes:** warm onion tart; lamb & mushroom pâté
in puff pastry; sticky stem ginger pudding. **Details:** off A377, between Exeter
& Barnstaple; L only, open Wed-Sat only; no Amex & no Switch; no smoking;
children: 14+.*

WINTERINGHAM, N LINCS   5–1D
Winteringham Fields   £ 55   A★★
DN15 9PF (01724) 733096
*"It's worth a lengthy detour" to find Annie and Germain Schwab's
16th-century manor house (which is "a lovely place for a weekend
break"); the "memorable" Swiss-French cooking provides a "wow!
experience", and it's delivered by "highly competent but relaxed"
service, in an "unpretentious" environment. / **Sample dishes:** pot-au-feu
of scallops; rack of lamb with caramelised chicory; chocolate, nougat & honey
pyramid. **Value tip:** set 2/3-crs L £18.50/£22.50. **Details:** 4m SW of
Humber Bridge; 9.30 pm; closed Mon & Sun; no smoking.
Accommodation: 7 rooms, from £85.*

WITHERSLACK, CUMBRIA
7–4D

Old Vicarage   £ 36   🄰★
Church Rd   LA11 6RS   (015395) 52381
"Superb Anglo-French cooking, using the highest-quality local ingredients" and "excellent, knowledgeable service" are two of the features which put this "delightful, old country house" a cut above the norm. / Sample dishes: Morecambe Bay shrimps with capers; Aberdeen Angus beef; parfait with chocolate & vanilla sauces. Details: from M6, J36 follow signs to Barrow on A590; 9 pm; no smoking. Accommodation: 14 rooms, from £44.

WOBURN, BEDS
3–2A

Paris House   £ 57
MK17 9QP   (01525) 290692
"Not many restaurants have their own deer", so as "a place to impress" this half-timbered house in the grounds of Woburn Abbey has quite a head start; some do praise "exquisite" cooking, but there's also quite a sentiment that the place is "resting on its laurels". / Sample dishes: duck confit with orange sauce; beef in red wine & shallot sauce; hot raspberry soufflé. Value tip: set 3-crs L & Sun L £26. Details: 9.30 pm; closed Mon & Sun D.

WOLLATON, NOTTS
5–3D

Mr Man's   £ 26   ★
Wollaton Park   NG8 2AD   (0115) 928 7788
"What a spread"; "every dish imaginable" – and many are "excellent" – is served at this efficient, large and lively Cantonese restaurant (which is quite a hit with the local Chinese community). / Sample dishes: deep-fried crab claws; sliced duck with ginger & fresh pineapple; ice cream. Details: 11 pm.

WOODSTOCK, OXON
2–1D

The Feathers Hotel   £ 50
Market St   OX20 1SX   (01993) 812291
This famous 17th-century hostelry, by the gates of Blenheim Palace, has many fans who applaud its "beautifully presented" modern British cooking and "pleasant" atmosphere; numerous gripes, however – poor table-spacing, "greedy" prices, and sometimes "unintelligible and embarrassing service" (for which there is a 15% charge) – conspire to dent the level of overall support. / Sample dishes: foie gras & split pea casserole; honey-roast duck with claret glaze; pear & almond tart. Value tip: set 2-crs L £17.50, set 3-crs Sun L £20.50. Details: 8m N of Oxford on A44; 9.15 pm; no smoking. Accommodation: 22 rooms, from £115.

WORCESTER, WORCS
2–1B

Brown's   £ 44   🄰★
24 Quay St   WR1 2JJ   (01905) 26263
With its "nice riverside location", this "converted warehouse, overlooking the Severn" (which has nothing to do with the eponymous brasserie chain) is a top, if rather "expensive", local choice on account of its "interesting" and "enjoyable" food and "friendly and well informed" service. / Sample dishes: grilled baby squid; calves' liver with pancetta mash; summer berry pavlova. Value tip: set 3-crs L £18.50. Details: 9.45 pm; closed Mon, Sat L & Sun D; no smoking area; children: 8+.

Pant Yr Ochan   £ 26   ★
Old Wrexham Rd LL12 8TY   (01978) 853525
*A "wide range" of dishes at "good-value" prices, a "beautiful
location" (and a "nice conservatory" too) make this Borders spot
a worthwhile destination. / **Sample dishes:** crispy pancake filled with
spinach & duck; braised lamb in rosemary & garlic sauce; strawberry pavlova
& honeycomb ice cream. **Details:** 1m N of Wrexham; 9.30 pm;
no smoking area; children: not permitted at D.*

Royal Oak Hotel   £ 38   𝔸
The Square RG18 0UG   (01635) 201325
*Famously "olde worlde", "wisteria-clad" inn, in the heart of the
village, offering "quality" modern British cooking and a "great",
"relaxed" atmosphere; some tip the bar snacks over the restaurant
fare. / **Sample dishes:** wood pigeon salad with celeriac; peppered tournedos
of hake; baked papillote of banana. **Value tip:** set 2/3-crs set L £12.50/£15.
Details: 5m W of Pangbourne, off B4009; 9.45 pm; closed Sun D;
no smoking. **Accommodation:** 5 rooms, from £115.*

Blue Bicycle   £ 34   𝔸★★
34 Fossgate YO1 9TA   (01904) 673990
*An "interesting and varied" menu, emphasising "lovely seafood"
and "the best fish ever", makes this "trendy", "relaxed" and
"friendly" candlelit spot "the best in town", by quite a margin.
/ **Sample dishes:** smoked venison with lime salsa; monkfish chowder;
chocolate & pear torte. **Details:** close to city centre overlooking River Foss;
10 pm; no smoking; children: not encouraged.*

Café Concerto   £ 25   𝔸★
21 High Petergate YO1 2EN   (01904) 610478
*"The nearest thing to the café/bistro of my dreams", this "little gem,
by the Minster" is "consistently excellent", thanks to its "generous
portions" of "beautifully presented" and "reasonably priced" cooking,
and "very friendly" service. / **Sample dishes:** Mozzarella, avocado
& tomato salad; cajun tuna steak; summer fruit pudding. **Details:** 9.30 pm;
no Amex; no smoking area; no booking at L.*

Delrio's   £ 26   𝔸
10 Blossom St YO24 2AE   (01904) 622695
*Specialists in the cuisine of particular Italian regions are a bit of a
rarity, so more credit then to this "welcoming" Sardinian, whose cellar
location offers a "cosy" and "comfortable" setting for some "good
value for money" cooking. / **Sample dishes:** fresh sardines baked with
garlic; fresh seafood; tiramisu. **Details:** nr station; 11 pm; D only, closed Mon.*

Kites   £ 30   𝔸★
13 Grape Ln Y02 1HU   (01904) 641750
*A "bistro with a plus", offering an "original" menu – "really nice
food, presented in a unique way" – and "friendly and helpful service".
/ **Sample dishes:** Thai crab cakes; fillet of grey mullet with roast toms; banoffi
pie. **Value tip:** set 2/3-crs set L £10.95/£12.95. **Details:** 10.30 pm; closed
Sun; no smoking area.*

Melton's   **£ 28**   ★

7 Scarcroft Rd YO23 1ND   (01904) 634341

*"Still good after many years" (well, nine), this small and "relaxing"
restaurant, housed in Victorian shop premises – the most mentioned
establishment in the town – offers a "consistently fine" but "ever-
changing" modern British menu, and at "good-value" prices.*
/ **Sample dishes:** *mackerel escabeche; chicken saltimbocca; apple & calvados
soufflé.* **Value tip:** *set 3-crs L & D £15.* **Details:** *10 mins' walk from Castle
Museum; 10 pm; closed Mon L & Sun D; closed 3 weeks at Christmas;
no Amex; no smoking area.*

Middlethorpe Hall   **£ 44**   A★

Bishopthorpe Rd YO23 2GB   (01904) 641241

*"The terrace is delightful on a summer's day" at this fine country
house hotel set in extensive gardens, a mile or so outside the city-
centre; the French cooking in the "stately" dining room is generally
lauded, but let-downs are not unknown.* / **Sample dishes:** *sole stuffed
with salmon & crab; roast rabbit and langoustines; crème brûlée.* **Value tip:**
set 2/3-crs L £14.50/£17.50 (Sun £18.50). **Details:** *next to racecourse;
9.45 pm; no Amex; jacket & tie; no smoking area; children: 8+.*
Accommodation: *30 rooms, from £145.*

Plunketts   **£ 26**   A★

9 High Petergate YO1 7EN   (01904) 637722

*The "amazing atmosphere" – "low-lit", "lively" and "fun" – draws
most commentary at this south west American-inspired venture,
which, with its "very accommodating" attitude is particularly
recommended as a good place for a group meal; the food (a sort
of go-faster Tex/Mex) is still complimented, however.* / **Sample
dishes:** *prawn quesadillas; Yucatan chicken with papaya salsa; lemon posset.*
Details: *in shadow of Minster; 11 pm; no Amex.*

Rubicon Vegetarian   **£ 19**

5 Little Stonegate YO1 8AX   (01904) 676076

*"A nice, little veggie", "tucked away in an atmospheric part of town",
by the Minster.* / **Sample dishes:** *Stilton, walnut & port pâté; baked
aubergine & goat's cheese; chocolate fudge brownie.* **Details:** *10 pm;
no smoking.*

UK & EIRE MAPS

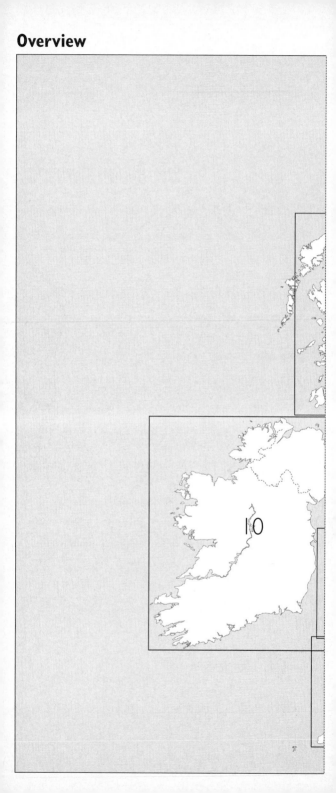

10

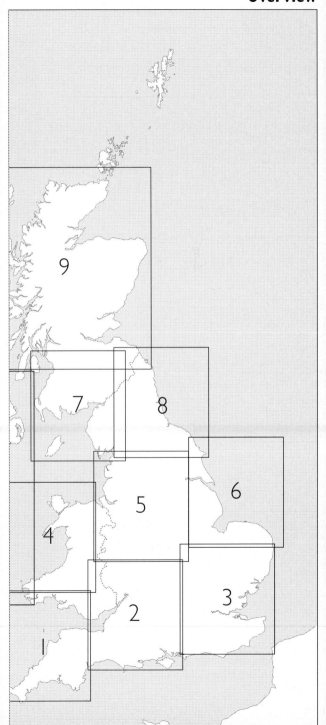

Map I

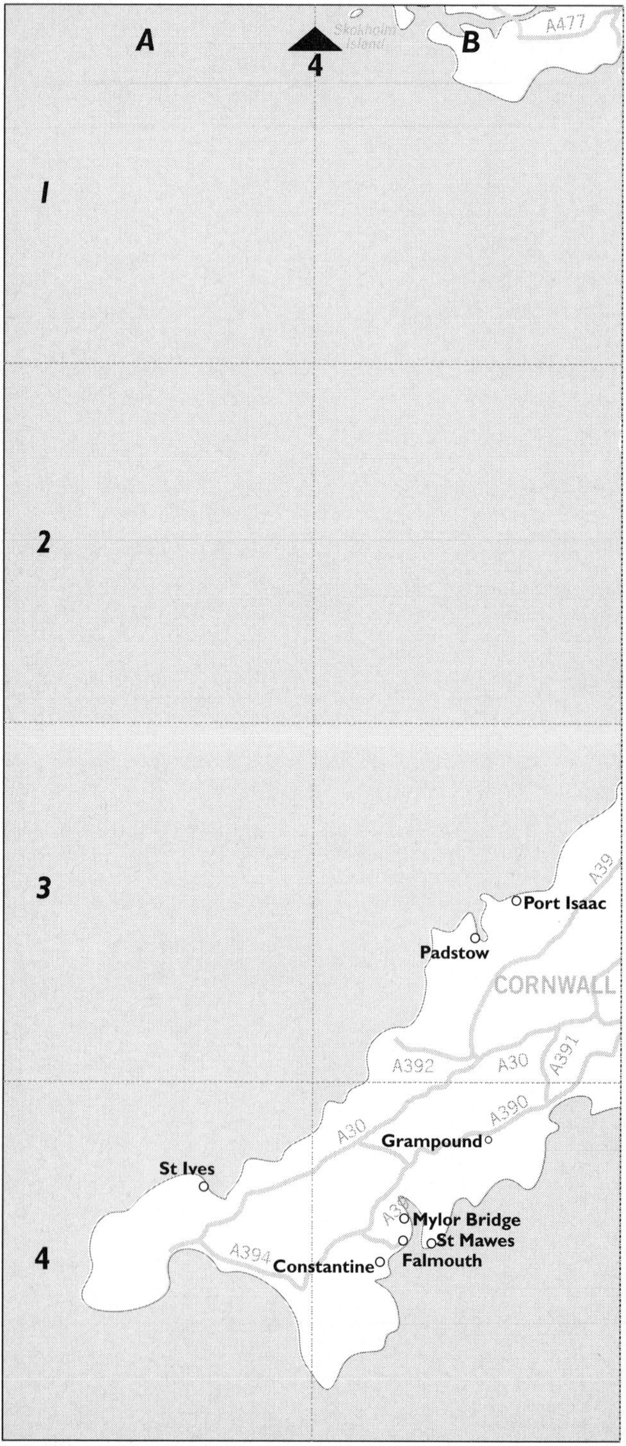

A   ▲4   B

A477

Skokholm Island

I

2

3

○ Port Isaac

Padstow ○

CORNWALL

A39

A392   *A30*   *A391*

A30   *A390*

Grampound ○

St Ives
○

○ Mylor Bridge
○ St Mawes
Constantine ○ Falmouth

A394

4

Map I

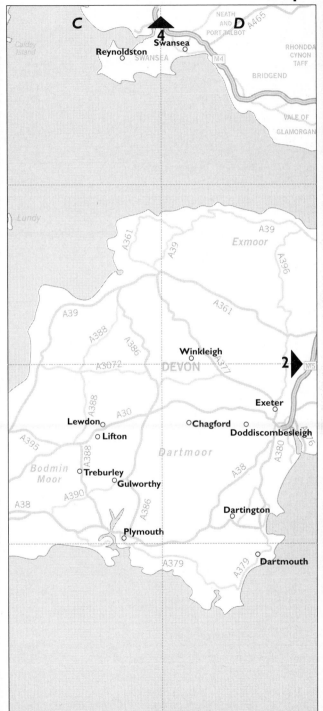

Map 2

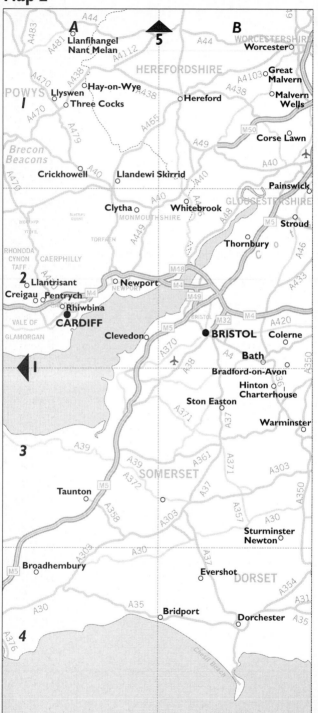

Map 2

WARWICKSHIRE

C

D

M5

A425

M1

A442

A46

Aston Cantlow

A46

Stratford upon Avon

5

A423

Stoke Bruerne

A44

A46

Evesham

Banbury

A43

A45

Paulerspury

A46

Broadway

Paxford

Blockley

Buckland

Moreton-in-Marsh

A422

Great Tew

A4

M5

Upper Slaughter

A4260

M40

BUCKINGHAM-SHIRE

Cheltenham

Lower Slaughter

Chipping Norton

A34

A41

A436

A40 s

A361

Woodstock

Birdlip

A429

Burford

OXFORD

Gibraltar

Long Crendon

A417

W

Cumnor

A40

A418

Thame

A419

OXFORDSHIRE

Chinnor

A420

A338

Great Milton

Maidensgrove

M40

A429

Brinkworth

A419

A361

Dorchester

Stoke Row

Britwell-Salome

Maidensgrove

A30

Henely-on-Thames

Moulsford

M4

A346

A34

Goring

BERKSHIRE

Yattendon

Sonning

A4

M4

A4

Stockcross

Newbury

Shipfield

3

Melksham

Rowde

A34

A339

WILTSHIRE

A342

A338

M3

Salisbury Plain

A303

Odiham

A36

A303

A80

A34

M3

HAMPSHIRE

A3

A30

A338

Sparsholt

Ovington

A31

Winchester

A272

A354

A338

A36

Romsey

(A31)

A32

Horton

A304

Stuckton

New Forest

A31

M27

Emsworth

A348

A35

Brockenhurst

New Milton

Lymington

Seaview

A351

Isle of Wight

A3055

Swanage

Map 3

A   6   **B**

A427   A605   A141

A43   A14   A1   CAMBRIDGESHIRE   A10   Ely

A14   A45   A6116

1   NORTHAMPTONSHIRE   A14   Huntingdon

A45   A6   A14   Histon   A14

Madingley   Bottisham

A428   Cambridge

A1198   Little Shelford

Bedford   A421   M11   Sawston

Fowlmere   Duxford   A1307

Milton   BEDFORDSHIRE   Melbourn

Keynes   A507   Heydon

A421   Houghton-Conquest

Flitwick   A505

BUCKINGHAM-   Woburn   A5 M1   A1(M)

SHIRE   Luton   HERTFORDSHIRE   A120

2   Ivinghoe   Harpenden   A602   A10

Aylesbury   Aston Clinton   Lemsford   M11

  Tring   M10

Prestwood   M25   Ongar   A414

Amersham   E Barnet   Loughton

Speen   Bushey   M1   M11

M40   **2**   Pinner   A406

Marlow   A41   Ilford   M25

Taplow   Bray   A40   **LONDON**   A13

Eton   Southall   A4   Bexleyheath

A4   Richmond

A329(M)   Ascot   A205   A2

3   Shepperton   Esher   Beckenham   Orpington

Chobham   Claygate   Locksbottom   M25

Brookwood   West   Weybridge   A232   M20

Byfleet   Cobham   M26

Ripley   A331

Guildford   SURREY   M25   A23   A22

Compton   Dorking   Reigate   Westerham   Tonbridge

A31   A25   A24   M23   Penshurst   Tunbridge

East   Wells

Grinstead   A26

Haslemere   Turners Hill   Langton Green

A3   A264   Slaugham   A26 A267

Lower   A22

Beeding   Fletching   Buxted

A272   A29   A272   A272   E. SUSSEX

4   WEST SUSSEX   Storrington   A23

Amberley   South

Chilgrove   Downs

Chichester   A27   A26   A22

A27   **BRIGHTON**

Seaford   Jevington

Map 3

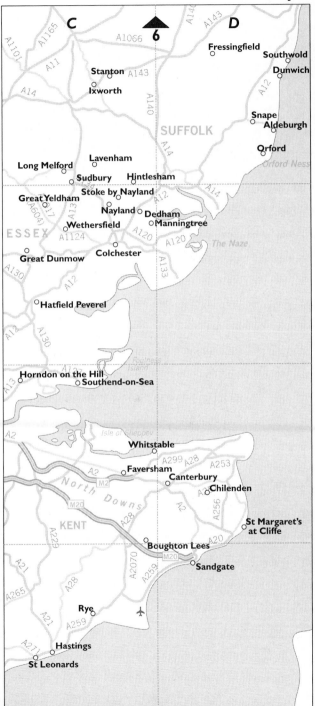

C **D**

A1066

6

A1165   A1143
A1101   A11   A143
A14

Fressingfield
Southwold
Dunwich

Stanton   A143
Ixworth

A12

SUFFOLK

A140   **Snape**
A14   **Aldeburgh**

Lavenham   **Orford**

Long Melford   *Orford Ness*
Sudbury   **Hintlesham**
Great Yeldham   **Stoke by Nayland**
A1017   A12   A14
A6041   **Nayland**   **Dedham**
A133   **Wethersfield**   **Manningtree**
ESSEX   A1124   A120   *The Naze*

Great Dunmow   **Colchester**   A120
A130   A133

A12

Hatfield Peverel

A130   A12

A130   *Foulness Island*

Horndon on the Hill
A13   **Southend-on-Sea**

A2   *Isle of Sheppey*

Whitstable

A299   A28
Faversham   A253
Canterbury
A2   A2   **Chilenden**
North Downs   M2   A256
M20

KENT   A28   **St Margaret's
at Cliffe**
A229   A2
A2070   A20
Boughton Lees
A259   M20
A21   **Sandgate**
A28

A265

A259   **Rye**
A21
A271   **Hastings**
St Leonards

Map 4

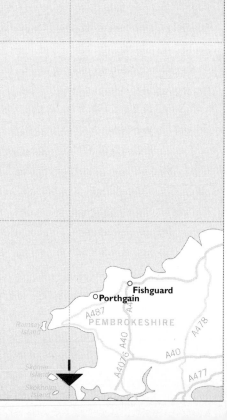

A B

I

Holy Island

2

Bardsey Island

3

4

Fishguard
Porthgain

A487
PEMBROKESHIRE

Ramsey Island

A40

A4076

A478

A40

A477

Skomer Island

Skokholm Island

Map 4

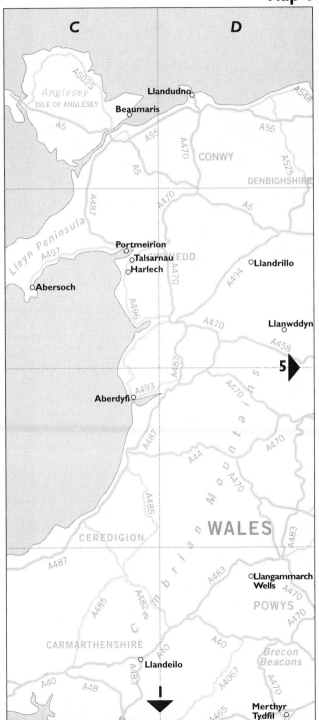

C

D

Anglesey
ISLE OF ANGLESEY

A5025

Llandudno

Beaumaris

A5

A55

A470

A55

CONWY

A5

A525

DENBIGHSHIRE

A487

A470

A5

Lleyn Peninsula

A497

Portmeirion

Talsarnau

Harlech

GWYNEDD

A494

Llandrillo

Abersoch

A496

A470

Llanwddyn

A458

5

A487

A493

Aberdyfi

A470

A487

A44

A470

A485

WALES

A487

CEREDIGION

Cambrian Mountains

A470

A483

A487

Llangammarch
Wells

A470

POWYS

A485

A482

A483

A470

CARMARTHENSHIRE

A40

A40

Brecon
Beacons

A483

Llandeilo

A4067

A470

A40

A48

A465

Merthyr
Tydfil

Map 5

Map 5

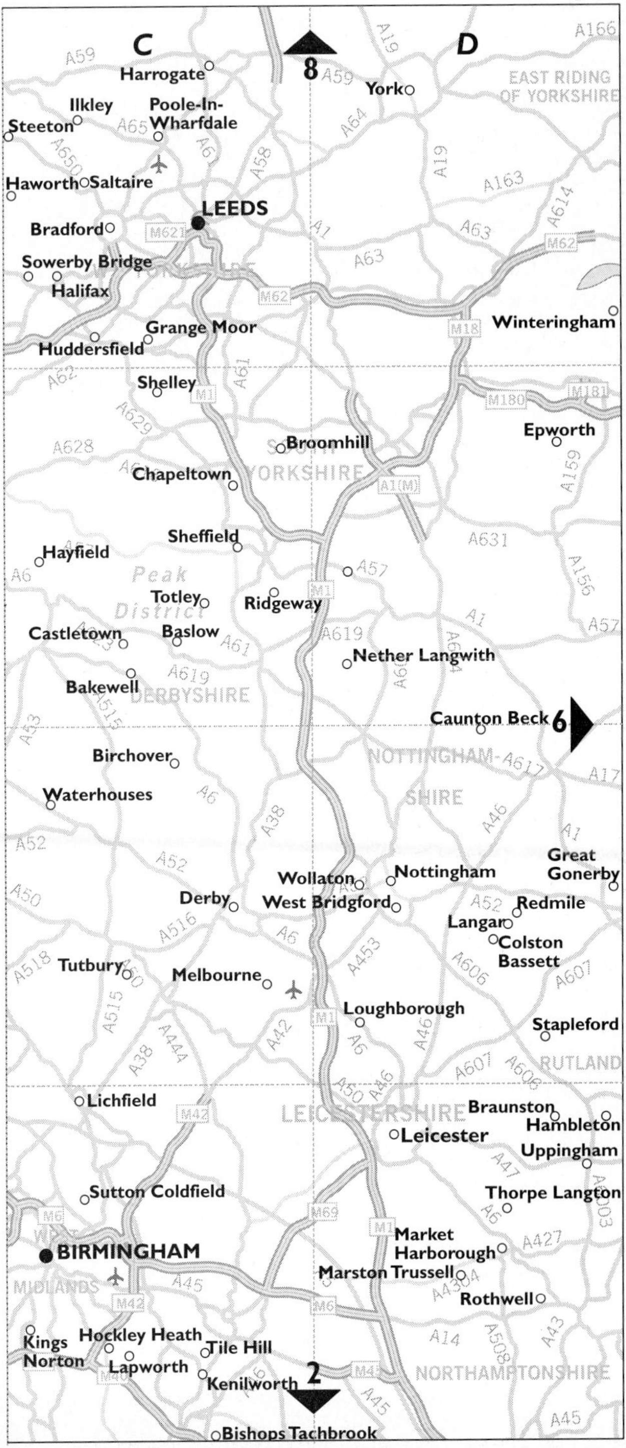

C

D

A59

Harrogate

EAST RIDING
OF YORKSHIRE

8

A59

York

Ilkley

Poole-In-
Wharfdale

Steeton

A65

A6

A64

A19

A166

A163

A614

Haworth

Saltaire

A58

A1

A63

M62

Bradford

LEEDS

M621

Winteringham

Sowerby Bridge

Halifax

M62

M18

Huddersfield

Grange Moor

A629

Shelley

M1

A61

Broomhill

M180

M181

Epworth

A159

A628

Chapeltown

SOUTH
YORKSHIRE

A1(M)

A631

A156

Hayfield

Sheffield

A57

A1

A57

Peak
District

Totley

Ridgeway

M1

A6

Castletown

Baslow

A61

Nether Langwith

Bakewell

A619

DERBYSHIRE

Caunton Beck

6

Birchover

A6

NOTTINGHAM-
SHIRE

A617

A1

Waterhouses

A52

A38

A46

A1

Great
Gonerby

A50

Wollaton

Nottingham

Derby

West Bridgford

A52

Redmile

Langar

A516

A6

A453

Colston
Bassett

A607

Tutbury

Melbourne

A606

Stapleford

Loughborough

M1

A6

A46

A607

A606

RUTLAND

Lichfield

M42

LEICESTERSHIRE

Braunston

Hambleton

Leicester

Uppingham

Sutton Coldfield

M69

A47

Thorpe Langton

A6003

BIRMINGHAM

M42

A45

M6

Market
Harborough

A427

Marston Trussell

A508

Kings
Norton

Hockley Heath

Tile Hill

2

Rothwell

A14

NORTHAMPTONSHIRE

Lapworth

Kenilworth

M40

A45

A45

Bishops Tachbrook

Map 6

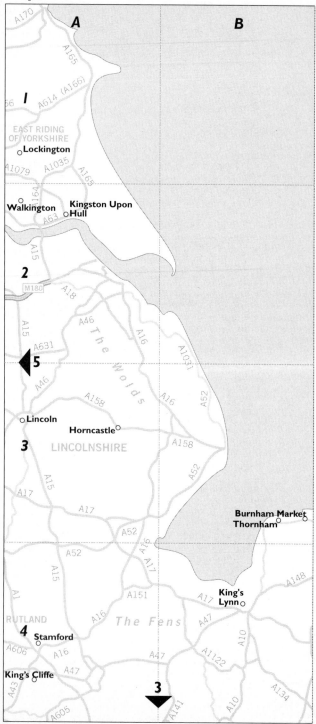

A   **B**

1

A170
A165
A614 (A166)
56

EAST RIDING
OF YORKSHIRE
○ **Lockington**

A1079   A1035   A165

○ **Walkington**   **Kingston Upon**
                   ○ **Hull**
A63

A15

2
M180
A18   A46   A16   A1031

A15
A631
◀ **5**
A46
A158   A16   A52

○ **Lincoln**
         Horncastle ○
3   LINCOLNSHIRE
                        A158

A17   A15   A52

A17

A52   A16   **Burnham Market**
            Thornham ○

A52   A17
A15
A1
RUTLAND   A16   A151   **King's**
                        Lynn ○
4   **Stamford**   A47   A10
        ○
A606   A16   **The Fens**   A1122
King's Cliffe   A47   A47   A148
A43
A605   A47   ▼ **3**   A141   A10   A134

Map 6

C

D

Wells-next-
the-Sea   Morston
  ○   ○
  A149
          Holt○   A148

A1065

          A140
      A1067
                    A149

  A47   ✈

NORFOLK   Norwich○   The
                    A47 Broads
          Stoke Holy   A146   A143
A11   Cross○
            3▼
          A140   A143

Map 7

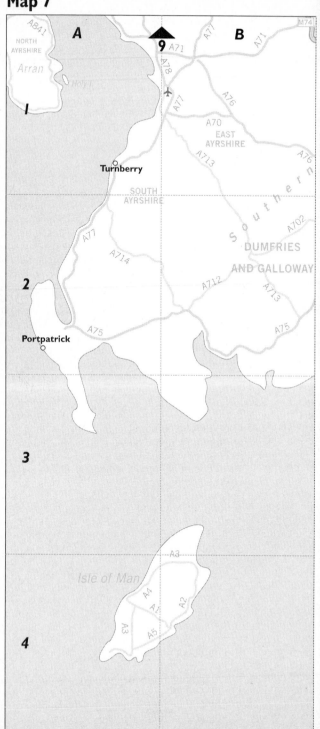

Map 7

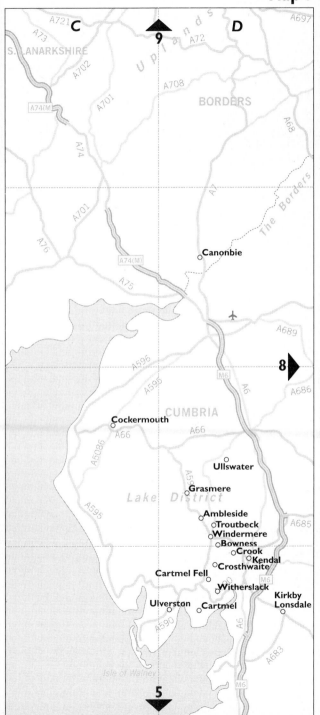

Map 8

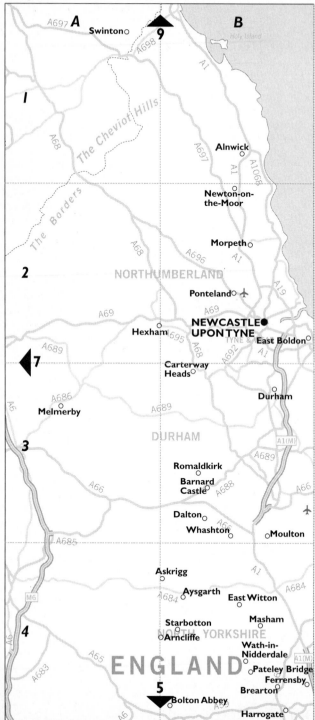

A697 **A** Swinton○ **9** **B**

1 The Cheviot Hills

A68 The Borders

Alnwick○ A697 A1068

A1

Newton-on-the-Moor○

A68 **Morpeth**○ A1

A696 A19

2 NORTHUMBERLAND

A69 A69 **Ponteland**○

NEWCASTLE UPON TYNE●

Hexham○ 695 A68 TYNE & **East Boldon**○

A692 A1

7 A689

Carterway Heads○

A686 **Durham**○

Melmerby○

A6 A689

A1(M)

DURHAM

3 A689

A66 **Romaldkirk**○ A66

Barnard Castle○ A688

Dalton○ A66

Whashton○ **Moulton**○

A685

A1

Askrigg○

Aysgarth○ A684

A684 **East Witton**○

M6 **Starbotton**○ **Masham**○

4 **Arncliffe**○ NORTH YORKSHIRE

Wath-in-Nidderdale○ A1(M)

A65 **E N G L A N D** **Pateley Bridge**○

A683 **Ferrensby**○

5 **Brearton**○

Bolton Abbey○

A6 **Harrogate**○

Map 8

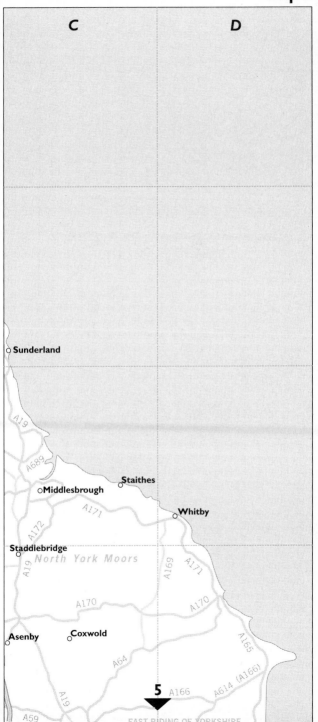

C

D

Sunderland

A19

A689

Staithes

Middlesbrough

A171

Whitby

A172

Staddlebridge

North York Moors

A19

A169

A171

A170

A170

Asenby

Coxwold

A165

A64

5

A166

A19

A614 (A166)

A59

EAST RIDING OF YORKSHIRE

Map 9

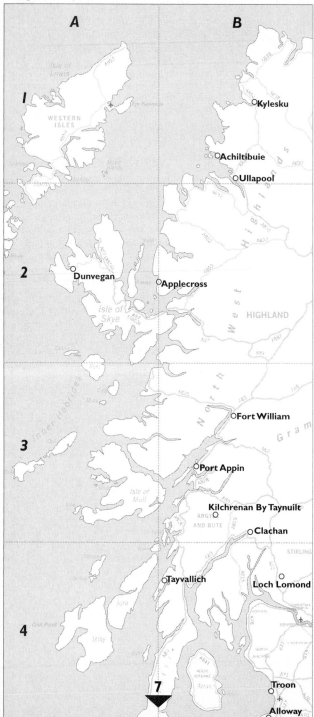

Map 9

Map 10

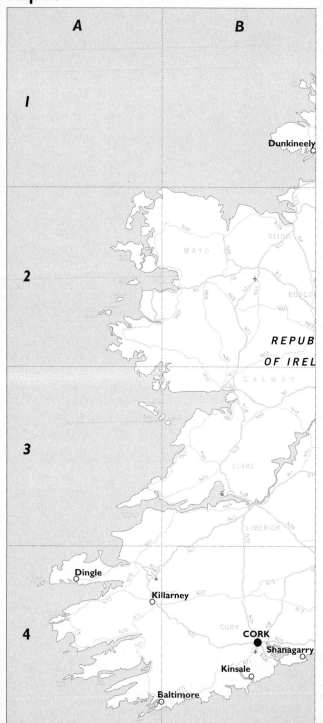

A

B

1

Dunkineely

2

MAYO   SLIGO   ROSCO

N5   N60

REPUB
OF IREL

GALWAY

3

CLARE

LIMERICK

Dingle

Killarney

4

CORK

Shanagarry

Kinsale

Baltimore

Map 10

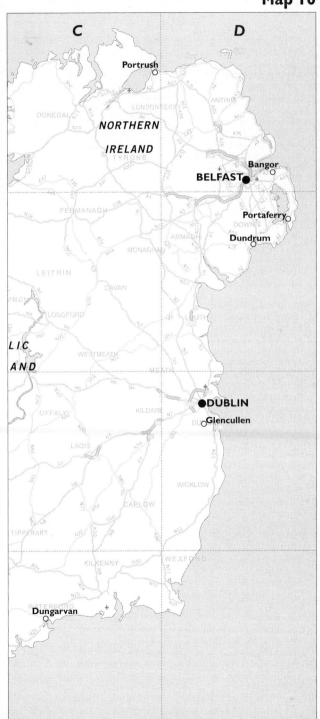

ALPHABETICAL INDEX

ALPHABETICAL INDEX

ALPHABETICAL INDEX

ALPHABETICAL INDEX

ALPHABETICAL INDEX